Walter Farquhar Hook

Lifes of the Archbishops of Canterbury

Walter Farquhar Hook
Lifes of the Archbishops of Canterbury
ISBN/EAN: 9783743435506
Printed in Europe, USA, Canada, Australia, Japan
Cover: Foto ©ninafisch / pixelio.de

Manufactured and distributed by brebook publishing software (www.brebook.com)

Walter Farquhar Hook

Lifes of the Archbishops of Canterbury

LIVES

OF THE

ARCHBISHOPS OF CANTERBURY.

VOL. VII.

Reformation Period.

LONDON
PRINTED BY SPOTTISWOODE AND CO.
NEW-STREET SQUARE

LIVES

OF THE

ARCHBISHOPS OF CANTERBURY.

BY

WALTER FARQUHAR HOOK, D.D. F.R.S.

DEAN OF CHICHESTER.

VOLUME VII.

REFORMATION PERIOD.

History which may be called just and perfect history is of three kinds, according to the object which it propoundeth or pretendeth to represent; for it either representeth a time, or a person, or an action. The first we call Chronicles, the second Lives, and the third Narratives or Relations. Of these, although Chronicles be the most complete and absolute kind of history, and hath most estimation and glory, yet Lives excelleth in profit and use, and Narratives or Relations in verity or sincerity. LORD BACON.

LONDON:
RICHARD BENTLEY, NEW BURLINGTON STREET,
Publisher in Ordinary to Her Majesty.
1868.

The right of translation is reserved.

CONTENTS

OF

THE SEVENTH VOLUME.

CHAPTER III.—*continued.*

THOMAS CRANMER.

Dissolution of monasteries.—Reform of Canterbury Cathedral.—Visit to England of German Protestants.—Treated with incivility by the King.—Their influence with Cranmer.—Discontent of the people.—Meeting of Parliament.—Whip with six strings.—Cranmer's conduct on the occasion.—Convocation consulted.—Persecution of Anabaptists.—Proclamation against Sacramentaries.—Persecution of John Lambert for denying Transubstantiation.—King Henry's zeal for Catholicism.—Other cases of persecution. How far Cranmer was concerned in them.—Mrs. Kyme, *alias* Ann Askew.—Joan Bocher.—Ann of Cleves.—Catherine Howard.—Fate of Crumwell.—Arbitrary proceedings of Cranmer.—Visitation of his diocese.—Vulgar errors.—Conspiracy against Cranmer.—Palace at Canterbury.—Cranmer supported by the King against a conspiracy in the Council.—Parts with his wife.—His domestic life.—Anecdotes.—His avarice.—Acceptance of monastic property.—II. Cranmer's theological opinions.—His zeal for circulating the translated Bible.—History of versions.—Cranmer's Catholicism.—His Sacramental doctrine.—When he renounced the dogma of Transubstantiation.—Cranmer denounced by foreign Protestants.—Violence of foreign Protestants against the Church of England.—Cranmer's Erastianism.—Became a sound Churchman.—The Apostolical Succession.—Crumwell's proceedings as Vice-gerent.—Crumwell's insolence.—Party movements.—The Book of Articles.—Synodical meeting of the two

Provinces.—Alexander Ales.—The Bishop's Book.—How far Cranmer had advanced in 1537.—New movement towards Liturgical Reform. —Homilies drawn up.—Necessary erudition or the King's Book.— Litany translated into English.—The Primer.—Archbishop active in repressing Protestant as well as Papist error.—III. Death of Henry VIII.—Cranmer celebrates Mass at the funeral.—Celebrates Mass in memory of Francis I.—Protector Somerset.—Edward VI.—Coronation.—Cranmer's arbitrary and unconstitutional proceedings.—The General Visitation.—Unjust deposition of Gardyner.—Disgraceful appointment of Poynet to the See of Winchester.—Bonner.—Northumberland.—Progress of the Reformation.—Discussions on the Eucharist.—Convocation.—First Revision of the Missal.—Commission appointed.—A review of our Liturgical Offices from Augustine to Osmund, from Osmund to Cranmer, from Cranmer to Juxon.—First Prayer Book of Edward VI.—Calvin and Calvinists violently opposed to Prayer Book and the English Reformation.—Second Prayer Book.—The Forty-two Articles.—The Reformatio Legum, a failure.—Northumberland's conspiracy.—How far Cranmer was implicated.—Death of Edward VI.—IV. Perplexity of the Reformers. —Gardyner and Bonner.—The Bloody Mary.—Cranmer unjustly accused.—His self-vindication.—Brought before the Star Chamber —Imprisoned in the Tower.—His comforting intercourse with Ridley, Bradford, and Latimer.—His delusive hopes.—A packed Convocation undoes the work of the Reformers.—Cranmer arraigned in Guildhall for treason.—Pleads guilty.—His letter to the Queen. —Sent to Oxford with Ridley and Latimer to dispute with a Committee of Convocation.—Unjustifiable proceedings. - Disputes with Harpsfield.—Summoned before a Synod of Presbyters.—Condemnation of Cranmer, Ridley, and Latimer.—Letter to the Council.—Not badly treated.—Pole's arrival in England.—Commission to degrade Ridley and Latimer.—Commission for degradation of Cranmer from the Pope.—Martyrdoms.—Persecutions.—Cranmer summoned to Rome.—Trial before Brookes.—His expectations of favour from the Queen.—Letter to the Queen.—Proceedings at Rome.—Cranmer's condemnation.—Bonner's harshness.—Cranmer's degradation.—His appeal.—The recantations.—His repentance.—His execution Page 1

SUCCESSION
OF
ARCHBISHOPS AND CONTEMPORARY KINGS.

Archbishops.	Consecration.	Consecrators.	Accession.	Death.	Contemporary Kings.
William Warham	1502	Rich. Winchester John Exeter Rich. Rochester	1503	1532	Henry VII. Henry VIII.
Thomas Cranmer	1533	John Lincoln John Exeter Hen. S. Asaph	1533	1556	Henry VIII. Edward VI. Mary.

TABLE

OF

CONTEMPORARY SOVEREIGNS.

A.D.	England.	Scotland.	Germany.	France.	Pope.	Spain.
1503	Henry VII.	James IV.	Maximilian I.	Louis XII.	Pius III. Julius II.	Ferdinand II. and Isabella.
1509	Henry VIII.	. .	. .	. .	. .	. .
1513	. .	James V.	. .	. .	Leo X.	. .
1515	. .	. .	. .	. .	. .	. .
1516	. .	. .	. .	Francis I.	. .	Charles I.
1519	. .	. .	Charles V.	. .	. .	Emperor Charles V.
1522	. .	. .	. .	. .	Adrian VI.	. .
1523	. .	. .	. .	. .	Clement VII.	. .
1534	. .	. .	. .	. .	Paul III.	. .
1542	. .	Mary	. .	. .	. .	. .
1547	Edward VI.	. .	. .	Henry II.	. .	. .
1550	. .	. .	. .	. .	Julius III.	. .
1553	Mary	. .	. .	. .	. .	. .
1555	. .	. .	. .	. .	Marcellinus II.	. .
1556	. .	. .	. .	. .	Paul IV.	Philip II.

LIVES

OF THE

ARCHBISHOPS OF CANTERBURY

BOOK IV.—*continued.*

CHAPTER III.—*continued.*

THOMAS CRANMER.

Dissolution of monasteries.—Reform of Canterbury Cathedral.—Visit to England of German Protestants.—Treated with incivility by the King.—Their influence with Cranmer.—Discontent of the people.—Meeting of Parliament.—Whip with six strings.—Cranmer's conduct on the occasion.—Convocation consulted.—Persecution of Anabaptists.—Proclamation against Sacramentaries.—Persecution of John Lambert for denying Transubstantiation.—King Henry's zeal for Catholicism.—Other cases of persecution.—How far Cranmer was concerned in them.—Mrs. Kyme, *alias* Ann Askew.—Joan Bocher.—Ann of Cleves.—Catherine Howard.—Fate of Crumwell.—Arbitrary proceedings of Cranmer.—Visitation of his diocese.—Vulgar errors.—Conspiracy against Cranmer.—Palace at Canterbury.—Cranmer supported by the King against a conspiracy in the Council.—Parts with his wife.—His domestic life.—Anecdotes.—His avarice.—Acceptance of monastic property.—II. Cranmer's theological opinions.—His zeal for circulating the translated Bible.—History of versions.—Cranmer's Catholicism.—His Sacramental doctrine.—When he renounced the dogma of Transubstantiation.—Cranmer denounced by foreign Protestants.—Violence of foreign Protestants against the Church of England.—Cranmer's Erastianism.—Became a sound Churchman.—The Apostolical Succession.—Crumwell's proceedings as Vice-gerent.—Crumwell's insolence.—Party movements.—The Book of Articles.—Synodical meeting of the two Provinces.—Alexander Ales.—The Bishop's Book.—How far Cranmer had advanced in 1537.—New movement towards Liturgical Reform. —Homilies drawn up.—Necessary erudition or the King's Book.— Litany translated into English.—The Primer.—Archbishop active in repressing Protestant as well as Papist error.—III. Death of Henry VIII.—Cranmer celebrates Mass at the funeral.—Celebrates Mass in memory of Francis I.—Protector Somerset.—Edward VI.—Coronation.—Cranmer's arbitrary and unconstitutional proceedings.—The General Visitation.—Unjust deposition of Gardyner.—Disgraceful appointment of Poynet to the See of Winchester.—Bonner.—Northumberland.—Progress of the Reformation.—Discussions on the Eucharist.—Convocation.—First Revision of the Missal.—Commission appointed.—A review of our Liturgical Offices from Augustine to Osmund, from Osmund to Cranmer, from Cranmer to Juxon.—First Prayer Book of Edward VI.—Calvin and Calvinists violently opposed to Prayer Book and the English Reformation.—Second Prayer Book.—The Forty-two Articles.—The Reformatio Legum, a failure.—Northumberland's conspiracy.—How far Cranmer was implicated.—Death of Edward VI.—IV. Perplexity of the Reformers. —Gardyner and Bonner.—The Bloody Mary.—Cranmer unjustly accused.—His self-vindication.—Brought before the Star Chamber —Imprisoned in the Tower.—His comforting intercourse with Ridley, Bradford, and Latimer.—His delusive hopes.—A packed Convocation undoes the work of the Reformers.—Cranmer arraigned in Guildhall for treason.—Pleads guilty.—His letter to the Queen. —Sent to Oxford with Ridley and Latimer to dispute with a Committee of Convocation.—Unjustifiable proceedings.—Disputes with Harpsfield.—Summoned before a Synod of Presbyters.—Condemnation of Cranmer, Ridley, and Latimer.—Letter to the Council.—Not badly treated.—Pole's arrival in England.—Commission to degrade Ridley and Latimer.—Commission for degradation of Cranmer from the Pope.—Martyrdoms.—Persecutions.—Cranmer summoned to Rome.—Trial before Brookes.—His expectations of favour from the Queen.—Letter to the Queen.—Sham proceedings at Rome.—Cranmer's condemnation.—Bonner's harshness.—Cranmer's degradation. —His appeal.—The recantations.—His repentance.—His execution.

CHAP. III.
───
Thomas Cranmer.
1533-56.

IN the great work which has consigned the name of Cromwell to an immortality of honour or disgrace—the dissolution of the monasteries—Cranmer took no active part. The story has been narrated in detail in the

Introductory Chapter, and need not be repeated here. In defending the regulars the archbishop and the secular clergy were not much interested, and a broad distinction was made between the property of the Church and the property of the monasteries. Although some were alarmed when Ucalegon's house was in danger, many more among the seculars were disposed to secure the safety of Church property, by sacrificing the monks to the cupidity of the courtiers and the avarice of the king. The monasteries, though connected with the Church, formed no part of the Church system. They were decidedly anti-episcopalian institutions; they had wasted large sums of money to purchase exemption from episcopal jurisdiction; an account of the contentions for this privilege occupies a large portion of the monastic chronicles; and it was not to be supposed that the bishops should be zealous in their defence. To this cause we may indeed attribute, in part, the ease with which they were overthrown.

To the confiscation of monastic property for the purpose of supplanting monasteries by schools and colleges, the public mind had been habituated from the time of William of Wykeham and Chicheley, to that of Cardinal Wolsey. Against their spoliation there was not a single protest from either house of convocation, whether in the province of Canterbury or of York.

I wish we could find a protest from Cranmer against the iniquitous proceedings of Crumwell, when that minister, in attempting to create a public opinion against the monks, permitted his followers to turn all religion into ridicule. As against the monks, Crumwell succeeded; but he created an alarm, which ended in a reaction, when he made it appear that by Protestantism his associates meant not a protest against popery, but a protest against all religion. In stage plays and interludes acted in desecrated churches the most sacred rites of Christianity were turned into ridicule, while the ministers of religion were exposed to the scorn and contempt of the grinning populace.*

Against these proceedings, some of the suffragans of Cranmer did protest, but Cranmer himself was overawed by Crumwell; and although, at this time, he saw little of his royal master, he applied to the *man* the legal fiction with which the law approaches the *king*, and imagined that Henry VIII. could do no wrong.

By Cranmer and his party Henry, indeed, was believed—and at this period of his reign, there is no reason why he should not be believed—when he declared it to be his intention, with the property of the monasteries, to erect schools, and to increase the number of bishoprics.

Of what took place at the gambling table in the palace, only the rumour would reach Lambeth; and, as the manner is with loyal subjects, the unwelcome rumour was disbelieved, or pronounced to be a gross exaggeration. We are continually to bear in mind that much of what is known to us was unknown or only partially known to contemporaries.

The promises of the king, like other royal promises, were forgotten amidst the calls of pleasure, or the pressure of business. They were recalled to his recollection, not by the eloquence of Cranmer, but by the alarming condition to which the country had been brought by Crumwell. The king was roused from the lethargy of dissipation by the disturbances in the north and by the Pilgrimage of

---

* See Maitland's Reformation, 236; and Burnet, i. 303. The subject is treated at length in the Introductory Chapter of this book.

Grace. As had been the case with Wolsey, so had it been with Crumwell; the king left to his minister the details of business, until there was an outcry among the people, and then Henry arose like a giant. He assumed the direction of affairs; he regained the popularity he dearly loved by throwing the blame of all past misconduct on the minister; and he was prepared to sacrifice the minister himself, if the sacrifice was demanded by the people.

The king was prepared to redress grievances, while he put down with a strong hand an insurrection which approached to the nature of a rebellion. Among other things, he redeemed his pledge to parliament; and new sees were established, though inadequately endowed, at Oxford, Peterborough, Bristol, Gloucester, and Chester. In certain conventual churches, in their respective dioceses, the cathedra, or throne, of the new bishop, was erected; and measures were taken to establish chapters of secular clergy in those ancient cathedrals from which the regulars had now been expelled.

The reader will remember the struggle of Dunstan and Lanfranc, predecessors of Cranmer, to place any cathedrals, to which their influence might extend, in the hands of the regulars. They partially succeeded, and it became a peculiarity of the Church of England, in the middle age, with a few exceptions, chiefly in Spain, that many cathedrals, instead of being governed by a dean and canons, were administered by a prior and his convent of monks. The seculars, who had been driven by Dunstan and Lanfranc from many of the cathedrals, were now, under Cranmer, restored to their ancient inheritance, and the monks were compelled to retire. The chapters of Canterbury, Winchester, Durham, Ely, Norwich, Worcester, Carlisle, and Rochester, were at this time composed of

CHAP. III.
Thomas Cranmer.
1533-56.

regulars. They were under the rule of priors, some of them mitred.

A mitred prior was the prior of Canterbury, who, when he officiated, was attired almost like a bishop. In each case, the relation of the bishop of the diocese to the priory in his cathedral was theoretically that of an abbot to his convent. These priories were now converted into colleges, and new arrangements of the chapter and of the inferior officers of the establishment became necessary. Hence there existed, and still continues to exist, in the Church of England two distinct classes of cathedrals: cathedrals of the old foundation, and cathedrals of the new foundation. With the old foundations, the reformers had no occasion to interfere. These cathedrals had from their foundation been administered by the secular clergy, and they were unmolested.* To the present hour they are regulated by statutes confirmed to them in the eleventh and twelfth centuries by the Norman kings, with powers of legislation, through which they have from time to time adapted themselves to the exigencies of the several ages through which they have passed. Although Queen Victoria has taken away the corpses formerly attached to the non-residentiary stalls, to endow new parishes or to increase the income of parishes badly endowed, those ancient stalls nevertheless remained and are claimed by the incumbents as freeholds.

As Canterbury was a cathedral administered by regulars; it required a reform amounting almost to a revolution. In effecting the change in his cathedral, the

---

* The cathedrals of the old foundation are York, London, Chichester, Exeter, Hereford, Lichfield, Lincoln, Salisbury, and Wells. Some of the old foundation cathedrals, it may be said, had new statutes given them; we may mention Lichfield for one. But I look on these rather as new promulgations or codifications of the old.

abilities of Cranmer, as a legislator, were called into play. In these matters, however, the king took a personal interest; and we must admit that the superiority of Henry in matters of detail—for he descended to details—is conspicuous.

There never was, nor was there likely to be, a good understanding between the archbishop and his chapter.

From the iniquities of the time, it was not to be expected, that the great convent of Canterbury would be entirely exempt; although we shall find the archbishop himself admitting that no charge of immorality, in the ordinary sense of the term, could be brought against that body. But that the respectable superiors of the monastery did not take steps to discover or prevent the impostures to which some unscrupulous members of the convent had recourse, we are compelled to suspect. They did not practise impostures themselves, but they must have been aware that of this offence some of the brethren were guilty, and they wilfully shut their eyes to the fact. The temptation was great. For centuries devotees had flocked to the shrine of St. Thomas, and now there was a tendency in the public to treat the history and the miracles of the martyr with a sneer scarcely concealed. To sustain the fading idea of a miraculous odour pervading the precincts of the cathedral, acts were resorted to which could be justified only by those who thought a righteous end would justify recourse to means of which righteousness could certainly not be predicated.

It is surprising to find how easily the pilgrimages to Canterbury were suppressed. One would have supposed that the whole city and county would have resisted the abolition of a custom which brought so much wealth to the inhabitants. But at this time, the wealthy seldom made pilgrimages to the shrine for the purposes of devotion; and the mob of pilgrims, in the absence of the wealthy, instead of enriching the inhabitants, made them their prayer. These came not to spend, but to beg. The grumblers, no doubt, were many, but when the authorities of Church and State had determined to suppress the superstition, the townspeople generally acquiesced, with a good grace; and fierce feelings of indignation were excited when they found that they had been all along victims of a delusion.

This feeling of disregard for the martyr had been gradually advancing of late years. When, in the time of Archbishop Warham, Erasmus visited Canterbury, he expressed himself perfectly astonished at the number of sanctified bones produced for his inspection; sculls, jawbones, teeth, hands, fingers, entire arms, all of which he and his companion, much to their disgust, were expected to kiss. He began to fear that the exhibition would have never come to an end, when the impatience of his companion interrupted "the zeal of the showman." It was thus he described the priest in his alb and with a lighted taper, who bent the knee as he indicated each sacred relic. But to the common showman a pilgrim so distinguished as Erasmus was not left; Dr. Goldwell himself, the lord prior, appeared to display certain treasures not exposed to the vulgar eye. The lord prior opened to them the shrine of which, resplendent with jewels, the least valuable part was the gold. With a white wand, Dr. Goldwell pointed out each jewel, giving its name and the name of its donor, and at the same time estimating its value. The principal gems were the gifts of sovereign princes who had knelt trembling before the queller of tyrants. In the sacristy was produced a box containing what the lord prior regarded as something more valuable than gold and precious stones—fragments of linen, originally filthy, and now filthier through age, with which St. Thomas had been accustomed "to wipe the perspiration from his face or neck, the runnings of his nose, and all the superfluities from which the most holy human frame is not free." Without a periphrasis, he exhibited the pockethandkerchief of Thomas à Becket.

The jocular, sarcastic, sneering tone of Erasmus, while observing all outward demonstrations of respect, was evidently not peculiar to himself. The worthy prior was accustomed to see an incredulous smile upon some from whom he had expected better things. We may mention the case of a lady—and ladies are the last to retire from acts of devotion long sanctioned : the easy, though well-bred, indifference manifested by Madame de Montreuil, when visiting the shrine, a few years after the visit just mentioned, of Erasmus, must have combined, with other circumstances, to convince the good and pious, but too credulous, prior Goldwell, and with him the wiser among his brethren, that, however much the treasures confided to their custody might be valued as works of art or as relics of piety, the time was passing, if it were not gone, when they could infuse into the admirers of St. Thomas a spirit of resistance to such a king as Henry VIII.

That with a convent so occupied Cranmer should have little or nothing in common is at once apparent; he regarded the prior and his brethren with contempt, and they looked upon him with mingled feelings of suspicion and fear; and yet, Thomas Goldwell, the last of the Benedictine priors of Christ Church, Canterbury, was not a contemptible person. Elected lord prior in 1517, he held the office till the dissolution of the monastery. He was a man against whose moral character the Protestant inquisitors were unable to bring the shadow of a charge, and he ruled his house well. Cranmer complained of

CHAP. III.
Thomas Cranmer.
1533-56.

him for not making grants sufficiently liberal to the archiepiscopal treasury, yet of the munificence of Prior Goldwell we have ocular demonstration to the present day. The student of history is reminded of Goldwell's good taste when he passes through the stately entrance into the precincts of Canterbury, which was planned and executed by the prior; by whom was also erected the central tower of the magnificent cathedral itself. He was contemplating the completion of Becket's crown. He is described by Erasmus—and a better witness could not be produced—as a man equally pious and judicious, and as by no means a bad Scotist. He complied, though not with a good grace, with the various changes which took place in the reign of Henry VIII., and had accepted the royal supremacy; he paid a retaining fee to Crumwell; but in theological opinions he differed from the archbishop. Cranmer, though holding no Protestant principles when he was appointed to the see of Canterbury, was nevertheless a man of progress, whereas Goldwell, though yielding to authority, was a decided conservative. He never willingly took a step in advance. Cranmer admitted that the prior acted up to the letter of any injunctions he might receive, but he complained that he was ever ready to evade or to explain them away. Such a one, standing in the relation of the prior to the archbishop, must have been peculiarly offensive to Cranmer; and in the letters of the archbishop, we find him desirous to have the prior of Canterbury removed, though it was long before he succeeded. At the same time, the prior and convent, though not prepared to show any great favour to their primate, quietly met his legal demands. They incurred—which was certainly unusual —the chief expense of the banquet at the archbishop's enthronisation, and we must admit, that the treatment they received from the archbishop was not always so gracious as might have been expected. On one occasion, for example, when the archbishop thanked the prior for some "good and kind token" he had received from "your brethren and mine, not deserved as yet;" he added, "nevertheless you should have done me much more greater pleasure if you had lent it me full of gold, not for any pleasure or delectation that I have in the thing, but for the contentation of such as I am indebted and dangered unto; which I assure you hath grieved me more of late than any worldly thing hath done a great season; in this I am bold to show you my necessity, thinking of good congruence I might in such lawful necessity be more bolder of you, and you likewise of me, than to attempt or prove any foreign friends. Wherefore, trusting in your benevolence and of all my brethren for the premises, I shall so recompense the same again, according as ye shall be well contented and pleased withal. Thus fare ye well."* There were faults on both sides. The convent gave less than they had been accustomed to give, but more than could be legally demanded of them. Cranmer felt the neglect, but could not compel them to give more.

Cranmer, no doubt, had Goldwell and several of his monks, to a certain extent, in his power. The prior and some of his brethren had been compromised in the affair of Elizabeth Barton; and the open advocacy of the imposture by two of the body cast suspicion upon all its members. But on the other hand, Goldwell, following the example which had been set by the superiors in other great monasteries, had secured the good offices of

* Letter lvii. Harl. MSS. 6,148, fol. 32, b. As abbot of the convent, the archbishop had probably some claim upon the revenues of the see, but no direct share in the dividends.

CHAP. III.

Thomas Cranmer. 1533-56.

Crumwell, and he sustained an interest in the vicegerent by sundry little attentions and presents. An ecclesiastic patronised by Crumwell might, if he acted with common discretion, assume an attitude of independence with regard to the primate.

Cranmer made no secret of his dislike of monastic institutions; he carried out his dislike even to the cathedral chapters, though he would have been glad to convert some of the religious houses into educational institutions. With respect to Canterbury, he did not hesitate to insinuate, that of the jugglery as to miracles which had been detected and exposed in other monasteries, the convent of Canterbury was not innocent. Although we acquit Goldwell of any direct patronage of the malpractices, in this respect, yet with respect to some of the monks his suspicions probably approached nearer to a certainty than those of the archbishop. But what the archbishop would expose, the prior would conceal. If wrong were done, the prior thought it were better to hush up the affair; and Goldwell would regard the offence as very venial, as it had for its object to increase the devotion of the people.

Cranmer watched the proceedings of the monastery very narrowly, and there were many persons ready to assist him in his observations and enquiries. At length, the archbishop openly declared his conviction that the blood of St. Thomas of Canterbury was but a feigned thing, and made of some red ochre or of such like matter, and he applied to the government for a commission to enquire and report.

There could be no doubt of the fact of the imposture, when once enquiry was made. Goldwell and his chapter therefore felt, that they were at the mercy of Cranmer and Crumwell, and were prepared to make the best bargain for themselves they could. An hostility of the townspeople against the monks, even when pilgrimages to St. Thomas's shrine were most popular, had always existed; and this hereditary animosity increased by the disrepute into which pilgrimages had fallen and by the spirit of the age amounting to a fanaticism against the monasteries, became inflamed to the highest pitch. In the destruction of other monasteries, Crumwell had sought to win the mob by hounding them on to plunder the monks of all that the commissioners had left; and the idea of a scramble was present to the minds, no doubt, of not a few. But the convent of Christ Church was not simply a monastery: it consisted of the members of the cathedral chapter, who were regulars, instead of being, as they ought to have been, secular clergy. It was not the intention of Henry to destroy the cathedrals; on the contrary, he took an interest in such establishments. The cathedral was saved because there stood the bishop's cathedra. But what has just been advanced will serve to show, why the prior and the convent were prepared to accept any terms proposed to them by the government.

A royal injunction, issued so early as 1536, for the abrogation of superstitious holidays or festivals, had its bearing upon the convent of Canterbury. As Cranmer complained to Crumwell, that the injunction, though emanating from the king, was not observed by the court, we may infer that it was issued at the instance of the archbishop, and that it had a political rather than a religious aspect. It was, indeed, with a special view to the abolition of the greatest of all the festivals of the Church of England as it then existed,—excepting those only which related to our Lord himself,—that orders were given that no festival should henceforth be kept during harvest time; that is, between the 1st of July and the

CHAP. III.
Thomas Cranmer.
1533-56.

29th of September.* Middle-class legislation is here perceptible. Land had been purchased by commercial men; they desired to make the most of their property; but owing to the multitude of holidays, during which the labouring classes were kept from work, they were by no means secure of carrying the harvest before the weather became foul. Readily did they, therefore, accept the injunction which Cranmer designed to be a step in advance towards the reformation of the Church.

The 7th of July arrived. It was the feast of the translation of St. Thomas of Canterbury. The archbishop was at his palace on the 6th, a day which his predecessors had long kept ostentatiously as a fast. No fast-day had been by the primates more strictly observed. Archbishop Cranmer took his place, however, in the centre of the high table in his hall, to which the public were freely admitted, and there they saw the Lord Archbishop of Canterbury enjoying a hearty meal, regaling, not on fish but on flesh.

What he did himself, he directed the prior and convent to do by command of the king. They obeyed; they feasted on the fast-day, and the day following was regarded as ferial.

> The dire ostent the fearful people viewed;

but if they were alarmed at first, lest the insulted saint should take vengeance on the Church and town, the alarm soon subsided, and the feast of the translation was extinct.

It was an easy and a pleasant triumph, followed by a remarkable proceeding, quite in character with the age, and conducted with a view not to satisfy the well-informed and educated portion of the community, but to

* Strype, 10.

make an impression upon the superstitious who required to be met on their own ground.

Men did not in those days regard death in the light of an annihilation of what was once alive. Death was regarded as the portal through which the sanctified passed into heaven; and those who, not dying in the odour of sanctity, had nevertheless been exempt from mortal sin, into purgatory. The soul of the saint was supposed to be endued with greater powers, and to be furthering invisibly the ends he had in view, when he was still in the flesh. Thomas à Becket was regarded as the personification of the principle of papal supremacy, as opposed to the supremacy of the crown. He had, in his death, triumphed over Henry II.; and Henry VIII. was determined to avenge himself upon the great enemy of his ancestor. He uncanonised the saint, who was henceforth to be called Bishop Becket. He would deal with that dead man as the papists had dealt with John Wiclif. He instituted legal proceedings against the traitor prelate. If the saint would work a miracle in vindication of himself, the king would submit to be defeated and disgraced. If the king with impunity scattered to the winds the bones of Bishop Becket, this would prove the reputed saint to be not a martyr but a traitor, who, if he possessed any powers, was now unable to defend himself, much less his worshippers.

Against "Thomas Becket," sometime Archbishop of Canterbury, "the king's attorney-general exhibited an information charging him with treason, contumacy, and rebellion." On the 24th of October, 1538, a pursuivant arrived at Canterbury, and straightway demanded admission into the cathedral. The monks knew why he had come, and he was received in solemn silence. With the insolence of an official arriving from the capital, and

CHAP. III.

Thomas Cranmer. 1533-56.

regarding the provincials with contempt, and with the irreverence also of one who, contemning superstition, had discarded all religion except that which the king's government commanded him to accept, the pursuivant hastened through the choir; he marched straight up to the shrine where thousands upon thousands had knelt in prayer, and, with a loud irreverent voice, he summoned the defunct archbishop to appear in the king's court of justice, in person or by proxy, to answer to the charge brought against him of high treason.

Silence ensued. Many were still prostrate before the shrine; their wavering hearts doubting, but not yet entirely rejecting, the legends relating to St. Thomas. They half expected some indication to be given of the martyr's anger, and they were there in an attitude to deprecate his wrath. For thirty days the summons was repeated.

When the last day came, all hope had expired. For the last time, the pursuivant stood before the shrine still resplendent with jewels and gold, his foot resting upon stones literally indented by the bare knees of the millions who had knelt there in earnest, if in mistaken, enthusiasm. There was a pause, and the imagination wandered to the crypt; and it did not require much exercise of the imagination to fancy that the lashes could be heard, as one after the other they fell upon the back of that proud king whom his prouder descendant was now avenging. The silence was broken by the hard unfeeling tone of the pursuivant's voice summoning the dead to judgment. Then there was silence again—

καὶ τῆς ἄγαν γάρ ἐστί που σιγῆς βάρος.

One by one the brethren retired, each for the last time bending the knee, as he passed it, to the shrine, which from childhood he had worshipped. The aged prior was left alone. His occupation was gone. When the shrine was demolished, what would be the use of Becket's crown? He pitied himself, the last lord prior. He pitied his brethren; from the consecrated palace of the King of Kings, which had been to many of them a happy home, from infancy to childhood, from childhood to old age—they were about to be driven homeless.*

On the 16th of November, a proclamation was issued setting forth the cause and manner of Becket's death—a proclamation which was drawn up with consummate skill and industry by Crumwell. All those points were dwelt upon which were seen to be most telling upon the public mind, which, however otherwise divided, was resolute in its resistance to the pope. The proclamation dwelt upon Becket's adhesion to a foreign potentate in opposition to the King of England, and represented his death as being inconsistent with the character of a saint. Instead of yielding his life with meekness, he defended it to the last with the ferocity of an outlaw. As the pope was hereafter to be spoken of only as the Bishop of Rome, so was St. Thomas of Canterbury ever afterwards to be described simply as Bishop Becket. His images and pictures were

---

* Wilkins, iii. 835, 836. Doubts of the authenticity of the narrative have been started because it rests on the authority of foreigners, Sanders, Pallini, and Paul III. Yet it seems to be confirmed by the proclamation of 1539, which is considered by Dr. Lingard and Dean Stanley, regarding the case from opposite quarters, to establish its authenticity. It is not improbable that, when some of the foreign Protestants represented the proceeding as absurd, Henry VIII. tampered with the documents relating to the affair, as he did with all the other public documents of the age. But neither Henry nor Cranmer were, at this time, Protestants, and the whole transaction is in accordance with the spirit of the age then passing away. They who take the opposite view dwell on certain mistakes in detail. It is not a point of much importance, but I have narrated the event, as according to the authorities, it occurred.

VOL. VII. C

to be destroyed. His festivals were to be abolished, the service, office, antiphons, collects, and prayers in his name were to be erased and put out of all books.*

The destruction of the shrine of St. Thomas may be regarded as the final overthrow of the monastic system in England, and of the worship of saints. Of this system, Thomas à Becket was the representative to the English mind; and if he were no longer to receive latria, it would be offered to none else. Hence the policy of the government to arm its officials with power in case of resistance; to surround the overthrow of Becket's shrine with legal pomp, and to make appeal to the prejudices of the people. It was the most decided step, next to the renunciation of the papal supremacy, which had as yet been taken. Upon this point Cranmer's mind never afterwards wavered; and Henry, by the retention of the abbey lands, had no choice but to support him.

The affairs of the cathedral, however, were not so bad as Prior Goldwell and his brethren had been led to suppose. When the cathedral was once more restored to the seculars, prebendal stalls, under the new constitution, were offered to those of the monks who might be willing to conform to the new statutes.

On the 20th of March, 1539, a commission was directed to the archbishop and others, authorising them to draw up a form by which, under the seal of the prior and convent, the priory of Christ Church might be surrendered to the king. They were required to make an inventory of the goods, chattels, plate, precious ornaments, and money, belonging to the unfortunate monks; and all that was movable was to be consigned to the master of the jewel-house in the Tower of London. The value of the jewels alone from the shrine of Becket must have

* Wilkins, iii. 848.

been incalculable. Of their disposal we hear little. They were soon dispersed, from the royal gaming table, among the Russells, the Seymours and the other courtiers who sprang from the royal favour to be, no doubt, a blessing to the country, as nutritious herbs from a dung-hill.

CHAP. III.
Thomas Cranmer. 1533-56.

The king, who had once more addressed his powerful mind to business, took measures for reconstructing the chapters in those cathedrals from which the usurping monks had now been ousted. It was a kind of employment in which Henry delighted, and he evidently found pleasure in letting Cranmer perceive that, occupied though he was by many things, he understood these matters quite as well as the archbishop, whose whole attention was given to ecclesiastical affairs. Henry, conscious of his intellectual superiority, took pride in causing it to be felt in every detail of office.

His readiness to discuss and his patience under contradiction, so long as the contradiction was confined to words, endeared him to all men of business, though perhaps many of them felt that the king, who to-day conversed with his minister like an intimate friend, might be as eager to sign his execution on the morrow as he had been to receive intelligence of poor Ann Boleyn's death.

The king himself drew up an extensive scheme, or, as Cranmer calls it, a device, for the re-establishment of the chapter of Canterbury Cathedral, which he intended should be a model for all the cathedrals of the new foundation. One of the reasons why the king took such a personal interest in these proceedings was that he sought, through the new dioceses he established, and through the reorganisation of the cathedral chapters, where such new organisation was required, to conceal or cover the iniquitous uses to which he had applied so much of the monastic property. He so prided himself

CHAP. III.
Thomas Cranmer.
1533–56.

upon his scheme or device for the reformation of Canterbury Cathedral that he directed Sadler, his ambassador to Scotland, to lay it before the Scotch king, "that he *might see the useful purposes to which religious houses might be applied.*" *

The scheme, a copy of which has been preserved, is admirable. He proposed to establish a provost, twelve prebendaries, six preachers, readers or professors of humanity, divinity, civil law, and physic; twenty students of divinity, ten to have exhibitions at Oxford, and ten at Cambridge; sixty grammar scholars, with a master; eight petty canons to sing in the choir, twelve singing men, ten choristers, a choir master, a gospeler, an epistoler, two sacristans, a butler and under butler, a caterer, a chief cook, an under cook, two porters, twelve almsmen, and various subordinate officers: all of them thoroughly endowed, having a separate fund for repairs, and for charitable distributions.†

Nothing was done in a niggardly spirit. All was designed to place the chapter of the Metropolitan Church on a footing which would enable it to maintain the character for a splendid hospitality by which it had been distinguished from the first foundation of our Church and its metropolitan cathedral by Augustine. A copy of the scheme was sent to the archbishop, and another copy to the prior and convent.

Cranmer objected—writing to Crumwell, for the archbishop was not the king's chief adviser and communicated with him through the only real minister of the crown at this time—to the appointment of prebendaries. He would have both name and office abolished. In fact, he was ambitious to have the sole management of the cathedral; but, as usual, he had no plan of

* Sadler's State Papers. † Remains, i. 291.

his own; he could only criticise the scheme or device which was sent to him. He begrudged the endowment of the prebendaries, amounting to about, £1,200 a year, according to the present valuation; and he maintained, that the money might be "altered to a more expedient use." He proposed that, instead of prebendaries, there should be established twenty divines, with a diminished income; and that the whole apparatus of readers and professors should be rejected as useless.

Although the cathedral establishments have not, of late years, been rendered so serviceable in the cause of religion as might have been wished, yet it is to the abuse of patronage that the fault is to be chiefly traced; and they will probably never become what they are designed to be, a provision for learned men—those who are not called to be pastors, but whose business it is to edify the body of Christ,*—until every canon or prebendary be compelled to perpetual residence, and be prohibited, under any pretence, from holding a living *in commendam* with a stall. A pastor should devote the whole of his time to his flock, but as God has appointed in His church not only pastors but also prophets and teachers, there ought to be provision made for those, who are to be employed in learned labours for the perfecting of the saints.

But although the archbishop had not shown much administrative wisdom in the management of the convent, and although he was obstructive rather than co-operative in the formation of the new chapter, he was anxious to secure for himself the patronage; and passing over the venerable and munificent prior, he urged the appointment of Dr. Crome as the first dean.† Of this no complaint can

---

* Ephes. iv. 10, 11.

† The influence of the archbishop with the king was not sufficient to prevent him from making a mere political appointment, and Nicolas

be fairly made, for Dr. Crome was a reformer, and Dr. Goldwell would have been a hindrance to the archbishop in many of the measures which he was already devising for the good of the Church. Dr. Goldwell was offered the first stall next to the dean in the new foundation, or a pension on his retirement. He naturally did not choose to take the second place in a cathedral over which he had long presided, if not wisely yet with munificence, and he accepted a pension equivalent to what would now amount to £800 a year.*

The pensions settled on other members of the priory, who refused appointments under the new system, were here, and elsewhere, considerable; and from documents in the augmentation office, we infer that they were regularly paid.

The treatment of the priory of Christ Church, which had, for many years, formed the chapter of the cathedral, is the more worthy of note since it tends to contradict the accusations brought wholesale against religious houses by Protestant inquisitors of Crumwell's appointment. Among the convents most maligned, was that of Christ Church, Canterbury. We have seen that in one respect, for the gross impostures of the inferior members winked at by the superiors, the convent deserved condemnation.

Wotton became the first dean of Canterbury under the new foundation. Cranmer's endeavour to obtain power over his chapter was only the continuation of an old controversy. To a secular chapter the diocesan was only the visitor; in a chapter of regulars he was regarded as the abbot, but there was a continual struggle to make his authority merely nominal. This dispute has prevailed at Canterbury from the earliest times. The archbishop's power as de jure abbot was reduced to the merest form in the twelfth century.

* It is presumed that Goldwell died in 1553, as his name does not appear in the exchequer return of pensions payable to retired members of religious houses in that or any subsequent year.

But the charge of immorality, beyond what is implied in this assertion, except among a few individuals, who were justly punished, is disproved by the fact, that of the twelve prebendaries appointed by the archbishop or the king, as they divided the patronage, eight had been monks of the dissolved monastery; or rather, we might say, all had been monks except two, for both Thomas Goldwell and William Wychope, though they preferred a pension, had each the option of a stall.

The ten minor canons and nine scholars, or choristers, were reappointed, and pensions or gratuities were offered to all for whom the dean and chapter were unable to find suitable situations.* We are consequently brought to this alternative — either the inquisitors appointed by Crumwell were libellers or Thomas Cranmer was a patron of immorality.

One transaction must be noted, as it tends to the credit of Cranmer's character. When the commission for regulating the constitution of the cathedral body was sitting, the reform of the school passed under review. The predominant middle-class feeling here displayed itself, and it was proposed to exclude the children of the poor.

The usual arguments, with which we were familiar some thirty or forty years ago, were produced. The children of husbandmen, it was said, were "more meet for the plough and to be artificers than to occupy the place of the learned sort." This notion Cranmer nobly combated. He pointed to the fact, that the children

* The amount of pensions granted to monks who were ousted from their houses throughout the country was considerable, and tells in favour of the monasteries. Men against whom no charge could be brought were bribed to resign. To the superiors of houses the pensions varied, according to modern computation, from £2,000 a year to £60. Priors of cells generally received from £130 to £200. This also speaks for the credit of the king's government.

CHAP. III.
Thomas Cranmer.
1533–56.

of the poor were often endowed " with more singular gifts of nature, which are also gifts of God, such as eloquence, memory, apt pronunciation, sobriety, and such like, and that also commonly they were more apt to apply to their study than is the gentleman's son delicately educated." He combated the vulgar notion that, " if the poor man's son received the same advantages of education as the son of the rich, there would be none to perform the humbler duties of life; and as we have, it was urged, as much need of ploughmen as of any other state, so that all sorts of men should not go to school."

He contended that to refuse to afford to children with high intellectual capabilities the means and opportunity of cultivating their endowments was to act directly in opposition to the God who gave them, and, said the archbishop with eloquent sarcasm :—" to say the truth, I take it that none of us all here, being gentlemen born (as I think),* but had our beginning that way, from a low base parentage: and through the benefit of learning, and other civil knowledge, for the most part all gentlemen ascend to their estate."

It was in the interests of learning, rather than in the interests of the poor, that Cranmer argued; though in doing so, the rights of the poor were vindicated. The difficulty, at this time, was to prevail upon men to accept a learned education. They were bribed to do so by the offer of a cheap education; and of that education the poor, if so minded, had as much right to avail themselves as the rich. Of that right the middle classes, now rising into importance, would have deprived the poor, the consequence of which exclusiveness would have been an insult to the industrial classes, while its tendency would have been also to diminish the number of scholars.

* Strype, 126. Was the parenthesis designed as an attack upon Crumwell? None of the commissioners were high-born.

This point Cranmer carried; but although the archbishop defended his cathedral, when attempts were made to compel the chapter to grant long leases in favour of the courtiers, his relations to the cathedral body, if not unfriendly, never became intimate.

We now revert to general history. It had long been an object with Cranmer to induce the king to establish political relations with the German princes; for he foresaw clearly that this would open the way to further reformations in the church.

At his suggestion Melancthon had been frequently invited by the king to visit England; and Melancthon had always declined. His reason, as assigned in his private correspondence, was his conviction that Henry had only a political and not a religious object in view.[*] This was probably the feeling prevalent among the German princes. But affairs on the Continent were so unsettled in the year 1538, that on the renewal of negotiations with them on the part of Henry they sent an embassy to England. It was a legation singular in its character, the members of it appearing before the king in a two-fold character, that of ambassadors and that of divines; ministers of man and ministers of God. They were not on that account the less welcome to Henry, who was not unwilling to display his abilities as a statesman and his learning, which was not inconsiderable, as a theologian. He even proposed to conduct a theological discussion with them in person. At the head of the embassy were Francis Burgrat, chancellor to the Elector of Saxony; George a Boyneburgh, a nobleman of Hesse; and Frederick Myconius, superintendent of the reformed church at Gotha.[†] They represented John Frederick, Elector of Saxony, and Philip, Landgrave of Hesse, and came for the

---

[*] Burnet, Strype, Seckendorf.   [†] Ibid.

ostensible purpose of forming a league against the pope, and, by a consultation with the English divines, of drawing up a common Confession of faith. But an obstacle presented itself at the commencement of their proceedings. It was proposed that the Church of England should accept as its doctrinal formulary the Confession of Augsburg. To this indignity Henry, always right-hearted when the honour of the country was concerned, would not for a moment consent. He had no objection to discuss the articles, and to hear what the Protestants had to say. He had no objection, if, after discussion, the Protestants were found to be Catholic or orthodox, to blend these articles with an English formulary; but a German formulary the Church of England must not accept; rather, on the contrary, the Germans must subscribe to a Confession of faith drawn up in England. Soon after the arrival of the legation, a royal commission was issued for a conference with the Protestants; and the commission represented fairly the two great sections of the Church of England, the men of the old learning and the men of the new learning. At the head of the former was the Bishop of Durham, Dr. Tonstal, and the latter were under the leadership of the Primate himself. While the discussion related to the chief articles of belief, there was little or no difference of opinion. The confession asserted the Catholic faith. But when the Protestants insisted on certain reforms requisite to reduce the Church of England to their own level, then were opened the flood-gates of controversy, which the king had no inclination, at the present time, to close. The archbishop laboured to effect a compromise between the opposing parties, and the position of his mind at this time, qualified him to act as a mediator. He would accept the regulations and the dogmas of the Church of England as they had been transmitted; but, with the exception of the dogma of transubstantiation, he was willing, or rather desirous, to make great concessions for the sake of peace. If he may be said to have had any definite object in view, it was to unite all parties who were opposed to the pope, by inducing or compelling them to adopt one Confession of faith.

On transubstantiation, ere long to become the test of orthodoxy on the part of the papist, the dogma for the denial of which life was to be sacrificed on the part of the Protestants, nothing was now said. The Lutherans had tacitly agreed, that it should be an open question, and well would it have been for the peace of Christendom if to that determination they had been permitted to adhere. Besides, the difference between consubstantiation and transubstantiation appeared so slight that they were willing to avoid discussion. But the points on which the Lutherans insisted were the administration of the Eucharist in both kinds, the renunciation of the practice of private masses,* and the constrained celibacy of the clergy.

On the latter point Cranmer felt a personal interest, but probably he would have preferred that the subject should not at this time be mooted.

The celibacy of the clergy was, as all admitted, not a divine law; it was a disciplinary regulation of the Church. A regulation of the Church, however, admitted of a dispensation from the Church. Dispensations for marriage had been occasionally granted by the pope; and the papal power to grant dispensations had now been conferred upon the Archbishop of Canterbury. He, being himself a married man, had granted his dispensations

---

* This was to them important, because their object was to convert the mass into a communion.

liberally, and many of the clergy had not acted with his own discretion. Instead of keeping their wives in a state of oriental seclusion, they had paraded them before the world, some of their wives having previously lived with them as concubines. This had militated against public opinion; a large majority of the laity being especially prejudiced against a married clergy. It would have been, therefore, for his advantage, and for the benefit of the clergy who had acted under his dispensation, to have avoided for the present any discussion on the merits of the case. On the other subjects, Cranmer's opinion accorded with those of the Germans, with this difference, that they considered as essential, what he desired to see reformed without admitting that a reform was obligatory, or to be immediately enforced. On the subject of auricular confession, his opinion was perhaps now, what in his catechism he declared it to be ten years later. At that time, he desired to leave it optional, but he did not wish to see the practice wholly abandoned.

Henry soon perceived, that the legation appeared at his court in the capacity of missionaries rather than as ambassadors; that what to him was of secondary was to them of primary importance; and he knew that in that character they were unpopular. When he came to converse with them on politics, he found that they were inclined to treat him as if the German princes were his equals, whereas the King of England was the equal not of the princes but of their emperor. The proud and patriotic Henry would not permit the German princes to approach him, except as an aristocracy seeking the protection of a sovereign. He was willing to form an alliance with the Germans against the pope, but not as one of a league; if a league was formed, the King of England must be their leader, and of that league the sovereign head.* He must be to them not less than the emperor now was. Henry was always a patriot; he was not a foreigner, or the son of a foreigner.

. It was this feeling on the part of Henry, which induced him to treat the legation with an amount of discourtesy and neglect which was perceived and resented. The archbishop complained of it; and in a letter which he wrote to Crumwell, we have a description of the kind of treatment to which the representatives of the German princes were subjected:—

Concerning the orators of Germany, I am advertised that they are very evil lodged where they be; for besides the multitude of rats daily and nightly running in their chambers (which is no small disquietness), the kitchen standeth directly against their parlour where they daily dine and sup, and by reason thereof the house savoureth so ill that it offendeth all men that come into it. Therefore, if your lordship do but offer them a more commodious house to demore in, I doubt not but that they will accept that offer most thankfully. Albeit, I am sure that they will not remove for this time. †

The conservatives, now supported by the king, refused to be persuaded by the archbishop, when he urged them

---

* Bishop Gardyner had urged this on another occasion. "The king," he says, "is a sovereign magistrate, vested with imperial jurisdiction; and in consequence of that prerogative, head of the Church of England: but the princes of Germany are but dukes at the highest. They are no more than subordinate governors, and such as make no scruple to own their emperor for their chief lord. Now, since we prove the king head of the Church of England, from his civil supremacy, it will follow by parity of reason that the emperor is head of the Churches in Germany. Things standing thus, which way can these princes be in a condition to perfect a treaty, or settle an agreement of religion, between us? Which way can this be done, without the consent of his imperial majesty the head of their Church?"—Collier, iv. 323.

† Remains, letter ccxxxi. Cotton MSS. Cleop. E. v. f. 212.

to concede to the very moderate proposals of the Germans; and all that the archbishop could obtain for his friends was a dismissal from the king so courteous and civil, as almost to amount to the incivility of showing, that the hour of their departure was an hour of relief to the royal mind.

This visit of the German Lutherans to England was, however, a crisis in the life of Archbishop Cranmer. Their private conversation made a more lasting impression upon the archbishop's mind, than their discussions in public; and at this period, those seeds of Protestantism were sown in his mind which, in the subsequent reign, produced such abundant fruit.

As regards the king, his attention was now withdrawn from continental affairs by the immediate exigencies of the home government. Henry, by virtue of his conceded supremacy, had decided upon the dissolution of the monasteries; but it did not follow that the confiscated property should all of it pass into the royal treasury. The heirs and representatives of the founders of religious houses, who had always reserved certain privileges for themselves, might fairly claim the property, if it were to be alienated from the uses to which it had been devoted by their pious ancestors. It is said, that Cranmer and some of the clergy who acted with him, proposed that a portion of it should be dedicated to the service of religion and charity. If the proposal was ever formally made, I have seen no proof of it; and I should doubt its ever having taken a more formal shape than that of a suggestion in the sermons of Latimer. The clergy did not concern themselves much about monastic property, and some of them, as was the case with Cranmer, shared in the spoils. Still, enough was said and done to render it necessary to secure it for the king by the provisions of an act of parliament. Crumwell therefore received orders to prepare a bill, or he may himself have suggested the proceeding, although for the introduction of such a measure a more inconvenient time could not have been chosen. The disturbances in Lincolnshire and the insurrection in Yorkshire, which assumed the high-sounding title of the Pilgrimage of Grace, and almost amounted to a rebellion, had indeed been put down by the strong arm and the energetic measures of the king. But no one can read the state papers of the period without perceiving, that the government had been thoroughly alarmed, and had still grounds for anxiety.* Henry, moreover, on enquiry, found that the strength of the insurrection lay in the honest fear that the king—led astray by his plebeian counsellor, more obnoxious, on account of his humble origin, to the common people than to the aristocracy—was about to overthrow the ecclesiastical institutions of the country, and with them the rights and liberties of the people—the very throne itself. As we have seen it to be invariably the case in all preceding insurrections, so was it now: loyalty to the king was proclaimed, and perhaps felt; it was only to rescue him from his counsellors that the people rose. Those counsellors had already confiscated the lesser monasteries; they had pronounced sentence on the abbeys and greater monasteries; and where was all this to stop? Monastic property having been confiscated, would not church property follow? At the same time complaint was made of new inventions, contrary to the law of God; it was felt to be a hardship that the Pater Noster was turned into an Our Father, and that the Ten Commandments should be said in English instead of the Latin, to which the people were accustomed. The feelings of discontent were not confined to the lower orders of society; the king became aware, that the lay lords in parliament, though ready to draw

* State Papers, i. 526.

their swords and to die, if need should be, in the king's quarrel, felt that the people had right on their side; and in both houses of parliament the reformations already accomplished were cordially supported by a minority of the lords spiritual.* The difficulties of the government were also increased by those blasphemous publications, of which mention has been made, and which, under pretence of zeal in the Protestant cause, had already made that cause to stink in the nostrils of peaceable and quiet subjects, who had meekly submitted to changes in the Church authorised by convocation and parliament, but who were piously alarmed when they found every species of wrong and robbery encouraged under the name of religion. These had been, by Crumwell, it will be remembered, countenanced, in order that the public mind might be inflamed against the monasteries; but it was very frequently found in the plays which he patronised, that while the monks were held up to ridicule, no fact or person was held sacred. His ability, when now he yielded to the superior judgment of the king, and was prepared to carry his measures, in being able to maintain his character as a man of God, among the Puritans, will be admired or censured, as it is viewed from the intellectual or the moral side.

The king was determined first to proclaim to the in-

* After the passing of the act, a contemporary Protestant wrote thus:—"How mercyfully, how plentifully and purely hath God sende his worde unto us here in England! Agayne, how unthankfully, how rebelliously, how carnally and unwillingly do we receive it! Who ys there almost that will have a Bible but he must be compelled thereto? How loth be our priestes to teach th' commaundements, the articles of the faith, and the Pater Noster in English! Agayne, how unwillinge be the people to lerne it! Yee they gest at it, calling it the new Pater Noster and new lernynge; so that as, helpe me God, if we amend not, I feare we shalbe in moare boudage and blindnes then ever we were."—Archæologia, xxiii. 59.

surgents that they had suffered themselves to be unnecessarily alarmed; and then to keep the advocates of Protestantism within certain limitations and boundaries, by introducing a bill—which afterwards became known and reprobated as the act of six articles, or, as the Puritans, who liked to give hard names to hard acts, were wont to call it, "the whip with six strings."

By this bill the King hoped to pacify the conservatives, whom the late events had rendered numerous. The bill was to satisfy them that no revolution was intended, and to give answer to the question, Where is this to stop? They would then, it was hoped, submit to the appropriation, on the part of the king, of the confiscated abbey lands; and the agents of Crumwell were busy among all classes of the people to win their assent. The old aristocracy felt that their claim to the lands their ancestors had given away was not likely to be admitted, and to them was held out a promise of due consideration when the spoils were divided. The younger courtiers and new-made lords were aware that by royal favour, so capriciously exercised, their own turn would come; or that by success at the royal gambling table, they would themselves profit by an act so profitable to the king. The House of Commons was satisfied by the prospect held out to it, that the enriched king would never more demand a subsidy of his people. Henry was, no doubt, sincere when he made a promise to that effect; but the sincerity of a gambler depends upon a cast of the dice. To pay his debts of honour was, in his opinion, more important than to keep his promise to the Commons.

This is not surprising; but what does surprise us is, to find that in this parliament, which gave the *coup de grâce* to the monastic institute, there sat twenty-seven abbots, of whom eighteen voted at the second, and seventeen at

CHAP. III.
Thomas Cranmer.
1532–56.

the third reading of the bill which transferred the property of their houses to the treasury of the king. There had been considerable jobbing in the monasteries, as soon as it was known that on their dissolution the king was determined. Long leases, which amounted to donations of estates, were made; and Crumwell probably had the means of exposing some of the abbots who with their brethren had acted thus dishonourably; although, in making the best of these circumstances, the abbots themselves may have thought that they were only doing what was perfectly justifiable. The abbots also and priors were liberally pensioned, and few suffered materially, so far as they were personally concerned.

So important in the eyes of Henry did the work of this parliament, which was to abolish for ever a time-honoured institution of the country, appear to be, that he determined upon opening it with more than ordinary ceremony, together with a solemn religious service. He was not one of those weak men who despise little things, and he fully appreciated the importance to all, except a few—rather pretenders to wisdom than really wise—of a *coup de théâtre*. Minutely did the king therefore arrange all the particulars of an equestrian procession from Westminster Palace to Westminster Abbey, and of the religious procession within the sacred walls of that splendid edifice. From the gentlemen and squires, who headed the procession, to the dukes, marquises, earls, viscounts, and barons, each with his squire at his side, and all on horseback, the king attended to every detail. The archbishop's horse awaited him, as he landed at Westminster, at the head of the steps; and riding by the side of the Archbishop of York, the two primates, each having his cross borne before him, headed the bishops and abbots.

When they dismounted at the king's "lighting place," the west door of the abbey was thrown open, and a splendid vista was revealed to the eye. The lord abbot was there *in pontificalibus*, with mitre, with pastoral staff pointing inwards, with his gloves, and his sandals: to all outward appearance, and except in minute particulars which did not attract the eye of the uninitiated, he was accoutred as a bishop. His brethren arranged themselves two and two in their splendid copes. When the king's procession entered the abbey, they proceeded on foot up the nave to the choir, where the king took his seat in "his place royal." At the south side sat the Archbishop of York, attended by his suffragans of Durham and Carlisle; the lords spiritual occupied the south side of the chancel, headed by the Archbishop of Canterbury, by whose side stood the Bishop of Rochester, his crossbearer.

Assisted by two abbots *in pontificalibus* the Bishop of Carlisle, as chaplain of the House of Lords, sang the mass of the Holy Ghost. When the mass, at which Cranmer assisted, was concluded, the archbishop, at the head of the House of Lords, proceeded to the Parliament House. Here the king, being seated on the throne, the Lord Chamberlain declared, in general terms, the causes and intent for which the parliament had been summoned. So carefully did Henry attend to every detail which might invest the present parliament with a character of more than ordinary importance, and so intent was he on shifting the blame of the dissolution of the monasteries from his own shoulders to those of the three estates of the realm, that he directed the Journal of the House of Lords to commence with this solemn sentence:—

A parliament commenced and held at Westminster on the

CHAP. III.
Thomas Cranmer.
1533-56.

28th day of the month of April, in the year of the reign of the most dread and powerful prince Henry the Eighth by the grace of God, King of England and France, Defender of the Faith, Lord of Ireland, and on Earth Supreme Head of the Church of England, the Thirty-first.

To the praise and glory of the Omnipotent God, the honour, decorum, peace, quiet, tranquillity, security, and reformation of the whole realm, commonwealth, and sovereignty of England, in the name of the holy and undivided Trinity, the Father, Son, and Holy Spirit, after solemn mass fitly and devoutly celebrated, and the Divine aid most humbly implored and invoked, on Monday, viz. the 28th day of the month of April, in the year of the reign of the said Lord King the thirty-first, on the first day of this Parliament, the Lord King himself in the Chamber, commonly called the Parliament Chamber, within his Palace of Westminster, sat on his royal throne, being then present the nobles and lords of the whole realm of England both temporal and spiritual, with the commons then summoned to Parliament and convoked by royal mandate.*

On consulting the journals, we discover no report of a debate, or even a hint that any discussion, at any time, took place; but we have indirect evidence, to which we shall presently refer, that some discussions certainly took place.

Business commenced on the 5th of May, when, at the king's suggestion, a committee was appointed to report upon the different opinions now in vogue on the subject of religion, and to suggest a measure for the promotion of unity. Here it was that the angry discussions must have occurred, if angry discussions there were. The committee was selected very fairly from members, as we should now say, of opposite sides of the house. At the head of the men of the "new learning" sat the Archbishop of Canterbury, while the men of the "old learning" found a leader in the Archbishop of York. It is

* Lords' Journals, i. 103.

probable that the committee was formed under the conviction that they would not be able to come to an agreement, and that therefore the suggestion of the measure to be adopted would be left to the government.

Crumwell was nominated to serve on the committee. This nomination must have placed him in an awkward position; he could not side with the Protestants, and certainly had no ambition to give a triumph to the Papists. He was appointed to serve on the committee out of deference to his office as vicegerent, but he probably never attended; for, while the committee was sitting, he was busily engaged in carrying through the house the great measure which he and the king had at heart: for the statute of six articles was not their first or chief object. The *dissolution* of the monasteries had been effected by an act of the royal supremacy; but the *appropriation* of the confiscated property by the crown required an act of parliament, without which the legality of sales and leases might have been called in question. How careful Henry was to produce on the minds of the public the right impression, may be seen from the preamble to the bill. The preamble to bills in this reign are of little service as historical documents, for the king had no special regard to truth; but they are serviceable as showing what the king wished to impress as truth upon the minds of his subjects. He first created a public opinion, and then sustained it.

Where divers and sundry abbots, priors, abbesses, prioresses, and other ecclesiastical governors and governesses of divers monasteries, abbathies, priories, nunneries, colleges, hospitals, houses of friars, and other religious and ecclesiastical houses and places within this our sovereign Lord, the King's realm of England and Wales, of their own free and voluntary minds, good wills, and assents, without constraint, coaction, or compulsion of any manner of person or persons, sithen the fourth day of February the twenty-seventh year of the reign of our now most dread sovereign Lord, by the due order and course of the common laws of this his realm of England, and by their sufficient writings of record, under their covenant and common seals, have severally given, granted, and by the same their writings severally confirmed all their said monasteries, abbathies, priories, nunneries, colleges, hospitals, houses of friars, and other religious ecclesiastical houses and places, and all their sites, circuits, and precincts of the same, and all and singular their manors, lordships, granges, meases, lands, tenements, meadows, pastures, rents, reversions, services, words, tithes, pensions, portions, churches, chapels, advowsons, patronages, annuities, rights, entries, conditions, commons, leets, courts, liberties, privileges, and franchises, appertaining or in any wise belonging to any such monastery, abbathy, priory, nunnery, college, hospital, house of friars, and other religious and ecclesiastical houses and places, or to any of them, by whatsoever name or corporation they or any of them were then named or called, and of what order, habit, religion, or other kind or quality soever they or any of them were then reputed, known, or taken, to have and to hold all the said monasteries, abbathies, priories, nunneries, colleges, hospitals, houses of friars, and other religious and ecclesiastical houses and places, sites, circuits, precincts, manors, lands, tenements, meadows, pastures, rents, reversions, services, and all other the premises, to our said sovereign lord, his heirs and successors for ever, and the same their said monasteries, abbathies, priories, nunneries, colleges, hospitals, houses of friars, and other religious and ecclesiastical houses and places, sites, circuits, precincts, manors, lordships, granges, meases, lands, tenements, meadows, pastures, rents, reversions, services, and other the premises, voluntarily, as is aforesaid, have renounced, left, and forsaken, and every of them hath renounced, left, and forsaken.*

From an examination of the Lords' Journals, I am led to the conclusion that, when a government measure was

* Statutes at Large, ii. 265.

introduced into the House of Lords, no division was called for, or permitted; but that those who declined to vote in favour of it obtained permission to stay away. The two archbishops and their suffragans assented to the confiscation of the monastic property; and though it is possible, as it is sometimes stated, that they suggested a better application of it, yet this does not appear. Of the abbots, as I have already had occasion to remark, eighteen sanctioned the second reading of the bill by their presence. We may presume that, at the third reading, some opposition was intended; for on that occasion the king himself attended, as if for the purpose of overawing the members. Henry was accustomed, throughout his reign, to attend occasionally the debates in the house. No one knew better than he how to assume, and when to throw off, the trappings of royalty; he made his appearance without ceremony on these occasions, and generally, as far as I can discover, when he had a personal object to carry. What is very remarkable is, that he never once attended when the bill was introduced which was intended to abolish diversity of opinion on certain articles concerning the Christian religion—"the whip with six strings."

The preliminary measures to the introduction of this bill were taken on the 16th of May. On that day, there was a full attendance in the house, and among the lords spiritual sat the Archbishop of Canterbury. It was natural that Crumwell should shrink from introducing a measure which, though he could not have anticipated all the clamour it excited among his former supporters and friends, he was quite aware would be to them very unpalatable. The bill, therefore, was confided to the Duke of Norfolk. He remarked that there was no probability of their receiving a report from the committee appointed on the 5th of May, and therefore he submitted the six articles to be freely discussed, not in committee, but by the whole house.

The six questions to be discussed were the following:—

1. Whether the Eucharist be really the body of our Lord without transubstantiation.

2. Whether the Eucharist should be given to the people in both kinds.

3. Whether vows of chastity made by men and women ought to be observed *de jure divino*.

4. Whether *de jure divino* private masses should be retained.

5. Whether it be lawful *de jure divino* for priests to marry.

6. Whether *de jure divino* auricular confession is necessary.

We cannot say that the house came to any hasty decision on these important questions; and it is necessary, for the elucidation of this portion of Cranmer's history, that, by a reference to the Lords' Journals, we should trace the passage of this bill through the house, and note the attendances both of the king and of the archbishop.

The questions were proposed, as we have just seen, on the 16th of May. On the 19th the king was present; but it was not to discuss these questions. The reason of the royal presence is to be found in the fact that this day was read, for the third time, the bill to enable the king to apply to his own purposes the confiscated property of the dissolved monasteries; nothing was said on the subject of the six articles.

The appropriation to the crown of the monastic property being the great work of the session, the parliament was prorogued by commission, on the 23rd of May. It had been found that the temporal peers had been unwilling to engage in a theological discussion; and instead of debating the articles in the whole house, they had appointed a committee of the lords spiritual to confer with the king as to the answer to be returned to the questions which had been already propounded. The king evidently assumed that whatever might be determined in a committee so constituted would be at once accepted and adopted by the house. Consequently, when parliament resumed its sittings on the last day of May, the lord chancellor brought a message from the king, stating that not only the lords spiritual, but his majesty himself acting with them, had studied the whole subject, and had laboured so as to have arrived at a unanimous conclusion. He desired, therefore, that a statute should be enacted, not, observe, to compel his subjects to subscribe to the articles, but, which is a very different thing, to prohibit them from speaking against the articles which would now become part and parcel of the law of the land. Two committees were then appointed, each to recommend the draft of the statute; the house reserving to itself the right of adopting, rejecting, or modifying them as might seem to the house expedient. The committees consisted, one of the Archbishop of Canterbury, the Bishop of Ely, the Bishop of St. Asaph, and Dr. Petre; and the other of the Archbishop of York, and the Bishops of Durham and Winchester, with Dr. Tregonwell.

It was probably foreseen that by the two committees thus formed and prepared to act on discordant principles, nothing satisfactory would be done; and again, therefore, the king took the matter into his own hands. A draft of a bill of pains and penalties was prepared by the king himself, and was introduced into the house on the 7th of

CHAP. III.
Thomas Cranmer.
1533-56.

June by the Archbishop of York.* Hence we may fairly suppose that the Archbishop of Canterbury, as he was not employed on the occasion, had given an opinion unfavourable to the proposed measure.

But other steps had been taken before the bill of pains and penalties was introduced. The judgment of convocation on the questions proposed for discussion had been sought for and obtained. The convocation held a session on the 2nd of June, and the lower house being represented by its prolocutor, the answers returned were:—

1. That in the blessed sacrament of the altar, by the strength and efficacy of Christ's mighty word, it being spoken by a priest, is present really the natural body and blood of our Saviour Jesu Christ, conceived of the Virgin Mary, under the form of bread and wine. And that after consecration there remaineth no other substance but the substance of his foresaid natural body. 2. That communion in both kinds is not necessary *ad salutem*, by the law of God, to all persons; and that it is to be believed and not doubted of, but that in the flesh and form of bread is the very blood, and in the blood under the form of wine is the very flesh, as well apart as though they were both together. 3. That priests after the order of priesthood received, as afore, may not marry by the law of God. 4. That vows of chastity or widowhood by man or woman made to God advisedly be to be observed by the law of God, and that it exempteth them from other liberties of Christian people, which without that they might enjoy. 5. That it is meet and necessary that private masses be continued and admitted in this our English Church and congregation, as

* That the bill was drawn by the king is a known fact.—Wilkins, iii. 848. Ex. MS. Cott. Cleop. E. v. fol. 313. It has been said that some of the more stringent clauses were inserted at the suggestion of the bishops, contrary to the inclination of the king. This gratuitous assertion is contradicted by facts. On the merits or demerits of the bill the bishops were divided. The primate and many of his suffragans were the chief opponents to the bill. And it is difficult to understand why the bishops should be truculent, and the murderer of his wives and friends have a monopoly of mercy.

whereby good Christian people ordering themselves accordingly do receive both godly and goodly consolations and benefits. And it is agreeable also to God's law. 6. That auricular confession is expedient to be retained and continued, used and frequented in the Church of God.*

Although, on the 7th of June, the bill was introduced by the Archbishop of York, yet Cranmer was in his place, that is to say, he was present when the bill was read the first time. All who were present voted for it; the member of the house who dissented from a measure signified his dissent by absenting himself. On the 9th of June the bill was read a second time, and on the 10th it was read the third time by the law officers of the crown. On both of these occasions Cranmer was in his place. He was also in the house on the 14th, when the bill was returned with amendments from the Commons, which amendments being accepted, the amended bill was read a first and second time. He was present on the 16th, when the bill was read a third time. He did not attend on the 17th, when no public business was transacted; and neither he nor the Archbishop of York was in his place on the 24th.

On that day there was a conference between the Lords and the Commons to make a slight alteration in the bill. It had not yet received the royal assent, but, as it had passed the two houses, it required all married clergymen to put away their wives on that very day—the feast of St. John the Baptist. This would have secured for the married clergy the respite of nearly a year, and it was now resolved that the act should come into operation on the 12th of the following month. Although Cranmer had been present at all the readings of the bill of pains and penalties

* Wilkins, iii. 845.   Ex. reg. Cranmer, fol. 9, et ex. reg. Convoc. et Excerpt. Heylin.

previously to this amendment, his absence from the third reading of the amended bill is no sign of his disapproving of the penalties, and he was present at a later hour of the same day, when the king in person gave to the bill his royal assent, and then prorogued the parliament. The king was not present on any single occasion when this bill was discussed;* and it is not probable, after the draft had been decided upon in the royal councils, that any opposition to it would be offered. But that there was a decided opposition to the bill, we know from the testimony of Cranmer himself, who appealed to Gardyner in the next reign, daring him to deny the assertion if he could. The king did in some way or other silence the opposition, but he was not unopposed; the objections made had been urged at the committee meetings.

That this act concerning the punishment of those who "either violate or impugn the articles aforesaid" is justly called a bloody act, if we have regard to its enactments, everyone will admit.

They are as follows:—

I. If any person by word, writing, printing, cyphering, or any otherwise do preach, teach, dispute, or hold opinion, that in the blessed sacrament of the altar, under form of bread and wine (after the consecration thereof), there is not present really the natural body and blood of our Saviour Jesus Christ, conceived by the Virgin Mary; or that after the said consecration there remaineth any substance of bread and wine, or any other sub-

---

* And yet in his address to the Devonshire rebels, in the next reign, Cranmer asserts that the bill would not have been passed unless the "King's Majesty had himself come to the Parliament House." Cranmer's memory perhaps failed him, as was not improbable after the lapse of several years, and he may have confounded the presence of the king at the discussions on the monastery bill with those that took place on the bill of six articles. His assertion is, however, of great value as stating the strength of the opposition.

stance but the substance of Christ, God and Man; or that in the flesh under the form of bread is not the very body of Christ; or that with the blood, under the form of wine, is not the very flesh of Christ as well apart as though they were both together; or affirm the said sacrament to be of other substance than is aforesaid; or deprave the said blessed sacrament: then he shall be adjudged as an heretic, and suffer death by burning, and shall forfeit to the king all his lands, tenements, hereditaments, goods, and chattels, as in case of high treason.

II. That if any person preach in any sermon or collection openly made, or teach in any common school or congregation, or obstinately affirm or defend that the communion of the blessed sacrament in both kinds is necessary for the health of man's soul, or ought or should be ministerd in both kinds; or that it is necessary to be received by any person, other than priests, being at mass and consecrating the same:

III. Or that any man, after the order of priesthood received, may marry or contract matrimony:

IV. Or that any man or woman which advisedly hath vowed or professed, or should vow or profess, chastity or widowhood may marry or contract marriage:

V. Or that private masses be not lawful, or not laudable, or should not be used, or be not agreeable to the laws of God:

VI. Or that auricular confession is not expedient and necessary to be used in the Church of God: he shall be adjudged to suffer death, and forfeit land and goods as a felon.

If any priest, or other man or woman, which advisedly hath vowed chastity or widowhood do actually marry or contract matrimony with another; or any man which is or hath been a priest do carnally use any woman to whom he is or hath been married, or with whom he hath contracted matrimony, or openly be conversant or familiar with any such woman: both the man and the woman shall be adjudged felons. Commissions also shall be awarded to the bishop of the diocese, his chancellor, commissary, and others, to enquire of the heresies, felonies, and offences aforesaid. And also justices of peace in their sessions, and every steward, under-steward, and deputy-steward, in their leet or law-day, by the oaths of twelve men, have authority to enquire of all the heresies, felonies, and offences aforesaid.*

Into the history of this act I have entered the more fully, that the reader may judge for himself how far a story current of Cranmer's conduct on this occasion is substantiated by a reference to facts. The authority for the story is Foxe, and his statement has been repeated, with more or less of eulogy or of rhetoric, by one writer after another. The following is Foxe's statement :—

> At the time of setting forth of the six articles mention was made before in the story of King Henry VIII., how adventurously this Archbishop Thomas Cranmer, standing, as it were, *post alone* against the whole parliament, disputing and replying three days together against the said articles.
>
> Insomuch that the king, when neither he could mistake his reasons, and yet would needs have these articles to pass, *required him to absent himself*, for the time, out of the chamber, while the act should pass, and so he did, and how the king afterwards sent all the lords of the parliament to Lambeth to cheer his mind again, that he might not be discouraged.

Foxe refers for his authority, when speaking of Cranmer, to Ralph Morice, his secretary, an authority we have before consulted and quoted; and that Morice was the authority of Foxe for this statement here made is certain from his employing the very peculiar expression adopted by Morice, "post alone." This interesting document remained in manuscript in the library of Corpus Christi College, Cambridge, until the year 1859, when it was published by the Camden Society, under the able editorship of Mr. Nichols, who has illustrated it by valuable and learned notes. The passage in Morice runs thus :—

> But if at the prince's pleasure in cause of religion at any tyme he was forced to give place, that was don with suche humble

---

* Parl. Hist. iii. 149.

protestation, and so knyt upp for the savegarde of his faithe and conscience, that it hadd byn better his good will had never byn requestid, than so to relente or give over. Which moste dangerouslie (besides sondrie tymes else) he speciallie attemptid when the VI articles by parliament passed, and when my lorde Crumwell was in the Tower, at that tyme the booke of articles of our religion was newlie pennyd; for even at that season, the hole rablemente, which he toke to be his frendes, being commissioners with hym, forsoke hym, and his opinion in doctrine, and so leaving him post alone, revolted altogether on the parte of Stephen Gardyner bisshopp of Wynchester, as by name bisshopp Heathe, Shaxton, Thirlby [*erased*], Daye, and all other of the meaner sorte, by whome theis so named were chiefelie advaunced and preservid unto thair dignities.*

CHAP. III.
Thomas Cranmer.
1533–56.

We have here a specimen of the manner in which Foxe could amplify and adorn a subject, without adhering strictly to the truth or violently opposing it. It has been justly observed that "Foxe speaks largely of the stand made by Cranmer against the six articles, while Morice says little."†

Foxe actually transfers to Cranmer's conduct in parliament what Morice says of his conduct when sitting in the conference upon the necessary doctrine and erudition of any Christian man.

The statement, with its full embellishments, as told in the story of King Henry VIII., is, after mentioning the act of six articles, thus presented to the reader:—

Everie man seeing the kings minde so fully addict upon politike respectes to have these articles passe forward, few or none in all that parliament would appeare, which either could perceive that was to be defended, or durst defend that they understood to be true, save onelie Cranmer archbishop of Canterbury who then being married (as is supposed) like a constant patron of God's cause, took upon him the earnest defence of the truth

* Narratives of the Reformation, p. 248.   † Nichols, 248.

CHAP. III.
Thomas Cranmer.
1533–56.

oppressed in the parliament, three daies together disputing against those wicked six articles, bringing forth such allegations and authorities as might easilie have helped the cause, *Nisi pars major vicisset, ut sæpe solet, meliorem.* Who in the said disputation, behaved himselfe with such humble modesty, and with such obedience in words towards his prince protesting the cause not to be his, but the cause of Almighty God, that neither his enterprise was misliked of the king, and again his reasons and allegations were so strong that well they could not be refuted. Wherefore the king (who ever bare speciall favour unto him) well liking his zealous defence, only willed him to depart out of the parliament house into the councell chamber, for a time (for a safeguard of his conscience) till the act should passe and be granted; which he notwithstanding, with humble protestation refused to doe.*

Everyone will be ready to believe that Cranmer did not hesitate to urge every objection which might occur to him against a measure which interfered directly with his domestic comfort; and until the political object of the bill was explained to him, and he was assured that it would not be carried out to its *full extent* for the repression of all religious opinion, it is very probable that his opposition was eager and eloquent. We have repeated instances of Henry's encouraging great boldness of speech in those whose real opinions he desired to elicit; but when the king's determination was known, that the bill, of which he himself produced the draft, was to pass, we know from better authority than that of Foxe that Cranmer gave in his adhesion. George Constantyne, reporting to Crumwell a conversation he had with the Dean of Westbury, mentions the complaint made by the dean that my Lord of Canterbury did not stick to his opposition. He adds the following remarkable sentence, which shows how cordially the bill had been supported by

* Wordsworth, Ecc. Biog. iii. 474.

Crumwell.* In answer to the complaint of the dean, George Constantyne said :—

> Well we know not the worke of God. If it be his pleasure it ys as easy for hym to overcome with few as with many; but I thinke veryly that my Lorde Privey Seale persuaded my Lorde of Cantorbury and that for other considerations than we do know; or els I am sure avoyding the kynges indignation he wold not haue subscribed, which in deade he shuld in conscience rather haue aventured, if he were not in conscience therto persuaded. I praye you what hath it avayled the Bishop of Rochester to subscribe: he had as good a charter of his life as the best of them? As I can heare, my Lorde Privey Seale ys utterly persuaded as the acte ys.†

The truth is, that neither Crumwell nor the king had any religious object in view, when this bill was brought into the House of Lords; and Cranmer was no doubt persuaded to withdraw his opposition by having its political object clearly set before him.

The abhorrence with which this statute has been regarded is to be traced, to a great extent, to the mistake of supposing, that it was a statute introduced through the influence of a religious faction to enable those by whom it was formed to persecute their opponents. That such a

---

* Archæologia, xxiii. 59.

† This is a proof that it was with a political, not a religious, motive that this statute was enacted. It was an act obtained by the government of which Crumwell was the head. If it were a religious act, and he took part in introducing the measure antagonistic to his conscience he was certainly not the saint which he is represented to be by party writers. If it was a political measure, he could justify his conduct, and we are the less surprised at his retaining his place at the head of the extreme or infidel Protestants. That the King did not consider the act as indicating any change in his religious views appears from his still keeping up his correspondence with the Germans, and in his refusal to marry the Duchess of Modena—a papist—and negotiating for a marriage with a Protestant Princess.

CHAP. III.
Thomas Cranmer.
1533-56.

measure it was not is proved by that which perplexes those who only view the subject in its religious aspect; the subjection of all parties, papist and protestant, to the penalties of the act. The government did not care for either party, but it was determined that those who on either side disturbed the peace of the realm, should be punished. The question was simply, will you obey the law—the law which requires you to admit the royal supremacy, and the law which requires you not to cavil against transubstantiation.

This subject has been thoroughly sifted by Dr. Maitland, a writer to whose accuracy of statement Mr. Hallam bears honourable testimony, though in his opinions on ecclesiastical affairs he differs from him widely. Maitland shows, that instead of there being any commission instituted in London, according to the statement of writers following the lead of Foxe, there was no enforcement of the act during the first year,*—a circumstance that establishes the fact, that it was not regarded as a party triumph; or rather we should say, that those who attempted to give it that character were immediately put down by the government. Foxe states, that those who refused to subscribe to the articles were so numerous "that they suffered daily." As the act was in force eight years, this implies some thousands of martyrdoms, taking the lowest estimate of one a day, whereas Dr. Maitland has shown that, during the eight years, there were only twenty-five prosecutions under the act; and with respect to these twenty-five, it is doubtful, whether it was for a violation of this precise law

* In decided opposition to the statement of Foxe, followed by Strype and others, George Constantyne, reporting to Crumwell his conversation with the Dean of Westbury, informs him :—" I told the Dean I could not hear of any Commission that was out for this last act." Nevertheless, he adds, with the caustic humour which all along pervades his narrative, " I will advise all my friends to keep out of danger." This was the object of the act, not to persecute but to terrify.

that they were condemned, or whether the persons said to have been prosecuted would not have suffered for treason or heresy even if this statute had not been called into existence.

I am not defending the statute, but I wish to impress it upon the mind of any reader who desires to study the history of this reign, that the statute was one which political circumstances, not religious rancour, called into existence, and that the object of the government was not to advance any particular religious system, but simply to prevent the peace of the country from being disturbed by that violence, by which the controversialists on either side too often disgraced their cause. It appears to me, that Dr. Maitland is correct when he says, " I believe that the king was roused by an idea that the church, of which he was resolved to be the supreme head, was likely to be overthrown by a torrent of what he considered infidelity and blasphemy, and that he devised and insisted on, and would have, and carried, such a measure as he thought was suited to check the frightful evil.

" Such I believe to have been the origin of the act. Subsequent events convince us, that it was meant to intimidate rather than to hurt, to pacify the people rather than to destroy and slaughter them by wholesale. Nothing but the spirit of party and passion, the withering blight of all truth in history, can represent it as a statute seriously intended to be executed according to the letter. But it did much without proceeding to such extremities as it threatened. It was meant to frighten the people, and it did frighten them. By those means it did two things which, whether right or wrong, good or bad, were undoubtedly of very great importance at that time, and in their consequences. In the first place, it caused many of the more violent partizans of the Reformation to quit

CHAP. III.
Thomas Cranmer.
1533–56.

the country, and secondly it made those who stayed at home more quiet and peaceable."*

Cranmer had sent his wife in his alarm to Germany, as soon as the act was passed, but from the manner in which the king joked with him upon the subject, it is clear that he did not intend that the penalties should be incurred by anyone who did not clearly defy the law. Some malignant persons might endeavour to involve an obnoxious neighbour in the meshes of the law; but the government, having secured the peace of the country, was tolerant, and, during the last years of Henry's reign, a protestant feeling increased among the people whom the late excesses of ultra protestantism had alarmed.

Henry VIII. was not a blood-thirsty tyrant, and never contemplated with delight the misery of others. That he could dandle his baby in his arms and fondle his wife, is mentioned as something extraordinary, by those who forget that a very tigress can purr round her young ones. The thing really extraordinary in Henry is, that he, who could one day demoralise his wife by making her an idol, and could, at another time, hang about the neck of his friend with the fondness of a school-boy, should the next day hear of their heads rolling on a scaffold stained by their blood, not only unmoved, not merely with complacency, but actually with exultation. The bell that announced to him the death of Ann Boleyn sounded a note of assignation to her rival. One day he could almost hug his children until in his embrace they were breathless, and on another day brand them with the mark of illegitimacy. And yet of this man it is no contradiction to say, that his cruelty was not that of one whose hardened heart knows not what humanity is; it was only the cruelty in the exercise of which upon

* Maitland, "Reformation," 270.

individuals, his vindictive rather than his malignant passions were indulged. And of this statute, which is called his bloody act, we must judge accordingly.

The story of Cranmer with reference to the passing of this statute is embellished by Foxe, and it has been repeated by others, with the object, of which they are more or less conscious, of making the good archbishop appear a bolder man than he really was, and with the object also of leaving an impression upon the mind, that being in advance of the age, he was opposed to what we call persecution, but what would appear to him as the prosecution of persons who had violated the law. There were, however, braver men than Cranmer who did not hesitate to admit, that in the service of Henry VIII. bold men might become cowards.

One man we know was "justus et tenax propositi," of whom it could be said,

> Non civium ardor prava jubentium,
> Non vultus instantis tyranni,
> Mente quatit solida.

More defied the tyrant by a passive resistance, and yet to Sir Thomas More, John, Duke of Norfolk, himself no craven, had the baseness to say, as Roper tells the anecdote, "By the mass, Mr. More, it is perilous striving with princes, for by God's body, Mr. More, indignatio principis mors est."

No one was more thoroughly convinced of this, than the archbishop whom the " vultus instantis tyranni " converted into the judge, and not a just one, of Sir Thomas More himself.

As to the persecution of heretics, it is absurd to suppose, that to this part of the act Cranmer had any objection. It was only in the preceding October, that he sat in judgment and sentenced to the stake, or rather

CHAP. III.

Thomas Cranmer. 1533-56.

handed over to the civil power, four unfortunate anabaptists, three men and one woman.

The reader will observe that a distinction is to be made between the Marian persecutions and those of the reign of Henry VIII. The Marian persecutions were generally the result of religious fanaticism; but though religion was the pretext, the persecutions of Henry VIII. were those not of the religionist, but of the politician. The elector of Hesse, himself a Protestant, had exhorted Henry not to tolerate the Anabaptists; and they had certainly done enough to alarm a politician anxious to restore a disturbed country to peace and quiet. The Anabaptists attributed the sacrament of baptism to the devil, an extreme assertion, in which the most vehement opponents of baptismal grace would scarcely in these days concur. This and other absurd religious tenets shocked the religious feelings of the age, but the real charge against them was that, to use a modern term, they were socialists. They had in Holland been hurried on by their enthusiasm into acts of violence, tumult and sedition. They had even formed a plan, fortunately detected in time, to reduce the city of Leyden to ashes. They had elected John of Munster their king, and to him it had been revealed, as it was said, that God had presented him with the cities of Amsterdam, Deventer and Wesel, and thither he despatched his emissaries to preach sedition and carnage. The amount of disturbance which they caused, and the support which they received, during a period of temporary success, are sufficient to attest their influence and power among the humbler classes of society.*

There is no doubt that the political opinions, if not the religious notions, of the Anabaptists had already spread in England. These were the men who rushed furiously,

---

* Mosheim, ed. Stubbs, iii. 112.

when Crumwell "let slip his dogs of war," upon the Universities; and what was to restrain them from attacking the castle of the noble, or the mansion of the merchant? When certain Dutchmen, holding the opinions of the Anabaptists, arrived in England, the government was aware that they came with a mischievous intent, and though they were few in number, and without influence, yet the amount of mischief which a few fanatics might accomplish, when religion was made the pretext for robbing men of their goods, was well known. As the manner then was, it was determined to proceed against these political offenders on the score of their religion. A royal commission was issued, in October, 1538, to Cranmer and others, for the purpose of "proceeding against them, of restoring the penitent, of delivering the obstinate to the secular arm, and of destroying their books." Cranmer delivered them over to the secular arm. The consequence was, that three men and a woman were brought before Paul's Cross with faggots tied to their backs. Two of the men appear, for some reason or other, to have received a respite, but one man and one woman were taken to Smithfield, and there burnt.*

A proclamation was issued, in the November following, against Sacramentaries as well as Anabaptists. The latter were required to leave the kingdom, and the Sacramentaries were warned to abstain from disputing about the Eucharist, under the penalty of forfeiting their lives. This penalty was incurred, almost immediately after the proclamation, by John Nicholson, alias Lambert, and in this persecution Cranmer bore his part and must share the obloquy.

The prosecution of John Lambert may appear to contradict what has been said of the political character of the prosecutions under Henry, but the contradiction is

* Stow's Annals, 526; Jortin's Erasmus, i. 357.

rather apparent than real. Henry's position was, that although the Church of England had renounced the pope, the Church adhered strictly to all Catholic doctrine. The Papists urged, on the contrary, that the renunciation of the Papacy led to the renunciation of all that was Catholic and orthodox in the Church. They pointed especially to the Sacramentaries, who denied that any grace was attached to the Sacraments and were vehement in their denunciation of the dogma of transubstantiation. That no toleration of heresy was permitted in his realm, by the king who had assumed the title of the supreme head of the Church of England, Henry determined to proclaim to the world, and he availed himself of the opportunity which now occurred, to do so.

John Lambert was born in Norfolk, and going to Cambridge, was converted from popery by Bilney. He afterwards became a friend of Frith and of the yet more illustrious Tyndale, to whom we are indebted to the present hour, for his version of the Bible, the basis upon which all subsequent translations have rested. In the time of the late archbishop he was brought into trouble by expressing his opinions too freely and was in custody at Warham's death, to be released by Cranmer when he was appointed to the primacy. He had been for some time at Antwerp, and, while he was abroad, he permitted himself to be hurried into the errors of ultra-Protestantism, and became a Sacramentary. On his return to England, he found few who would sympathise with him in his extreme opinions, and when those opinions were making some progress in the world, there were still fewer who cared to assert them openly. He lived, therefore, in retirement, and earned a scanty livelihood by keeping a school in London. As his opinions advanced, his scholars declined in number, and he had now taken up his freedom in the Grocer's Company, with a view of supporting himself by trade. He was attracted on one occasion, to St. Peter's Church, Cornhill when Dr. Taylor, afterwards bishop of Lincoln, was preaching. The preacher attacked the principles of Zuinglius, and Lambert could not restrain himself: he waited upon Dr. Taylor in the vestry, and, in terms of civility and respect, offered to dispute with him on the dogma of transubstantiation. Dr. Taylor declined, on the plea that he had not leisure to enter into a discussion. Lambert, whose blood was now up, committed his thoughts to paper; and Dr. Taylor, with no evil intention, showed the paper to Dr. Barnes, himself a Protestant.

By a Protestant Dr. Barnes meant a Lutheran, and a Lutheran held the doctrine of consubstantiation. He regarded the extreme opinions of the Sacramentaries as peculiarly dangerous, because they seemed to him to present a serious impediment to the progress of the Reformation. He advised Taylor to institute proceedings against Lambert in the archbishop's court, evidently expecting that, under a threat of prosecution, Lambert would modify his statements.

We have seen in the case of former archbishops, that they shrunk, in general, from proceeding against heretics; and to avoid a prosecution they first endeavoured privately to prevail upon the reputed heretic to recant. In the present instance, the Bishop of Worcester, Dr. Latimer, was staying with the archbishop, and the two prelates laboured, but in vain, to persuade Lambert to save his life by subscribing to the dogma of transubstantiation. Cranmer then cited the Sacramentary to stand upon his defence in the archbishop's court. Lambert appealed to the king. The king determined to avail himself of the opportunity of proving to the world the

Catholicism or orthodoxy of the supreme head of the English Church. He sat himself in the court of appeal. A summons was issued to all the magnates of the realm to attend. In "the king's palace called the Whitehall, a throne or seat royal was erected for the king's majesty, scaffolds for all the lords, and a stage for Nicholson or Lambert."* The place is thus described by Hall.† On the day appointed the king appeared seated upon the throne "all in white." The king's guard was in white, and the cloth of state was white. The lords spiritual sat on his right hand, the lords temporal on his left. The judges were also present and the king's counsel. There was an incredible number of spectators. Before this remarkable assembly Lambert was summoned. He had not anticipated that his trial would be conducted with such circumstances of worldly pomp, and was evidently embarrassed. He was not prepared for such an array, and though his determination never forsook him, he became nervous, confused, and abashed. His whole demeanour, nevertheless, was that of a perfect gentleman, ready to show all courtesy to others, but resolute to maintain his own position. But as in a man so circumstanced we might expect, while from his conclusions which he had before arrived at, he would not shrink, the arguments which had antecedently satisfied him he could not command. The business of the day was commenced by a speech from the Bishop of Chichester, Dr. Sampson. He stated that the meeting had not been convened to call in question any article of faith, for though his majesty had

---

* Foxe says that the king was urged to take this step by Gardyner, for which there is not a particle of authority. Crumwell was at this time Henry's adviser; but Foxe, Burnet, and other writers of that school attribute every wrong doing in this reign to Gardyner, and most ridiculously claim for Cranmer everything that was done right. This course is peculiarly provoking to the honest enquirer.

† Hall, 826.

emancipated his church and realm from papal usurpations, he was determined to maintain the Catholic religion intact; but the king, being supreme head, had determined to confute and condemn the heresy of the man who stood before him. It is worth while to remark on the coarseness and vulgarity of the king's conduct, because it shows that a judge did not at that time feel it necessary to comport himself as a gentleman—a circumstance which ought to be borne in mind when we shall have to record similar unfeeling coarseness in subordinate judges hereafter. As a counsel in these days thinks he may browbeat a witness, we find a similar system of browbeating on the bench itself, down to the time of the Revolution.

The king exclaimed, with his usual jocular familiarity of manner: "Ho, ho, good fellow, and what is thy name?" On learning that the culprit had two names, the king in the same tone exclaimed, that he would not trust a man who had two names, no, not though he were his brother. Lambert pleaded on his knees, that he was driven to the expedient by persecution; and began with courtesy,—for in a man determined to maintain his own, it were unfair to call it flattery,—to pay a compliment to the king both for his learning and for his benignity in condescending personally to see justice done to his subjects, however humble. He was proceeding in a speech evidently prepared, when the poor man, already showing symptoms of nervousness, was "worse confounded" by an interruption on the part of the king: "I came not here to hear my praises pointed out in my presence. Briefly, without further purpose, go to the matter." Thus rebuffed—interrupted in the speech which he had prepared, the accused stood speechless. The king, seeing but not pitying, his perplexity, sternly cried out, "Why standest thou still; answer plainly. Is the Body of Christ in the Sacrament of the Altar or not?"

CHAP. III.
Thomas Cranmer.
1533-56.

"I reply," said Lambert, "in the words of St. Austin, Our Lord's Body is present in the Eucharist after a certain manner." "Answer me not," exclaimed the royal theologian, "out of St. Austin or any other, but tell me plainly, Is the Body of Christ there or not?" Lambert saw that he was now to pursue his own line of defence and vindication, and his spirit being roused, he raised himself and manfully, emphatically, and as he was required, briefly said: "I deny the Eucharist to be the Body of Christ." "Mark well, then," rejoined the king, "thou shalt be condemned by Christ's own words. *Hoc est corpus meum.*"

This argument was supposed to be irrefragable in regard to those who were willing to abide by the Bible and the Bible only; and here the king, as if in triumph, paused.

The controversy now devolved upon the Primate and the other divines who had been summoned to attend. Cranmer evidently commiserated the unfortunate man—he could sympathise with one whose nerves were unstrung when called upon to act so conspicuous and unexpected a part; and even if he could not have sympathised with him, Cranmer must have admired the noble simplicity with which, when Lambert was not permitted to guard his position by certain explanations, he at once avowed his belief. The kindness and courtesy of Cranmer's address may be contrasted favourably with the unfeeling manner of the king, so utterly devoid of Christian courtesy. "Brother Lambert," said the Archbishop of Canterbury, "let this matter be argued between us so indifferently, that if I convince you this your argument to be false by the Scriptures, you will willingly refuse the same; but if you shall prove it to be true by the manifest testimonies of the Scriptures, I promise I will willingly embrace the same." *

---

* Burnet, for some reason or other, speaks of Cranmer as holding now the dogma of consubstantiation. Cranmer himself, when asked

Perhaps there is nothing which redounds more to the credit of Cranmer, than the manner in which he comported himself at this trial. Of the argument with Lambert the archbishop had clearly the best. Lambert maintained that our Lord's body could not be in two places at one and the same time. The archbishop referred to our Lord's appearance to St. Paul on his way to Damascus, to show that, as the rays of the sun may be in many places on earth, while the sun nevertheless remains stationary in the firmament, so there might be a sense in which our Lord, though at the right hand of power, might cause his presence to be felt on earth.

Lambert could only defend his own position by lapsing into the most fearful rationalism, and by denying the reality of our Lord's appearance to St. Paul. Lambert's whole argument must have damaged his cause. The Bishop of Winchester is said to have been provoked by the archbishop's calmness and kindness to the prisoner, and to have rushed into the argument before his turn. But, however that may have been, the discussion continued until it was dark. The torches were already lighted in the hall, and the wearied king thought it time to bring the controversy to a close.

The king reverted to what had been previously said, that the object of the meeting was not to discuss an article of faith, which every one of his subjects was bound to believe because it was the law; but that its intent was to convince the gainsayer, if possible, and if not, to condemn him: therefore he now adroitly asked Lambert whether he were satisfied by what he had heard; whether it was his resolution, in short, to live or die.

To have given a triumph to the royal theologian by

what doctrine he held at Lambert's trial, said, "He maintained then the Papist's doctrine."

appearing to have been convinced by his argument, would have gained for Lambert not life only, but honour. But wearied and worn though he was, he did not relax in his manner, and continued *tenax propositi*. He replied that he committed his soul to God, and his body to the clemency of the king's majesty. The king, without any symptom of pity, exclaimed: "Then die you must; for a patron of heretics I will never be;" and Crumwell immediately rose to read the sentence of condemnation.

The sentence was carried into execution; and the death of Lambert was attended by circumstances of peculiar horror, into which it is not necessary here to enter.

By party writers, on one side an attempt is made to represent Cranmer as a persecutor, and on the other, to explain away his share in the religious persecutions under the reigns of Henry and Edward, and to make him appear as tolerant as—so far as the rack and the stake are concerned—men are compelled to be in the nineteenth century.

As usual, the truth lies between the two extremes, and this perhaps is the fittest place to consider the subject. The case of Lambert has been presented to the reader, who will see from the narrative, how easily, by the suppression of some of the circumstances, Cranmer may be painted to us as a willing, or, on the other hand, as an unwilling agent in the condemnation of that noble-minded, although much mistaken man.

But in the other two cases it is difficult to see how Cranmer is even indirectly implicated.

In the prosecution of Mrs. Kyme the archbishop clearly was not called upon, even officially, to act. Mrs. Kyme was the sister of a Lincolnshire knight, Sir Philip Askew. She married Mr. Kyme; and the husband and wife differed so entirely upon the subject of religion, that they separated, apparently by mutual consent, and not probably by any sentence of an ecclesiastical court, against the jurisdiction of which the lady would have protested. Although she professed to be guided by the Bible only, she considered herself divorced, and assumed her maiden, which has become her historical name, Ann Askew.* She rendered herself conspicuous in violating the statute of the six articles, and was committed to custody previous to a trial for denying the dogma of transubstantiation. At the same time, for the same offence, Cranmer's friend Shaxton, who on the passing of the statute had resigned his bishopric, was committed to prison. As had always been the custom, certain divines were appointed to confer with the accused, and if possible to induce them to renounce their reputed heresy. On this occasion, the Bishop of London, Dr. Bonner, the Bishop of Worcester, Dr. Heath, Dr. Robinson, and Dr. Redmayn visited Bishop Shaxton and Mrs. Kyme or Ann Askew. With Bishop Shaxton, no doubt to Cranmer's great delight, these divines succeeded.† Bishop Shaxton became a

CHAP. III.
Thomas Cranmer. 1533–56.

---

* She was probably an Anabaptist. It is stated, on the authority of Melanchthon, that the Anabaptists held that the marriage between a person holding Anabaptism ceased to be valid if the husband or the wife of an Anabaptist refused to conform to his creed. The passage is quoted in the brief history of Anabaptism in England. London, 1738, p. 48.

† Cranmer at this time held the dogma of transubstantiation, and must have rejoiced to know that his friend had saved his life by accepting what Cranmer believed to be the truth. Shaxton knew what his recantation meant—it meant that he was henceforth to leave the party to which he had been hitherto attached. Having accepted the distinguishing dogma of the Papists, he henceforth became more and more devoted to that party. He is hardly dealt with by those who treat his consistency as a crime. His conduct rather shows that he did not merely recant to save his life, but that he was really persuaded to return to a dogma in the acceptance of which he had been educated.

believer in transubstantiation, and immediately endeavoured to persuade Mrs. Kyme to follow his example. "He came to me," she said, "and counselled me to recant, as he had done. I said to him that it had been good for him if he had never been born."

The lady persevered in repudiating the dogma, and was handed over to the civil power, and died a martyr to her opinions. It is a sad story, and it raises indignant feelings in a modern reader, but what had the Archbishop of Canterbury to do with it? She was cited before her ordinary, who was not the archbishop, but the Bishop of London. If the Archbishop of Canterbury had presided, in the court of his suffragan, the thing was so contrary to all precedent that it would have been noticed, and certainly Bonner was not the man to tolerate an insult offered to himself and his court.

The other case is perplexing to the panegyrists of Cranmer, as it rests on the authority of one who was, in general, accustomed so to colour his facts as to reflect credit on the archbishop. Foxe perhaps did not think the archbishop in error in burning Joan Butcher, or Bocher, sometimes called the maid of Kent, but he repeated a story without investigation which he thought tended to elevate the character of another hero whom he would present to us as overflowing with the milk of human kindness, the boy-king Edward VI. His story is repeated by Burnet and Strype, and so has passed into our histories. It runs as follows:—

He (the king) always spared and favoured the life of man, as in a certain dissertation of his once appeared, had with Master Cheke, in favouring the life of heretics; in so much that when Joan Butcher should be burned, all the council could not move him to put to his hand, but were fain to get Dr. Cranmer to persuade with him, and yet neither could be with much labour induce the king so to do, saying, What, my Lord, will you have me to send her quick to the devil, in her error? so that Dr. Cranmer himself confessed, that he had never so much to do in all his life, as to cause the king to put to his hand, saying, that he would lay all the charge thereof upon Cranmer before God.*

Now for this story Foxe does not assign any authority. It rested on hearsay: and even the report of the supposed transaction was not widely current, or it would have reached Sanders, by whom not the slightest allusion to the story is made. This is the more remarkable, since he does refer to the taunt which Joan Bocher addressed to her judges, when she said:—

"It is a goodly matter to consider your ignorance. It was not long ago since you burned Anne Askew for a piece of bread, and yet ye came yourselves soon after to believe and profess the same doctrine for which you burned her. And now, forsooth, you will needs burn me for a piece of flesh, and in the end you will come to believe this also, when you have read the Scriptures and understand them." †

On reference to the Privy Council Book we find, that Joan Butcher or Bocher was executed under a writ *de hæretico comburendo*, addressed to the Sheriff of London, and issued out of the Court of Chancery, upon the authority of a warrant not signed by the king, but by the council. The young king was not accustomed to attend the council, neither was he consulted, except on special occasions when his attendance was required by a committee. At this meeting of council, moreover, Cranmer was not present. The persons present on the day referred to were—the Lord Chancellor, the Lord High Treasurer, the Lord Privy Seal, the Lord High Chamberlain, the Lord Chamberlain, the Lord Paget, the Bishop of Ely, Mr. Treasurer, Mr. Comptroller,

* Soames, Hist. Ref. iii. 544.   † Soames, Hist. Ref. iii. 546.

Master of the Horse, Mr. Vice-chamberlain, Sir Ralf Sadler, and Sir Edmund North. The council were the *de facto* rulers of the kingdom, and on the 27th of April 1550, the following is the entry on their journal:—" A warrant to the Lord Chancellor to make out a writ to the Sheriff of London for the execution of Joan of Kent, condemned to be burnt for certain detestable opinions of heresy." In short, Edward did not sign the document. Cranmer felt certainly no eager desire to enforce a punishment which he knew would be inflicted as a matter of course, or he would have attended the council; and all the tears of the young king, and the difficulty of Cranmer to persuade him to put his hand to the warrant, is an affecting incident, which, repeated by all writers of this period of history, has no foundation in fact.* That young Edward was not a youth easily moved to compassion we may judge from his heartless conduct towards his uncle; and his entry with respect to the execution of Joan Bocher is so cold, as in itself to give the lie to the charge brought against Cranmer of being " importunate for blood ":—

May 2. Joan Bocher, otherwise called the Maid of Kent, was burnt for holding that Christ was not incarnate of the Virgin Mary, being condemned the year before but kept in hope of conversion. And on the 30th of April the Bishop of London and the Bishop of Ely were to persuade her; but she withstood them and reviled the preacher at her death.†

We have already seen that Cranmer was by nature a mild, indulgent, kind-hearted man. He was not a man likely to take pleasure in human suffering, and if a heretic could be induced to recant, no one assuredly would have

---

* Mr. Coxe, in his preface to Cranmer's works, has gone through this case concisely and with much ability.

† Edward's Journal, in Burnet.

rejoiced more than he. It is not probable, that he should have been sent to persuade a headstrong boy; for he was much more likely to have shed the tears of pity than the fanatical youth, who not long after proved that, of the two, his will was the stronger, since he persuaded Cranmer to commit an offence for which the Primate afterwards repented, and perhaps lost his life. At the same time, it were absurd to suppose, that Cranmer would not have signed the warrant, if he had been present at the trial. He might have pitied the culprit, even as George III. may have pitied Dr. Dodd while signing his death-warrant; or as a magistrate, at a later period, might have commiserated the criminal who had stolen a sheep to save his family from starvation. That the sensibilities of a generous nature would have been moved had Cranmer witnessed the sufferings of a fellow-creature, is perfectly compatible with his deciding, when the question was considered in the abstract, that a heretic ought to die. In the very first year of his primacy, one of the most learned and amiable of the Reformers, John Fryth, died for denying the dogma of transubstantiation, and of his case Cranmer could write carelessly to his friend Hawkins:—

"Other news have we none notable, but that one Fryth which was in the Tower in prison, was appointed by the King's grace to be examined before me, my Lord of London, my Lord of Wynchestre, my Lord of Suffolke, my Lord Chancellor, and my Lord of Wylteshere, whose opinion was so notably erroneous, that we could not dispatch him, but was fain to leave him to the determination of his ordinary, which is the Bishop of London. His said opinion is of such nature that he thought it not necessary to be believed as an article of our faith, that there is the very corporeal presence of Christ, within the host and sacrament of the altar, and holdeth of this point most after the opinion of Œcolampadius, and surely I myself sent for him three or four times to persuade him to leave that his imagination, but for all that we could do therein, he would not apply to any counsel: notwithstanding now he is at a final end, with all examinations, for my Lord of London hath given sentence and delivered him to the secular power, where he looketh every day to go unto the fire. And there is also condemned with him one Andrew, a tailor of London, for the selfsame opinion."*

In the case of Joan Bocher, the archbishop was the judge who sentenced her to death, and so far from being ashamed of it, the whole process, together with others of the same kind, ranging over four years, from 1548 to 1551, is carefully narrated in Cranmer's register. In the Commission for the trial of Joan Bocher, we find the name of Hugh Latimer, as well as that of Thomas, by Divine permission, Archbishop of Canterbury, Primate of all England and Metropolitan. They found her guilty of asserting "the accursed and intolerable error, the damnable and scandalous opinion, opposed, contradictory, and repugnant to the Catholic faith, that although she believed that the Word was made flesh in the Virgin's womb, yet she did not believe that Christ took flesh of the Virgin; because the flesh of the Virgin being the outward man, was sinfully gotten and born in sin, but the Word, by the consent of the inward man, of the Virgin was made flesh. To this damnable error, directly contrary to the Catholic faith, she with malicious pertinacity obstinately adhered; and therefore the aforesaid Thomas, Archbishop of Canterbury, Primate of all England and Metropolitan, with his assessors, acting under the advice of certain persons learned in the law, and certain professors of theology, having first excommunicated her, delivered her up to the secular power." The sentence was proclaimed on the ast day of April, in the year 1549, in St. Mary's Chapel, in the Cathedral of St. Paul, in the presence of

* Letter xiv. Harl. MSS. 6148, fol. 23.

the assessors of the archbishop, among whom sat Hugh Latimer.*

During the year which elapsed between the sentence and its being carried into execution, the unfortunate woman was lodged first at the house in Smithfield, usually occupied by Lord Rich, the chancellor; and she was afterwards removed to the priory of St. Bartholomew. She was not, therefore, treated with undue severity, and every attempt was made to induce her to recant. She had long been a notorious or celebrated character, and from time to time, had caused some trouble to the government. Before the free circulation of the Bible was allowed, she was a vendor of Tyndall's Testaments, and clandestinely disposed of them among the ladies of the court. She had also been the friend of Mrs. Kyme.

We have thus the history of Cranmer's mind as regards those prosecutions, which we have happily learned to regard as persecutions. He may have been as tender-hearted as many a modern judge, whom we have seen weeping on the bench; but the feelings of the man were not to interfere with the duties of the magistrate. Perhaps, too, with all her heroism, Joan's conduct may not have been such as to conciliate her judges. When, on the 2nd of May 1550, she was burnt at Smithfield, and a sermon, as usual, was preached to improve the occasion, her last dying speech and confession was, "You lie like a rogue; go read the Scriptures."

Upon another occasion we find Cranmer inflicting, without compunction, a barbarous punishment upon a poor man of whom the archbishop complained to the Privy Council that he had forged a grant to himself of the office of beadsman in the city of Canterbury. The council ordered the

* Reg. Cranmer, fol. 74, b. The processes are printed from the Register in Wilkins, iv. 39, 45; and in Burnet, v. 246, ed. Pocock.

archbishop to cause one of the criminal's ears to be nailed to the pillory on the next market-day, to remain in that situation during the market, with a paper declaring his offence in large letters. The archbishop obeyed.*

These are horrible things to record, and the sentence passed upon a heretic is narrated with the more disgust from the terrible nature of the punishment. But there is no reason why we should expect Cranmer to be in advance of his age; nor can he be charged with inconsistency when, as a judge, he punished the culprit, whom as a man he pitied.

I have wished to bring this whole subject under one point of view without attending to the sequence of events. We must now return to the historical position from which we have digressed, and we find Cranmer implicated in the miserable case of the Lady Ann of Cleves.

The only event of interest in the history of Queen Jane, the successor of Ann Boleyn, in which Cranmer was personally concerned, is that which relates to the baptism of her child, to whom the king, with hearty English feeling, gave the popular name of Edward. The archbishop was associated as sponsor with the Lady Mary, afterwards Queen of England, and the Duke of Norfolk. No theological differences of opinion, at that time, kept religious parties separate. The court was divided in its sympathies between joy for the birth of the prince and grief for the death of the queen his mother; who, if we set aside her heartless conduct towards the late Queen Ann, had conducted herself, as Lord Herbert says, with discretion, and had borne her faculties meekly. Twelve hundred masses were said for the repose of her soul, and a solemn dirge at St. Paul's. If there was a tendency to Protestantism on the part of the king and of Cranmer—the king who

* Proceedings of Privy Council, 117, 118.

ordered these masses and the archbishop who officiated at them—it was not at this time much developed.

Great as was the king's grief, yet for the sake of his country he overcame it. His mind reverted to the policy of his great minister Wolsey, and with a view of strengthening his alliances abroad, he determined to select a foreign princess for his wife.* The Duchess Dowager of Milan and Mary of Guise refused him—the last-named lady because she was betrothed to the King of Scots; the former, indicating the estimation of Henry's character abroad, because she had only one head. If she had possessed two heads, she would gladly have placed one of them at the disposal of his majesty. He also thought of one of the two sisters of Mary of Guise, but insisted that they should be first brought for inspection to Calais—a proposal rejected by the gallantry of Francis I.

Henry had also been an admirer of Madame de Montreuil.† But there would probably have been an insurmountable obstacle to any one of these marriages, in that they would have required a dispensation from the pope. When the emperor heard, that the king was projecting a matrimonial alliance with one of the German princesses, he offered his services to prevail upon the Duchess of Milan to give him her hand. When, however, the subject came seriously under consideration, the king declined to stultify himself and to retrace his steps by receiving a dispensation from the pope, whose authority he had rejected; and at last, he made up his mind to wed the Lady Ann, a sister of the reigning Duke of Cleves. Aware of the ridicule to which he had exposed himself in requiring the King of

---

* State Papers, i. 574.

† Among the State Papers, i. 583, in a letter from Penison to Crumwell, there is a curious account of the presents made to this lady on her journey through England.

CHAP. III.
Thomas Cranmer.
1533-56.

France to produce the ladies of his court for inspection, as a horse-dealer would trot out his horses at a fair; he was contented with demanding that lady's portrait—a circumstance which led to much inconvenience, and eventually into a violation of the moral law, in which Cranmer was involved.

I have entered, at some length, into the history of these royal flirtations, or rather matrimonial speculations, because they tend to refute the notion that the marriage with Ann of Cleves was the result of a grand manœuvre, on the part of Crumwell and the Protestants, to force the king into a Protestant alliance. The notion, that the Protestants and Papists formed at this time, two clearly defined parties in the state, each contending for the formation of a ministry, Gardyner at the head of one and Cranmer at the head of the other, is certainly not borne out by historical evidence. All the country was agreed on one point, namely, the rejection of the papal and the assertion of the royal supremacy. The men of the new learning would push the reforms consequent upon this fact to an extreme; the men of the old learning were conservatives, and would advance no further. And what was the Protestantism of Henry and Cranmer? Henry had defined his position with firmness—a rejection of the pope but a maintenance of old Catholic or orthodox truth. The only difference between him and Cranmer was, that Cranmer had discovered, that some portion of what was now assumed to be Catholic truth, held "from the beginning everywhere and by all," was not really such; and Henry was not unwilling, when Cranmer could prove his assertions, to accept and enforce them; but as for Protestantism, as the word was then understood, the only point on which the Church of England accorded with the foreign Protestants was that both rejected the pope.

As regards Crumwell, his religion was purely political: when he desired to rouse the people against the monks, he patronised the most violent preachers of the Protestant faction; when that was accomplished, he was prepared, in order to preserve the peace of the country, to support the statute of the six articles.

That Henry was influenced by Crumwell to select the Lady Ann, and that the latter in consequence fell under the royal displeasure, when the king repudiated his marriage with that princess, is a purely gratuitous assertion, contradicted by facts. For it is certain, that after the marriage Crumwell not only continued but increased in favour, and was advanced to the Earldom of Essex.

But, be this as it may, a treaty of marriage was entered into with the little court of Cleves; and the sister of the Duke was selected to become the Queen Consort of England. Courtiers and painters thought fit to pay their homage to the rising sun; and the lady, though marked with the small-pox,* was, from the omission of any allusion to that defect, painted as a beauty and described as perfection.† Although at this period, Protestantism was unpopular in England, yet the people, from political

---

* Even after her arrival in England, to those who only saw her at a distance she appeared, in the words of Hall, as "a brave lady," and her "good visage" is mentioned. We may presume, therefore, that the personal disgust which Henry felt was from her disfigurement, not seen at a distance, by the small-pox.

† Thus was she represented to Henry, when he had determined upon the marriage, but I find among the State Papers a letter which shows that Crumwell had been otherwise informed. Hutton, writing to Crumwell in December, 1537, says:—"The Dewke of Clevis hathe a daughter, but I here no great preas neyther of hir personage nor beawtie." (State Papers, viii. 5.) After this Crumwell would hardly have taken an active part in promoting the match if he had not seen that his royal master was determined upon it.

CHAP. III.
Thomas Cranmer.
1533-56.

considerations or prejudices, were decidedly in favour of the marriage with the Lady Ann.

When all the preliminaries were arranged, preparations were made for her reception in England on a scale of magnificence never surpassed. A full description of it may be found in the Chronicle of Hall.

The archbishop repaired to Canterbury, where the representatives of all parties in the state were assembled. The Duke of Norfolk, Lord Dacre, Lord Montjoye, and a large company of knights and esquires, with the lords of the exchequer, all in the richest uniforms, were commissioned to welcome her to England. The primate was attended by the Bishops of Ely, St. Asaph, and St. Davids, together with the suffragan of Dover. The queen elect had landed at Deal on St. John's day, the 27th of December. Here the Duke and Duchess of Suffolk, and the Bishop of Chichester, Dr. Sampson, received her, and she was conducted by them to Dover Castle; she rested till the following Monday, when she commenced her progress to London. The primate and the other magnates of the land who had assembled at Canterbury, met her on Barham Downs, and escorted her into the city. She was not entertained by the primate; but was lodged at St. Augustine's, which had now lapsed to the Crown, and here she was entertained at the king's expense. The archbishop seems to have preceded her to London, or rather to Greenwich, there to make ready for the marriage.

Hall is again grandiloquent in describing the meeting of Henry and the Lady Ann, at Greenwich. Here, in the king's procession, which must have been a magnificent display, the primate rode, attended by his suffragans, "apparelled," as the chronicler informs us, "in black satin."

On the feast of the Epiphany, 1540, under circumstances of unusual splendour, Archbishop Cranmer performed the marriage ceremony, and afterwards celebrated mass in the king's closet. After mass, he partook of wine and spices. It does not appear, that Cranmer was admitted into the secrets of the king, or that he was, at this time, aware of the antipathy which Henry felt against the unfortunate lady, whom he had selected for his wife. But this subject soon came officially before the archbishop. Into the offensive and disgusting details of the divorce case I am not about to enter. What must be said may be stated briefly. The king determined to put away his wife; and Archbishop Cranmer was required to conduct the repudiation of that injured and insulted lady,* according to those forms of law which the king loved to observe, whenever they could be rendered subservient to his will. The case was regularly submitted to convocation; and when the judgment of convocation had been given, an act of parliament, based upon that judgment, was obtained. It is to be remarked how all parties sought to divide the blame. The archbishop, instead of deciding the case in his own court, first took the precaution of consulting the convocation; as to the members of convocation, they were so fearful of being personally responsible, that they, to the number of two hundred, gave their assent to the divorce.† In the act of parliament it is said, that the

---

* If anyone were in duty bound to expose the character of Henry VIII., an investigation of this case would prove him to be void of the common feelings of a gentleman, a Christian, a man. Perhaps there is not in historical literature a viler document than that in which he assigned his reasons for seeking a divorce. He cared not what he did or said, if only he could carry his object.

† I give the numbers as I find them; but there must be some mistake. There are not two hundred members of the Convocation of Canterbury.

marriage, as solemnised by the king and the Lady Ann of Cleves, is by the judgment of the clergy of the Church of England in their convocation adjudged and pronounced to be void. To this sentence the Lady Ann had given her consent, and therefore it was enacted that the king "shall be at liberty to marry any other woman, and she any other man." In what follows we have another, out of the many instances that might be adduced, of the little account, at this time taken of human life, for it is enacted, that "it shall be high treason by word and deed to account, take, judge or believe the said marriage to be good, or to do or procure anything to the repeal of this act."

I have already had occasion to remark, that while all reference to the proceedings against Ann Boleyn has been erased from the register at Lambeth, the divorce case of Ann of Cleves is given in full. And hence we infer, that the two cases were regarded by the archbishop with very different feelings; and indeed the delight of the Lady Ann of Cleves in escaping, with her life, from the embraces of her husband, was so evident as, in her instance, to render the divorce, if an act of injustice, still an act of mercy. It was well, indeed, for the country that the Lady Ann of Cleves was a woman of no strong passions.* She preferred the enjoyment of a splendid establishment in England, which was afforded her, to the precarious support she was offered in a petty continental court. After the first great wrong to which she submitted, without remonstrance, she had no cause for complaint. To all who did not oppose his will, or involve him in trouble, Henry was one of the kindest and best humoured of men. When

* From the conversations reported to have taken place between her and her ladies, we are to infer, after making due allowance for the manners of the age, that she was a coarse-minded woman, who took a utilitarian view of all things brought under her notice.

Ann of Cleves retired from his bed, he was at all times careful, that every mark of attention and even of kindness should be manifested towards her; and the people, commiserating the fate of a lady who had been so grossly insulted by the king, regarded her with feelings of respect and pity.

The absurdity of supposing the king to be sincere in the alarm which he professed to feel, and which he required his courtiers to express, lest at his death there should be a disputed succession to the throne, is glaringly apparent on this occasion. He had done all he could to vitiate the claim to be made upon the throne by his daughters; his son was a child, not in vigorous health, and if Henry were to have issue by another marriage, a pretender to the throne might have easily disputed the legitimacy of the divorce from Ann of Cleves, obtained under circumstances so unparalleled and unprecedented. But Henry cared not for his theories when his passions were roused; and he caused the proceedings against his insulted wife to be conducted with the greater expedition, as he had fallen in love—I again use the word love, in his instance, under a protest—with Catherine Howard.

In this case also Cranmer was concerned, and acted with discretion and kindness so far as circumstances would allow. Catherine being the daughter of Lord Edmund Howard, was a niece of the Duke of Norfolk and a cousin-german of Ann Boleyn. It was as suitable a match as that which had been just dissolved; for an English duke is more than the equal of a German prince, and royal blood flowed in the veins of the Howards. She had been appointed maid of honour to the Lady Ann of Cleves, the late queen; but it is supposed that she was unnoticed by Henry until she excited his admiration at a dinner given by the Bishop of Winchester; when the mighty monarch professed himself her slave. In regard to the time when the marriage between the king and Catherine took place, there is as much mystery as there was about the marriage of Ann Boleyn; and gossip among the courtiers insinuated that the marriage was consummated before it was solemnised.*

All that is known is, that on the 8th of August 1540, the Lady Catherine was introduced by Henry at Hampton Court as his queen. The amorosity publicly evinced by a bridegroom, not young but " burly and big," towards a blooming, bright-eyed girl still in her teens, and remarkable for being in stature small and slender, provoked a smile in the English court, and was mentioned, for the amusement of his royal master, by the Ambassador of France. From this happy dream Cranmer was to awaken his royal friend. While the young queen was sharing with her devoted husband the splendid hospitalities, by which the aristocracy of the North endeavoured to win back the royal favour, and to prove, that it was not against the king, but against his ministers, that rebellious thoughts were lately entertained; while Catherine by her inimitable grace was winning all hearts; a man named Lossells, or Lascelles, came to Cranmer and informed him, on the authority of his sister, who had been servant to the Dowager Duchess of Norfolk, that the queen had before her marriage been seduced by one Francis Derham, and had been guilty of gross acts of immorality. To the Lord Chancellor and the Earl of Hertford, who were the ministers left in charge of the government, the archbishop communicated the disclosure. It was agreed between them, that the fact ought not to be concealed from the king. The archbishop " could not find it in his heart " to make the statement verbally, and he determined to

* Dépêches de Mérillac.

communicate it to his majesty in writing. Cranmer acted with delicacy and caution. He waited till the royal family returned to Hampton Court, desirous, probably, of being at hand to assist in consoling the king, whose affliction he knew would be as passionate as his anger. He went with the council to Hampton Court, and there he was told, that, on the festival of All Saints, the king had determined to receive the Holy Communion with his queen, and that he had directed his confessor, the Bishop of Lincoln, Dr. Holbeach, to draw up a form of thanksgiving, that he might express his gratitude to Almighty God for the blessing he now enjoyed in an amiable and loving wife. It would seem that Cranmer had not the heart to interfere with the enjoyments of that day. It must be borne in mind that he had not come to accuse the queen of adultery, but merely to disclose certain disreputable actions in her unmarried life. He possibly thought, as we gather from his conduct afterwards, that the amorous monarch might overlook the past, if he could obtain a proof of his wife's fidelity to her marriage vow, and a pledge of that fidelity for the time to come. The archbishop permitted that day to pass.* On the morrow, being the feast of All Souls, the king, the queen, and Cranmer all assisted at mass; and as they were returning from mass, Cranmer placed in the king's hands a paper which he requested the king to read in private.

Henry would not, at first, believe what he read. For reasons already mentioned more than once, and from the

* This is the order of events as I gather it from the letter of the Privy Council to Paget. The statement is confused. The 1st of November was and is All Saints' day, the 2nd all Souls' day. Allhallow's day was a synonym of All Saints' day; but, by an oversight, the title of Allhallows is applied by the Council to All Souls' day.

destruction of the official documents, it is impossible to return a verdict either of guilty or of not guilty, in this or in any public trials of this reign. We may say, that from the evidence we possess, the case is not proved against the queen; and we may, with this proviso, venture upon an opinion. I have no occasion to enter further into the subject; but having read the proceedings of the Privy Council and the various State papers, I may be permitted to say, that while no one doubts the truth of the charges brought against the poor girl before the time of her marriage, I think that everything tends to show, that she was not guilty of adultery; but that after she had become the king's wife, she conducted herself with great propriety. I suspect that, though she was only nineteen, and he old enough to be her father, she was truly attached to the king, and that it was by the real affection evinced by her, that the king was fascinated. But her story is one of the saddest of the many sad stories which history has to tell. She had lost her mother in early life, and she never had a maternal friend. She lived in the house of her grandmother; but that grandmother, the Dowager Duchess of Norfolk, not only did not rule her family well, but, being an unprincipled woman, of a violent temper, sometimes applied her fists to the correction of the men as well as the women of her household, and at other times treated as a joke what, in any but a disorderly house, would be regarded as a grave offence. Francis Derham, a bold man, occupied an inferior position in her family, though distantly related to the Howards. He availed himself of his opportunities to seduce Catherine while she was yet little more than a precocious child. She was, though frivolous, quick and clever, not absolutely beautiful, but of such superlative grace as to be more admired than persons whom an artist would have regarded as handsomer. She was short of money, and was not able, except through Derham's assistance, to procure the little elegancies pertaining to her station. While flattered by his admiration of her, before she had attracted the notice of others, she placed herself under obligations to him, until at last she could deny him nothing. When people remarked, that he took liberties with her which, as she was approaching womanhood, ought not to be permitted, he called her his little wife, and she did not repudiate the title. The old duchess, who appears to have been folly itself, looked upon this as a flirtation carried rather too far; but talked loosely on the subject.

At length they parted. No one knew what became of Derham, but he was supposed to be engaged in acts of piracy; for in that age, persons calling themselves gentlemen did not lose their gentility by being suspected of robbery by sea or by land; it was in detection that, with the penalty, came the disgrace. Those persons, however, of the duchess's household who knew or suspected what had occurred, were more in number than could have been the case if it had not been part of Derham's policy, to make it appear that he was merely romping with a child; but they too had been dispersed. The woman who knew most of these miserable circumstances, who had been most in the confidence of Catherine, who had acted as her secretary, and communicated with her paramour until all communication with him had ceased—Joan Bulmer—was settled at York. To say that a person had migrated from the South of England to York amounted almost to what would be meant in these days if we were to say of a man that he has gone to the colonies.

All seemed to have been forgotten; and Catherine, taught by past experience, the experience of a poor girl without a female friend to advise her, became the model of propriety. By nothing about her was the king, according to his own statement, more enamoured, than by her "notable appearance of honor, cleanness, and maidenly behaviour."*

As soon as Catherine became Queen Consort of England, they who had been the witnesses or abettors of the sins, we might almost say of her childhood, came out of their secret hiding-places, or from the retirements of private life, and were seen at court. By their very appearance, they were demanding an amount of hush money, or an equivalent in high appointments, which the poor young queen could not supply or procure. A terrible letter came from York, from the wickedest of the destroyers of the queen, which must have made her very sick at heart. She struggled to free herself, but what could she do? This question is easily answered by those who can view this subject dispassionately from a distance. We can say, that she ought *not* to have done the things which she did. She committed indiscretions; how were they to be avoided? Here was the terrible Francis Derham, a man imbruted in selfishness and without a single feeling of a gentleman. He, to the last, confirmed the assertion of the queen; they both admitted that they had, at one time, lived together as man and wife, but both denied that there had been the slightest familiarity between them after Catherine's marriage with the king. But there was the fact, that she could not refuse him, when he demanded, a place in her royal household. All who knew anything of her past misconduct were ever in her presence, their very looks bringing daggers to her soul. Any one of them might utter a word which would be her doom. We are not surprised to read of secret messages, and various communications made through Lady Rochford, the purport of which is not

* See letter from Cromwell to Paget, 352.

known, though we feel sure, that they related to the one subject.

There was a near relation of the queen, named Culpepper, whom she made her confidant; and with whom, through Lady Rochford, she had frequent communications by letter. When the Court was at Pontefract, the queen had an interview with her kinsman Culpepper in the night, in the presence of Lady Rochford; he declared to the latest hour of life, defying the rack as well as the axe, that there never was anything approaching to criminality in this or any other interview with the queen; and where there were such obvious reasons why there should be such interviews, and why they should be clandestine, we may believe him, if we are charitably disposed; and the side of charity is generally the side of justice. But that interview cost Culpepper his life.

This is the story, as far as we can gather it from existing materials. There was the original offence—this is admitted, but it is not proved; perhaps we shall some of us think the opposite position fully established—that Catherine was not guilty of that adultery which was laid to her charge, and for which she died.

The king at first hoped, that the accusation brought against his wife for immorality before her marriage would prove to be unfounded. So convinced was he of her innocence, that he caused her at first to be treated with great consideration, and was careful to prevent any scandal injurious to her reputation that might arise from the secret investigation into her conduct which he appointed. When it was admitted by the queen herself, that she had kept this secret from him, his vindictive passions were roused, and could only be satiated by her blood.

Cranmer, who was peculiarly free from vindictive feelings, and who easily forgave, did not understand his royal master. He supposed, that all the king required was a divorce; and the archbishop therefore urged the queen to admit the existence of a precontract between herself and Derham. This she pertinaciously refused to do. If she would admit the precontract, then the archbishop could pronounce sentence of divorce, and the poor young woman would be dismissed with a tarnished reputation, but with her life. She still refused. It is difficult to understand why, unless it was from such hatred of Derham, that she revolted from what would have bound her to him for life, if the lives of both were spared.

The archbishop was commissioned to have an interview with her, and to obtain a confession of her guilt. There still exists a letter from the archbishop to the king, very touching; the poor girl being terrified almost to death; and evidently feeling affection for the king, whose love, on the contrary, had turned into hatred.

Cranmer laboured earnestly in her cause; but in vain. A bill of attainder passed through parliament, and on the 13th of February 1542, England was degraded by another legal murder. One is filled with horror at the nature of the man, who could give orders that the head should roll on the scaffold which a few weeks before had reclined on his breast—the head of one who, with all her faults, was as an angel of light compared to the wretched being who pronounced on her the sentence of death, and then revelled on his blood-stained throne. The confessions in this reign made on the scaffold were either previously composed by the government; or, if other words were uttered, the reporter shaped them according to the will of him whose will it was death to gainsay. Catherine was attended to the scaffold by her confessor, the Bishop of Lincoln; and afterwards, when Henry too had gone to his account, he recorded the last words of Catherine Howard to have been—

> As to the act, my reverend Lord, for which I stand condemned, God and his holy angels I take to witness, on my soul's salvation, that I die guiltless, never having so abused my sovereign's bed. What other sins and follies of youth I have committed I will not excuse; but am assured that for them God hath brought this punishment upon me, and will in his mercy remit them, for which I pray you, pray with me unto his Son and my Saviour Jesus Christ.*

By those who determine to find a religious motive for all the actions of this reign, as they attribute the death of Ann Boleyn to a conspiracy on the part of the Papists, so they opine that a Protestant conspiracy led to the death of Catherine Howard. The facts of history do not bear out either suspicion. That there was a conspiracy against Ann Boleyn we must admit, but the leading spirit in that conspiracy was, we can little doubt, Thomas Crumwell, who is regarded as the head of the Protestant party; it remains to be proved whether there were any conspiracy at all against Catherine Howard. The most bitter of her enemies were men of the old learning; and so far from her having been under the influence of Norfolk or Gardyner, we hear not the name of the latter after the dinner-party at which the king fell in love with her; while in a family feud Catherine took part against her uncle the duke, who became her enemy. It is ridiculous to suppose, that the counsellors of such a king as Henry could have imagined that he would have tolerated the interference in political affairs of a girl of nineteen, or that such a girl as Catherine would do anything but defer to the judgment, opinion, and will of such a husband as Henry.

I have entered more fully into this subject, because it

* Speed, 1030.

has been insinuated that Cranmer, afraid of sharing the fate of Crumwell, was at the head of this conspiracy; that he conspired with Norfolk and Gardyner to ruin the unfortunate queen. Not only is this disproved, but the very assertion is directly opposed to the whole character of Cranmer. If we are told, that through fear, moral more than physical, he was at any time induced to belie his principles, we might give credit to the assertions of the accuser; but Cranmer's was a character simple and unsuspecting even to weakness; his whole nature would have revolted from anything so degrading as a conspiracy merely to sustain that political power which, in point of fact, he neither possessed nor desired to possess. Both these points are established by what little remains to be told of Cranmer's history during the reign of Henry VIII.

It seems as if Henry delighted to raise his favourites to a giddy pinnacle of greatness, that their fall might be the heavier when, in his caprice or his vengeance, he thought fit to hurl them to the bottom of the pit. Not long before the execution of the fifth queen of Henry VIII., Thomas Crumwell, Earl of Essex, had to plead in vain for his life, in terms the more offensively abject when contrasted with his previous haughtiness of demeanour. His letter to the king concluded in the following terms: "Written at the Tower with the heavy heart and trembling hand of your Highness most miserable prisoner and poor slave. I cry for mercy, mercy—mercy!"

Let the reader compare the abject cowardice of Crumwell with the Christian courage exhibited by Sir Thomas More.

Self-confident, self-reliant, returning frown for frown with the proud peers, who ill brooked to see the plebeian upstart take precedence of all but royalty in the land, the Earl of Essex appeared in his place in the House of Lords on the morning of the 10th of June, 1540. Before evening he was a prisoner in the Tower. He was arrested at the council board under a charge of high treason, by the Duke of Norfolk.

It is impossible to discover the real grounds of his apprehension, unless light shall be hereafter thrown upon the subject by communications made to foreign courts. The principal evidence against him has been suppressed, because probably it would have implicated the king, whose "slave" he had been. He was condemned under the iniquitous statute, which admitted of attainder without trial. It is incorrect to state, as is sometimes done, that he was the author of that statute; he was rather the reviver of it. The preamble tells us nothing except the fact, which is patent, that he took bribes to hold people harmless who had violated the law. The enormous wealth which he had accumulated within a very few years, is sufficient to show how unscrupulous he must have been as to the means by which it was raised; but it was impossible to substantiate against him a charge of high treason. It was only by the will of a Parliament as stern and arbitrary as its master that he could be condemned as a traitor! Why Crumwell should be given up to the vengeance of the people, at this particular juncture of affairs, it is difficult to surmise and useless to conjecture. So it was; he who was yesterday all powerful, found himself on the next day a friendless traitor. When it was known that Crumwell was in the Tower, the joy of the whole nation, and of all parties in the nation, was as if a victory had been won. The peers envied and hated him; the clergy feared him, for he had hinted significantly, that the Church property might share the fate of the monastic property; the men of the old learning abhorred the innovator; and although Protestants, in after ages, under the leadership of Foxe, have declared him to be "a most valiant soldier and captain of Christ, studious in a flagrant zeal, to set forth the truth of the Gospel,"* yet, at the time of his death, he was reputed even by them as one who had betrayed their cause, who had supported, if he did not suggest, the statute of the six articles. Cranmer alone had the boldness to come forward in his defence, knowing that, whatever his faults may have been, he certainly was not a traitor to the king. Cranmer was never admitted into the secret counsels of the king, for Henry respected his virtue too much to employ him in his dirty work. Cranmer looked therefore upon the case unprejudiced, and judged it on its own merits. He speaks of Crumwell as his friend. This was especially generous at the time. The word friend, however, is not to be regarded in the real depth of meaning which may be attached to that sacred word. He merely meant what is still meant in parliament, when one member speaks of another, with whom he has happened to be associated in politics, as his honourable friend.† They who read the correspondence of Cranmer and Crumwell will be aware, that there was not much either of intimacy or congeniality between the two great men. Cranmer's letter to the king on behalf of Crumwell has not been found entire. For what has been preserved of it we are indebted to Lord Herbert. It must be presented to the reader‡:—

I heard yesterday in your grace's council that he (Crumwell) is a traitor, yet who cannot be sorrowful and amazed that he should be a traitor against your majesty, he that was so ad-

---

* Foxe, v. 403.

† It would appear from letter cclvii. that Crumwell was, for some reason or other, in Cranmer's pay. The archbishop sent him £20 for his half-year's fee.

‡ Lord Herbert, 519.

vanced by your majesty; he whose surety was only by your majesty; he who loved your majesty, as I ever thought, no less than God; he who studied always to set forwards whatsoever was your majesty's will and pleasure; he that cared for no man's displeasure to serve your majesty; he that was such a servant in my judgment, in wisdom, diligence, faithfulness, and experience, as no prince in this realm ever had; he that was so vigilant to preserve your majesty from all treasons, that few could be so secretly conceived, but he detected the same in the beginning? If the noble princes of memory, King John, Henry II.,[*] and Richard II., had had such a counsellor about them, I suppose that they should never have been so traitorously abandoned and overthrown as those good princes were. . . . I loved him as my friend, for so I took him to be; but I chiefly loved him for the love which I thought I saw him bear ever towards your grace, singularly above all other. But now if he be a traitor, I am sorry that I ever loved him, or trusted him, and I am very glad that his treason is discovered in time; but yet again I am very sorrowful; for who shall your grace trust hereafter, if you might not trust him? Alas! I bewail and lament your grace's chance herein. I wot not whom your grace may trust. But I pray God continually, night and day, to send such a counsellor in his place whom your grace may trust, and who for all his qualities can and will serve your grace like to him, and that will have so much solicitude and care to preserve your grace from all dangers as I ever thought he had . . . (14 June, 1540).[†]

As we have often to complain, the conduct of Cranmer did not correspond with his words. On referring to the journals of the House of Lords, we find the bill of attainder introduced on the 17th of June. The archbishop was not present. The bill was read the second and third time on the 19th of June, when Cranmer was in his place, and it was read without a dissentient voice. He was present at all

---

[*] Cranmer was not profound in his history. Henry is certainly the name given in Cranmer's letter; for Henry read Edward.

[†] Remains, letter cclviii.

CHAP. III.
Thomas Cranmer.
1533–56.

the other processes of the bill, until it had received the royal assent. Had proof been, in the meantime, introduced sufficient to satisfy the archbishop's mind, or, having expressed his opinion, was he overawed? To speak openly and then to obey, this was his avowed principle as a politician. Crumwell was beheaded on the 28th of July, 1540.

It is frequently supposed that Cranmer, after this, retired from public life, and that the king for the rest of his reign committed the affairs of state to the Bishop of Winchester, Dr. Gardyner. But this assertion is more easily made than proved; it is, indeed, to apply the notions and principles of the nineteenth century to the interpretation of the actions of the sixteenth. A minister in the time of Henry VIII. was as different from what a minister is, in the reign of Queen Victoria, as a clerk in a public office in these days differs from the head of his department. When a minister obtained influence over the royal mind he was called a favourite, and it was as a favourite that he retained that influence. Wolsey was all powerful because he *managed* the king; he saved the king trouble, and though he ruled, he never showed that he ruled. Crumwell was employed by the king to replenish the treasury, as he had promised to do, but he was not admitted to his friendship; and when the king had delighted the people by the condemnation of Crumwell, Henry sought counsel from no one. He became, in the strongest sense of the word, his own minister. This is proved by the State Papers of his time. Even when Wolsey was in power, there were some occasions on which Henry did not consult his favourite minister; and it may be inferred that there were many more on which he acted without the advice of his council.*

* Proceedings of the Privy Council, vii. pref. p. xii. Two remarkable examples of the secret manner in which Henry VIII. sometimes

Cranmer never intruded an opinion except when asked, and was very little about the Court. The same may be said of Gardyner. Henry's insight into character was one of the characteristics of his powerful mind; and that he understood the character of Gardyner is clear from what he said of him to Sir Anthony Browne: "that none could use or rule Gardyner but his royal self, so troublesome was his nature, and so certain was he to cumber all with whom he was associated."*

Such a man was not likely to gain much influence over Henry's mind; and Gardyner was well aware that Henry would not tolerate the proffer of advice unasked. Both Wolsey and Crumwell fell, partly at least, from jealousy on the part of the king. They had made themselves so useful, that in both instances, the "Ego et Rex meus" was implied even if the presumptuous formula was not actually used.

The exclusion of Gardyner from the Regency of Edward VI., by the will of Henry VIII., is sufficient to show, that he had not that power, in the latter years of Henry, which is sometimes attributed to him; and for the withdrawal of which those who gratuitously assert the existence of his power are unable to account.

---

conducted affairs are given in the "State Papers." Part of the instructions with which Dr. Knight, the principal secretary, was furnished on his mission to Rome, in 1527, were concealed even from Wolsey himself (vol. i. 277); and in August, 1541, when Henry contemplated an interview with James V. of Scotland, for which purpose passports under the Great Seal were indispensable, he directed the Lord Chancellor to prepare them, without disclosing the circumstance to any member of the Privy Council in London; and he was commanded to make no more persons privy to the instruments than could possibly be avoided, all of whom were to be solemnly sworn to the strictest secrecy. (Ibid. pp. 680, 681.)

* Ridley's Ridley, 183.

CHAP. III.
Thomas Cranmer.
1533–56.

It is a remarkable circumstance, that while under the act of supremacy, the administration of which the king had confided to Crumwell, the persecutions were so numerous as to defy calculation; under the statute of six articles, more apparently blood-thirsty, they were comparatively few. We may doubt, if the administration of the last-mentioned statute had been confided to Gardyner, whether this would have been the case. The object with Henry was to prevent any party from having the predominance; and to have placed the power in the hands of a party leader would have been to stultify the whole policy of the king. The king's policy was to preserve the tranquillity of the country, and for the furtherance of this object the Privy Council was invested with enormous, almost inquisitorial, powers. These powers were employed not only in the detection of treasonable designs, and the punishment of sedition; but if the public peace were likely to be disturbed the Privy Council would descend to the investigation of the grounds of a family dispute, or it would take part, not always the part of justice, in a private quarrel. In their body, parties were formed, and party hatred could only be appeased by the blood of an opponent. But the king's eye was upon the council. Henry knew the character of every man he employed, and if any, instead of labouring for the public good, were furthering objects either of malice or self-aggrandizement they were not likely to escape detection. He suffered no man to defraud the country but himself; and though he allowed Crumwell to take his percentage out of the spoils of the monasteries, when he exceeded what the king regarded as his fair perquisites, it was by his blood only that he could expatiate his offence.

Of this we shall presently have a remarkable instance; but we must first follow the archbishop to his diocese.

As an administrator Cranmer had not been successful. In some things, he was sufficiently arbitrary, calling in the royal authority, when his powers as metropolitan were disputed. Nothing could have been more arbitrary, as we have seen, than the measures he adopted to silence the clergy, immediately after sentence of divorce had been pronounced against Katharine I. He knew that if the expectants of preferment would be cautious, yet the feelings of the great body of the clergy were in accordance with those of the nation in general, and that against the iniquitous divorce they would have exerted their eloquence. In consequence he prohibited all the clergy of his diocese from preaching, except those who had obtained a license from himself. Cranmer was not the hero whom the countenance of an urgent tyrant could not move. With the same object in view, that of preventing the clergy from denouncing the divorce, he had entered upon a metropolitical visitation in 1535, of which we have spoken before, and which evinced on his part more of zeal than of sound judgment.

In the next reign, we shall find Cranmer guilty—never of cruelty, but still of harsh measures, to silence opponents; no measure being more arbitrary than that which subjected the Church to a royal visitation. Because a metropolitical visitation was opposed by his suffragans, he seems, as a punishment, to have resorted to that extraordinary measure of appointing a royal commission of enquiry.

But, not to anticipate; now in 1543, the archbishop had leisure for a diocesan visitation. A proof that the statute of the six articles was not vigorously enforced is to be seen at once, in the condition of the diocese. Superstitions were still prevalent, and by many of the clergy encouraged as religious observances. Images were retained in the churches, and it was said, that they had power to heal those among the sick who paid to them their devotions. Holy Water was esteemed as efficacious against thunder, lightning, and evil spirits. Holy Candles were employed for the purposes of vindictive sorcery. In one place red-hot coals were poured upon the grave of one who had been chaplain to the archbishop, to signify the death such a heretic deserved. Such was superstition in the one extreme; on the other side, there were men of the new learning who spoke of the ordinances of the Church as mere acts of conjuring to fill the pockets of the clergy, who were represented as professors of legerdemain. Others taught it to be the bounden duty of a Christian man to eat eggs, butter, and cheese in Lent.* All this is intelligible, but we are surprised to find, that some there were, who went so far as to decline preaching in favour of the royal supremacy. Even against the archbishop's chaplain, Dr. Ridley, and against his brother, Archdeacon Cranmer, charges were brought; against the first, for teaching that, although auricular confession was a godly means through which the sinner might come to the priest for counsel, yet it was simply a law of the Church, and not appointed by scripture; against the archdeacon, for removing candles from before a high altar in Canterbury, and for destroying a sacred image. A prebendary of the cathedral was indicted for declaiming against prayer in the vulgar tongue.

It redounds to the credit of Cranmer, that he resorted, under these circumstances, to no harsh measures of coercion or repression. Although the statute of the six articles prevented him from defending the reformers, so many men of the old learning might have been brought

* An amusing list of the cases which came before the archbishop on this occasion is given in **Strype**, I. cxxv.

to destruction for neglecting to assert the royal supremacy, that, if his temper had been vindictive, he might have wrought the death of many who now reviled him and hoped, through the statute, to bring the archbishop and his followers into difficulties. Instead of this, and knowing the king's intention, that the act should only give him powers which he might use at his discretion, Cranmer did what he could to prevent it from being perverted into the means of persecution, by obtaining permission from the king to introduce a measure, sometimes spoken of as a mitigation of the preceding act, although, more properly speaking, it was explanatory of it. He represented to the king, that the extreme severity of the penalties by which the articles were enforced rendered the enforcement of them a thing impossible. It was provided, therefore—to render it almost impossible to apply the statute to the purposes of religious faction—that no person should be put to trial for any offence against the six articles but upon the oath of twelve men; that the presentments should be made within one year after the offence had been committed; that no person should be arrested for any such offence before he should be indicted; and that any accusation for speaking in opposition to the act should be preferred within forty days of the alleged delinquency. The moderation of the archbishop was less efficacious, because wherever he went he appeared as a party man—not indeed as a Protestant, but as an advocate of the men of the new learning; and the reactionary spirit against the reformation, prevalent throughout the country, was especially strong in Kent.

There was in the Privy Council a strong party of the men of the old learning. That Gardyner, in whose mind, as in that of Bonner, a reaction had already taken place, had

CHAP. III.

Thomas Cranmer. 1533–56.

much influence in the Council is highly probable; but the circumstances we are about to relate show, that he was not more in the secret councils of the king than any other of the counsellors. Gardyner cordially hated Cranmer, and was the leader, with the Duke of Norfolk, of that faction which hoped to work his disgrace and ruin. At one period of his life, expecting the archbishopric, Gardyner had been most zealous in the cause of the divorce and of the supremacy, but the elevation of Cranmer had rendered him no longer zealous in supporting the king, though he dared not oppose him. His party was in communication with the reactionaries, and especially with the discontented people in Kent. It appears, that a supposition prevailed that the king had changed his opinions; and a conspiracy was consequently formed against Cranmer. Evidence was to be produced before the Council, that the archbishop had deterred people from preaching, unless they were friendly to the men of the new learning; that he had caused certain images to be removed, though they had not been abused to superstitious purposes; that he had corresponded with the German reformers, and had contributed to the support of some of their friends. We can hardly imagine anything weaker than their cause, and certainly Cranmer could not, as yet, have gone far in the direction of Protestantism, when his most malicious enemies could not bring against him any accusation stronger than this. All would depend upon the humour of the king. The majority of the Council were to be shocked at such a deviation from the royal will, the king was to be exasperated, and Cranmer sent to the Tower.

But nothing could escape the vigilance of the king, resolved as he was to preserve the peace of the country. To him the conspiracy became known.

The archbishop was at Lambeth. He heard the sound of music on the water; such as betokened the passing of the royal barge. He immediately repaired to the bridge or quay, to salute his royal master as he passed. The king was on his way to Chelsea; but when he saw the archbishop, he told the watermen to pull near the shore, and desired the archbishop to come on board. No sooner was he seated, than with a merry voice he said: "Ah, my chaplain, I have news for you; I now know who is the greatest heretic in Kent." He then pulled out of his sleeve a paper containing the charges brought against the archbishop; signed by certain prebendaries and justices of the county. He desired the archbishop to inspect the document. To the astonishment and amusement of the king, the archbishop, as the custom then was in addressing royalty, bent his knee and entreated the king to appoint a commission, by which the truth of what was alleged might be ascertained, "so that from the highest to the lowest they might be well punished, for an example to others, if they had done otherwise than became them."* "Marry," said the king, "that will I do, for I have such affiance and confidence in your fidelity, that I will commit the examination hereof wholly unto you and such as you shall appoint." Morice, the archbishop's secretary, who is our authority, tells us: "Then said my Lord Cranmer, that will not, if it please your grace, seem indifferent." "Well," said the king, "it shall be none otherwise; for surely I reckon you will tell me the truth; yea, of yourself, if you have offended. And, therefore, make no more ado; but let a commission be made out to you and such other as you shall name, whereby I may understand how this confederacy came to pass." "And so," continues Morice, "a commission was made

---

* Morice, 252.

out to my Lord Cranmer, Dr. Coxe, his chancellor, and Dr. Bellasis, a master in Chancery, afterwards Archdeacon of Colchester, and Mr. Hussey, his registrar;" and proceeding to Canterbury,* the commissioners entered upon their investigation. The chancellor and registrar—appointed in the spirit of fairness on account of their official position by the archbishop—were men of the old learning, and his secret enemies. Through their artifices nothing was discovered or disclosed, and it seemed that their report would be that a false alarm had been raised. Morice, however, the archbishop's secretary, saw through their manœuvres, and communicated his suspicions to Dr. Butts, the royal physician, with whom, through Shakspeare, we are all of us acquainted. By Dr. Butts the king was informed of what was taking place, and to the surprise of the chancellor and registrar, even of the archbishop himself, Mr., afterwards Sir Anthony Denny, and Dr. Leigh, made their appearance as additional members, by the king's appointment, of the commission. They immediately nominated nine or ten gentlemen to search the houses of the suspected prebendaries and magistrates; and in a wonderfully short space of time a correspondence was discovered, which not only proved the conspiracy, but involved in its guilt some persons of greater political importance than the prebendaries of Canterbury and the magistrates of Kent. Several of the conspirators were committed to prison, there to remain during the archbishop's pleasure. All that he required of them was, that they should give him some security not to conspire against him for the time to come. "And so," says Morice, "a parliament being at hand, great labour was made by their friends for a general

---

* Strype says they sat at Faversham, but Morice was present at the proceedings.

pardon, which wiped away all punishment and correction for the same, specially my Lord Cranmer being a man that delighted not in revenging." *

The archbishop was deeply grieved to find among the conspirators some who had been distinguished by his patronage, and whom he had hitherto regarded as his friends. He generously, however, forgave them all; and even, with respect to these, received them back into favour.

To add to the troubles of the archbishop, at the end of this year the palace at Canterbury was burnt to the ground, and in the flames perished some of his friends, his brother-in-law being one. The archbishop was on this account exempted from the expense of maintaining the Viceroy of Sicily, in making preparations for whose entertainment the accident occurred.

When the parliament assembled, notwithstanding the generosity of the archbishop in not opposing the bill of indemnity, which was to whitewash those who had lately conspired against his fair fame and his life itself, considerable animosity against him was displayed. Sir John Gostwick, M.P. for Bedfordshire, accused the primate of heresy against the sacrament of the altar. On that point Cranmer certainly had not yet expressed any change of opinion, and it was only on vague report that Sir John made his attack. The speech was reported to the king, "who marvellously stormed at the matter, calling openly Gostwick a varlet, and said he had played a villainous part so to abuse in open parliament the primate of the

---

* Foxe of course implicates Gardyner in the conspiracy, and is followed by most writers, but his name is not mentioned by Morice. A nephew of his was one of the conspirators, and the bishop made no secret of his hostility to the primate, though he does not appear to have committed himself to the present plot.

realm, specially being in favour with his prince as he was. 'What will they (quoth the king) do with him if I were gone?' Whereupon the king sent word unto Mr. Gostwick after this sort: 'Tell that varlet Gostwick that if he do not acknowledge his fault unto my Lord of Canterbury, and so reconcile himself towards him that he may become his good lord, I will surely both make him a poor Gostwick and otherwise punish him to the example of others.' Now Gostwick, hearing of this heinous threat from the king's majesty, came with all possible speed unto Lambeth, and there submitted himself in such sorrowful case, that my lord out of hand not only forgave all the offence, but also went directly unto the king, for the obtaining of the king's favour again, which he obtained very hardly, upon condition that the king might hear no more of his meddling that way."*

From this time till the year 1545, the archbishop lived in peace, pursuing his studies as we have before related, and preparing for those further reforms which Henry encouraged him to design, and which were carried into effect in the next reign. But in the year just mentioned he lost his great friend in the council, the Duke of Suffolk, and his enemies were prepared once more to attempt his ruin.

The archbishop was at Lambeth, and had retired to rest, when at about eleven o'clock a boat arrived from the opposite side of the river, and Sir Anthony Denny was announced as the bearer of a message from the king. The archbishop was required "incontinently" to wait upon the king's majesty at Westminster. He immediately took boat for the palace. Henry had that morning been informed by his Privy Council that "the archbishop, with his learned men, had so infected the whole realm

* Morice, 254.

with their unsavoury doctrine, that three parts of the land were become abominable heretics; and that it might prove dangerous to the king, being like to produce such commotions and uproars as were sprung up in Germany. And therefore they desired that the archbishop might be committed unto the Tower, until he might be examined." The king was very strait in granting this. They told him "that the archbishop, being one of the Privy Council, no man dared to object matter against him, unless he were first committed to durance: which being done, men would be bold to tell the truth, and say their consciences."*

The persons who thus applied for the king's permission to commit Cranmer are the persons who are generally supposed to have made Henry their puppet, for it is not uncharitable to assume that the Duke of Norfolk and the Bishop of Winchester were the persons who took the lead in this factious movement in the Privy Council. If they could have controlled the king in private they would not have thus come before him as a deputation from his council. The king yielded to their solicitation, and permitted them to call the archbishop before them the next day, and if they saw cause to commit him to the Tower.

We are glad to know that Henry had still left in him some sense of justice, and felt what was due to a man on whose friendship he could under all his difficulties rely. He thought more of Cranmer's heart than his head, while he was flattered by knowing how entirely on the king's judgment the archbishop relied.

On reaching Whitehall the archbishop found the king pacing the long gallery in great perturbation of mind. Henry immediately mentioned what had happened in the morning. He stated the charges brought against the

* Strype, I. 177.

archbishop by the council, and acknowledged that he had yielded to their petition that he should be committed to the Tower. He concluded with saying: "but whether I have done well or no, what say you, my lord?" The archbishop thanked the king for his consideration and kindness in thus giving him warning, and added that he was contented to be committed to the Tower for the trial of his doctrine, so that he might be " indifferently heard ; " and he expressed his conviction that his majesty would see him fairly used. I give the rest of this scene in the words of Morice, which may be regarded as the *ipsissima verba* of Cranmer himself. The king, after the archbishop had expressed his willingness to go to the Tower, exclaimed :—

Oh Lord God! what fond simplicity have you: so to permit yourself to be imprisoned that every enemy of yours may take vantage against you. Do you not think that if they have you once in prison, three or four false knaves will be soon procured to witness against you and to condemn you, which else now, being at your liberty, dare not once open their lips or appear before your face. No, not so, my lord (quoth the king); I have better regard unto you than to permit your enemies so to overthrow you, and therefore I will that you to-morrow come to the council, who no doubt will send for you, and when they break this matter unto you, require them that being one of them you may have thus much favour as they would have themselves, that is, to have your accusers brought before you; and if they stand with you, without regard of your allegations, and will in no condition condescend unto your requests, but will needs commit you to the Tower, then appeal you from them to our person, and give to them this ring (which he delivered unto my Lord Cranmer, then), by the which (said the king) they shall well understand that I have taken your cause into my hand from them, which ring they well know that I use it to none other purpose but to call matters from the council into my own hands to be ordered and determined. And with this good advice my

Lord Cranmer, after most humble thanks, departed from the king's majesty.*

Strype and those who follow him give this speech with the embellishments due to the imagination of Foxe, not always improvements. The next day occurred the scene with which we are familiar in the pages of Shakspeare. Shakspeare adheres as usual to his authority, putting in one or two of those master strokes which give life to the picture.

I must briefly advert to what is so well known. The archbishop, after his interview with the king, returned to Lambeth in no very comfortable frame of mind; for when many enemies are bent upon one man's destruction, the probability is that they will eventually succeed. The next morning his Grace was summoned to the Council. Intending to take his seat as usual at the board, he was rudely repulsed at the Council Chamber door. There the first peer of the realm remained with the serving men and lackeys, while members of the council were passing and repassing—all these insults indicating a foregone conclusion. The archbishop's secretary, Morice, to whose account we adhere as that of an eye-witness of what took place, was naturally indignant at the insult offered to his master. On the former occasion, as we have narrated, he communicated with the king's physician, Dr. Butts, and he either sent for or called upon him now. Dr. Butts immediately went to the Council Chamber door, " to keep my lord company." But before the archbishop was called into the council, and while the faction which ruled the council were debating how to proceed, it was arranged that Dr. Butts should go at once to the king. Henry was always accessible to his subjects, and Dr. Butts now told

* Morice, 256.

his majesty that he had seen a strange sight. "What is that?" quoth the king. "Marry," replied Dr. Butts, "the Archbishop of Canterbury is become a lackey or a serving man, for well I wot he hath stood amongst them this hour almost at the Council Chamber door—so that I was ashamed to keep him company any longer." "What!" quoth the king, "standeth he without the chamber door? Have they served me so? It is well, enough; I'll talk with them by-and-by."

It is evident that this was a relief to the royal mind. Henry, willing to oblige the council, had acceded to their request for the apprehension of the archbishop. He repented of his promise; he communicated with the archbishop; he promised to assist him; but still he was in a delicate position, until the council had now placed themselves in the wrong, or, at all events, afforded him an opportunity of simulating just indignation and anger.

Meantime the archbishop was commanded to appear before the council. "'It was declared to him, that a great complaint was made of him both to the king and to them, that he and other by his permission had infected the whole realm with heresy, and therefore it was the king's pleasure that they should commit him to the Tower, and there for his trial to be examined.' My Lord Cranmer required, as is before declared, with many other both reasons and persuasions, that he might have his accusers come there before him, before they used any such extremity against him. In fine, there was no entreaty could serve, but that he must needs depart (to) the Tower. 'I am sorry, my lords (quoth my Lord Cranmer), that you drive me unto this exigency, to (appeal) from you to the king's majesty, who by this token hath resumed this matter into his own hands, and dischargeth you thereof;' and so delivered the king's ring unto them. By-and-by the Lord Russell sware a great oath, and said: 'Did not I tell you, my lords, what would come of this matter? I knew right well that the king would never permit my Lord of Canterbury to have such a blemish as to be imprisoned, unless it were for high treason.' And as the manner was, when they had once received that ring, they left off their matter, and went all unto the king's person both with his token and the cause. When they came unto his highness, the king said unto them, 'Ah! my lords, I had thought that I had had a discreet and wise council; but now I perceive that I am deceived. How have ye handled here my Lord of Canterbury? What! make ye of him a slave, shutting him out of the Council Chamber amongst serving men? Would you be so handled yourselves.' And after such taunting words, said: 'I would you should well understand that I account my Lord of Canterbury as faithful a man towards me as ever was prelate in this realm, and one to whom I am many ways beholden, by the faith I owe unto God (and so laid his hand upon his breast); and therefore who so loveth me (said he) will regard him thereafter.' And with these words all, and specially my Lord of Norfolk, answered and said: 'We meant no manner hurt unto my Lord of Canterbury in that we requested to have him in durance. That we only did because he might, after his trial, be set at liberty to his more glory.' 'Well,' said the king, 'I pray you that you use not my friends so. I perceive now well enough how the world goeth among you. There remaineth malice among you one to another; let it be avoided out of hand, I advise you.' And so the king departed, and the lords shook hands every man with my Lord of Canterbury, Cranmer, against whom never more no man durst spurn during king Henry's life."*

* Morice, 257.

The scene thus graphically described by a contemporary, we may almost say by Cranmer himself, since he was his secretary's authority, is of considerable value. It shows us Henry's skill in managing men; the mixture in his character of much humour with a fierceness which kept men sometimes in a state of suspense, whether all was to end in a comedy or whether to some there would be a tragical termination.

Henry had as much faith in the tendency of a good dinner, to effect a reconciliation between parties at variance, as Homer himself. On the passing of the statute of six articles, the king had commanded the archbishop to invite the House of Lords to dine with him at Lambeth; and now all differences were to be made up by a similar entertainment, which the archbishop was glad to give, at the king's command, to the Lords of the Council.

It had been, nevertheless, with a very heavy heart that Cranmer obeyed the royal mandate with respect to the hospitality he was expected to show on the passing of the statute just mentioned.

By no one was the effect of the passing of that act more painfully felt than it was by Cranmer. It broke up his happy home. It divorced him from his wife for a season, and separated him from his children. How deeply affected Cranmer was upon the occasion we learn, through the gossiping propensities of Alexander Ales, in a document which has been lately discovered among the State Papers. Alexander Ales, through the patronage of Crumwell, had become a professor at Cambridge. Crumwell employed him for his own purposes, made him the lion of the town for a season, and then neglected him. In 1539, the professor had come to London to solicit from Crumwell the payment of his salary then in arrear. Ales was, though a priest, a married man, and the archbishop, whose care for his friends was one of his amiable characteristics, sent for him to Lambeth. He wished to warn him, that the protection which he had hitherto extended to a married priest could be extended no longer. He advised him to leave England without loss of time, exclaiming:—

"Happy man that you are, you can escape. I wish that I could do the same! Truly my See would be no hindrance to me. And now you must make all haste to quit the island before a blockade is established, unless you are willing to sign the decree, as I have done. I have sealed it, compelled by fear. I repent of what I have done; and if I had known, that my only punishment would have been deposition from my archbishopric—as I hear my Lord Latimer is deposed—of a truth I would not have subscribed. I am grieved that you have been deprived of your salary for three years by Crumwell, that you have no funds for your travelling expenses, and that I have no ready money. I dare not mention this to my friends, lest the king should become aware that I have given you warning to escape, and that I have provided you with the means of travelling. I give you, however, this ring as a token of my friendship. It at one time belonged to Thomas Wolsey, and it was presented to me by the king when he gave me the archbishopric." *

They parted, in this world never to meet again. Cranmer's wife was already gone.

> His true and honorable wife,
> As dear to him as were the ruddy drops
> That visited his sad heart.

It may be expedient here to pause, in order that we may place under one point of view what may be gathered

* State Papers, Elizabeth, 533. The report of this conversation, given by Ales himself to Queen Elizabeth, is important as throwing light upon the character of the archbishop, as well as upon the king. Crumwell refused to assist Ales, whom he had formerly patronized. He said he did not dare to speak to him. To solicit his dismissal, or to give him anything, would be to offend the king. He promised to send what he owed him into Germany.

from various sources, relating to Cranmer's private life and domestic relations. Various little anecdotes have been preserved, which throw light upon his character, and, to a certain extent, explain and qualify certain objectionable points in his political career.

His clandestine marriage, as he had foreseen, subjected him to continual annoyances. It not unfrequently involved him in difficulties, and placed his wife in painful situations.

The husband and wife were well aware, that throughout the reign of Henry VIII. they might, at any moment, be compelled to separate, and that they were surrounded by enemies, who would have found, in their separation, an indulgence to their malignant passions or vindictive feelings. In the lingering immorality of mediævalism, clerical concubinage, though denounced by the canons, was winked at by society; and Cranmer was probably enabled to live with his wife, by rendering it difficult, if not impossible, for his adversaries to prove that a marriage between him and Margaret had ever taken place.* But this placed her in a position which must have been painful to her husband and annoying to herself. Mrs. Cranmer was, however, not a woman of much sensibility or refinement. One would have supposed that the widow of such a man as Cranmer would have retained her weeds to the hour of her death, and have regarded them with

---

* Under the statute of the six articles it was constituted felony for a cleric to live with his wife. There can be little doubt that this was a blow aimed at Cranmer. They were indebted for their security to the uncertain character of the king. Cranmer was known to be a favourite with the king, and no one knew what might be the fate of any informant against the archbishop. The king, who knew everything, knew of the marriage, and if he winked at it who would dare to find fault. In the preceding chapter the proclamation against the married clergy is given.

pride. But after the archbishop's execution she was twice married. She was first wedded to Edward Whitchurch, the printer; and on his death, in 1561, the widow of Cranmer and Whitchurch was again wedded, in 1564, to Bartholomew Scott, Esq., a justice of the peace for the county of Surrey.*

In the gossip of the day, various stories were afloat concerning the primate and his wife. As an example, we may mention one. It was reported that on certain occasions, when the archbishop was travelling in state, his wife was packed up in a chest and carried with him. Once upon a time, the story goes, the precious chest was consigned to a porter who was not made aware of the treasure it contained. Poor mistress Cranmer was in the first place tossed and jolted on the man's shoulders, and then in the barrow of the porter. She kept, however, her sorrows to herself, until at length the burden was deposited at the palace door, but topsy turvy. She was now obliged to scream, and the servants rushing to her rescue, compelled the astonished porter to surrender his precious burden.

This story, first told, if not invented, by Sanders, has been handed on by succeeding writers down even to Dr. Milner, though we presume that it will find credit with no one who has not a party end to serve by turning a great man into ridicule. But this and similar stories are not without their historical value. They would not have

* Collect. Topog. et Genealogica, iii. 145. Both Whitchurch and Scott resided at Camberwell. In the epitaph of the latter his first wife (for Scott married three times) is described as " Marget ye wido of ye right Rev. Prel. and Martyr, Tho. Cranmer, Archbish. of Canterburie." By Todd and those who follow him she is called Ann. Todd does not give his authority, and he is usually accurate. She may have had two Christian names. Her eldest daughter was Ann, her second Margaret.

been told, unless the inventors of them had been certain that they would be received as something possible. Whether true or not, they were at the time believed. They prove that though the marriage was known, it was not publicly announced, and that although Mrs. Cranmer was visited by the archbishop's personal friends, yet on public occasions she was kept in the back ground. We may mention, as confirmatory of this, that when we look at the dates attached to Cranmer's letters, we find, that he resided for the most part at one or other of the country residences attached to his see; at Croydon, at Otford, but chiefly at Ford. Ford was conveniently situated, being near to Canterbury, and not far from Herne, the parish of Ridley. The manor house—the most ancient except the palace at Canterbury—had been given to the see by Ethelbert, and had lately been rebuilt by Archbishop Morton. The archbishop was, as we have before recounted, a keen sportsman, and the park we know was filled with game; for it is recorded that his successor, Archbishop Whitgift, who was equally fond of field sports, was accustomed here to follow the chase.

Cranmer's love of retirement, where only he could enjoy that intercourse with his beloved family for which he sacrificed so much, rendered him unpopular at Canterbury, where the citizens expected the archbishop to live in splendour; and although when he visited the metropolis he kept great state and hospitality at Lambeth, yet the Londoners were not well pleased, as their countless barges passed the gates of Lambeth, to see that the manor house was only occupied when the primate was compelled by business to attend the Parliament, the Convocation, or the Privy Council; or when he was summoned to wait upon the king at Westminster.

The secret of his marriage may also, to a certain extent, account for Cranmer's extreme subserviency to the king. Henry must have known that Cranmer had a family, but he forbore to enquire whether the mother of the archbishop's children were his wedded wife. We find Wolsey, though not a profligate man, making provision for one child at least; and so obfuscated had become the moral perceptions of men, through the constrained celibacy of the clergy, that Henry would not have regarded Cranmer's cohabitation with a concubine any serious impeachment of the moral character of a prelate. The truth had, however, become known to the king during the passing of the statute of six articles. It was in favour of Cranmer, that, in his proclamation, the king directed his attack only upon those of the clergy who had *openly declared* their marriage, or should *hereafter* enter into the marriage state.* Henry took an opportunity, indeed, of informing Cranmer that the act should not be put in force against him, when it was evident that his adversaries thought they had at length a case against the archbishop. The king, in familiar conversation, stated that the archbishop's obedience to the statute was questioned, when Cranmer declared that his opinion had always been against the passing of the bill, but that since it had become an act of parliament he had scrupulously observed it. The king, assuming an air of pleasantry, demanded whether his chamber would stand the test of the articles. The archbishop solemnly declared that this test he could stand, since immediately after the passing of the act he had sent his wife back to her friends in Germany.

This was a good-natured way of imparting to Cranmer the fact, that Henry had penetrated the designs of his enemies, and that while it became the archbishop to

* Strype, Book i. c. 18.

act with caution, he had, nevertheless, a friend in the king.

How far the king was, antecedently to this, acquainted with his secret, Cranmer did not know; but this he *did* know, that the king might at any moment be prompted to make the enquiry; and aware of the uncertain temper and the despotic disposition with which he had to deal, he felt that his happiness, his station, and his very life were in the king's hand. To conciliate the king was, therefore, with him a matter of policy; and the course marked out by prudence it was the more easy to follow, since with the natural admiration which a weak mind feels for a strong one, and with the abundant gratitude with which a generous spirit accepts little acts of kindness from a superior, Cranmer loved Henry, and Henry, sagacious to perceive that Cranmer's attachment to him was personal, regarded the archbishop with as much of the holy feeling of friendship as a character so selfish is capable of experiencing.

Of Cranmer's domestic habits we have some account from his private secretary, Morice.* His usual hour of rising was five o'clock. The first four hours of the day were generally given to devotion and reading. He did not, in reading, trust to his memory, but had his commonplace book always at hand; and instead of taking his ease in his chair, he read standing at his desk. His custom of early rising and of standing while he read was certainly conducive to his health, although, in regard to either practice, some strength of constitution is required. At

---

* "A declaration concernyng the Progeny, with the maner and trade of the lif and bryngyng upp, of that most Reverent Father in God, Thomas Cranmer, late archbishop of Canterbury, and by what order and meanes he came to his prefermente and dignitie." Printed by the Camden Society from a MS. in L.C.C.C.

nine o'clock he received visitors, and transacted business till one, the usual hour for dinner. After dinner, he was prepared to hear any suitor or petitioner who claimed his attention, and by his courtesy and kindness of manner he won the goodwill of all who approached him, even though in their suit they might have been unsuccessful. When such business was over, he enjoyed, if in the country, the healthy field sports in which he always excelled, or else he indulged himself in a game of chess, or in looking over the game as played by his children. At five o'clock, he repaired to his chapel; there, until the year 1549, or during the first sixteen years of his primacy, to assist in the office of the Breviary, and after that time, in that revision of the Breviary which has assumed the shape of our Book of Common Prayer. He devoted the interval, between chapel and supper time, to recreation, and when the weather permitted it, to out-door exercises. Supper was not with him a formal meal. He frequently did not partake of it; but he always appeared in the hall, where he welcomed his guests, and remained in the enjoyment of their society till nine o'clock, when he retired to rest.

His establishment was well ordered, and his servants were bound to him by ties of affection and gratitude. The officers of his extensive household maintained a strict discipline; and every Friday the archbishop himself held, as it were, a court, at which any of the servants who thought themselves wronged might appeal to his Grace.

Never was the family so happy, as when Hugh Latimer was a guest of the archbishop; and towards the close of his life he lived with him entirely. He was the wit of the "new learning," the Sydney Smith of the age. He was not always decorous in his manners, and sometimes his merriment was ill-timed. When the primate was, on one occasion, presiding at a court which was to decide upon the legal murder of Sir Thomas More, the illustrious prisoner was required to withdraw. The day was hot, and More declined going into the garden, but took his seat at a window from which he could see all that was passing below. "And I saw," he said, "Master Latimer very merry, for he laughed and took one or twain by the neck so handsomely, that if they had been women I should have weened that he waxed wanton."*

Although Cranmer entertained for Latimer a sincere friendship, and received him, at the close of his life, as a regular inmate of his family, yet he was aware of the weaknesses as well as of the virtues of his eccentric friend. Latimer's eccentricities occasionally involved the more prudent archbishop in difficulties. On one occasion, he had preached at Bristol a sermon in favour of the divorce of Queen Katharine and the royal supremacy with his usual vehemence, jocosity, and want of judgment; and a disturbance was the consequence, a regular riot ensuing between the men of the old learning and the men of the new. For extending his patronage to such a man the archbishop was censured, and bravely did Cranmer meet his assailants. He knew that the king loved to hear an outspoken man, especially on the supremacy and divorce, and he used his interest with Crumwell to have Latimer appointed one of the Lent preachers at Court. At the same time, he felt rather anxious when the experiment was to be made, and addressed the following letter, full of worldly wisdom, to Latimer:—

"I commend me unto you, &c. These be to certify you of the king's pleasure, how that his grace is contented that ye shall be admitted to preach on all the Wednesdays of this next Lent before him. Whereupon I thought it very expedient, for divers

* Roper's More, 179.

considerations reasonably moving thereto, to admonish you of certain things in no wise to be neglect and omitted on your behalf, in time of your preaching; which to observe and follow according to mine advice hereafter to you prescribed, shall at the length redound to your no little laud and praise.

"First, therefore, take this order (if ye will), reading over the book ye take for your purpose some processes of Scripture, the Gospel, Pistill, or any other part of Scripture in the Bible, and the same to expound and declare according to the pure sense and meaning thereof; wherein above all things it will be most convenient, that ye do not at all persuade for the defence of your own causes and matters lately in controversy; but that ye rather do seem utterly (to pass over) those your accusations, than now in that place any sparkle or suspicion of grudge should appear to remain in you for the same. This done, that likewise ye be very circumspect to overpass and omit all manner speech, either apertly or suspiciously sounding against any special man's facts, acts, manners or sayings, to the intent your audience have none occasion thereby, namely to slander your adversaries, which would seem to many that you were void of charity, and so much the more unworthy to occupy that room. Nevertheless, if such occasion be given by the Word of God, let none offence or superstition be unreprehended, specially if it be generally spoken without affectation.

"Furthermore, I would ye should so study to comprehend your matters, that in any condition you stand no longer in the pulpit than an hour, or an hour and a half at the most, for by long expense of time the king and the queen shall peradventure wax so weary at the beginning that they shall have small delight to continue without with you to the end. Therefore let the effect of the premises take no place in your mind, specially before this circumspect audience, to the intent that you in so doing need not to have any other declaration hereafter against the misreports of your adversaries. And for your further instruction in this behalf I would ye should the sooner come up to London, here to prepare all things in areadiness, according to such expectation as is had in you."*

* Remains. Letter cxxx. Harl. MS. 6148.

The archbishop was not in advance of his age on the subject of toleration, when the law was to be maintained; but whenever he was personally or privately concerned, he evinced a liberal mind and a mild disposition, the more remarkable, as it seemed to be scarcely intelligible to those with whom he was associated. Morice, for example, tells us that the lenity with which the archbishop overlooked offences provoked Dr. Hethe, afterwards Archbishop of York, with unoffending sarcasm one day to say to him: "I know how to win all things at your hands well enough." "How so?" quoth my lord. "Marry!" replied Dr. Hethe, "I perceive I must first attempt to do you some notable displeasure, and then by a little relenting obtain from you what I desire." Whereat, continues Morice, "my lord bit his lip, as his manner was when he was moved, and rejoined, "You say well, and yet you may be deceived."

This characteristic anecdote is worth much, and the reader will remember how admirably it is noticed by Shakspeare :—

> "The common voice I see is verified
> Of thee, which says thus: Do my Lord of Canterbury
> A shrewd turn and he is your friend for ever."

Many faults in such a man were overlooked by his contemporaries, and may be passed over with complacency by posterity. It was thought by those around him, that he carried this virtue to an extreme, that he gave encouragement to his enemies and discouraged his friends. He, on his part, complained that many Protestants, by their "outrageous doings," placed a stumbling-block in the way of those who had not yet come to a knowledge of the Gospel. He determined to tread in the steps of his Divine Master, and to remember that those who erred from ignorance of the truth were to be beaten with only a few stripes, while the many stripes were intended for such as acted in opposition to the dictates and warnings of conscience. This principle, we shall find, he carried out in the "Reformatio Legum;" and on this principle he acted in interceding for the Lady Mary, when her exasperated father thought of sending her to the Tower for refusing to relinquish the title of Princess, or to renounce the supremacy of the Bishop of Rome.

In the autobiography of Edward Underhill, who was regarded, or who accounted himself, a man of more than ordinary piety, we have another instance of the archbishop's lenity—his culpable lenity, as it appeared to Underhill. This "man of God" had a quarrel with Henry Moore, the vicar of Stepney, abbot formerly of Eastminster.* In the lawless reign of Edward VI., Underhill apprehended the unfortunate vicar, and carried him off to Croydon, where the archbishop was at that time residing. The charge against the vicar was, that when strange preachers forced themselves into his pulpit he disturbed them. Sometimes the godly preachers were disturbed in their discourse by the ringing of the bells. At other times, when the sermon was not half done, the hour of divine service had arrived, and the singing in the choir commenced. At other times the vicar would, in his own church, challenge the preacher who had taken possession of his pulpit. Mr. Underhill's neighbours were "weary of the vicar of Stepney, especially those who lived at Limehouse, Mr. Dryver, Mr. Ive, Mr. Poynter, Mr. Marche, and others," and probably the vicar was rather provoking. But those eminent men— Mr. Dryver, Mr. Ive, Mr. Poynter, and Mr. Marche—

---

* Henry Moore had been Abbot of St. Mary de Grace, near the Tower of London. MS. Harl. 6956, p. 74. He was presented to the vicarage of Stepney on the 6th of March, 1544. Newcourt, i. 740.

"durst not meddle with him until it was my hap to come and dwell among them. And for that I was the king's servant I took upon me, and they went with me to the archbishop, to witness those things against him. The archbishop was too full of lenity. A little he rebuked him and bade him do so no more. 'My lord,' said I, 'methinks you are too gentle with so stout a papist.' 'Well,' said he, 'we have no law to bind them by.' 'We have, my lord,' said I; 'if I had your authority, I would be so bold as to unvicar him, or minister some sharp punishment to him and such other. If ever it come to their turn they will show you no such favour.' 'Well,' said the archbishop, 'If God so provide we must abide it.' 'Surely,' said I, 'God will never con you thanks for this, but rather take the sword from such as will not use it upon his enemies.' And thus we parted."*

But although the temper of Cranmer was naturally mild, and such as won the esteem of all who approached him, he could on principle, as we shall hereafter see, become occasionally stern and even harsh. In juxtaposition with the statements just made we may place the following letter to Thirlby, Archdeacon of Ely. It is dated May, 1534. The occasion is not known:—"Master Archdeacon, I commend me unto you; signifying to you that I have received your letters, with a billet from the King's Highness in them enclosed, whereby amonges other things I perceive your ambitious mind in seeking your own glory and advancement of your name, and that unjustly without your deserts, in that you desire to have me confess by writing your diligence, laying to my charge that heretofore I have been a testimony of your negligence. If you have hitherto been accounted negligent, there is nothing as me seemeth as yet commenced and

* Autobiography of Edward Underhill, 157.

done on your behalf whereby you do not declare yourself indeed the same man that I spake in word; although you have changed the kind of negligence from a slow negligence to a rash negligence. For so negligently you have run of heed in this matter that you have advertised me never a word of those things which I desire to know the king's pleasure in."

We are pleased with Cranmer's attention to the courtesies of life and minor morals of society. We find him not forgetful of his old college friends, and I doubt not that my readers will peruse with interest the following little note, preserved by chance among his papers, and addressed to Dr. Capon, the master of Jesus College, Cambridge:—

" In my right hearty wise I commend me unto you, &c. And so certifying you that I send you here a buck to be bestowed amonges your company within your college. And forasmuch as you have more store of money and also less need than I at this season, therefore I bequeath a noble of your purse towards the baking and seasoning of him. And whensoever I have so much money beforehand as I am now behindhand I shall repay you your noble again. And thus fare you well. From my manor of Croydon, the xxvi. day of June.

" To the Master of Jesus College in Cantabrige." *

He had, when he was first appointed, to look after his supply of venison, which, no doubt, was an important item in his expenses, when he was obliged to maintain a large establishment and to entertain much company. The Earl of Arundel evidently hoped to escape a customary payment; but Cranmer looked carefully after his dues, as the following letter will show.

To Lord Arundel.

" In my right hearty wise I commend me unto your good lordship, &c. And where I am credibly informed of a certain

* Letter xvi. Harl. MSS. 6148, f. 22, b.

composition concluded between my predecessors and yours, concerning the game and other liberties in the forest of Arundell, for the number of thirteen bucks or stags in summer, and for so many does or hinds in winter, which as is more plainly specified are yearly due unto the Archbishop of Canterbury's larder, within his manor of Slyndon: in consideration hereof, and forasmuch as the store of my other parks and games are now, by reason of this last vacation, utterly wasted and decayed, whereby I am at this season destitute of venison, both for myself and my friends; and so am thereby also now constrained more effectually to require of you this my said duty herein, I most heartily desire your lordship, that I may have these my said bucks or stags at your pleasure at this time. And hereafter when my game is better increased and replenished I shall be as glad again to accomplish your requests in such like matters from time to time &c.

"To my very singular good Lord, my Lord of Arundell."*

To various members of his family he was an affectionate kinsman and a benefactor. According to Thoroton and Todd, the elder branch of his family was indebted to the archbishop for an increase of the family property. To his nephew the archbishop assigned the advowson of the rectories of Aslacton and Whatton, which the archbishop purchased in the first year of Edward VI., and which had belonged to the dissolved monastery of Welbeck. Todd affirms that this monastic property was assigned to his nephew on the condition, that the archbishop's wife, if she survived him, should enjoy the revenues, and that after her death the rectories and manors should be the united property of the head of the Cranmer family. Possessed of both, this nephew died, and to his heir they descended. The same affectionate disposition is discernible in the following letter addressed to his brother-in-law, Harold

* Letter xxxviii. Harl. MSS 6184, fol. 30.

Rosell, Esq., of Radcliffe-on-Trent, who had married the archbishop's sister Dorothy.

CHAP. III.
Thomas Cranmer. 1533–56.

"Brother Rosell, in my right hearty wise I commend me unto you, and in likewise to my sister your bedfellow, &c. And where I understand that your son is very apt to learn, and given to his book, I will advise you therefore that ye suffer not him to lose his time, but either that ye set him forth to school at Southwell, or else send him hither unto me, that at the least between us he utterly lose not his youth, &c. Further I pray you have me commended unto your father and mother. And thus fare ye well. From my manor of Otteforde, &c."*

The amiable qualities of Cranmer's character sometimes degenerated into weakness. It will be difficult to justify his proceedings with respect to the promotion of his brother Edward. Next to a bishopric the most lucrative preferment in the Church was the archdeaconry of Canterbury. On Cranmer's appointment to the See of Canterbury, this profitable and important office was held by William Warham, a nephew of the late archbishop. Not only did the new archbishop interfere with the archdeacon's leases in favour of one of his servants, but he actually persuaded or compelled him to resign both the archdeaconry and the provostship of Wingham, in March, 1534; and Edward Cranmer received the two appointments. What added to the offence was, that the resignation was effected through a simoniacal contract. The resigning archdeacon, with the privity and consent of the primate, was to receive a pension of sixty pounds a year out of the archdeaconry, and twenty pounds a year out of Wingham. It was amiable in the archbishop to desire to make his brother a sharer of his own good fortune; it was desirable that he should have an archdeacon in whom

* Harl. MSS. 6148. fol. 31.

he could confide, and what was done was probably not done, at that careless period, without a precedent. Nevertheless, one who had avowed his intention to correct abuses in the Church of England ought not to have commenced his career by an act of simony.

To this we must add the fact, that in the correspondence of Cranmer, there are several requests made to the king's vicar-general, for grants out of the Abbey lands in favour of his friends. In one he asks for the suppression of Rocester or Crockesden, that his servant Francis Basset might have a lease of one of the houses.

As this part of Cranmer's life is either slurred over or ignored by his apologists, I shall present to the reader the following document, by which it will be seen that he obtained, in the reign of Edward VI., the confirmation of grants made to him in the time of Henry VIII.*

"March 20. 1 Edw. VI.

"Indenture between the king of the first part, Edward Duke of Somerset Lord Protector, Sir William Paulett Knight, Lord Saint John, Sir John Russell, Knight, Lord Russell, Sir John Dudley, Knight, and others of the second part, and Thomas Cranmer Archbishop of Canterbury of the third part.

"Reciting that the late king by his will directed that all grants, &c. not perfected should be completed by his executors, and that his counsellors were to perform all necessary acts during the minority of Edward VI.

"And reciting that the Lord Protector and other his co-executors knowing that the late king intended, in consideration of true and faithful service done by the Archbishop of Canterbury, as also for £429 14s. 2d., to have granted to him and his heirs for ever the site of the late Priory of Arthington, Co: York, together with all lands pertaining, and also the site of the late monastery of Kirstall in the same county with all lands pertaining, and also the parsonages and churches of Whatton and As-

* Deeds of Purchase and Exchange, Edw. VI. Nos. 31 (a & b).

lacton, Co: Nottingham, to the late monastery of Welbeke in the same county lately belonging, and the advowsons of the same, and also the manor of Woodhall, Co: Nottingham, late parcel of the lands of Thomas Graye, Esquire, and also the advowson of Kingsnorth, Co: Kent, to hold to the same archbishop his heirs and assigns for ever by the service of the twentieth part of a knight's fee, at the yearly rent of 12s. for Arthington, £6 0s. 1d. for Kirstall, 33s. 4d. for Whatton, 16s. 8d. for Aslacton, and to hold Woodhall and Kingsnorth of the king as of his castle of Nottingham, by fealty only, in free socage and not in chief, and reciting that the grant of the premises were not made in the lifetime of the said late king.

" Therefore the king agrees by patent to be made before the Nativity of St. John the Baptist next, to grant the same premises unto the Archbishop his heirs and assigns for ever."

Cranmer's family consisted of two daughters, Ann, who died in her father's lifetime, and Margaret, who survived him, with a son who bore the same Christian name as himself. His son Thomas was deprived of the monastic estates with which the archbishop had thus endowed his family—lands belonging to the monastery of Kirkstall and the nunnery of Arthington—in the reign of Queen Mary. He petitioned Queen Elizabeth to be restored to the woods and lands pertaining to the monastery of Kirkstall and the nunnery of Arthington, on the ground of his being his father's heir, restored in blood by an act of parliament, February 27, 1562-3.*

The tenderness with which this part of Cranmer's conduct is sometimes approached, is occasioned by his apologists overlooking the fact, that the transaction was not regarded by Cranmer, his nephew or his son, with those feelings which have been prevalent since the time of Spelman. By many persons who treat of the

* Original MS. Lansdown MSS., No. 107, Art. 72.

dissolution of the monasteries, the monastic property is confused in their minds with Church property. The monastic property, however, was no more Church property than is at the present day the property belonging to the colleges of Oxford and Cambridge. The colleges are more closely allied to the Church of England than were the monasteries. The monasteries being, for the most part, opposed to the discipline of the Church and the regimen of the bishops. A secular clergyman did not regard the spoliation of the regulars with an evil eye, and when the property was on sale, they did not imagine that the purchase of it was sacrilege. This has been an after-consideration—and we must not approach the conduct of the sixteenth century with a sentiment which only came into vogue at a subsequent period.

It is fair to make this observation in passing, although it is with the fact, not with the exculpation of Cranmer, that we are here concerned: the fact is indisputable that, however we may account for it, Archbishop Cranmer invested his money in the confiscated property of the monasteries, and purchased the forfeited Abbey lands.

I confess, that I find it more difficult to account for or to palliate Cranmer's conduct in another particular. The king having squandered and gambled away the estates of the monks, began now to cast a longing eye upon the lands of the secular clergy. It seems that parliament had empowered ecclesiastical corporations, sole and aggregate, to exchange estates with the king; or to alienate ecclesiastical property in his majesty's favour. The pretence was, that the king and the clergy might thus benefit the Church by a redistribution of the Church estates. The principle was the same as that on which the present Ecclesiastical Commission has been established; for its misapplication by Henry, Cranmer is not responsible. We have again only to record the fact, that, under this act of parliament, Cranmer alienated to the king twelve good manors of the See of Canterbury; and he conveyed to him the parks, and splendid residences of the archbishops, at Otford, at Knowle, and at Mayfield.

It is difficult not to suspect that by the surrender of the Church property the means were provided for enabling Cranmer to settle a portion of the monastic property upon his wife and children.

Cranmer had acquired one important quality in a statesman—he had a perfect command of his countenance, and never betrayed his feelings. He was said to be imperturbable. Certainly, under every change of circumstance whether of prosperity or of adversity, he was to outward appearance the same.

To the king Cranmer was always acceptable as a friend, though I cannot discover, from his correspondence or from any other source, that he was such a constant counsellor of Henry VIII. as modern historians, following Foxe, have represented him. Certainly, during Crumwell's existence, Cranmer approached the king only or chiefly through the minister; and he did himself, through the same channel, receive the royal commands. It was not likely that Henry, when gambling away the monastic property, should invite the archbishop more frequently than was necessary, to a court which had become in this respect what is not now mentioned to ears polite; and Crumwell was not very willing to have a rival near the throne, especially as we know that Cranmer was not satisfied with the way in which the confiscated property was disposed of, and that moreover he did not sympathise with those ribalds whom the vicar-general patronised, and who in ridiculing popery permitted their wit not unfrequently to degenerate into blasphemy against Christianity. The personal feeling of attachment to Cranmer on the part of Henry was, however, no secret to the courtiers. The archbishop's secretary records, that he heard the Lord Crumwell say one day at dinner to my Lord Cranmer:* "You were born in a happy hour, I suppose, for do or say what you will the king will always take it at your hand. And I must needs confess that in some things, *I have complained of you*; but all in vain, for he will never give credit against you, whatsoever is laid to your charge; but let me or any other of the council be complained of, his grace will most severely chide and fall out with us." †

This may seem to some persons to contradict the statement made in the preceding paragraph; but to my mind the anecdote is confirmatory of the assertion there made. It was a speech such a statesman, secure of his superiority, might be willing to make, in flattery to one contented to act a subordinate part, and who was satisfied with the appearance of power without possessing the reality. Cranmer was happy to be the king's friend; Crumwell, a keen observer of men, saw that this was Cranmer's ambition and pride, and he knew how to apply the harmless flattery.‡

We have seen, on more than one occasion, that Cranmer was accused of not keeping up the hospitality for which his predecessors in the see of Canterbury had been cele-

---

* In those days the title of lord was not confined to the office; it was attached to the person. We occasionally read of my Lord Cranmer, my Lord Latimer, my Lord Ridley. In modern times, when a bishop resigns his see he is simply styled bishop, though still addressed as my lord.

† Morice, 259.

‡ So attached was Cranmer as a friend to Henry VIII., that after that king's death, he ceased to shave; he let his beard grow as a sign of mourning.

brated. The world indeed is difficult to please. One person is sometimes blamed for doing the very thing which has elicited men's praise for others. There had been an outcry against the bishops at the commencement of Henry's reign for their sumptuous living, and a sumptuary law was introduced by the bishops, of which we have the following memorandum :—

CHAP. III.
Thomas Cranmer.
1533-56.

"In the yere of our Lord MDXLI it was agreed and condescended upon, as wel by the common consent of both th' archbishops, and most part of the bishops within this realme of Englande, as also of divers grave men at that tyme, both deanes and archdeacons, the fare at their tables to be thus moderated.

"First, that th' archbishop should never excede six divers kyndes of fleshe, or six of fishe on the fishe dayes, the bishop not to excede five, the deane and archdeacon not above four, and al other under that degree not above three.

"Provided also, that the archbishop might have of second dishes four, the bishop three, and al others under the degree of a bishop but two, as custard, tart, fritter, cheese, or apples, peares or two of other kyndes of fruites.

"Provided also, that if any of the inferiour degree dyd receave at their table any archbishop, bishop, deane or archdeacon; or any of the laitie of lyke degree, viz. duke, marques, earle, vicount, baron, lorde, knyght, they myght have such provision as were meete and requisite for their degrees.

"Provided alway, that no rate was limitted in the receavyng of any ambassadour. It was also provided, that of the greater fyshes or fowles there should be but one in a dishe, as crane, swan, turkey cocke, hadocke, pyke, tench; and of lesse sortes but two, viz. capons two, pheasants two, conies two, wodcockes two. Of lesse sortes, as of partriches, the archbishop three, the bishop, and other degrees under hym two. Of blackburdes the archbishop six, the bishop four, the other degrees three. Of larkes and snytes, and of that sort, but twelve. It was also provided, that whatsoever is spared by the cuttyng off of the old superfluities, shoulde yet be provided and spent in playne meates for the relievying of the poore."*

So unpalatable were these regulations to those, who had been accustomed to feast at the expense of the bishops, that soon after, an outcry was raised against them from the opposite quarter, and they were accused of covetousness. To keep hospitality and to bid all comers welcome was still considered the duty of great men in Church and State; and upon this point the enemies of Cranmer thought to establish a charge against him. Sir Thomas Seymour, " being of the privy chamber," was employed to bring odium upon the archbishop, by complaining to the king that he kept no hospitality or house correspondent with his revenues or dignity. It was said, that he sold his woods, and realised a large property by fines, to enrich his family. The king was always ready to take the part of Cranmer, and said : " I do marvel that my Lord of Canterbury should keep no hospitality, for I have heard the contrary." No notice was at first taken of the accusation; the king was as though he either heard not, or heeded not the accusation. Suspecting, however, that there was a conspiracy to undermine the archbishop in his esteem, the king called Sir Thomas Seymour to him, as he was going to dinner about a month afterwards, and said, " Go ye straightways to Lambeth, and bid my Lord of Canterbury come and speak to me at two of the clock in the afternoon." The rest shall be stated in the quaint language of the archbishop's secretary, Morice, from whom we have the account, and through whose language the state of the case is brought vividly before us. He says :—

* Wilkins, iii. 862. Ex. MS. C.C.C.C. et apud Hearn, Append. par. ii. ad Lelandi Collectanea, p. 38.

Incoutynently Mr. Seymour came to Lambeth, and being brought into the halle by the porter, it chaunced the halle was sett to dyner, and when he was at the skrene and perceyvid the halle furnished with iij principal messes, besides the reste of the tables thoroughlie sett, having a giltie conscience of his untrue reporte made to the kinge, recoylid backe, and wolde have gone into my lorde by the chapell awaie. Mr. Nevill being stewarde, perceyving that, rose uppe and wente after hym, and declaird unto hym that he could not goom (sic)* that wey; and when he came to my lord, and had done his message, my lord caused hym to sit downe and dyne with hym. But, making a short dyner bycause he would bring the kinge wourde againe of his message, he departid and came to the kinge before he was rysen frome the table. When he came to the kinge's presence, saied the kinge, "Will my lord of Canterbury come to us?" "He will wayte on your majestie (saied Mr. Seymour) at ij of the clocke." Then said the kinge, "Had my lord dyned before ye came?" "Noo, forsothe (saied Mr. S.), for I founde hym at dyner." "Well (saied the kinge) what chere made he you?" With these wourdes Mr. Seymour knelid downe and besought the kinge's majestie of pardon. "What is the matter?" (saied the kinge). "I do remembre (saied Mr. Seymour) that I tolde your highnes that my lorde of Canterburye kepte no hospitalitie correspondent unto his dignitie; and nowe I perceyve that I did abuse your highnes with an untruth, for, besides your grace's house, I thincke he be not in the realme of none estate or degre that hath suche a halle furnyshed, or that fareth more honorablie at his awne table. "Ah! (quod the kinge), have you espied your owne faulte nowe?" "I assuer your highnes (said Mr. S.) it is not so moche my faulte as other mennys who semed to be honeste men that enformede me herof, but I shall hensforthe the nowisse truste theym whiles thei lyve." Then, saied the kinge, "I knowe your purposes well enough; you have hadd emonge you the commodities of the abbeis, whiche you have consumed some with superfluous apparell, some at dice and cardes, and other ungratious rule, and nowe you wolde have the

---

* Query. Goo in.

bishopp landes and revenewes to abuse likewise. Yf my lorde of Canterbury kepe such a halle as you say, neither being terme nor parliamente, he ys metelie well visited at those tymes, I' warrante you. And if th' other bisshopps kepe the like for their degre, they had not nede to have anything taken from them, but rather to be aided and holpen. And therefore set your harte at reste; there shall no such alteration be made whiles I lyve" (quod the kinge). So that in very dede, where some had pennyd certeyn bookes for the altering of that estate in the nexte parliamente, thei durst never bring them forthe to be redde. Whereupon also it came to passe that when the kinge understode that, contrary unto the reporte, my lorde C. hadd purchased no manner of landes, his highnes was contente upon th' onelie motion of D. Buttes, without my L. C. knowledge, that he shoulde have that abbey in Notynghamshere, whiche his wife *nowe enjoyeth, to hym and his heires.**

Of Cranmer's munificence we have nothing to say, if we institute a comparison between him and some of his predecessors, such as Chichely, Bourchier, and Morton; but when we find his house the resort of the learned foreigners who were invited to England, at a later period of his life, it would be to make a statement contrary to fact, if we should speak of him as failing in the rites of hospitality. When Latimer resigned his bishopric he was domiciled with the archbishop; and while Cranmer did not diminish the charities for which the primates of England had for centuries been distinguished, we may mention to his credit the fact, that when the sick and wounded soldiers engaged in the French wars landed in Kent from Boulogne, his residence at Bekesbourne was converted into a hospital for their reception; and his almoner was directed that when they were cured he should pay their expenses until they reached their respective homes.

Nevertheless, the charge of avarice was brought against

* Morice Anecdotes, 263.

him to the last; and Cecil, who was accused of a similar vice, thought he was acting the part of a friend in bringing the subject under the archbishop's notice. We are under an obligation to him for so doing, as it provoked a reply which speaks much to the archbishop's honour.

"As for your admonition," he says, "I take it most thankfully, as I have ever been most glad to be admonished by my friends, accounting no man so foolish as he that will not bear friendly admonishments. But as for the saying of S. Paul, 'Qui volunt ditescere incidunt in tentationem,' I fear it not half so much as I do stark beggary. For I took not half so much care for my living when I was a scholar of Cambridge as I do at this present. For although I have now much more revenue, yet I have much more to do withal: and have more care to live now as an archbishop than I had at that time to live like a scholar. I have not so much as I had within ten years passed by 150*l.* of certain rent, beside casualities. I pay double for everything that I buy. If a good auditor have this account, he shall find no great surplusage to wax rich upon."*

What his difficulties were when he was first appointed to the see, we have had occasion already to mention; and the shifts to which he was subjected, in order to raise the necessary supplies to support his establishments in different parts of the country, may have given rise to the charge brought against him of avarice. He knew the value of money, he had a family, he was economical, and he contended for his dues.

He gratefully received pecuniary assistance from the Abbot of St. Augustine's, "besides Canterbury," who, in the threatening aspect of public affairs, desired to conciliate the primate; and he complained of the prior of his own convent, when from the chapter of Canterbury he received a sum of money less than he had been led to

* Letter cclxxxvii. Sir W. Hicks's MSS.

expect.* But his difficulties were to be really traced to the unprincipled conduct of the king. The estates of the see during the vacancy had been sequestered, and the king, as sequestrator of the manors, let many of them on long leases to his favourite courtiers: such leases were almost tantamount to donations. Cranmer, as a man of business, introduced the rule which in Queen Elizabeth's reign became the law of the land, that leases of ecclesiastical property should be limited to three lives or twenty-one years. In other respects also, the king had appropriated during the vacancy to his own use what belonged to the Church; but in doing so he could plead the example of his ancestors; and Cranmer was not the man to call upon Henry VIII. to render an account of his stewardship. He only ventured so far as to apply through Crumwell for a loan of a thousand pounds to be paid through the treasury; but Crumwell was too busy in filling his own coffers from the overflowings of the public purse to press the archbishop's suit; and Cranmer, after a long delay, was obliged to be contented with a grant of 500*l*. These and similar circumstances are to be taken into consideration before we accuse the economical primate of avarice, or reprove him for his want of munificence.

How little interest Cranmer really had even in matters ecclesiastical, while Crumwell lived, may indeed be gathered from the fact, that we possess five letters written by him to Crumwell to obtain some small preferment for his friend Mr. Newman, and that to his long suit no attention was paid. At the same time, it is due to Cranmer to show that he could maintain his own, and when Crumwell, who thought he could make every patron submit to his dictation, applied under circumstances which seemed

* Letter vi. Harl. MSS. 6148, fo. 22. Letter lvii. Harl. MSS. 6148, fo. 36.

to imply a simoniacal contract to Cranmer, he received a just rebuke. Crumwell, having persuaded the prior of St. Gregory's, Canterbury, to retire from his post, requested the archbishop to place the nomination of his successor at Crumwell's disposal. There was probably a simoniacal contract such as had already enriched the vicar-general. The answer of the archbishop, excellent in itself, is important as throwing light upon Cranmer's principles.

"Master Crumwell, as touching this behalf, or any other thing wherein I may lawfully show you my pleasure, ye shall be as well assured of the same, as ye would be willing to desire it of me. But the truth is, that, in my mind, I am entirely resolved to prefer to the same office, and all such other when the same shall be void, some such one person as was professed in the same house, et *sic de eodem gremio,* if any such shall be found apt and meet in the same house for it; for as long as there may be had some one meet for that room in the same house, I do think it much inconvenient for many considerations to provide a stranger to be head and ruler there. If there be none so apt and meet in the said house for the said office as the law will require, then I will be glad to provide the most meetest that can be found in any other place, of the same rule, habit, and religion, of whose sufficiency and ability I ought, if I do my office and duty, to have good experience and knowledge myself, afore that I will admit or prefer him; and forasmuch as I do not know the person whom ye would prefer to this office, and to the intent also that I may enquire of his learning, living, and of other his good qualities, I pray you that I may be ascertained of his name, and of the place where he doth demore; and that done, I will hereafter in this behalf make you such further answer as I trust ye shall be pleased withal; albeit the bringer of your letters and bearer hereof showed me, that ye did write your said letters for him and in his favour, which thing, I assure you, moveth me to take longer respite in this behalf. Ye do know what ambition and desire of promotion is in men of the Church, and what indirect means they do use, and have used, to obtain their purpose; which their unreasonable desires and appetites, I do trust that ye will be more ready to oppress and extinguish than to favour or further the same; and I remit to your wisdom and judgment what an unreasonable thing it is for a man to labour for his own promotion spiritual. At Mortelake, the 6th day of May.*

"Your own assured,
"THOMAS CANTUAR.

"To the Right Worshipful and my very loving friend Master Crumwell, of the King's Grace's most honourable council."

Cranmer had generally a clear perception of what was right; and he had the moral courage to declare his sentiments; but whenever he was threatened he succumbed. This was the secret of the kind feeling towards him on the part of the king. Henry liked to have his opinions canvassed; it was a new source of enjoyment to him, when he found a man who would openly tell him his mind, when he knew all the while that this same man would, when the king's will was distinctly declared, eat his words and obey. His courtiers in general assented to all he said, and promised obedience, but Henry knew that when the time for action came, if their interests or prejudices interfered, they would either evade their promises, or offer impediments tending to the frustration of the royal intentions.

By a very natural process of self-deception, Cranmer represented to himself his natural weakness in the light of a principle. That principle he revealed when, in writing to Queen Mary, he asserted, that he considered it to be his duty to "show his sovereign his mind in things pertaining to God" and "if his representations failed, to submit patiently, thinking himself discharged."

* Crumwell's Correspondence.

For "to private subjects," he observed, "it appertaineth not to reform things, but quietly to suffer what they cannot amend."* Even if we were to admit this passive obedience, he forgot that the primate of all England was something more than a private person.

After the passing of the statute of the six articles, Cranmer retired from the turmoil of public life, and the years were passed with much profit to himself. Separated from his wife and family, he continued his studies; and, assisted by his chaplain Ridley, he was, with the king's full consent, employed in preparing for further reformations in the Church of England. Much of what was accomplished in the reign of Edward, was planned in that of Henry. Henry VIII. had no objection to reforms; he desired to promote them to the last; only he required that they should be introduced at a proper time, not when a violent reaction was, through the violence of Cromwell's reign of terror, setting in, and that the principles he had laid down for his guidance should be strictly observed. They required that, in abolishing any ancient practice or in restoring to its primitive simplicity any doctrine which had been by modern glosses obscured, there should be no deviation from the standards of the Church, which were Catholic. He distinguished what was papistical—introduced by papal authority— from what was Catholic or orthodox.

Having brought the history of Cranmer to this point, I propose, in one distinct section, to review his theological opinions, or to give a history of his mind. As connected with this subject, and to bring all under one head, I have reserved the consideration of certain facts which took place in Henry's reign, and shall anticipate

---

* Remains, i. 563.

some transactions which belong chronologically to the reign of Edward.

II. For Cranmer's own character as a public man, it was a misfortune that he was appointed to the primacy, and obliged, from his high position, to take part in public affairs before his principles were formed. For the Church of England this was a blessing. Had Cranmer been a greater man, he would, like his contemporaries, have founded a sect; as it was, he was a humble instrument in the hands of God for reforming the Church. When he returned from Germany to England, and consented (I believe him when he says most reluctantly) to become Archbishop of Canterbury, he was resolute in two points only; but those were important points. He was determined to emancipate the Church of England from all papal usurpation, and, at the same time, to secure for the people an authorised version of Scripture, to be freely circulated—to be placed in the hands of all who could read. Let men have the Bible, and the Church would reform itself.

He had himself experienced the consolation, the joy of the Holy Ghost, which a heart, sanctified by grace, must always find in the perusal of those words, which were written by holy men of old as they were moved by the Holy Ghost, for doctrine, for reproof, for instruction in righteousness: and, as faith is charity in the germ, and charity is the perfection of faith, he desired to impart to others what had brought his own soul into communion with his God and all the sanctities of heaven.

On public grounds, if the Bible is the only book composed by miraculous inspiration, containing in it all that man can be called upon to receive *de fide*, it must be to this test that every doctrine, every practice, of the Church must be brought; every doctrine propounded must rest on the authority of Scripture, and we must indulge in no practice, which is opposed to those principles which Scripture lays down for our guidance. The Church must be judged by Scripture; this is the basis of all reform. To the law and the testimony; if they speak not according to this word, it is because there is no light in them. Cranmer thought that all men should be placed in the situation of the good Beræans of old. When the Church preached to them they ought to have power to search the Scriptures, to see whether those things were so. The Church was to act towards them as the woman of Samaria in the Gospel. She was to preach the Gospel, the glad tidings, and they, after the study of Scripture, might be able to say, Now we believe, not because of thy saying; for we have heard Him ourselves, and know that this is indeed the Christ, the Saviour of the world.

Ever since the reign of Edward III. and the preaching of John Wiclif this feeling, that the people had a right to the Scriptures, and through the Scriptures to ascertain whether what the Church was teaching was in accordance with the written word of God, had been gaining ground. They who dreaded a revolutionary movement, and were, at the same time, aware that the Church, as it then existed, could not stand the test, had shifted their ground. They no longer combated the principle, that the people ought to have the Scripture in the vulgar tongue; but they attacked all existing translations, as so full of error that they, in fact, promulgated heresy. The weakness of this objection soon became apparent, and when the principle was conceded, that the people might possess the Scriptures, the demand was for an authorised version—a version to be made by the Church with the special object of avoiding the error complained of.

CHAP. III.
Thomas Cranmer.
1533-56.

The thoughtful among the clergy joined in this demand. Few of them could read Greek. The Vulgate was only a translation. If they were to read a translation, they would rather have it in the vulgar tongue. For an authorised version of Scripture they, the clergy, had made application to the king, in the time of Archbishop Warham; that is to say, they desired that the king would appoint a Commission to make a translation, or cause it to be made, to be subjected afterwards to the two houses of Convocation. In the first convocation under Cranmer, that application was renewed. Upon this point Cranmer appears always to have had a strong party in convocation; although the party opposed to him was powerful, from the fact of its including some persons of learning and influence, including Bishop Gardyner and Bishop Bonner.

It will be expedient to pause here, that we may take a rapid view of the versions of Scripture at this time made, and of the attempts to introduce them into the Church.*

Of Wiclif's translation—that noble work—many copies had been clandestinely circulated; but it was only in manuscript. Admirably, too, as the work, considered as a whole, was executed, still it was only the translation of a translation, and by the late labours of Erasmus, the Vulgate had declined in repute.

We have already seen that in the reign of Henry VIII., before the commencement of Cranmer's primacy, attention

---

* The reader may be referred generally to Lewis's Hist. of Translations of the Bible; Newcome's Historical View of English Biblical Translations; Anderson's Annals of the English Bible; Cotton's editions of the Bibles and parts thereof; and also to a work of extraordinary labour by Mr. Fry, a Description of the Great Bible of 1539 and the six editions of Cranmer's Bible.

had been called to this subject. William Tyndal, assisted by John Firth, and William Roye, translated the New Testament from the original Greek, and published it anonymously, at Hamburg or Antwerp, about the year 1526. This is the first translation into English of any part of the Holy Scripture that issued from the press. It is said to have been incorrectly printed, but More and Tunstal, through their puerile attempt to prevent its circulation, by committing all the copies they could purchase to the flames, enriched the publisher, and enabled him to prepare an improved edition. With the assistance of Miles Coverdale, Tyndal now undertook to prepare for the press a version of the Old Testament also. In 1530, he published at Hamburgh a translation of the Pentateuch, with prefaces abusive of the clergy; and in the following year he was able to produce a more correct version of the New Testament. In 1531, he published a translation into English of the prophet Jonah. He was proceeding to the translation of the other books, when his labours were brought to a cruel termination. Having been imprisoned by the emperor, he was condemned by a decree made in an Assembly at Augsburg, and died a martyr's death at Villefort near Brussels in the year 1536.

To Miles Coverdale, sometime Bishop of Exeter, belongs the high praise of having presented the Church of England with the first version of the entire Bible. It professed to be translated "out of the Douche and Latin into English." Neither name of printer nor notice of place where it was printed is given; whether it was printed at Zurich, or Frankfort, or Cologne, is doubtful. Coverdale had assisted Tyndal, and availed himself of his labours.

Cranmer's business was now not so much the translation

of the Scripture, as its circulation. The work was done to his hand. How was he to enable the people to enjoy the treasure which the Church of England at length obtained? this was the question. In anticipation of the version just mentioned, he obtained, this year, a unanimous vote, or, at all events, a commanding majority, in convocation, in favour of a petition to the king, requesting him to authorise a translation of the Bible with a view to its greater circulation.

The royal assent was obtained. Crumwell, anxious to do a popular act, when his conduct with respect to the oath of supremacy and the dissolution of the monasteries was causing a strong feeling against him throughout the country, put himself forward on this occasion, and so managed affairs as to connect his name with the first authorised edition of the translated Scriptures.

Early in the year 1536, as vicar-general or vicegerent in ecclesiastical matters, Crumwell issued injunctions to the clergy, by the king's authority, of which the seventh was:—

"That every parson, or proprietary of any parish church within the realm, before August the 1st, should provide a book of the whole Bible, both in Latin and in English, and lay it in the choir, for every man that would look and read therein; and should discourage no man from reading any part of the Bible, either in Latin or English, but rather comfort, exhort, and admonish every man to read it as the very Word of God, and the spiritual food of man's soul."

This was a great step gained. A demand was created, and was met at once. A folio edition of the Bible appeared in 1537 from the pens of Grafton and Whitchurch. It was a revision of the Bible published by Tyndal and Coverdale, by John Rogers, under the assumed name of Matthews. A copy of this was laid before Crumwell by the archbishop, who had not easy access, at that time, to the king; with a request that the vicegerent would obtain the king's permission for the free use of this version among his subjects. The royal licence was granted, and an injunction was issued in 1538, ordering the clergy to provide, before a certain festival, one book of the whole Bible of the largest volume in England, and to set it up in some convenient place within their churches—wherever their parishioners might most commodiously resort and read it.

This created a great sensation: churches were crowded. Here the learned few continued, hour after hour, to read the Scriptures to attentive crowds of illiterate men and women trying to understand what they eagerly heard. Some aged persons, eager to avail themselves of a privilege newly acquired, were actually seen to be taking lessons in the art of reading.

We have evidence in his correspondence of the activity of Cranmer in this good cause, and of his attention to details. I shall present the reader with the correspondence which took place on the occasion.

The first letter is addressed to the Right Honourable, and my especial good lord, my Lord Privy Seal (Crumwell).

"My very singular good lord, after my most hearty commendations, this shall be to signify unto your lordship that Bartelett and Edward Whitechurche hath been with me, and have, by their accounts, declared the expenses and charges of the printing of the great Bibles, and by the advice of Bartelett I have appointed them to be sold at 13s. 4d. a piece, and not above. Howbeit, Whitechurche informeth me that your lordship thinketh it a more convenient price to have them sold at 10s. a piece, which, in respect of the great charges, both of the paper (which in very deed is substantial and good), and other great hindrances, Whitechurche and his fellow thinketh it a small price. Nevertheless, they are right well contented to sell them for 10s., so that you will be so good lord unto them as to grant henceforth none other licence to any other printer, saving to them, for the printing of the said Bible; for else they think that they shall be greatly hindered thereby, if any other should print, they sustaining such charges as they already have done. Wherefore I shall beseech your lordship, in consideration of their travail in this behalf, to tender their requests; and they have promised me to print in the end of their Bibles the price thereof, to the end the king's liege people shall not henceforth be deceived of their price.

"Further, if your lordship hath known the king's pleasure concerning the preface of the Bible, which I sent to you to oversee, so that his Grace doth allow the same, I pray you that the same may be delivered unto the said Whitechurche, unto printing, trusting that it shall both encourage many slow readers, and also stay the rash judgments of them that read therein. Thus our Lord have your good lordship in His blessed tuition. At Lambeth, the 14th day of November.*

"Your own ever assured,
"T. CANTUARIEN.

"To my singular good lord, my Lord Privy Seal."

But, although contented with this version of Scripture to meet the present exigencies of the Church, the archbishop was not satisfied with any of the translations, and desired to have a revision made by a committee of the convocation which might afterwards receive the synodical consent. He determined to propose the subject, as one of the agenda, to the convocation of Canterbury, which was summoned to meet on the 20th of July, 1541-2.

Cranmer proceeded in his usual state and magnificence to open the convocation. He embarked on board his

* State Papers, vol. i. pt. 2. Letter cxv. Remains, i. 289. This letter is placed in the State Papers in the year 1538, but Dr. Jenkyns assigns good reasons for supposing it to belong to 1540. The reference to the preface proves its date to be at that time, or in 1539.

barge at Lambeth, and landed at Paul's wharf. Thence, attended by the officials, with his cross carried before him, he proceeded on foot to St. Paul's Cathedral Church. The Bishop of London, Dr. Bonner, was there to receive him; and the bishop proceeded to the high altar, where he officiated at a mass of the Holy Ghost. The sermon was preached, as is still the case, in Latin, by Dr. Richard Cox, Archdeacon of Ely, who took for his text, "Ye are the salt of the earth." Dr. Richard Gwent, Archdeacon of London, was chosen prolocutor.*

Although Cranmer had been primate nearly eight years, it was not till this convocation of 1541 that any decided measures were adopted in favour of a reformation of the Church. It was now decreed, that images should be removed from churches, and that the Lord's Prayer, the Creed, and the Decalogue, should be taught the people in the vulgar tongue. A step was taken towards a reform of the liturgy. The Use of Sarum was to be observed in all churches with a view of producing uniformity, and the archbishop declared, that it was the king's pleasure, that all mass books and breviaries in the Church of England should be examined, and cleared of legends of Popish saints, &c. The correction of these books was entrusted to the Bishops of Sarum and Ely. To this subject we shall revert when the history of the further revision of the services which terminated in the Book of Common Prayer will come under consideration.

We confine ourselves, at present, to what was done with reference to the translation of the Bible. On the 3rd of February, the question was put by the archbishop to the upper house whether it would be possible, without

---

* Fuller, iii. 196; transcribed by his own hand out of the Records of Canterbury. Wilkins, iii. 860. Joyce, 404.

scandal to the Church, to retain the Great Bible as at that time translated. The reference was probably to the Bible published in 1539, called Crumwell's Bible, as published under his auspices. It was decided by a majority of the bishops that this Bible should not be retained, but that it should be examined and amended, *according to that Bible which is usually read in the English Church*, that is, Cranmer's Great Bible of 1540. Certain prelates were then appointed to examine different portions of Scripture. The prolocutor, and the rest of the clergy, attended the upper house, and the archbishop pointed out to the united synod the errors in the translation of the Old Testament.* On the 13th of February, the prolocutor of the lower house exhibited the result of their examination of the Old Testament, and gave a list of the passages which required reconsideration. The upper house on the same day, appointed a joint committee to examine both the Old and the New Testament. The New Testament was committed to the Bishops of Durham, Winchester, Hereford, Rochester, and Westminster, together with Doctors Wotton, Day, Coren, Wilson, Leighton, May, and others of the lower house. The Old Testament was committed to the Archbishop of York, the Bishop of Ely, with Redman, Taylor, Haynes, Robertson, Cocks, and others who were well versed in the Hebrew, Greek, and Latin languages.

So much has been said of the ignorance of the clergy at this period, by men more ignorant than they, that these circumstances are worthy of notice. The majority of convocation was so decidedly with the reforming party, that the opposition only counselled caution and delay. On the 17th of February, the Bishop of Winchester, Dr.

* Wilkins, Conc. Mag. Brit. iii. 861.

Gardyner, produced a list of one hundred words and phrases in Latin, concerning which he argued that they must be either retained in Latin, on account of their peculiar significance, or translated into English with as little alteration as possible. Mistranslation might lead to the inculcation of false doctrine, and this, when a provincial synod was undertaking to set forward an authorised version, was to be avoided. The fact that some of the words have been retained to the present day in their Latin form, shows that the selection of words was carefully made; though, comparing the Bishop of Winchester's present proceedings with other portions of his conduct in what relates to the translation of Scripture, we may, without any breach of charity, conclude that his object was to perplex rather than to assist the committee.

So fully was Cranmer convinced of this and so fearful of Gardyner's influence with the convocation, where it had always been great, that the archbishop determined to take the matter of the translation out of the hands of that body. He proposed to the king, and obtained the royal consent, that the committee of translators should not be appointed by and out of the members of convocation, but should be selected from the two universities.

The reader has had the state of the universities at this period, brought under his notice more than once. The active party in both universities now consisted of young Masters of Arts, all inclined, more or less, to the new learning. A measure which the convocation was too slow to adopt, and which a good politician like Gardyner might have frustrated, would be accepted with alacrity by the universities, and it was expected that there the work would be undertaken with enthusiasm.

On the 10th of March, when the convocation was proceeding to business, the archbishop declared the king's pleasure to be, that nothing further should be done, until the version of the Old and New Testament had been examined for the purposes of revision by the two universities. The members of convocation were far more independent than the members of parliament; the opponents of Cranmer did not hesitate to remonstrate against the royal command of which he was the bearer. They had the best of the argument when they contended that such business belonged not to the universities, but rather to an ecclesiastical synod. They also showed, that they were quite aware of the object in the proposed transfer of the business; for they attacked the universities. It was stated that the universities had sunk considerably in public estimation, that the affairs were managed by a majority of young men, and that without maturity of judgment there was no relying on the result. But Cranmer contented himself with repeating the royal mandate; and, by his power to prorogue the convocation when he chose, the archbishop's rule was despotic. He asserted that "he should stick by his master's will and pleasure," and that no decision should be come to in convocation until the universities had examined the translation. The convocation perhaps abstained from further resistance, knowing the uselessness of opposing the king, or that if the archbishop refused to maintain their authority, it could be done by no one else.

Cranmer's Bible continued to be used in the churches until it was superseded by a Bible projected by Archbishop Parker, and known as the Bishop's Bible. The consequence of the present interference of Henry VIII. was that the Church of England possessed no authorised version of Scripture till the reign of James I., when that translation appeared which is still in use.

We have thus given the result of Cranmer's labours in a matter which he had much at heart, but we have not yet stated his principle. The Bible he held to be the word of God; but the Bible was, in his opinion, not the word of God unless it be rightly interpreted. The Bible rightly interpreted is the rule; but who is to decide what the right interpretation is? This was not a difficult question as it presented itself to Cranmer's mind, and he would consider that there was only one way of answering it. It must always be remembered, that Cranmer was born a churchman, or rather became a churchman immediately after his birth. As a churchman he deferred to the authority of the Church, and admitted that " it has authority in matters of faith." He did not suppose that men were to take their Bible, and then chalk out from it a religion for themselves. He professed himself, to the last hour of his life, to be a Catholic. A certain form of religion had been transmitted to him. He accepted it. There were certain acts and doctrines done or asserted which revolted his moral nature; he went to his Bible, and perceived at once, that these things formed no part of religion as it came from God, the Source of revelation. He at once removed them. When the Church and the Bible were antagonistic the one to the other, he adhered to the Bible. But when it was doubtful whether a doctrine was or was not expressed in Scripture—when, as in all language and writings must be the case, expressions were doubtful or ambiguous, he appealed from the present to the early Church. He enquired how was the Scripture understood before controversies arose, to which the ambiguity is traceable? What was the Catholic doctrine in the primitive ages, anterior to mediæval corruption? He expressly declares, that he accepted the rule of Vincentius Lirinensis, who taught plainly " that the canon of Scripture is perfectly sufficient in itself for the truth of the Catholic faith; and that the whole Church cannot add one article of the faith, although it may be taken as a necessary witness for receiving and establishing the same, with these three conditions, that the thing we would establish thereby hath been believed in all places, at all times, and of all men."*

So careful was the king, as well as the archbishop, to warn people, that in renouncing popery they were not deserting Catholicism, that they were reforming the ancient Church of England not substituting for it a new sect, that we find the following assertion of a theological principle in an act of parliament:—

"Provided always, that this act, nor any thing or things therein contained, shall be hereafter interpreted or expounded, that your grace, your nobles, and subjects intend by the same to decline or vary from the congregation of Christ's Church in any things concerning the very articles of the Catholic faith of Christendom, or in any other things declared by Holy Scripture and the Word of God necessary for your and their salvations, but only to make an ordinance by policies necessary and convenient to repress vice, and for good conservation of this realm in peace, unity, and tranquillity, from ravin and spoil, insuring much the old ancient customs of this realm in that behalf; not minding to seek for any relief, succours, or remedies for any worldly things and human laws, in any cause of necessity, but within this realm at the hands of your highness, your heirs, and successors, kings of this realm, which have and ought to have an imperial power and authority in the same, and not obliged in any worldly causes to any other superior." †

Cranmer's conduct with respect to the doctrine of transubstantiation illustrates his principle. The words of Scrip-

---

* Remains, iii. 23. The ultramontanes, finding that what is papistical is distinguished from what is catholic, have given up this appeal to the primitive Church and tradition, and represent the Pope as empowered and inspired to add new doctrines to the Church at his will.

† Statutes at large.

ture, "This is my body, this is my blood," if taken literally, establish the position of the Papists. Cranmer therefore, receiving the doctrine of transubstantiation as prevailing in the Church, and finding it confirmed by the words of Scripture barely considered, for a long time maintained the dogma. When he found that it had not always been held in the primitive Church, he then renounced it.

"Touching my doctrine of the sacrament," he said, "and other my doctrine, of what kind soever it be, I protest that it was never my mind to write, speak, or understand anything contrary to the most holy Word of God, or else against the holy Catholic Church of Christ; but purely and simply to imitate and teach those things only, which I had learned of the sacred Scripture, and of the holy Catholic Church of Christ from the beginning, and also according to the exposition of the most holy and learned fathers and martyrs of the Church.

"And if anything hath peradventure chanced otherwise than I thought, I may err, but heretic I cannot be, forasmuch as I am ready in all things to follow the judgment of the most sacred Word of God, and of the holy Catholic Church, desiring none other thing than meekly and gently to be taught, if anywhere (which God forbid) I have swerved from the truth.

"And I protest and openly confess, that in all my doctrine and preaching, both of the sacrament and of other my doctrine, whatsoever it be, not only I mean and judge those things as the Catholic Church and the most holy fathers of old, with one accord, have meant and judged, but also I would gladly use the same words that they used, and not use any other words, but to set my hand to all and singular their speeches, phrases, ways, and forms of speech, which they do use in their treatises upon the sacrament, and to keep still their interpretation. But in this thing I only am accused for an heretic, because I allow not the doctrine lately brought in of the sacrament, and because I consent not to words not accustomed in Scripture, and unknown to the ancient fathers, but newly invented and brought in by men, and belonging to the destruction of souls, and overthrowing of the pure and old religion."

CHAP. IU.

Thomas Cranmer
1533-56.

We are employed in tracing the growth of his principles in Cranmer's mind, and in remarking upon their influence upon his conduct; having already, therefore, touched upon transubstantiation, we will now proceed to consider this subject especially.

Before the year 1533, the public attention in England was almost exclusively directed to the question of the royal supremacy; and Cranmer took little interest, when he was in Germany, in the discussion of a dogma, which he, for a long time, regarded as of only secondary importance. It was indeed the opinion of most of the men of the "new learning" in England, as expressed by Tyndale, that it was expedient to leave the Presence as an indifferent thing to be discussed in peace, and at leisure of both parties. But it was gradually discovered that the whole controversy turned upon this fact. Protestants of all shades of opinion were united on this one point, that the mass should be turned into a communion. The mass was regarded as a sacrifice of our Lord for the quick and the dead: this the Reformers one and all denied; they maintained that it was a communion, through which the faithful were united to God; and that the sacrifice was the offering of themselves, their souls and bodies, to God's service in common with the hosts of heaven. The controversy was perplexed, as it still is, by the fact, that the Reformers did not deny that in the Eucharist there is a sacrifice; but the question is, what kind of sacrifice? It is one thing to offer Christ as a sacrifice for sin, and another thing for those who have been accepted through Christ as God's servants, to offer themselves as a sacrifice, a body of persons prepared to serve God, in body and soul. The Church from the beginning had regarded the Eucharist as a sacrifice in the last sense of the word—a memorial before God of the great work once and once for all done upon the cross, and at the same time, a dedication, a Eucharistic sacrifice of the Church, as a whole and in all its parts, to the service of God. In process of time, the Western Church, instead of offering itself as a sacrifice on the merits of the one full perfect and sufficient sacrifice, oblation, and satisfaction, once and once for all, made upon the Cross, regarded itself as offering the Lord Jesus Christ Himself.

But if He was to be offered, He must be corporeally present; He could only be corporeally present by the transmutation of the substance of the bread and wine into the body and blood of Christ.

Viewed not from the sacrificial, but from the sacramental point—not with regard to what man does to God, but to what God does to man, there is a Real as distinguished from a Corporeal Presence. So that the worthy recipient receives Christ, as Christ has promised in all the sacred influences of His spiritual presence.

This was the reason why Luther adhered to the doctrine of consubstantiation; that is, a Real not a Corporeal presence, in, under, and along with the bread and wine.

Distinguish between the sacrifice and the sacrament, and we arrive at the ground of Luther's adherence to his system.

As regarded the sacrifice, what was offered to God was the Church militant and triumphant, with the present communicants and Christ its Head—not, as the Papists contended, Christ considered as the Lamb of God. Luther did not, therefore, require the dogma of transubstantiation. But regarded as a sacrament, what is offered to the communicant is the indwelling Saviour, and therefore he believed our Lord to be for that purpose actually present.*

---

* See Waterland on the Eucharist, for this whole subject.

CHAP. III.
Thomas Cranmer.
1533-56.

The English Reformers did not accept Luther's view of the *manner* in which our Lord is present; that is, through consubstantiation; they simply, and without explanation, asserted the fact. They did not hold that the sacrifice consists in the offering of Christ, therefore they did not require a belief in transubstantiation; nor, as regards the sacrament, did their system require the Lutheran, or strictly Protestant, doctrine of consubstantiation. Without this, they believed that Christ can be really present to the worthy recipient. They admitted that the Lord's body is in heaven; in like manner as they admitted that the sun is in the firmament. As the sun, though in the firmament, may be present on earth by its rays, and though in one sense present wherever there is solar light, yet may be present more in one place than in another: so by His Spirit, Christ the Sun of Righteousness, though in heaven, may be still on earth, and in one place on earth more than in another, in the heart of a saint more than in the soul of the careless. In the Lutheran system, the Res sacramenti, as in the Romish system, is created by the consecration: our Reformers considered the Res sacramenti to depend on consecration *and* on the worthy receiving: not the receiving without the consecration, but the consecration *with* the receiving.

With reverence be it spoken, as reverence must be always invoked when we compare the things of heaven with things earthly, when a money bill is drawn out, it is drawn for the purpose of becoming money, though the paper is not changed into gold; and yet it does not acquire its real value until it is endorsed by the person to whom it is directed. Just so, argued the English reformers, the bread and wine, when consecrated, are intended to become, to all intents and purposes, that blessed thing which they represent, but such they do not become in fact, until the worthy recipient has made it such to himself by faith. He then rejoices, for that he has received his Lord.

If we carefully examine the progress of Cranmer's mind, we shall find that this point he reached before he died; although some there are who persevere in saying that he was never orthodox on this subject.*

The Papists saw that the controversy on the Eucharist was not what it at first appeared to Cranmer, or as it appears to some even at the present time, a mere metaphysical question of no real importance. One feels a repugnance to write the sentence, but the vulgar notion was that the priest in the mass created his Redeemer, and then offered Him as a propitiatory sacrifice for sin. The order of men, who were endued with a power to do this, must be superior to all civil power; and it was now more than ever the policy of Rome to make the civil power subservient to the sacerdotal. This dogma was made therefore the test to which men were to be brought, when the question was, whether they were loyal to the pope rather than to the crown.

It was long before Cranmer could see the subject in this point of view: he did not perceive how it bore, indirectly but with great force, upon the supremacy. When he understood this—when he saw that the Reformers, however much they differed on other points relating to the Eucharist, were as one man in their rejection of the

---

* "And in that Catechism I teach not, as you do, that the body and blood of Christ is contained in the sacrament being received, but that in the ministration thereof, we receive the body and blood of Christ; whereunto if it may please you to add, or understand this word spiritually, then is the doctrine of my Catechism sound and good in all men's ears, who know the true doctrine of the sacraments."

dogma of transubstantiation, he began to waver in his opinion.

Even after his desire to act with his party and the other Reformers with reference to the controversy, he was at a loss for arguments to satisfy his mind. Here was the Bible which he regarded as the book to be appealed to, as the authority in matters of faith, saying expressly that our Lord spake of the bread and the wine as His Body and Blood, and this not only at the institution of the Holy Communion, but also in the sixth chapter of St. John. Might anyone, to serve a special purpose, explain away the assertions of Scripture? This Cranmer declined to do on his own responsibility or through reliance upon the rationalistic arguments of those writers, who, instead of asking what has God revealed, disputed on what they called the absurdity of the tenet. The amount of blasphemy in which men indulged when disputing on this subject, was revolting to a pious mind and reached such a pitch, that the government itself at length found it necessary to interfere.

But if not a few self-sufficient individuals, but the primitive Church, rejected the dogma, then Cranmer was quite prepared to reject it too. The primitive churches had preserved as a tradition, what the apostles had taught when they established the churches, and this interpretation of a disputed Scripture was, therefore, to Cranmer's mind authoritative.

It was when the archbishop was in this hesitating state of mind that his chaplain Ridley* called his attention to a remarkable treatise by Ratramn or Bertram, which was published in opposition to Paschasius Radbert, who in the

---

* Cranmer himself says, "he did confer with me, and by sending persuasions and authorities of ancient doctors, drew me quite from my opinion in favour of transubstantiation." Remains, iv. 97.

ninth century had asserted the dogma of transubstantiation.* From this work, which is sometimes attributed to Duns Scotus, he learned that if he applied to this doctrine the test of Vincentius Lirinensis, it had not been always taught, it had not been everywhere received, it was not accepted by all Churches. Ratramnus supplied him with quotations from several of the fathers, including St. Ambrose and St. Augustine ; and Cranmer, with his usual assiduity and accuracy, carried on the investigation.† When he stood to be cross-questioned before the commissioners at Oxford, he gave that memorable challenge, which has been more than once repeated : "If it can be proved by any doctor, above a thousand years after Christ, that Christ's body is there in the Eucharist, really (corporeally) present, I will give all over."

The date of the archbishop's renunciation of the dogma of transubstantiation is doubtful.‡ It certainly was not before Henry's death, because, as we shall presently see, he celebrated mass on that occasion, at the coronation of Edward VI., and again, when the obsequies were celebrated of Francis I. At all events, he could not, therefore, at that

---

* The history of this controversy is given in the Life of Lanfranc. The dogma of Paschasius Radbert approached more nearly perhaps to consubstantiation than to the decided assertion of transubstantiation. Ratramn's work has been translated and printed, and is a production which is instructive even to the modern reader. In my copy it commences Incipit liber Ratramni de corpore et sanguine Domini. Bertram was a corruption of the original name.

† There is a collection of citations on this subject in the British Museum, and another at C.C.C.C.

‡ In the year 1537, in a letter to Joachin Vadianus, or Wat, he condemned in strong terms the errors of Zuinglius and Œcolampadius, and he declared that though he had read almost every modern publication on this subject, he adhered to what he then thought the ancient faith respecting the true presence of Christ's body in the Holy Sacrament. Archiv. Eccles. Tigurin. clxxxvii.

time have seen the relation of this dogma with the great controversy of the day. The dogma of transubstantiation was only wanted, when, as in the mass, it was supposed that Christ, corporeally present, was offered for the quick and the dead; when Cranmer celebrated mass, this sacrifice he offered. Logically, he required a belief in transubstantiation. But he had perhaps already renounced it abstractly as a dogma; but did not at first perceive the end at which the renunciation of the dogma would land him. His own expressions relative to the date of his change of opinion are indecisive; he only mentions, that not long before he published his Catechism, he was in error with respect to the Corporeal Presence. In the Embden edition of the *Defence*, the preface of which is attributed to Sir John Cheke, the year 1546 is mentioned, but doubtfully. It is probable, that it was about this time that Ridley placed in his hands the book of Ratramn, and it is not likely that a man so slow and cautious as Cranmer would at once commit himself.

So cautious, indeed, was Cranmer, that when, in 1548, he published the translation of the Catechism of Justus Jonas—which, whether executed by himself or not, was published as expressing his own sentiments—the Sacramentarians regarded the work as a declaration against themselves: and to the present time it is a question whether he had advanced beyond consubstantiation. He probably still desired, like some of the continental reformers, to leave these as open questions.

It is observed by Mosheim, that there was at this time a desire on the part both of Lutherans and of Sacramentarians to seek an agreement in words though not in sentiment. This may account for the doubt which is sometimes entertained of Cranmer's orthodoxy on the doctrine of the sacraments. If, however, Cranmer's object was conciliation, he did not succeed, for John Burcher, writing to Bullinger, says:—

"The condition of our England is such as I can neither much commend or find fault with. A more sincere and pure feeling of religion has begun to flourish with success; but Satan, through his hatred of this, has been endeavouring to throw everything into confusion by means of dissension. The Archbishop of Canterbury, moved, no doubt, by the advice of Peter Martyr and other Lutherans, has ordered a Catechism of some Lutheran opinions to be translated and published in our language. This little book has occasioned no little discord; so that fightings have frequently taken place among the common people, on account of their diversity of opinion, even during the sermons. The government, roused by this contention, have convoked a synod of the bishops to consult about religion. God grant they do not produce some prodigy.* So much respecting religion."

Of the violence with which he was attacked by the foreigners, we may give, as a specimen, the following quotation from a letter † written by John ab Ulmis to Bullinger.

"I would have you know this for certain, that this Thomas has fallen into so heavy a slumber, that we entertain but a very cold hope that he will be aroused even by your most learned letter. For he has lately published a Catechism, in which he has not only approved that foul and sacrilegious transubstantiation of the Papists in the Holy Supper of our Saviour, but all the dreams of Luther seem to him sufficiently well grounded, perspicuous, and lucid."

The attacks made upon this work, which if not translated was published by Cranmer, rendered it necessary for him to enter into explanations, and to arouse himself

* Original Letters, Eng. Ref. ccxcviii.
† Ibid. clxxxv.

from his lethargy, if lethargic at this time he really was. In making explanations, his own opinions, as is frequently the case, became even to himself more clear and defined. He consulted Peter Martyr and John à Lasco; the former probably as a Lutheran, the latter as a sacramentarian. Both Peter Martyr and Martin Bucer were regarded as the representatives of Lutheranism in England. John Hooper, writing to Bullinger in 1549, says:—

"I hear that East Friesland has received the Interim. If this be the case, Master à Lasco will soon return into England. I greatly regret his absence, especially as Peter Martyr and Bernardine so stoutly defend Lutheranism, and there is now arrived a third (I mean Bucer), who will leave no stone unturned to obtain a footing. The people of England, as I hear, all of them entertain right notions upon that subject. Should not Master à Lasco come to us in a short time, I will send him your letter with the writing. But, if it please God, I could wish to meet the parties in person." *

The conferences between the archbishop and Peter Martyr concluded with the publication by the latter, of a disputation and treatise, of which the one was written by the archbishop's request, and the other was introduced by a dedication to his Grace. Peter Martyr here modified his views as a Lutheran, but the publication did not give satisfaction. Martin Bucer, in a letter to Bullinger, writes thus:—

"I am as sorry for Master Martyr's book, as anyone can be; but that disputation took place, and the propositions were agreed upon, before I arrived in England. At my advice he has inserted many things in the preface, whereby to express more fully his belief in the presence of Christ. Among the nobility of the kingdom those are very powerful, who would reduce the whole of the sacred ministry into a narrow compass, and who

* Original Letters, Eng. Ref. xxx.

are altogether unconcerned about the restoration of Church discipline.... While they seek to provide against our bringing down Christ the Lord from heaven, and confining him in the bread, and offering him to the communicants to be fed upon without faith—a thing that none of our party ever thought of— they themselves go so far as, without any warrant of Holy Scripture, to confine him to a certain limited place in heaven, and talk so vapidly about his exhibition and presence in the Supper (nay, some of them cannot even endure these words), that they appear to believe that nothing else but the bread and wine is there distributed. No one has as yet found fault with me for my simple view of this subject; nor have I ever heard of anyone who has been able to confute it from any solid passage of Scripture, nor indeed has anyone yet ventured to make the attempt. Their principal argument is, that the mysteries of Christ can be well and intelligibly explained (which would be true, if they would add "to faith, but not to reason"). They now assume, that it cannot with reason be supposed of Christ that he is in heaven, without being circumscribed by physical space; and since he is thus in heaven, as they take for granted, they insist, not only upon what no one will allow them, but also, without any solid reason, that it cannot be understood that the same body of Christ is in heaven and in the Supper: and when we reply, that no one supposes a local presence of Christ in the Supper, they again say that the body of Christ cannot be understood to be present anywhere without being locally circumscribed. The sum, therefore, of their argument is to this effect. Reason does not comprehend what you teach respecting the exhibition and presence of Christ in the Supper; therefore they are not true, and the Scriptures which seem to prove them must be otherwise interpreted. Let us pray for these persons. I have as yet met with no real Christians who were not entirely satisfied with my simple view of the subject, as soon as it had been properly explained to them." *

---

* Original Letters, Eng. Ref. cclii. Still Bucer advocated the use of ambiguous terms, so as to create an apparent agreement where it did not really exist. This was the ground of his complaint.

Nevertheless from this time the opinions of the archbishop were given in a more decided tone. Bartholomew Traheron, writing to Bullinger in 1548, says:—

"On the 14th of December, if I mistake not, a disputation was held at London concerning the Eucharist, in the presence of almost all the nobility of England. The argument was sharply contested by the bishops. The Archbishop of Canterbury, contrary to general expectation, most openly, firmly, and learnedly maintained your opinion upon this subject. His arguments were as follows:—The body of Christ was taken up from us into heaven. Christ has left the world. 'Ye have the poor always with you, but me ye have not always,' &c. Next followed the Bishop of Rochester, who handled the subject with so much eloquence, perspicuity, erudition, and power, as to stop the mouth of that most zealous papist, the Bishop of Worcester. The truth never obtained a more brilliant victory among us. I perceive that it is all over with Lutheranism, now that those who were considered its principal and almost only supporters, have altogether come over to our side."*

All this shows how decidedly inclined to Lutheranism some of the leading Reformers in England had hitherto been.†

John ab Ulmis writes, still speaking not very courteously of the archbishop, in the same year:—

"The bishops entertain right and excellent opinions respecting the Holy Supper of Jesus Christ. That abominable error and silly opinion of a carnal eating, has been long since banished, and entirely done away with. Even that Thomas (Cranmer) himself, about whom I wrote to you when I was in London, by the goodness of God, and the instrumentality of that most upright and judicious man, Master John à Lasco, is in a great measure recovered from his dangerous lethargy."‡

Even Hooper was soon after inclined to take a more impartial view of Cranmer's conduct, although he betrays

---

* Original Letters, Eng. Ref. clii.
† On this point, see Archbishop Laurence's Bampton Lectures.
‡ Original Letters, clxxxvi.

the malevolence of a puritan mind in imputing to selfish and worldly motives the course suggested by prudence. Writing to Bullinger, he says:—

"The Archbishop of Canterbury entertains right views as to the nature of Christ's presence in the Supper, and is now very friendly towards myself. He has some articles of religion, to which all preachers and lecturers in divinity are required to subscribe, or else a licence for teaching is not granted them, and in these his sentiments respecting the Eucharist are pure and religious, and similar to yours in Switzerland. We desire nothing more from him than a firm and manly spirit. Like all the other bishops in this country, he is too fearful about what may happen to him. There are here six or seven bishops who comprehend the doctrine of Christ, as far as relates to the Lord's Supper, with as much clearness and piety as one could desire, and it is only the fear for their property that prevents them from reforming their churches according to the rule of God's Word. The altars are here in many churches changed into tables. The public celebration of the Lord's Supper is very far from the order and institution of our Lord. Although it is administered in both kinds, yet in some places the Supper is celebrated three times a day. Where they used heretofore to celebrate in the morning the *mass* of the apostles, they now have the *communion* of the apostles; where they had the *mass* of the blessed Virgin, they now have the communion, which they call the *communion* of the blessed Virgin; where they had the principal, or high mass, they now have, as they call it, the high communion. They still retain their vestments and candles before the altars; in the churches they always chant the *hours* and other hymns relating to the Lord's Supper, but in their own language. And that popery may not be lost, the mass-priests, although they are compelled to discontinue the use of the Latin language, yet most carefully observe the same tone and manner of chanting to which they were heretofore accustomed in the papacy.*

* Original Letters, xxxvi.

The bishops of whom he thus uncharitably speaks—because, while willing to reform the Church, they were unwilling to destroy and replace it by a Protestant sect—were the Archbishop of Canterbury, Dr. Cranmer; the Bishop of Rochester, Dr. Ridley; the Bishop of Ely, Dr. Goodrich; the Bishop of St. David's, Dr. Farrar; the Bishop of Lincoln, Dr. Holbeach; the Bishop of Bath, Dr. Barlow.

In the year 1550, all doubts were removed as to the opinions of the archbishop by the publication of his "Defence of the True and Catholic Doctrine of the Sacrament of the Body and Blood of our Saviour Christ." It was published, as he himself tells us, "to the intent that it might hereafter neither of the one party be contemned or lightly esteemed, nor of the other party be abused to any other purpose than Christ himself did first ordain and appoint the same."*

The work is divided into five books, in one of which he expounds what he regards as the true doctrine of the Holy Sacrament, in the other he refutes the arguments of his opponents, contending against transubstantiation, the Corporeal Presence of our Lord, the eating and drinking of Christ by the wicked, and the Propitiatory Sacrifice of the Mass.

He rejected the notion of the Corporeal Presence, that he might refute the doctrine of a Propitiatory Sacrifice; the notion of a Propitiatory Sacrifice having, during the last seven hundred years, superseded the idea of that Spiritual Sacrifice which consists of a presentation to God of the Church, militant and triumphant, to do God's will. But though he rejected the *Corporeal* Presence, the *Real* Presence he strongly asserts.

"That the cup is a communion of Christ's blood that was shed

* Remains, ii. 289.

for us, and the bread is a communion of His flesh that was crucified for us; so that, although in the truth of His human nature Christ be in heaven, and sitteth at the right hand of God the Father, yet whoever eateth of that bread in the Supper of the Lord, according to Christ's institution and ordinance, is assured, of Christ's own promise and testament, that he is a member of His body, and receiveth the benefits of His passion which He suffered for us on the cross."

In this work we look in vain for any display of genius; such is not to be found in any of Cranmer's writings. The author does not come before us as an original thinker; but he evinces throughout the clearness of his mind, its logical precision, and a sound judgment in the selection of his authorities. This work, coming from such a quarter, made a profound impression upon the public mind, and provoked replies from Dr. Smyth and Bishop Gardyner. The replies are not deserving of that sweeping condemnation which has been poured upon them by party writers; and the archbishop felt himself called upon to publish an answer both for the cause of truth and for his own vindication. Perhaps there does not exist a better specimen of controversial fairness than the answer to Gardyner published by Cranmer; but, as we have already touched upon the controversy, it is not necessary to enter on it any further. Another reply was published by Gardyner under a fictitious name and in Latin. To this Cranmer was preparing a rejoinder, when, by the death of Edward VI., the reformers of England were called upon to serve their Divine master by endurance rather than by action.

In giving the history of Cranmer's mind, we must notice the charge which is sometimes brought against him of Erastianism. Here, however, we must bear in mind the fact that he began life, as he ended it, a churchman: his object was to reform the Church; but his mind was formed on the principles of the age, and he had never heard the doctrine of the apostolical succession assailed. He was a party assenting to the ancient ordinal, in the revision of which he assisted. That preface commences thus: "It is evident to all men diligently reading the Holy Scripture and the ancient authors that, from the apostles' time, there have been three orders of ministers in Christ's Church, bishops, priests, and deacons."

We will consider what would be the meaning of these words at the time when the committee was appointed to revise the ancient ordinal of the Church of England. At that time, as in the time of "the ancient authors," a bishop was a minister of God not of man, who was distinguished from priests or presbyters and deacons, by having the sole right to ordain or send new ministers into the vineyard of the Church. The word bishop had no other meaning; it was held that as the Lord Jesus Christ was sent by the Father, so the Lord Jesus sent the apostles; as the Lord Jesus sent the apostles to be his ministers and to govern his Church, so the apostles sent the first race of bishops; thus the first race of bishops ordained their successors, and so down to the present time; the existing bishops going back from generation to generation, thus trace their succession from the apostles. So careful has the Church ever been on this subject, that although consecration by one bishop is *valid*, no consecration is *canonical* unless it be administered by three at least.

This doctrine is asserted in the "Institution of a Christian Man," a work which received full synodical sanction, and was subscribed by both of the archbishops in 1537.* Cranmer at that time held, "that Christ and his apostles

* Formularies of Faith, 101.

did institute and ordain in the New Testament, besides the civil powers and governance of kings and princes, that there should also be continually in the Church militant certain other ministers and officers, who should have special power, authority, and commission under Christ to preach and teach the Word of God to His people, to dispense and administer the Sacraments of God unto them, and by the same to confer and give the graces of the Holy Ghost."

It is further stated, " this office, this power, this authority was committed and given by Christ and his apostles to certain persons only; that is to say, to priests or bishops, whom they did elect, call, and admit thereunto by their prayer and imposition of hands."*

In the "Necessary Doctrine," or the king's book, printed first in 1543, we find the opinion of the king in concurrence with that of convocation; for it is expressly stated that:—

"Order is a gift or grace of ministration in Christ's Church, given of God to Christian men, by the consecration and imposition of the bishop's hands upon them; and this sacrament was conferred and given by the apostles, as it appeareth in the Epistle of St. Paul to Timothy, whereby it appeareth that St. Paul did consecrate and order priests and bishops by the imposition of his hands. And as the apostles themselves, in the beginning of the Church, did order priests and bishops, so they appointed and willed the other bishops after them to do the like, as St. Paul manifestly sheweth in his Epistle to Titus, saying thus: 'For this cause I left thee in Crete, that thou shouldest ordain priests in every city, according as I have appointed thee.' And to Timothy he saith, 'See that thou be not hasty to put thy hands upon any man.'" †

Both convocation and the archbishop were very

* Formularies of Faith, 104.
† Formularies of Faith in the Reign of Henry VIII., p. 276.

careful to guard against any misrepresentation of their doctrine upon this topic. After the assertion, as against the pope, of the supremacy of the crown, and of the duty of the civil power to see, that the bishops and clergy do execute truly and faithfully "the power, office, and jurisdiction conferred upon them by God, according to all points as it was given them by Christ and his apostles," it is added:—

"We may not think that it doth appertain unto the office of kings and princes to preach and teach, to administer the sacraments, to absolve, to excommunicate, and such other things belonging to the office and administration of bishops and priests, but we must think and believe that God hath constituted and made Christian kings and princes to be as the chief heads and overlookers over the said priests and bishops, to cause them to administer their office and power committed unto them purely and sincerely, and in case they shall be negligent in any part thereof, to cause them to supply and repair the same again." *

To the articles and other documents of the Church, wicked men have occasionally—to share in its emoluments—attached their signature, while denying the truths which these documents express; we can show, however, that Cranmer is not to be numbered among these, for in one of his latest works, the translation of the Catechism of Justus Jonas, he would have even children to be taught that:—

"After Christ's ascension, the apostles gave authority to other godly and holy men to minister God's Word, and chiefly in those places where there were Christian men already, which lacked preachers, and the apostles themselves could not longer abide with them. For the apostles did walk abroad into divers parts of the world, and did study to plant the Gospel in many places. Wherefore where they found godly men and meet to preach

* Formularies of Faith, 121.

God's Word, they laid their hands upon them and gave them the Holy Ghost, as they themselves received of Christ the same Holy Ghost, to execute this office. And they that were so ordained, were in deed, and also were called, the ministers of God, as the apostles themselves were, as Paul saith unto Timothy. And so the ministration of God's Word (which our Lord Jesus Christ Himself did first institute) was derived from the apostles unto other after them, by imposition of hands and giving the Holy Ghost, from the apostles' time to our days. And this was the consecration, orders, and unction of the apostles, whereby they at the beginning made bishops and priests; and this shall continue in the Church, even to the world's end. And whatsoever rite or ceremony hath been added more than this, cometh of man's ordinance and policy, and is not commanded by God's Word." *

These were the deliberate opinions of Archbishop Cranmer; and knowing this to be the case, we must make the due allowance, when, in the heat of controversy, he occasionally was hurried into assertions not always in keeping with what we know to have been his deliberate judgment. We are not attempting to defend a man, who was too often inconsistent while feeling his way to the truth, but we desire to ascertain what were the principles into which he subsided. The inconsistencies of Cranmer are not to be denied; but if we look upon them impartially and regard him, not as a Protestant of the modern type, but as a Catholic labouring to reform the Church, we must admit that his inconsistencies were not so glaring as they are sometimes represented to be.

At the present time, the Lord High Chancellor is appointed, and may be removed, by the Sovereign. But before his appointment to that post by the crown, he was a man called to the bar by an authority independent of the crown. The king can make a Lord Chancellor,

* Sermon on the Authority of the Keys, 196.

but he cannot make a lawyer; and though he can nominate to the chancellorship, yet, by the practice of the constitution, his nomination must rest upon some one who has been previously made a lawyer.

What Cranmer contended for was,—the right of the king, when his supremacy was conceded, to act with respect to bishops as he did with respect to his other ministers. The king did not make the bishops, but he might appoint any man, being a bishop, to preside over a diocese in his kingdom, and at his discretion he might remove him. The person removed would still be a bishop; but he would be—as such bishops were then seen in the bishops *in partibus*, and as they are seen now in retired colonial bishops—a bishop without a see. That the distinction was clearly understood is seen at once by the fact, that Bishop Coverdale officiated at Archbishop Parker's consecration, though Bishop Coverdale had been deprived of his see; he had ceased to be a diocesan, but not a bishop.

Both Henry and Cranmer in the application of this principle often acted despotically, but it does not prove that Cranmer by being its advocate was of necessity or consciously an Erastian. The judges in our courts of law were, at one time, removable at the will of the Sovereign; and the mischief was so great, that the legislature interfered, and the lawyers appointed to judicial situations by the crown are now irremovable; so it has been with reference to our diocesans, but even now a diocesan may resign and subside into a simple bishop.

We should be more correct, were the anachronism allowable, if we speak of Cranmer as an ultra-tory. He was one of those who pushed the prerogative so far that at last it became an intolerable burden, and ultimately led to the temporary suspension of the kingly government.

He was the first archbishop who ventured to affirm that the king held his crown of hereditary right, without the consent of the people or of the Church. In former times, hereditary right was claimed; but there was a power to set aside a particular person in favour of the next in succession, or some other member of the royal family. This had been done throughout the Norman dynasty. The mischievous effects were sufficiently visible, and we readily acquiesce in the doctrine of hereditary right as the general rule: but even in Henry VIII.'s reign the king and parliament assumed the right of regulating the succession to the crown; and perhaps it was from some fear lest Mary should dispute the crown with Edward, that Cranmer went out of his way, at the coronation of that young king, to set aside what had hitherto been the law of the land. The eldest son of a king departed, had claimed the crown, demanding of the people their homage; this they might render or refuse at the coronation; when the claim had been admitted, the archbishop or his deputy proceeded to consecrate the sovereign by anointing him. The form is still observed in our church's order for the coronation of a sovereign, but has become, like the *congé d'élire* in the appointment of a bishop, a form, and nothing else.

When Cranmer determined to advocate the royal supremacy in opposition to the papal, he had not previously determined in his mind the amount of power which this conveyed to the prince. He took only a negative view of the subject: the papal supremacy was to be renounced; upon this point he was clear and firm. But he had not considered how far the royal supremacy was to extend, and this occasionally involved him in difficulties and in some of the inconsistencies to which we have alluded.

It is to this that we are to attribute the usurpation, as we may call it, of Crumwell. When that unprincipled man was at the head of affairs, he sought to carry his objects by exalting the powers of the supremacy on the one side, and encouraging the extreme views of Protestants on the other side, including under that designation all the free-thinkers and the most unprincipled of those who were disturbing the public peace.

The convocation had conceded, as we have had occasion before to remark, the title of Supreme Head of the Church of England to Henry VIII., so far as the law of God permitted; and when this was corroborated by Parliament in 1534, an explanatory document was added, stating that, in conceding this title to the king, no new authority was given him, but that the Church and State only recognised his possession of such power " as to a king of right appertaineth, by the law of God, and not that he should take any spiritual power from spiritual ministers that is given to them by the Gospel." *

It was all along maintained, that King Henry only claimed the authority and power which had always been inherent in the kingly office, although it had not been always maintained by his ancestors.

Nevertheless, this question was open to misunderstanding and abuse. The opinion of Henry VIII., to which Cranmer humbly deferred was, on this matter, not always uniform. When he had no particular object in view, his clear understanding enabled him to perceive how far the supremacy was to extend; but he permitted his authority to be stretched beyond its due limits when, exercising

* In the introductory chapter it is shown that Queen Elizabeth, as well as Queen Mary, repudiated the title, which has never subsequently attached to the Crown of England.

it to suppress the monasteries, Crumwell promised to replenish his treasury, and to give free scope to his gambling propensities. . .

Crumwell's argument was this:—The royal supremacy invests the king with the powers hitherto exercised by the pope. The pope, when he desired to correct any abuse, or to enforce any special object, would appoint a legate, with plenary powers to represent the pope and to act in his name. Therefore the king might do the same. He might from time to time appoint a legate. Although the papal legate *a latere*, while generally a cardinal, was sometimes a deacon and might be a layman, he, in the execution of his office, superseded, for the time being, all metropolitans, and had precedence of archbishops. Crumwell caused himself to be appointed vicar-general, or, as he preferred being called, vicegerent, and he assumed the functions, precedence, and authority of a legate. The title and office were anomalous, and were never, after Crumwell's death, renewed.

Archbishop Cranmer supinely acquiesced in the arrangement, as a temporary measure.

But although the legatine office thus conferred upon Crumwell answered its real purpose, that of suppressing the monasteries, and of diverting the property into the king's treasury and his own, it presented an impediment to the progress of the Reformation: of this the archbishop had experience in what occurred in the Convocation of 1536.

The convocation met on the last day of June in that year. The Bishop of Worcester, Dr. Latimer,* was

---

* Hugh Latimer had been consecrated on the 26th of September, 1535, by the primate, Dr. Cranmer; by the Bishop of Winchester, Dr. Stephen Gardyner; and the Bishop of Sarum, Dr. Nicholas Shaxton. As the

appointed to preach the sermon. The Archbishop admitted Mr. Gwent into the office of prolocutor, to which he had been elected by the lower house. Crumwell insulted the convocation by sending a certain William Petre to represent him, and, in the name of the vicar-general, to challenge for himself the first place in the synod. It was bad enough for the king to appoint Crumwell as his representative, but the representative of a representative was more than the convocation could stand, and the feelings of indignation were such, that at the second session Crumwell himself appeared. In this convocation, parties were pretty evenly balanced in point of talent, as well as of numbers; and in politics they were united. The "new learning" party, as it was called, was headed by the primate, Dr. Cranmer; the Bishop of Ely, Dr. Goodrich; the Bishop of Sarum, Dr. Shaxton; the Bishop of Worcester, Dr. Latimer; the Bishop of Hereford, Dr. Fox; the Bishop of Rochester, Dr. Hilsey; and the Bishop of St. David's, Dr. Barlow. The "old learning" party was led by the Archbishop of York, Dr. Lee; the Bishop of London, Dr. Stokesley; the Bishop of Durham, Dr. Tonstal; the Bishop of Winchester, Dr. Gardyner; the Bishop of Lincoln, Dr. Longland; the Bishop of Chichester, Dr. Sherborne; the Bishop of Carlisle, Dr. Kite.

They were all men of competent learning, and, as far as we know, they all of them sustained a high character for morality and religion.

They were united all by one great principle, a determination to uphold the royal supremacy against the pope; and it must not be forgotten that Cranmer and

bishop to be consecrated generally selects the prelates who are to assist the primate, it would appear that Gardyner and Latimer were at this time on friendly terms.

his party were, at this time, as ready to burn men for denying the dogma of transubstantiation, as were Gardyner or any bishop on the "old learning" side. The "old learning" party, alarmed by the excesses which Crumwell had encouraged, were under the influence of reactionary feelings; and they desired no further changes in the Church of England, than those which the renunciation of the papal supremacy rendered absolutely necessary. The "new learning" party were desirous of correcting all abuses, and of testing the received doctrines which had been assailed by the Lutherans, through an appeal to Scripture.

The first party movement took place in the fourth session, June 20, when the prolocutor presented to the upper house a list of erroneous opinions commonly preached in the province of Canterbury.

The preamble to the presentation contained an ample declaration of loyalty to the king, and of a determination on the part of the house, that "they minded in no wise by any colorable fashion to recognise privily or apertly the Bishop of Rome or his usurped authority, whose inventions, rites, abuses, ordinances, and fashions were to be for ever renounced, forsaken, extinguished, and abolished." The erroneous opinions are then reduced to sixty-seven articles. Complaint is justly made of that amount of irreverence to which we have before adverted, and then in denouncing the errors, there is such a strange jumble of truth and falsehood, that it is clearly shown that the new learning party required a leader, such as Cranmer at this time, certainly was not, and perhaps ought not ever to have become.

Complaint was also made that certain books which had been examined by a committee of convocation and were pronounced by it to be full of heresy and heterodoxy, had nevertheless not been expressly condemned by the upper house, and were still in circulation.*

The next movement was on the part of the men of the "new learning." The protestation just received gave proof that no peace could be expected in the Church, unless some standard formulary should be adopted which would at least be as a polar star for the guidance of those who were now tossed about by every strange wind of doctrine. On the 11th of July, the Bishop of Hereford submitted to the upper house a book of articles, as it was called, or a rough draft of certain articles of faith, for which he solicited the ratification of the synod.†

On this occasion Cranmer spoke, and we possess his speech. On the remonstrance of the lower house it appears that sundry warm debates had arisen. To these discussions the archbishop, as president of the convocation, adverts, and describes such "babbling and brawling" as unbecoming in men of learning and gravity. He reminded his brethren that "the controversies now moved and put forth had not reference to ceremonies and light things, but to the understanding and the right difference between the law and the gospel. They had to consider questions relating to the way and manner in which sins are to be forgiven, to the comforting of doubtful and wavering consciences, and by what means they may be certified that they please God, seeing they feel the strength of the law accusing them of sin; of the true use of the sacraments, whether the outward work of them doth justify man, or whether we receive our justification by faith. Item, which be the good works, and the true service and honour which pleaseth God; and whether the choice of meats, the difference of

* Collier, iv. 341.   † Wilkins, iii. 803.

garments, the vows of monks and priests, and other traditions which have no word of God to confirm them, whether these, I say, be right good works, and such as make a perfect Christian man or no? Item, whether vain service and false honouring of God and man's traditions do bind men's consciences or no? Finally, whether the ceremony of confirmation, of orders, and of annealing, and such other (which cannot be proved to be institute of Christ, nor have any word in them to certify us of remission of sins), ought to be called sacraments, and to be compared with Baptism and the Supper of the Lord or no?"*

He concluded with exhorting them to the serious consideration of these things. The articles submitted to convocation, familiarly known as the Articles of 1536, refer to—I. The Creeds; II. Baptism; III. Penance; IV. The Sacrament of the Altar; V. Justification; VI. Images; VII. Honouring Saints; VIII. Prayers to Saints; IX. Rites and Ceremonies; X. Purgatory.

The king was desirous to have something definite to produce on the authority of the Church, to pacify the insurgents in the north of England. That the articles were the production of the king is sometimes affirmed, but such statement is not corroborated by the introduction prefixed to them, and is contradicted by the fact, that he desired that copies of them should be dispersed among the insurgents, that the clergy and others in the north "might understand that it was a proper act of the Church, and *not* an innovation of the king and a few of his counsellors." †
That the formulary was revised by the king before it was submitted to convocation is probable, as scarcely any public document appeared, before it had been shaped to his wishes by his revision thereof. In the preface he

* Remains, ii. 17.   † Strype, 40.

speaks of having in his own person many times taken great pain, study, labour, and travail on these subjects. That it was revised by the archbishop also is proved by a draft for the articles on images, and on prayers to saints, with the corrections of Archbishop Cranmer and of Bishop Tunstall, still preserved at Lambeth.

This formulary was published under the title of "Articles devised by the kinge's highnes majestie, to stablyshe Christen quietnes and unitie amonge us, and to avoyde contentious opinions: which articles be also approved by the consent and determination of the hole clergie of this realme, anno MDXXXVI."

When we are tracing the progress of Cranmer's mind, this work is of considerable importance. It shows us how little advanced on the side of reformation the archbishop and the men of the new learning at that time were.

The political object of the king himself oozes out in the preface. The excesses and licentiousness encouraged by Crumwell, and which were now exposing the king to censure and the kingdom to disturbance, had provoked an insurrection in the north of England and the king desired to calm the storm which had been raised. The king, having perceived that it was his duty to remove all occasion of dissent and discord from his subjects in the matter of religion, declared that he had, in his own person, taken great pain, study, labour, and travail in this cause; and not only this, "we also," he continues, "have caused our bishops, and other the most discreet and best learned men of our clergy of this our whole realm, to be assembled in our convocation, for the full debatement and quiet determination of the same. Where, after long and mature deliberation, and disputations had of and upon the premises, finally they have concluded and agreed upon the most special points and articles, as well such as be commanded of God, and are necessary to our salvation, as also divers other matters touching the honest ceremonies and good and politic orders, as is aforesaid, which their determination, debatement and agreement, for so much as we think to have proceeded of a good, right and true judgment, and to be agreeable to the laws and ordinances of God, and much profitable for the establishment of that charitable concord and unity in our Church of England, which we most desire, we have caused the same to be published, willing, requiring and commanding you to accept, repute, and take them accordingly."*

With reference to the "Principal articles concerning our Faith," the document insists on the acceptance of the three creeds, of which a short abstract is given; and ordains that all "bishops and preachers" ought and must utterly refuse and condemn all those opinions contrary to the said articles, which were of long time past condemned in the four holy councils, that is to say, in the council of Nice, Constantinople, Ephesus, and Chalcedonense, and all other sith that time in any point consonant to the same."

The necessity of baptism and of infant baptism is affirmed. In regard to penance, it is said, "we will that all bishops and *preachers shall instruct* and teach our people committed by us to their spiritual charge, that they ought and must certainly believe that the words of absolution pronounced by the priest, be spoken by authority given to him by Christ in the Gospel."

In the article of the sacrament of the altar the Corporeal presence is without qualification maintained. Justification is made to depend upon contrition joined with faith and charity. The use of images was allowed " to the intent, the rude people should not from henceforth take such superstition, as in time past it is thought that the same hath used to do; we will that our bishops and preachers diligently shall teach them, and according to this doctrine reform their abuses, for else there might fortune idolatry to ensue, which God forbid. And as for censing of them, and kneeling and offering unto them, with other like worshippings, although the same hath entered by devotion, and fallen to custom; yet the people ought to be diligently taught that they in nowise do it, nor think it meet to be done to the same images, but only to be done to God, and in His honour, although it be done before the images, whether it be of Christ, of the cross, of our lady, or of any other saint beside." *

Saints were to be honoured, and prayer to them was permitted. The article on rites and ceremonies is interesting, as showing the observances of the Church at that period.

"As concerning the rites and ceremonies of Christ's church, as to have such vestments in doing God's service, as be and have been most part used, as sprinkling of holy water to put us in remembrance of our baptism, and the blood of Christ sprinkled for our redemption upon the cross; giving of holy bread to put us in remembrance of the sacrament of the altar, that all Christian men be one body mystical of Christ, as the bread is made of many grains, and yet but one loaf, and to put us in remembrance of the receiving of the holy sacrament and body of Christ, the which we ought to receive in right charity; which in the beginning of Christ's church, men did more often receive than they use nowadays to do; bearing of candles on Candlemas Day, in memory of Christ the spiritual light, of whom Simeon did prophecy, as is read in the church that day; giving of ashes on Ash Wednesday, to put in remembrance every Christian man in the beginning of Lent and penance, that he is but ashes and earth, and thereto shall return; which is right necessary to be uttered from henceforth in our mother tongue always on

* Formularies of Faith, xxviii.

the same day; bearing of palms on Palm Sunday, in memory of the receiving of Christ into Jerusalem, a little before his death, that we may have the same desire to receive him into our hearts; creeping to the cross, and humbling ourselves to Christ on Good Friday before the cross, and there offering unto Christ before the same, and kissing of it in memory of our redemption by Christ made upon the cross; setting up the sepulture of Christ, Whose body after His death was buried; the hallowing of the font, and other like exorcisms and benedictions by the ministers of Christ's church; and all other like laudable customs, rites, and ceremonies be not to be contemned and cast away, but to be used and continued as things good and laudable, to put us in remembrance of those spiritual things that they do signify; not suffering them to be forgot, or to be put in oblivion, but renewing them in our memories from time to time. But none of these ceremonies have power to remit sin, but only to stir and lift up our minds unto God, by whom only our sins be forgiven." *

Purgatory and prayers for the dead were allowed.

Such was the formulary which was signed by Crumwell as the king's representative or legate; and not only by the Archbishop of Canterbury but also by the Archbishop of York. It is well known that on certain important occasions the northern prelates appeared in the convocation of the southern province.

So far had Cranmer's opinions advanced in 1536.

The convocation consisted of practical men, rather than of men determined to carry some favourite theoretical scheme. It was clear from the articles that the men of the "new learning" were willing to make as much concession as they could to the opposition, and the men of the "old learning" now gave way when a motion was made on the opposite side of the House to abolish many

* Formularies of Faith, xxxi.

of those Church festivals which had been the cause of idleness.

The feast of dedication of churches was ordered to be kept on the first Sunday in October and on no other day.

The feast of the patron of any Church, commonly called the wake, was to be a day of business. All feasts falling in harvest time or term time, were also made days of business. The festivals of the Apostles and of the Virgin Mary and all those festivals in which the judges do not usually sit at Westminster were excepted. Priests and clerks, regular and secular, were, however, allowed to perform the accustomed services in the Church, provided they did not do it in a solemn manner, or compel others to attend. It is remarkable that this was evidently a point insisted upon by Cranmer, and not by the crown, for Cranmer, through Crumwell, on one occasion remonstrated with Henry that the repealed festivals were observed at court. This is the more unaccountable as the non-observance of the festivals, and other determinations of the synod were afterwards published by Crumwell as royal injunctions. A practical question was also put to the convocation on the 20th of July; and this was, whether the king lay under any obligation to attend the council lately summoned by the pope to meet at Mantua. The determination was signified to the king in an instrument which set forth the advantages resulting from general councils, but which at the same same denied the right of the pope or of any one prince to convoke such a synod. It could only be called by the consent of all the princes in Christendom. This important subject appears to have been brought frequently before this assembly and to have been discussed in the Privy Council. There is a speech attributed to Cranmer relating to general councils, of which Burnet gives an outline. There are indications of some modern touches by the hand of the reporter, but from this speech it would appear that, although Cranmer was not very clear on the subject, he saw that the authority of the first general councils rested on the fact, not of their defining the faith, but upon that of the bishops having, at the emperor's call, assembled to bear witness of the tradition they had received. Later councils had taken upon themselves to define articles of faith, which was a useless labour, since for articles of faith we should go to the scriptures.* Whether this speech was delivered at this time, or when, or where, it is impossible to say.

Cranmer was a diligent student, and during the next two years his mind advanced considerably. Whether by his advice or not, a synod consisting of a union of the two convocations of Canterbury and York was convened to meet in 1537. The king had been both annoyed and alarmed by the disturbances in the North, and probably summoned the Northern metropolitan and his suffragans to meet in London, in order that the people in the North of England might perceive that his ecclesiastical policy met with the sanction of the entire Church of England. By the right of his conceded supremacy, and on the principles advocated in the debate on general councils, the king himself convened the synod. As Constantine had presided at Nice, Henry claimed to be its president; as the pope had in former times presided through his legates, so the king was represented by his vice-gerent.† The summons to attend the synod was obeyed with the readiness with which obedience was rendered to every command of Henry VIII., and indeed with such alacrity as to elicit the thanks of the king. The upper house was addressed by the vice-

---

* Burnet mentions a copy of this speech among the Stillingfleet MSS. But such copy cannot now be found.

† This title was assumed by Lord Crumwell, with a new patent in 1536, with the view of giving him more importance at the synod of 1537.

CHAP. III.

Thomas Cranmer. 1533–56.

gerent in the following speech, as it were, from the throne.

"Right reverend fathers in Christ, the king's majesty giveth you high thanks that ye have so diligently, without any excuse, assembled hither according to his commandment; and ye be not ignorant that ye be called together to determine certain controversies which, at this time, be moved concerning the Christian religion and faith not only in this realm, but also in all nations thorow the world. For the king studieth day and night to set a quietness in the church, and he cannot rest until all such controversies be fully debated and ended through the determination of you and the whole parliament. And he desireth you, for Christ's sake, that all malice, obstinacy, and carnal respect set apart, ye will friendly and lovingly dispute among yourselves of the controversies moved in the Church; and that ye will conclude all things moved by the word of God. Ye know well enough that ye be bound to shew this service to Christ and to his Church; and yet, notwithstanding, his majesty will give you high thanks if ye will set and conclude a godly and perfect unitie. Whereunto this is the only way and means, if ye will determine all things by the Scripture, as God commandeth you in Deuteronomie, which thing his majesty exhorteth and desireth you to do." *

The bishops rose simultaneously, and desired to return thanks to the king's majesty not only for his great zeal towards the church of Christ, but also for his most godly exhortation, so worthy of a Christian prince. †

Parties in the synod continued much the same as they had been in the convocation of the preceding year, and there still remained on both sides a conciliatory disposition encouraged by the king.

At this synod Crumwell, who was profoundly ignorant on all theological subjects, had by his side a Scottish divine, of whom mention has been made before, Alexander

* Wake, 584. † Atterbury, 397.

Aless, evidently introduced, as an amicus curiæ to advise him. The presence of this person does not appear to have given offence so long as his advice was only whispered in the ear of the vice-gerent. It is probable that other strangers were admitted to hear the debates, and Aless had several personal friends among the bishops, including the primate. But their surprise was great, when Crumwell, unable to give an opinion on a theological question himself, desired Aless to address the synod, the subject of the sacraments being under discussion. It must be confessed that the opinions of Aless were more clear and defined than those of the archbishop or any other of the members of the synod. He took high ground and represented the question to be, whether a sacrament was an ordinance of the Lord Jesus Christ, appointed to "signify a signal and special grace of the Gospel, or whether, on the other hand, it was a ceremony which might be taken of any holy thing." If the latter were the meaning, then the word sacrament might be given, not to seven ordinances only, but to any number they might name. If the former were the meaning of the word, then he concluded, with St. Augustine and other fathers, that there were only two sacraments, baptism and the supper of the Lord.

The Bishop of London replied to the Scot, and, to the amusement of some of his hearers, lost his temper. Arguing from the decretals, he maintained that the sacraments were seven, neither more nor less. The allusion to the decretals brought up the archbishop, his strong point having been attacked, the sufficiency of Scripture. Among other things, he affirmed that to appeal to any other authority than Scripture, especially in a synod, was not becoming the character of a bishop. The archbishop was supported by the Bishop of Hereford, Dr.

Fox. Fox had been the king's ambassador in Germany, and he held up the example of the Germans who had translated the Scriptures; upon which, rather than upon commentaries and glosses, it were wise to rely. The Bishop of London treated with disdain the notion "that there is no other word of God than that which every cobbler may read in his mother tongue."

As the synod was too excited to come to any calm decision upon this important subject, it was prorogued for the day.

The archbishop joined with the other bishops in remonstrating with Crumwell upon the impropriety of introducing a stranger and foreigner, for such at that time a Scotchman was, into the synod, and the intrusion of Aless was not repeated.*

The discussions of the synod led to an important result. The bishops of the new learning suggested to the king, the importance of carrying out to a greater extent, and after longer deliberation, "the principle on which the articles of the late convocation had been based." The bishops of the old learning could not oppose this proposal, or perhaps dared not when it had the sanction of the king and his cordial support.

The king accordingly issued a commission, for the production of a formulary, larger and more complete than the book of articles. Both parties were fairly represented in the commission, the Archbishop of Canterbury, Dr. Cranmer, the Bishop of London, Dr. Stokesley, the Bishop of Winchester, Dr. Gardyner, the Bishop of Chichester, Dr.

---

* Crumwell had some justification for his conduct, for Aless was at this time what was called a king's scholar, a scholar receiving a salary from the king, so appointed no doubt through the influence of Crumwell, who required a privy councillor in his house to advise him on theological questions.

Sampson, the Bishop of Norwich, Dr. Repps, the Bishop of Ely, Dr. Goodrich, the Bishop of Worcester, Dr. Latimer, the Bishop of Salisbury, Dr. Shaxton, the Bishop of Hereford, Dr. Fox, the Bishop of St. David's, Dr. Barlow, with others of the inferior clergy.

They met at Lambeth, and the primate was of course the chairman. As might be expected from such a commission, the debates at first were long and angry. The prelate who took the most active part in the proceedings, was the Bishop of Hereford, Dr. Fox, who was assisted by the zeal, if not the learning of the Bishop of Worcester, Dr. Latimer. The result was the production of what was called the Bishop's book, "The Institution of a Christian man." When it was nearly completed, Bishop Latimer, writing to Crumwell, says that "his prayer to God is, that when it is done, it may well and sufficiently be done, so that we shall not need to have any more such doings:" he adds, "It is forsooth a troublous thing to agree upon a doctrine in things of such controversy with judgments of such diversity, every one, I trust, meaning well, and yet not all meaning one way. But I doubt not but now in the end, we shall agree both one with the other, and all with the truth."*

I quote this passage, for it shows that by the reforming party the publication of the Institution was regarded as a final measure. They were prepared to take their stand here and to go no further. In another letter Latimer informs Crumwell that their joint work will be forwarded to him for transmission to the king by the archbishop, " to whom also, if there be anything praiseworthy, bona pars laudis optimo jure debetur."†

It will be observed that Cranmer had not direct access to the king: indeed he never had during the ascendancy

---

* State Papers, i. ii. 563. † Ibid. 556, 562, 563.

of Crumwell, if at any other time. It will be also observed that to the Institution, or the Bishop's book, we are to look for the theological opinions of Archbishop Cranmer in 1537. If he was a protestant at this time, in any sense except in that of being anti-papal, we can only say that protestantism was at that time something very different from what it is now.

The Institution of a Christian Man contains an exposition or interpretation of the Apostles' creed, of the seven sacraments, of the ten commandments, of the Pater noster, of the Ave Maria, of justification and of purgatory. It is dedicated to King Henry VIII. by Thomas Archbishop of Canterbury, by Edward Archbishop of York, and all other the bishops, prelates and archdeacons of the realm. It maintains that the Church of England is a catholic church and denies to the Church of Rome any exclusive claim to that title, although regarding it as one branch of the Church catholic.* The twelve articles of the creed are to be received; and all opinions are condemned which are contrary thereto or which are condemned in the four holy councils of Nice, Constantinople, Ephesus and Chalcedon.† Baptismal regeneration is asserted to its full extent, and infants are to be baptized because they are born in original sin, "which sin must needs be remitted, which

---

* Institution, 54, 55. Although the word καθολικὸς properly signifies universal, yet they (the ancient fathers) commonly used it in the same sense as we do the word orthodox, as opposed to a heretic, calling an orthodox man a Catholic, that is a son of the Catholic Church; as taking it for granted, that they, and they only, which constantly adhere to the doctrine of the Catholic or Universal Church, are truly orthodox, which they could not do, unless they had believed the Catholic Church to be so. And besides that, it is part of our very creed that the Catholic Church is holy, which she could not be except free from heresy, as directly opposite to true holiness. Beveridge, Works, ii. 197.

† Institution, 62.

can only be done by the sacrament of baptism, whereby they receive the Holy Ghost."[*]

In the exposition of the sacrament of penance, Cranmer insists on the necessity of auricular confession, and directs the bishops and clergy to warn the people that they must give no less faith and credence to the same words of absolution, so pronounced by ministers of the Church, "than they would give unto the very words of God himself if He should speak with us out of heaven, according to the saying of Christ, 'Whose sins soever you do forgive, shall be forgiven, whose sins soever you retain, they are retained.' And again in another place Christ saith, 'Whosoever heareth you heareth me.'"[†]

From the article on the sacrament of the altar, we find Cranmer asserting the Corporeal presence of our Lord in that holy ordinance.

In speaking of the charge brought against him of Erastianism, we have already quoted from the exposition of the sacrament of orders. Cranmer clearly distinguished between the authority received by a bishop from Christ our Lord through the Apostolical succession, and the right to exercise that authority in any particular realm, which must be a concession of the state. The outward and visible sign in the sacrament of orders he describes to be prayer and the laying on of the bishop's hands; the grace conferred he affirms to be nothing else but the power, the office, the authority of the ministry.[‡]

The subject of the sacraments had been frequently discussed. Cranmer and the men of the new learning determined, as we have seen, that to baptism, penance, and the Lord's Supper the name of sacrament should be confined. We have seen, however, that in the convoca-

---

[*] Institution, 93.   [†] Ibid. 98.   [‡] Ibid. 105.

tion of 1536 angry disputes arose upon this question. In preparing The Institution there was a compromise: the archbishop and the bishops of his party were willing to concede the name, provided the opposite party would admit an explanation which would distinguish "baptism, penance, and the sacrament of the altar" from the other ordinances, the divine appointment of which they did not deny. The chapter, if it may so be called, on the sacraments concludes in these words:—

"Thus being declared the virtue and efficacy of all the seven sacraments, we think it convenient that all bishops and preachers shall instruct and teach the people committed to their spiritual charge; that although the sacraments of matrimony, of confirmation, of holy orders, and of extreme unction, have been of long time past received and approved by the common consent of the catholic Church, to have the name and dignity of sacraments, as indeed they be well worthy to have (forasmuch as they be holy and godly signs, whereby, and by the prayer of the minister, be not only signified and represented, but also given and conferred some certain and special gifts of the Holy Ghost, necessary for Christian men to have for one godly purpose or another; like as it hath been before declared); yet there is a difference in dignity and necessity between them and the other three sacraments, that is to say, the sacraments of baptism, of penance, and of the altar, and that for divers causes. First, because these three sacraments be instituted of Christ, to be as certain instruments or remedies necessary for our salvation, and the attaining of everlasting life. Second, because they be also commanded by Christ to be ministered and received in their outward visible signs. Thirdly, because they have annexed and conjoined unto their said visible signs such spiritual graces, as whereby our sins be remitted and forgiven, and we be perfectly renewed, regenerated, purified, justified, and made the very members of Christ's mystical body, so oft as we worthily and duly receive the same." *

* Institution, 128.

The Jewish sabbath is clearly distinguished from the Lord's Day. After an eloquent discourse on the spiritual rest, or the rest from sin which is enjoined upon all Christians, it is added that although to this spiritual rest all Christians are bound,

"Yet the Sabbath day which is called the Saturday, is not now prescribed and appointed thereto, as it was to the Jews; but instead of the Sabbath day succeedeth the Sunday, and many other holy and feastful days, which the Church hath ordained from time to time; which be called holydays, not because one day is more acceptable to God than another, or of itself is more holy than another, but because the Church hath ordained that upon those days we should give ourselves wholly without any impediment unto such holy works as be before expressed; whereas upon other days we do apply ourselves to bodily labour, and be thereby much letted from such holy and spiritual works." *

It is added :—

"That all they do break this commandment also, which in mass time do occupy their minds with other matters, and like unkind people remember not the passion and death of Christ, nor give thanks unto Him; which things in the mass time they ought specially to do; for the mass is ordained to be a perpetual memory of the same. And likewise do all those, which in such time as the common prayers be made, or the word of God is taught, not only themselves do give none attendance thereto, but also by walking, talking, and other evil demeanour, let other that would well use themselves. And likewise do all they which do not observe but despise such laudable ceremonies of the Church as set forth God's honour, or appertain to good order to be used in the Church." †

From this book and from the other we find that Cranmer did not advocate the great Lutheran doctrine of justifica-

---

* Institution, 144.   † Ibid. 146.

tion by faith only; faith was to be united with good works.*

In the exposition of the Ave Maria is seen the progress already made. The Ave Maria was declared not to be a prayer. It was merely appended by custom to the Pater noster as a hymn, laud and praise, partly of our Lord and Saviour Jesus Christ for our redemption, and partly of the blessed Virgin for her humble consent given and expressed to the angel at this salutation.

Cranmer believed, at this time, in purgatory and in the efficacy of prayers for the dead.

This formulary, signed as we have seen by the two archbishops and by all the suffragans in their respective provinces, was by them transmitted to the lower house of convocation, where it received the signatures of the clergy.†

Cranmer speaks of it as the production of a most learned council of archbishops, bishops, and other learned men of this kingdom consulting on affairs of religion.‡

Although it never received the formal authority of Henry, yet it was printed by the royal printer, to indicate that it had received the king's imprimatur; and the king sent a copy of it to King James V. of Scotland, in the hope thereby to induce him to make the like reformation in the realm of Scotland as was in process in England.§

---

* Institution, 209.

† Dr. Samuel Ward gives a list of the clergy in the lower house of convocation who signed, but it was incomplete. Collier, iv. 402, and Heylin, who consulted existing extracts from the convocation register, speaks of the book as authorised by convocation.

‡ Wilkins, iii. 827.

§ Heylin, i. 40. In the second volume of Cranmer's Remains, the reader will find two interesting papers: Henry VIII.'s corrections of the Institution, and Cranmer's annotations on the same. The corrections of the king are the remarks of a theologian and a scholar desirous of showing his ability and his learning. They are for the most part

The plague was raging in London, and the commissioners were, by the king's permission, dismissed from their labours. It was especially prevalent at Lambeth, where people were dying even at the very gates of the manor house, now the palace. The archbishop retired to Ford, not a little pleased at the work which he had accomplished, and which he had reason to hope would be final; and that it would preserve the peace of the Church.

CHAP. III.

Thomas Cranmer. 1533–56.

Well would it have been for the Church if all who desired its reformation had shown the same moderation as the Archbishop and Bishop Ridley; but there was already a body of violent men who aimed not at the reform but at the overthrow of the Church; and who desired to see in its place a protestant sect, though what protestantism was scarcely two persons were prepared to say. The violence, the irreverence, the blasphemies of the protestant party alarmed the government, and the government was the more alarmed because equally violent and intolerant and profane men were their opponents, who were generally denominated papists.

Heretic and papist were terms hurled about from one side to the other, until the disturbances which

verbal criticisms. In the article of orders he was evidently angry at the restrictions upon the royal authority, though he would not deny the correctness of the statements. Although Henry VIII. would tolerate no opposition to his will, when his passions were roused, yet he encouraged in his courtiers great freedom of speech. He loved to engage in an argument. Cranmer had no hesitation therefore to reply freely to his royal critic, and the scholarship, both of the king and of the primate, is seen to advantage. Henry's sole object appears, however, to have been to show how superior the work would have been if he had been on the commission; but this did not imply that he did not approve of the Formulary as a whole, which is proved by his sending it to the King of Scots. On the other hand, Cranmer was not pledged to every statement, as no one is who may append his signature to a document in which there is nothing of which he disapproves, though he thinks some things might have been done better.

threatened the peace of society were, to all appearance, likely to terminate in a civil war.*

The king had lost all confidence in Crumwell, who, having served his master by doing his dirty work, was, like a filthy instrument no longer serviceable, cast aside; and Henry took the reins of government into his own hands, being for the rest of his reign his own minister. To create uniformity, as he called it, he caused the statute of the six articles to be carried through the two houses of parliament in the year 1539.

Of this statute we have already spoken at some length, and we have shown its object to have been, not to give a triumph to any one party, but to keep both parties in check. The king, who was alone responsible for the policy, said in effect to the reformers, who had indulged in great excesses, "You have abused the liberty I gave you. We must retrace our steps; we must go back to the place from which we started, and proceed more wisely in our reforms." The reformation proceeded steadily, though slowly, during the last eight years of Henry's reign; and if we may judge from facts and not from party statements and surmises, Henry never ceased to be a reformer; a protestant he never was, a reformer he continued to the last. He was much too wise a man to suppose that he could discard the papal supremacy and let things remain as they were before. We have the archbishop's own authority for saying that although, for political reasons, he acted cautiously, the king was to the last determined upon carrying out the reformation further. In conversation with his secretary, Morice, after Henry's death, he said:

"I am sure you were at Hampton Court when the French king's ambassador was entertained there at those solemn ban-

* See A Proclamation for Uniformitye in Religion. Brit. Mus. Cleop. E.V. 303. "Oon parte of them calling the other papist, the other parte called the other heretic."

quetting houses, not long before the king's death; namely, when after the banquet was done the first night, the king, leaning upon the ambassador and upon me; if I should tell what communication between the king's highness and the said ambassador was had, concerning the establishing of sincere religion then, a man would hardly have believed it. Nor had I myself thought the king's highness had been so forward in those matters as then appeared. I may tell you it passed the pulling down of roods, and suppressing the ringing of bells. I take it, that few in England would have believed that the king's majesty and the French king had been at this point, not only within half a year after to have changed the mass into a communion (as we now use it) but also utterly to have extirpated and banished the Bishop of Rome and his usurped power out of both their realms and dominions.

"Yea, they were so thoroughly and firmly resolved in that behalf, that they meant also to exhort the Emperor to do the like in Flanders and other his countries and seignories, or else they would break off from him. And herein the king's highness willed me (said the Archbishop) to pen a form thereof to be sent to the French king to consider of." *

On the 24th of February, the bishops on the motion of the primate directed, that no candles should burn in the front of images, and that the candelabra should be removed. They likewise, at his suggestion, took measures for the reformation of all portuases,† missals and other books, and for the erasure of the names of all popes, and of Thomas à Becket. Directions were at the same time given for the instruction of the people in the Lord's Prayer, the Apostles' Creed, and the Ten Command-

* Remains, i. 321. Although the authority referred to by Dr. Jenkyns for this anecdote is Foxe, yet Foxe stated that he had it from Morice himself. I do not find it in Morice's Anecdotes in the C.C.C.C. Library, but I think that there is intrinsic evidence of its authenticity.

† A word formed from portiforium, a manual, the name given to the breviary.

ments, which they were required to repeat in the vulgar tongue.

Attention was called by the lower house, through the prolocutor Archdeacon Gwent, to the profanation of God's name, and to the infamous profanity of the stage where plays were acted of a character perfectly blasphemous. The archbishop replied, that he and the other bishops would bring the matter under the notice of the king, and consult with his majesty on the subject. It is presumed, that in making the complaint the lower house named certain persons, such as Crumwell, who had encouraged these blasphemies and profanations, for the archbishop enjoined the lower house not to repeat out of doors what the two houses had, in convocation, freely discussed.

In the next session, which took place on the 3rd of March, the first step was taken in favour of that liturgical reform which ended in the formation of the Book of Common Prayer. The expediency was discussed of providing one formulary of public devotion for the whole province. The bishops decided, that the Use of Sarum should be adopted in all their churches. They were perhaps the more ready to do this, as an edition of the Use of Sarum had been lately published from which the name of the pope had been expunged, as being contrary to the last statute.* As the clergy were frequently getting into difficulties by omitting to make the necessary erasures, one would have supposed that they would have availed themselves of a book which was in print and published under the royal sanction. But either some of the bishops

* Portiforium secundum usum Sarum noviter impressum, et a plurimis purgatum mendis. In quo nomen Romano Pontifici falso adscriptum omittitur, una cum aliis quæ Christianissimo nostri Regis statuto repugnant. Excusum Londini per Edvardum Whytchurch, 1541. Cum privilegio ad imprimendum solum. Bibliothec. Cott. Cleop. E. v. 259; apud Coll. v. 106.

did not issue their injunctions, or some of the clergy neglected to obey, for in the convocation which met in February 1543, N.S., the archbishop brought down a message from the king, in which it was stated to be his majesty's will that all mass books, antiphoners, portuases in the Church of England should be newly examined, corrected, reformed, and "castigated from all manner of mention of the Bishop of Rome's name; from all apocryphas, feigned legends, superstitious orations, collects, versicles, and responses; that the names and memories of all saints, which be not mentioned in the Scripture or authentical doctors, should be abolished and put out of the same books and kalendars; that the services should be made out of the Scriptures, and authentic doctors; for the eschewing of inconveniences, which daily chance to his subjects of the clergy for their negligence in not abolishing such things and names, as by his majesty's injunctions and proclamations have been commanded to be stricken out, cancelled and abolished." *

It was not considered expedient to force the observance of the Use of Sarum in every instance, and therefore in pursuance of the royal mandate it was determined by the upper house, that the service books should be submitted for revision to the Bishop of Ely (Dr. Goodrich), and the Bishop of Salisbury, together with a committee to consist of six members of the lower house. The lower house waived the privilege of furnishing this committee, and the whole affair was left in the hands of the bishops. They seem to have submitted their proposals to the entire convocation, for, during the two succeeding sessions, the business of reforming the prayer books of the Church of

* Wilkins, iii. 863. Convocatio prælatorum et cleri provinciæ Cant. ad 29 diem Martii continuata. Ex reg. convoc. et Excerpt. Heylin. et reg. Cranmer, fol. 9, 9b, 10a.

England was under discussion, and the way was thus prepared for the great event of the reign of Edward VI. So important was this work esteemed, that the archbishop brought a message from the king to the effect, that during the discussion on the reformation of the missals, no one should absent himself without leave under the penalty of the royal displeasure.

During the sessions of this convocation certain homilies composed by some of the prelates* were introduced with the view of enabling those of the clergy who had not ability to preach, nevertheless to instruct their people. What became of these homilies, or whether they were the composition of Cranmer, we know not. An order, however, was made with the view of instructing the people " that every Sunday and holiday throughout the year, the curate of every parish church, after the Te Deum and Magnificat, should openly read unto the people one chapter of the New Testament in English, without exposition, and when the New Testament was read over, then to begin the Old." †

This important convocation,—in which the archbishop carried so many essential points,—when voting a subsidy to his majesty appended to the instrument which conveyed the grant the following four requests, as articles of the clergy to be presented to the king: 1. That the ecclesiastical law should be reformed; 2. That some improprieties with reference to the solemnisation of marriage in Bethlehem hospital, Bishopsgate, should be amended; 3. That an act of parliament should be made for the

---

* It is presumed that these homilies were corrected and amended by Cranmer, and in the reign of Edward VI. they were published. The homilies then published still form our first book of homilies now nearly obsolete.

† Wilkins, iii. 863.

consolidation of poor benefices; 4. That provisions for just payment of tithes should be enacted by parliament."*

During the whole of this period, Cranmer was engaged in the revision of the Institution, or the Bishops' Book, and in preparing the Necessary Erudition, or the King's Book. This work was commenced in 1540, but not completed till 1543. In the year first mentioned, the king appointed two commissions, one to draw up "an exposition of those things which were necessary for the institution of a Christian man," and the other to examine "what ceremonies should be retained, and what was the true use of them." The primate was of course the chairman, and the commissioners fairly represented the two great parties of the old learning and the new.

What occasioned a delay so long in the production of this work it is difficult to surmise, unless it be that the minds of the commissioners were perplexed by the discussion of such subjects as faith, justification, and the merit of good works, subjects lately brought upon the *tapis*. Of these it is said by the king in his preface: "Forasmuch as the heads and senses of our people have been embusied, and in these days travailed with the understanding of free will, justification, good works, and praying for the souls departed; we have, by the advice of our clergy, for the purgation of erroneous doctrine, declared and set forth openly, plainly, and without ambiguity of speech, the mere and certain truth in them." †

The formulary thus drawn up is valuable to us as indicating the progress of Cranmer's mind in 1543. There may have been certain parts of the formulary which, if he had been alone concerned in drawing it up, he might have expressed differently; but we have here what he

* Wilkins, iii. 863.   † Formularies of Faith, 217.

thought sufficient for the teaching of the Church.* The authority of the Church itself in articles of faith, though subordinate to that of the Scriptures, he still maintained. "All those things," it is said, "which were taught by the Apostles, and have been by a whole universal consent of the Church of Christ ever sith that time taught continually, and taken always for true, ought to be received, accepted, and kept, as a perfect doctrine apostolic."†

The formulary vindicated to the Church of England the title of the Catholic Church in England, saying with reference to the Church of Rome, that the Roman Church,

"being but a several church, challenging that name of catholic above all other, doeth great wrong to all other churches, and doeth only by force and maintenance support an unjust usurpation, for that church hath no more right to that name than the church of France, Spain, England, or Portugal, which be justly called catholic churches, in that they do profess, consent, and agree in one unity of true faith with other catholic churches. This usurpation before rehearsed, well considered, it may appear that the Bishop of Rome doeth contrary to God's law in challenging superiority and preeminence by a cloke of God's law over all." ‡

We have already had occasion to refer to the assertion, in this document, of the fact of an Apostolical succession in the Christian Church. We revert to the subject because it has been thought by persons not versed in ecclesiastical history, that this historical fact is a novel invention. That persons belonging to a denomination of Christians, the

---

* He gave to the Erudition his support in Convocation; he upheld it in his diocese; in a draft of a letter for the king, in 1546, he made Henry to refer to it as "his, the archbishop's own book." He certainly says of the Institution, that he had acquiesced in things which "he never well understood," but that he did so because there was "no evil doctrine therein contained."—See Jenkyns' Pref. to Remains, xxxix.

† Formularies of Faith, 221.

‡ Ibid. 278.

ministers of which cannot prove their succession, should regard the fact as of no importance, is perfectly intelligible; but to account for the reason why it should excite the ire of persons who belong to a church by whom the advantage is possessed, when the fact is asserted, would be perplexing, if we had not experience that party-feeling is the result not of reason but of passion.

In treating of the sacrament of baptism he enunciates with equal lucidity the doctrine of baptismal regeneration. It will not be necessary to enter further into detail, as the work only professed to be a revised edition of the Institution, rendering the ambiguous expressions in that formulary conformable to the six articles passed by act of parliament. The assertion of transubstantiation in this account is rendered more explicit, and transubstantiation was still a doctrine for denying which Cranmer was prepared to send an unbeliever to the flames. The Erudition was superior to the Institution, from its greater conciseness and perspicuity of expression. The practice of praying to the saints was cleared of much superstition; justification is explained carefully, but still there is a shrinking from the Lutheran assertion that we are justified by faith only. The ability shown in handling the articles on faith, freewill, and good works, is very great; and we may say of both these formularies, the Institution and the Erudition, that whether we agree with the doctrinal statements or not, they are in point of style very wonderful productions considering the age in which they were composed; and indeed, without this consideration we may add that, even in the nineteenth century, they would be treated as remarkable works.

An attempt has been made to claim the authorship for the Bishop of Winchester, Dr. Gardyner. But we possess an acknowledged work of Gardyner's, and judging from this, we may at once deny that the claim can be established. In point of doctrine and argument the Erudition differs little from the Institution; it is superior to the Institution in point of style, and the style of Gardyner, in a later production is as bad as confused sentences and incorrect collocation of words can make it. Cranmer's style was his strong point, and perhaps we shall not be far wrong, if we conclude that the work was revised by him, assisted by the Bishop of Rochester, Dr. Heath, a man admitted to be both a scholar and a divine.

Bishop Gardyner probably laboured to retain whatever tended to further the views of the old learning party, and this may have been one of the causes for retarding the publication. Tradition has always given to Cranmer the articles on freewill, justification, and good works.

Great pains and care were, as we have seen, taken in a work which was expected to be for ever the doctrinal formulary of the Church of England. Three years were occupied in the composition of it, although it was little more than a revision of the Bishops' Book. Questions were submitted to certain sub-committees, and when the answers were returned, two persons were appointed to collate them. When the convocation met in 1543, first the exposition of the Lord's Prayer and the Ave Maria were submitted by the upper to the revision of the lower house. This was on the 20th of April. The next day the explanations of the first five commandments were handed by the archbishop to the prolocutor. On the 24th of April, the last five commandments and the sacraments of baptism and the Lord's Supper. And thus day by day, the examination continued until, on the 30th of April, a message through the prolocutor, was sent to the bishops, stating that the lower house accepted the articles sent down to them, as Catholic verities and religious truths; they returned sincere thanks to the bishops for the great labour, pain and trouble which they had undergone in the cause of religion and of the realm, and also for the sake of unity.

Thus did the book obtain that full and synodical authority to which the king in the preface refers. This work, published four years before the death of Henry VIII., gives us, so late as the year 1543, Cranmer's deliberate opinion of Church authority. The precision with which in a few words the doctrine of the Apostolical succession is asserted, has never been surpassed. It is stated that "order is a gift or grace of ministration in God's Church, given of God to Christian men, by the consecration and imposition of the bishop's hands upon them. . . . As the Apostles themselves, in the beginning of the Church, did order priests and bishops, so they appointed and willed the other bishops after them to do the like, as St. Paul manifestly showeth."* It then goes on to show that the power thus divinely given is to be exercised, subject to the laws of the realm.

This assertion in the authorised exposition of doctrine in this reign should be taken into consideration when, from chance expressions of Henry and of Cranmer, they appear to broach Erastian opinions.

The king at the same time was desirous of having this formulary published with the full sanction of the three estates of the realm in parliament assembled. The confidence in the bishops evinced by parliament is very remarkable. In 1540 the king notified to Parliament the appointment of the commission mentioned above. The parliament waited for their report, and when it was not presented, a vote was passed to the effect that "all decrees and ordinances which, according to God's Word and Christ's

* Formularies of Faith, 277, 278.

Gospel, by the king's advice and confirmation of his letters patent, shall be made and ordained by the archbishops, bishops, and doctors appointed or to be appointed in and upon the matter of Christian religion and Christian faith, and lawful rites, ceremonies and observations of the same, *shall be in every part thereof believed, obeyed, and performed, to all intents and purposes*, upon the grounds therein contained, provided that nothing shall be ordained and decided which shall be repugnant to the laws and statutes of the realm."*

This was the struggle in the reign of Henry. The nation represented by him might decide as to what the truth is; this was a step towards Protestantism, but what the nation as a nation might do in opposition to the pope, an individual, whether right or wrong, might not do in opposition to the king.

When the parliament met in 1543, an act was passed "for the advancement of true religion and the abolition of the contrary," in which it was declared expedient to ordain and establish a certain form of pure and sincere teaching, agreeable to God's Word and the true doctrine of the Catholic and Apostolic Church.

The necessary Erudition then received the acceptance of parliament, being represented as a document the more important at a time when controversies affecting "the Catholic and Apostolic Church of England" were prevalent; such controversies being urged as rendering it necessary to place some restrictions on the perusal of the English Bible.

When the book was published in the king's name, it was called the King's Book, to distinguish it from the Institution, which was known as the Bishops' Book.

The next step taken appears to have been suggested

* Statutes at large, II. 291.

by the king himself. In the year 1543, a plentiful crop had raised expectations of a good harvest, which were doomed to be disappointed. As the time of harvest approached, "a plague of rain" marred the prospects of the husbandman, and created an alarm lest a famine should ensue. The primate was required to issue his commands to his suffragans, enjoining them to supplicate the Divine mercy by appointing a prayer of procession and litany.

The order was obeyed, but the litany was sung in some places in Latin and in some places in English. It may be also conjectured that some of the enjoined alterations were not very strictly observed.

A litany in English was not an unusual thing. In the middle ages, the mass was always in the Latin language, but from time immemorial there had been translations in the vulgar tongue of the Lord's Prayer, the Creed, the Commandments, and also of the Litany.*

But there was no uniformity, and for uniformity Henry VIII. had a special vocation: he wished to see everything done by rule.

He issued a further order of council in 1544, requiring the archbishop "to take order incontinently that from henceforth, through his province, processions should be kept constantly on the accustomed days and none other, and be sung or said as the number of the quire shall serve for the same, in the *English tongue*, to the intent that there might be authority in every place."

The uniformity, so far, related to the fact that an

---

* The Litany might be said in church by a layman in some side chapel, with people kneeling round him. I have seen this done in foreign churches. At Lincoln Cathedral, some years ago, the Litany was always chanted by laymen till we came to the Lord's Prayer, when the priest is directed to take up the service. It is to be hoped that this right of the Laity handed down from primitive times has not been abolished in that Cathedral.

English instead of a Latin litany should be used; the selection of the one or of the other having been till this time, optional. But the English litanies, though each resembled the other, were not identical in expression, and there was some carelessness as to the erasures required by law. The archbishop was commanded, therefore, to translate a litany which might be published by authority. To no fitter hands could such a work have been consigned, and when it was completed the archbishop addressed the following letter to the king:—

"It may please your majesty to be advertised, that according to your Highness' commandment, sent unto me by your Grace's secretary Mr. Pagett, I have translated into the English tongue, so well as I could in so short time, certain processions to be used upon festival days, if after due correction and amendment of the same your Highness shall think it so convenient. In which translation, forasmuch as many of the processions in the Latin were but barren, as me seemed, and little fruitful, I was constrained to use more than the liberty of a translator; for in some processions I have altered divers words; in some I have added part; in some taken part away; some I have left out whole, either for by cause the matter appeared to me to be little to purpose, or by cause the days be not with us festival days; and some processions I have added whole, because I thought I had better matter for the purpose than was the procession in Latin; the judgment whereof I refer wholly unto your Majesty; and after your Highness hath corrected it, if your Grace command some devout and solemn note to be made thereunto (as is to the procession which your Majesty hath already set forth in English), I trust it will much excitate and stir the hearts of all men unto devotion and godliness: but in mine opinion, the song that shall be made thereunto would not be full of notes, but as near as may be, for every syllable a note; so that it may be sung distinctly and devoutly, as be in the matins and evensong, *Venite*, the hymns, *Te Deum, Benedictus, Magnificat, Nunc Dimittis*, and all the psalms and versicles; and in the mass

Gloria in Excelsis, Gloria Patri, the Creed, the Preface, the *Paternoster*, and some of the *Sanctus* and *Agnus*. As concerning the *Salve festa dies*, the Latin note, as I think, is sober and distinct enough; wherefore I have travailed to make the verses in English, and have put the Latin note unto the same. Nevertheless they that be cunning in singing can make a much more solemn note thereto. I made them only for a proof, to see how English would do in song. But by cause mine English verses lack the grace and facility that I could wish they had, your Majesty may cause some other to make them again, that can do the same in more pleasant English and phrase. As for the sentence I suppose will serve well enough. Thus Almighty God preserve your Majesty in long and prosperous health and felicity. From Bekisbourne, the 7th of October.*

" Your Grace's most bounden chaplain
　　　　and beadsman,
　　　　　　" T. Cantuarien.
" To the King's most excellent Majesty."

This authorised Litany † was published in the year 1544 under the following title: "An exhortation unto prayer thought meet by the king's majesty and his clergy ‡ to read to the people in every church after processions. Also a Litany, with suffrages to be said or sung in time of the said processions."

The reader who would see the great superiority of Cranmer as a master of the English language, may compare this translation with that which occurs in a Primer published by Bishop Hilsey in the year 1535. We have not space to insert the long list of saints, occupying three or four pages in the original Litany of the

---

* Remains, i. 315.

† State Papers, 1. Letter cxcvi. The date 1543 is given, and I think correctly, as it appears that Cranmer advised the convocation on that subject during the first session of this year.

‡ It therefore had the sanction of convocation.

Use of Sarum, who are invoked to pray for us; but we may remark, that Cranmer reduced the three or four pages to three sentences. Cranmer, in the year 1545, taught the people to ask the prayers of the Virgin Mary, and to call upon angels and archangels, patriarchs and apostles, martyrs, confessors, and virgins to pray for us. But with the omission of these passages and the deprecation of the Bishop of Rome and all his detestable enormities, among which Cranmer did not reckon prayer to saints departed, the Litany we use in the nineteenth century is the translation made from an old Latin Litany of our Church in the sixteenth, and is a lasting testimony to the great ability of Cranmer, at a period when the syntax and rhythm of our language were not yet settled.

So acceptable was this translation of the Litany to the Church, that it was determined to publish a Primer, to be drawn up on the same principle; that of making the devotions of the people as much as possible conformable to the received doctrine of the Church.

The title of Primer had been given in the Church of England, from the fourteenth century downwards, to certain forms of devotion translated for private use. The earliest form of these translations may, perhaps, be traced to times antecedent to the Conquest, when the Creed, the Lord's Prayer, and the Ten Commandments were taught the people in the vulgar tongue. To these were added gradually, other offices of devotion, until, in the fourteenth century, the collection obtained a certain amount of uniformity, though admitting of alterations to meet the peculiarities of different dioceses. It was published sometimes in English, sometimes in Latin, sometimes in English and Latin. One of its objects was to provide the people with a translation of those portions of Divine worship with which they were more directly concerned.

But as different dioceses had different Primers—though in principle one yet varying in detail—Henry's love of uniformity determined him to have one Primer for the whole Church of England.*

The Primer, when completed, was submitted to the two houses of Convocation, and it was under the title of "The Primer set forth by the king's Majesty and his clergy, to be taught, learned, and read, and none other to be used throughout his dominions."

If to the king we give the merit of suggesting this work, the credit of its compilation and of the translations belongs to Cranmer. If the reader will take the trouble of comparing this, which is generally called Henry VIII.'s Primer, with the Salisbury Primer, he will, after making all allowances for the improved state of our language during the interval, be deeply impressed with the archbishop's superiority as a writer. There is a strain of piety running throughout the work from which we may infer that there were many holy and humble men of heart who in those troublous times were worshipping God in secret and who were seeking not to inflame their passions by the fierce polemical writings which abounded, but to worship their God in spirit as well as in truth. The table of contents does not describe the volume in

---

* Maskell's Monumenta Ritualia, and Burton's Three Primers. The notion prevails that the object now was, in opposition to the existing order of the church, to supply the people with English prayers. The object was simply to secure uniformity. Two books, sometimes called Primers, had been published in Henry's reign. Marshall's Primer in 1535, and Bishop Hilsey's in 1539, but these were not really Primers, they were manuals of devotion published by individuals without ecclesiastical authority. It was just as if a man in these days should publish a Prayer Book of his own, and call it the Book of Common Prayer For Hilsey's Manual, Crumwell's authority may be quoted, but probably it was for the very reason that the authority was insufficient that Cranmer had nothing to do with it.

its fulness. The Lord's Prayer, the Ave Maria, the Creed, and Ten Commandments are given. There are Prayers for Matins, Evensong and Compline. There are the seven Psalms, the Litany as before published, the Dirige, the Commandments, the Psalms of the Passion, the Passion of our Lord, and some admirable prayers, including private prayers for morning and evening, and graces to be said at meal times.

The translation of the Missal and the Breviary, or the formation of a book of Common Prayer, would have been the natural consequence of these proceedings; and on Cranmer's own authority we can affirm that before Henry's death, it had been determined to revise the service books, to abolish several superstitious usages, and to digest a new code of ecclesiastical law. For the revision of the service books it would appear that a commission had absolutely been appointed and had nearly completed their work. For the abolition of certain superstitious ceremonies we find Cranmer writing thus sensibly to the king in January 1546:

"As concerning the ringing of bells upon Alhallow Day at night, and covering of images in Lent, and creeping to the cross, he thought it necessary that a letter of your Majesty's pleasure therein should be sent by your Grace unto the two archbishops; and we to send the same to all other prelates within your Grace's realm. And if it be your Majesty's pleasure so to do, I have, for more speed, herein drawn a minute of a letter which your Majesty may alter at your pleasure. Nevertheless, in my opinion, when such things be altered or taken away, there would be set forth some doctrine therewith, which should declare the cause of the abolishing or alteration, for to satisfy the conscience of the people: for if the honouring of the cross, as creeping and kneeling thereunto, be taken away, it shall seem to many that be ignorant, that the honour of Christ is taken away, unless some good teaching be set forth withal to instruct them sufficiently therein: which if your Majesty command the Bishops of Worcester and Chichester with other your Grace's chaplains to make, the people shall obey your Majesty's commandment willingly, giving thanks to your Majesty that they know the truth; which else they would obey with murmuration and grutching. And it shall be a satisfaction unto all other nations, when they shall see your Majesty do nothing but by the authority of God's word, and to the setting forth of God's honour, and not diminishing thereof."*

Justice is not done by modern writers to the wise and judicious policy of Henry VIII., and the orderly manner in which the Reformation was conducted in his reign. Of course, if men choose to assume that Cranmer and Henry were Protestants, who ought to have risked everything to establish Protestantism, there is an end of the matter. They were, in reality, firm and consistent Catholics, who saw that the Church required reform, but in what particulars they had no previous conception. Preconceived theories they neither of them had. When they saw what was wrong they sought to amend it; when they discovered what was right they endeavoured to establish it. But their minds were only gradually enlightened. Of Cranmer's opinion on transubstantiation, we have spoken. In 1546 he had not yet given up the dogma; and, in all matters of doctrine, the king's mind was sure to travel slower than that of the theologian. Sometimes, urged on by his avarice or his other passions, the king would bring the country to the brink of a revolution; but when he could act on his own sound judgment, he encouraged Cranmer to advance in his opinions, while he himself acted as the drag to prevent his advanced opinions from endangering the gradual progress of the Reformation. At the end of Henry's reign, the archbishop might look back with some satisfaction to his past career as an

* Remains, i. 318.

ecclesiastic. The papal supremacy had been abolished; the translation of the Bible had been authorised, and if the reading of it had been restricted to educated persons, this was only a temporary measure; various superstitions had been abolished; a formulary of doctrine had been established, not exactly in accordance with what we should now account orthodox, but certainly in advance of the age; the manuals of private devotion had been reformed; the reform of the public services, as well as of the canons of the Church, was designed: and all this had been done at a time when it required a strong hand to preserve the peace of the country, and to prevent, on the one hand, reform from becoming revolution, and, on the other hand, conservatism from being reactionary. Although the despotic temper of Henry led sometimes to an exertion of the prerogative repugnant to modern notions, and into expressions, uttered in the haughtiness of an irritated mind which sometimes belied his principles; yet, in his deliberate actions, he observed the forms of law in regard to affairs both temporal and spiritual; so that an historian, more attached to the Regale than the Pontificale, is fully borne out in his remark:—

"Upon serious consideration, it will appear that there was nothing done in the reformation of religion, save what was acted by the clergy in their convocations, or grounded upon some act of theirs precedent to it, with the advice, counsel, and consent of the bishops and most eminent churchmen, confirmed upon the post-fact, and not otherwise, by the civil sanction according to the usage of the best and happiest times of Christianity."*

One of the first measures adopted by the archbishop,

---

* Fuller, v. 188. Mr. Joyce, in his able and learned History of Sacred Synods, brings proof for the confirmation of this assertion in every particular.

when Edward VI. ascended the throne, was to produce a book of Homilies which had been long in hand.

Although from the proceedings of convocation we see that, among the clergy, there were men of worth and learning, yet the abolition of chantries and private masses had a tendency to place in a wrong position many who had been willing to explain and enforce the "new learning," but who had not sufficient education or ability to fulfil the task. They had sought admission into holy orders to earn a scanty livelihood by performing the routine duties which private masses implied. Unless they had received benefices from the king and the archbishop they would have starved; and now that,—as regarded their temporal requirements,—they had been provided for, it was necessary to supply them with spiritual food.*

So early as the year 1540, an attempt had been made to meet the demand from this quarter, through the publication, by royal allowance, of "Postills or Homilies upon the Epistles and Gospels," with certain " sermons drawn forth by dyverse learned men for the instruction of all good Christian persons, and in especial of priests and curates." The subject had also been discussed in the convocation of 1542, when it was determined " to stay such errors as were then by ignorant preachers sparkled among the people." For some reason or other, perhaps owing to the publication of the "Necessary Erudition,"

---

* When the mass was turned into a communion, the fate of the chantries was settled. The chantries were established for priests to say mass for the dead, and to offer the sacrifice for sin, for the dead as well as for the living. When the Eucharist was declared to be not such a sacrifice as this, but a sacrament, a means of conveying Christ to living souls, and of thus inspiring them to offer themselves, their souls, and bodies a living sacrifice to God, chantries were not needed. As means of propagating false doctrines they were denounced: they were abolished, and the courtiers scrambled for the spoils.

which may have been regarded as sufficient for the purpose, the Homilies did not appear till 1547.

The Archbishop of Canterbury had solicited the assistance of his suffragans: to what extent he succeeded is not known. We happen to know, indeed, that the sermon, "Of the Misery of Mankind," proceeded from the pen of Bishop Bonner, so unhappily distinguished in the persecutions of Queen Mary's reign. It forms one of the Book of Homilies which has a quasi authority in the Church, as in the thirty-fifth of the Thirty-nine Articles it is declared "that they contain a godly and wholesome doctrine necessary for these times."* But the chief management of the publication rested with the archbishop, and we may

---

* It is found almost verbally with the same title among the Homilies put forth by Bishop Bonner in Queen Mary's reign. We hear this homily sometimes quoted by persons whom Bonner would have burnt, and who would themselves have burnt Bonner. The Homilies are not read now, but the principle of reading homilies is recommended by the Spectator, when he advises the younger clergy to read printed sermons from the pulpit. This is not advisable when there is ability to deliver extempore or to write a sermon. But as the object of preaching is to do good, it may be recommended when a pastor finds a sermon written by another calculated to explain a truth better than he could do it himself. When we look at the House of Commons, and see, out of five hundred, how many, as a blessing to the country, are "dumb dogs;" when we read the foolish speeches which are made, which would be unreadable unless they were "cooked" for publication by the reporter; when even, of public men who are obliged to speak, the number is small who are really eloquent, we ought not to expect that among eighteen thousand clergy every one should have the ability to compose and deliver more than a hundred original sermons in a year. It is remarkable rather that on the average so many good sermons are delivered. When printed sermons are used by a preacher, he is reading a homily, the difference between the practice of the sixteenth and nineteenth century being, that the choice of the homily is left to the preacher. One of the most eloquent assailants of preaching in a liberal journal, when called upon to address a public meeting, failed so miserably, that he told the writer "he should as an honest man cease to ridicule the clergy."

safely infer from them that during the intervening four years his mind had advanced. The Homilies, which, if we accept a tradition, supported by some external evidence, were composed by Archbishop Cranmer, are the Homilies, "Of the Salvation of Mankind," "A Short Declaration of the True and Lively Christian Faith," "Of Good Works Annexed unto Faith," three out of twelve. Some persons attribute also to the archbishop "The Exhortation to the Reading and Knowledge of the Holy Scripture."

The publication is historically valuable, for it shows that the archbishop's attention was directed to repress Protestant error, as well as to reform his Church from papistical superstitions. The excesses of the Anabaptists are quite sufficient to account for a precaution taken by Henry on the conservative side, without supposing that he or Cranmer had relaxed in their determination to effect a complete reform of the Church. Against the prevailing antinomianism of the age the Homilies are a continual protest. This was one of the great evils against which, quite as much as against those who, in their dread of Antinomianism, had fallen back upon the papistical superstitions, the archbishop and his friends had to take precautions at the commencement of King Edward's reign. Hooper, himself a narrow-minded man and vehement in asserting what he regarded as Protestantism, was against this phase of Protestantism equally violent. Writing to Bullinger, he says:—

"The Anabaptists flock to this place, and give me much trouble with their opinions respecting the incarnation of the Lord; for they deny altogether that Christ was born of the Virgin Mary according to the flesh. They contend that a man who is reconciled to God is without sin, and free from all stain of concupiscence, and that nothing of the old Adam remains in his nature; and a man, they say, who is thus regenerate cannot sin. They add, that all hope of pardon is taken away from those who, after having received the Holy Ghost, fall into sin. They maintain a fatal necessity, and that beyond and besides that will of His which He has revealed to us in the Scriptures, God hath another will by which He altogether acts under some kind of necessity. Although I am unable to satisfy their obstinacy, yet the Lord by His word shuts their mouths, and their heresies are more and more detested by the people. How dangerously our England is afflicted by heresies of this kind, God only knows, I am unable indeed from sorrow of heart to express to your piety. There are some who deny that man is endued with a soul different from that of a beast, and subject to decay. Alas! not only are those heresies reviving among us which were formerly dead and buried, but new ones are springing up every day. There are such libertines and wretches who are daring enough in their conventicles not only to deny that Christ is the Messiah and Saviour of the world, but also to call that blessed seed a mischievous fellow and deceiver of the world. On the other hand, a great portion of the kingdom so adheres to the popish faction, as altogether to set at nought God and the lawful authority of the magistrates; so that I am greatly afraid of a rebellion and civil discord. May the Lord restrain restless spirits, and destroy the counsels of Achitophel! Do you, my venerable father, commend our king and the council of the nation, together with our Church, to God in your prayers." *

Cranmer's opinion of the nature of the sacraments,† as here expressed, has more weight than his opinions generally

---

* Original Letters, xxxiii.

† In those days the controversy about the sacraments assumed a character of importance. By baptism, called in the Homilies "The Sacrament of Regeneration," the unbaptized were united to Christ; by the Lord's Supper the baptized were continued in union with Christ. These two ordinances, by the fact of their uniting us to Christ, differ in essence from all other ordinances. The other five may be means of grace, but not of *this* grace. The two, therefore, it was contended, should differ in name from all other rites. At a time when all sects exterior to the Church disconnect regeneration and renovation from baptism and the Supper of the Lord, the dispute about the number of the sacraments is a mere dispute about words.

have; for what he has here said, we still pronounce to be a wholesome doctrine. It is thus stated:—

"Although absolution hath the promise of forgiveness of sin, yet, by the express word of the New Testament, it hath not this promise annexed and tied to the visible sign, which is imposition of hands. For this visible sign, I mean laying on of hands, is not expressly commanded in the New Testament to be used in absolution, as the visible signs in baptism and the Lord's Supper are; and therefore absolution is no such sacrament as baptism and the communion are. And though the ordering of ministers hath his visible sign and promise, yet it lacks the promise of remission of sin, as all other sacraments besides do. Therefore neither it, nor any other sacrament else, be such sacraments as baptism and the communion are. But in a general acceptation, the name of a sacrament may be attributed to any thing, whereby an holy thing is signified. In which understanding of the word, the ancient writers have given this name, not only to the other five, commonly of late years taken and used for supplying the number of the seven sacraments; but also to divers and sundry other ceremonies, as to oil, washing of feet, and such like; not meaning thereby to repute them as sacraments, in the same signification that the two forenamed sacraments are. And therefore St. Augustine, weighing the true signification and exact meaning of the word, writing to Januarius, and also in the third book of Christian doctrine, affirmeth, that the sacraments of the Christians, as they are most excellent in signification, so are they most few in number; and in both places maketh mention expressly of two, the sacrament of baptism, and the Supper of the Lord. And although there are retained by the order of the Church of England, besides these two, certain other rites and ceremonies about the institution of ministers in the Church, matrimony, confirmation of children, by examining them of their knowledge in the articles of the faith, and joining thereto the prayers of the Church for them, and likewise for the visitation of the sick; yet no man ought to take these for sacraments, in such signification and meaning as the sacrament of baptism and the Lord's Supper are: but either for godly states of life, necessary in Christ's Church, and therefore worthy to be set forth by public action and solemnity, by the ministry of the Church; or else judged to be such ordinances as may make for the instruction, comfort, and edification of Christ's Church." *

In order that I might bring the theological opinions of Cranmer, their gradual formation and their ultimate settlement, before the reader, I have, in some measure, deviated from the historical order of events. The archbishop did not take an active part in political affairs, and, with his enlightened chaplain Ridley, he was busy in investigating the all-important subject of transubstantiation. Henry had given his sanction to a review, with reference ultimately to a revision of the breviary and the missal. As the most important, the missal was first to be considered. Was it a mass? Was it the sacrifice of our Lord for the quick and the dead? or was it merely a communion? The English reformers regarded it as the means of conveying Christ to the believer, so that, as food blending with his body becomes one with the man who eats, Christ, received by faith, may become one with the believer, and thus become the sustenance of his soul; to the end that the believer, being one with Christ, might offer himself, with all the sanctified in heaven and in earth, a sacrifice to God, an offering of holy persons ready to do God's will.

This was the bearing of the question as it put itself to Cranmer's practical mind. If you adhere to the mass, then must you adhere to transubstantiation; if the Eucharist is to be received, on the principles of the primitive Church, as a communion, and not as a mass in the mediæval sense of the word, the dispute about transubstantiation is a mere logomachy, against which Cranmer's mind revolted. He had begun to hesitate, but he had not

* Corrie, Homilies, 355.

decided. He still devoutly celebrated mass; and celebrating mass, he could not deny the dogma of transubstantiation.

In the January of 1546-7 the archbishop was pursuing his investigations and studies at his manor of Croydon. He consoled himself for the absence of his wife by learned discussions with Ridley, and by a moderate enjoyment of those field-sports in which, through life, he indulged. He had long been anxious about the state of the king's health; but he had no reason at this time for feeling more anxiety than usual. The king had a wife who, though her heart was given to another, attended to his wants, and bore with his caprices. Henry was only fifty-six years of age, and so he had, comparatively speaking, youth on his side; but self-indulgent in all things, he had lately given himself to the pleasures of the table; whole estates, conferred originally upon the fasting monks, were thrown with carelessness into the lap of cooks and confectioners who could by new inventions pamper his palsied appetite. He had become so unwieldy and corpulent that he could not move from one part of his room to another without assistance. As is often the case with sensualists, he indulged in a kind of maudlin sentimentality. But this emotional piety was no indication of a softened heart. Was that heart of stone ever converted into a heart of flesh? God knows. All *we* know is that his last conversation with Cranmer related to the execution of a heretic, whose heresy might have been pardoned, if, in the assertion of it, he had not reflected on the character of the king himself. There is something very awful in hearing that the last *act* of Henry VIII. was to sign the death-warrant of his long-tried minister, the Duke of Norfolk—the uncle of two of his murdered queens, and his own uncle-in-law—the great commander who had added to the glories of his reign and the security of his throne by the victory of Flodden Field. Norfolk was condemned to suffer on the 29th of January, and although he had been no friend to Cranmer, still the sympathies of the archbishop, the most forgiving of men, must have been excited at the approaching end of one whom he had been accustomed to meet day after day at the council board, and whose sentence was a sermon on that insecurity of life of which every counsellor of Henry must have been painfully aware.

It was a gloomy time: the reigning king was a capricious tyrant; the heir apparent was a boy. On the 28th of January, an unexpected summons came to the archbishop to attend upon the king, without loss of time, at Westminster. When he arrived, he found Henry speechless. Cranmer reminded the dying sinner, who had caused the death of many a better man, that even to the last there is hope to the penitent who seek salvation through a Saviour Almighty to save. Henry VIII. turned his glazed eye towards the only man in the wide world who felt for him as a friend; he squeezed the archbishop's hand, and died. The rich man died and was buried.

Every mark of respect was shown to the memory of the king, whose death was the more deeply felt from the anxiety occasioned by the fact that his son was a minor. Henry was buried at Windsor, and Cranmer sang the mass. When Francis I., King of France, followed his friend Henry VIII., another criminal before the throne of the King of kings, his obsequies were celebrated in England, and the mass was chanted by Cranmer. The archbishop, as the head of the council, ordered a dirge to be sung in all the churches of London, and himself, assisted by eight other bishops in their rich mitres and pontificals, sang a mass of requiem.*

* Ridley's Ridley, 210.

By the will of Henry, the Archbishop of Canterbury was placed at the head of the regency which was to govern the country during the minority of the young king. It was an advantage to the country that Cranmer, who was not endued with much administrative ability or political sagacity, was not a worldly or ambitious man. He readily acquiesced in the arrangement which conferred the title and power of Lord Protector on the Earl of Hertford—or, as we shall henceforth style him, the Duke of Somerset, such being his historical name. It might have been well for both Somerset and the country if there had been in the privy council nominated by Henry VIII. sufficient foresight and wisdom to limit the powers of one who, though constituted by themselves only a *primus inter pares*, was soon afterwards invested, by the child upon the throne and a careless parliament, with power almost despotic.*

By the archbishop support was given to the Lord Protector so long as he continued in office, with the understanding that, in legislating for the Church, the Protector should act under the advice of the Primate. By some writers Cranmer is accused of an ungenerous pusillanimity in deserting his friend the Protector when, after a few years' trial, he was driven from office. But it remains to be proved, that any personal friendship, at any time, existed between these two great men. I believe that I have consulted most of the private letters and public documents relating to the domestic affairs of our country at this time, and I do not recollect having seen anything to show that Somerset received from Cranmer anything more than that general support which was accorded to him by the other members of the council until the majority had determined on a change of ministry. At

* Tytler, 53: Burnet, ii. 98, Append.

the same time we are certain that, from several of the measures adopted by the Protector, Cranmer withheld his support, and to some he offered a decided opposition.

Although Cranmer had not always the courage to abide by his principles, yet his religion was a religion of principle, and not of mere emotion. The very opposite to this may be predicated of the Protector. Cranmer's faults were few, even if they were glaring; and among his minor faults we may complain of his want of imagination and his inability to comprehend how man arrives at the truth not by reason only, but by a balance of the several faculties of his nature brought to bear upon one particular point: his tendency was to rationalism rather than enthusiasm. Somerset was a creature of impulse. He sought to relieve the sufferings of the people by the adoption of measures which sometimes alarmed the conservative selfishness of the other members of the council, and we may give him credit for generous inclinations.* At the same time, when corrupt motives were imputed to him, as they will be by the base and selfish in all cases; or when he met with opposition where he had expected support; he showed himself impatient, arrogant, and quick-tempered. Cranmer, on the other hand, was one of the mildest and most placable of men. On grand occasions, Cranmer would appear with mitre and cope and in full pontifical display, the cross of Canterbury being carried before him; yet, in private life, his manners were simple and unostentatious. Somerset, on the other hand, affected a regal state, and, through a puerile assumption of dignity, excited the indignation of the ancient aristocracy, already envious of the honours which a man so lately ennobled heaped upon himself. He revelled in the spoils of the monasteries, and equalled Crumwell himself in his love of riches. If he was godly, he certainly found, in his

* Strype, Memorials, i. pt. i. 146.

own case, that godliness was gain. He had received from Henry VIII. the grant of three religious houses; and one of the first of his acts as Protector was to endow himself with five or six more. Among these were the splendid monastery of Sion near Brentford, and the Abbey of Glastonbury. The latter he had the bad taste and feeling to turn into a worsted manufactory. On the site of what still retains the name of Somerset House, he determined to build a palace; and his religion was so far removed from superstition, that to make way for his palace he destroyed the parish church of St. Mary-le-Strand; and when materials were wanted, orders were issued to blow up by gunpowder the foundations of the church of St. John of Jerusalem, that the stones which the late prior had employed in the restoration of the house of his God, might be more usefully applied to the edification of the palace of the king's uncle. Time, taste, and money the last prior of the knights of St. John had expended—we think not wasted; for though he was reduced to beggary for his superstition, there are some who think superstition not worse than sacrilege. None of the council equalled the Duke of Somerset, either in his rapacity or in his display; but as Fuller quaintly expresses it, "Courtiers keep what they catch, and catch what they can."

Extensive offices were required for the liveried servants whom, in defiance of the law, the duke, almost royal in his establishment, maintained. To create apartments for his menials, the town houses of three bishops were demolished, their chapels were desecrated, and pleasure-grounds were formed, reaching to St. Paul's churchyard, for this religious Sybarite, whose patronage of the Protestantism by which he was enriched, has secured for him the undeserved character of a saint.* He permitted

---

* Stow, 595. "This Somerset House is so tenacious of his name, that it would not change a duchy for a kingdom, when solemnly proclaimed

Thomas Cranmer. 1533–56.

his religious principles to carry him to extremes which would scarcely be, in modern times, approved. He refused to pray for the dead; and he did more, he denounced monuments erected to their honour; and he treated with scientific scorn the bodies of the departed. The charnel-house and chapel in St. Paul's Churchyard were destroyed, and the neighbouring fields were whitened by the bones of the dead, which, scattered over them, were utilised into manure. So active, we are told, was the "good duke's zeal" against the religion or superstition of monastic establishments, that he had consigned Westminster Abbey to destruction. He was diverted, we are informed, from his purpose by timely gifts of land; although it is difficult to understand how, so far as principle is concerned, by the gifts of land, so timely conceded, any alteration was made in the state of the case.

Cranmer was never a popular character. He had not the art of winning the applause of the masses, or of appealing to their feelings, although no one desired more sincerely to promote their real and permanent welfare. Among his private friends, however, and by all who came in contact with him, Cranmer was always beloved; and the longer he was known, the more endeared he was to his friends. Somerset, on the contrary, was the most popular character of the age. Wherever he went, the cheers of the populace awaited him. At the end of twenty years, it might be, that a man would find that he was not one whit more dear to the duke than he was at the first warm greeting he received; but still there was the kind look, and the right word expressed at the right time and to the

by King James Denmark House, from the King of Denmark's lodging therein, and his sister Queen Anne her repairing thereof. Surely it argueth that this duke was well beloved, because his name made such an indelible impression on this his house, whereof he was not full five years peaceably possessed."—Fuller, Ch. Hist. iv. 87.

right person. When he was not provoked to anger, he knew how to administer the flattery of which a concourse of persons are as susceptible in the mass, as is everyone individually of which that mighty mass is composed. Flattered by their cheers, such a one flatters them in their turn; and anecdotes are passed from mouth to mouth in proof that the flattery offered is deserved. But unflattered at the council table, Somerset was there continually giving offence. Forgetting that his nephew was his king, he treated the precocious youth as a boy, regarded him as a puppet in his own hands, subjected him to restraint, and made him feel, as Edward once expressed it, like a prisoner in his own palace. Cordially did the royal youth hate his uncle, and heartily glad he was to be emancipated from his control.*

Somerset's popularity was only with his own party; and as our chief authorities for this portion of English history were—until the publication of the State Papers—Protestant, he has received a character for excellence which he certainly does not deserve. From the facts before us we infer, that although the Reformation had many and eminent supporters in the midland counties, in the towns,

---

* The entries in his diary on what relates to the trial and death of Somerset, are sufficient to show that the character of young Edward was as stern as that of his father. The unprincipled Lord Seymour, the admiral, Edward's other uncle, tried to win the boy's favour by encouraging him to communicate with him clandestinely, and by inducing him to resent the Protector's discipline. The notes from the State Paper Office are printed in Tytler, i. 112. When the Protector was deposed, Cranmer, Paget, and Wingfield, writing to the council, say of the king: "The king's majesty, thanks be to the living God! is in good health and merry, and this day after breakfast came forth to Mr. Vice-chamberlain, and all the rest of the gentlemen, whom, I promise your lordships, he bade wellcome with a merry countenance and a loud voice, asking how your lordships did, when he should see you, and that you should be wellcome whensoever you come: the gentlemen kissed his highness' hands, every one much to their comfort."—Tytler, i. 242.

CHAP. III.

Thomas Cranmer. 1533-56.

and especially in the metropolis, the opposition was at the same time so strong, that when Somerset was disgraced, his partizans, though strong enough to raise a clamour, failed to excite an insurrection in his favour: in truth, a reaction, caused by his violent and unjust proceedings, had already commenced.

This reaction Cranmer evidently foresaw, dreaded, and desired, if possible, to avert. Therefore, proceeding in our reference to facts in order that we may show, in justice to Cranmer, that no cordiality of friendship existed between him and Somerset, and that even when acting together, they were not always carrying out the same principle, I will at once observe that the Duke of Somerset was, at the commencement of Edward's reign, far in advance of the archbishop. Both were decided antipapists. The duke was not merely a reformer such as Cranmer, but he was a Protestant; he was more than a Protestant, in the strict sense of the word. He was not of the Lutheran school, he was a Calvinist; hence the enthusiasm with which his history has been written. He was prepared to go all lengths with his party. The excesses of which many of his party were guilty ere Henry VIII. was wellnigh cold in his grave, had been so lightly repressed by him, that it might almost be said, and by his enemies it was said, that he encouraged them.

Cranmer appears at the beginning of the new reign in a new character. It is said that he had encouraged Henry to advance further in the direction of the reformed doctrines; and although I am not aware that any proof of this fact exists, it is highly probable. But in conversation with his private secretary, who urged him to proceed with the reformation, the archbishop said, as his secretary reports, "It was better to attempt such reformation in king Henry VIII.'s days, than at this time, the king being in his infancy. For if the king's father had set forth anything for the reformation of abuses, who was he that durst gainsay it? Marry, we are now in doubt how men will take the change and alteration of abuses in the Church."* The foreign reformers of the Calvinistic school complained of Cranmer, that he was lethargic and lukewarm, unwilling to carry out the Reformation to its full extent, even when the cards were in his hands; and one of the reasons assigned by the Duke of Northumberland in 1552, for desiring the preferment of John Knox, —or as his Grace writes, Mr. Knocks,—to the bishopric of Rochester was, that he would be "a whetstone to quicken and sharpen the Bishop of Canterbury, whereof he hath need."† A person who could thus speak in private could have no confidence in the government, and was not likely to offer any strong opposition to a change of ministry, when the time for such change had arrived.

To some of the measures adopted at the suggestion of the Protector a direct opposition was offered by the Primate. The parliament had granted to Henry VIII. what Henry condescended to accept as a mark of their confidence and as a proof of their sense of his moderation, a right to deal with the property devised, in times past, for the maintenance of colleges, free chapels, chantries, hospitals, fraternities, brotherhoods, and guilds,‡ and

---

* Remains, i. 321.   † Tytler, Orig. Letters, ii. 142.

‡ It may be convenient to mention that a chantry "was a little church, chapel, or particular altar in some cathedral, church, &c, endowed with lands or other revenues for maintenance of one or more priests daily to sing mass and perform divine service, for the use of the founders and such others as they appointed. Free chapels were independent on any church, and endowed for much the same purpose as the former. The obit was the anniversary of any person's death; and to observe such day with prayers, alms, and other oblations, was called the keeping of the obit. Anniversaries were the yearly returns of the day of the death of persons, which the religious regis-

all similar institutions, the funds of which were to be employed in procuring masses for the dead. The confiscated property was to be "converted to good and godly uses,"—the foundation of almshouses and grammar schools, the endowment of populous parishes ruined by the dissolution of the monasteries to which they had been formerly attached,—and the repairs of harbours, piers, embankments, and other public works. As Henry in his will directed masses to be offered for the repose of his soul, we may presume that he felt some compunction in thus robbing others of a privilege which he valued for himself. On the subject of purgatory we may also presume, that Cranmer's own mind was not made up. He did not hesitate to offer masses for the repose of Henry VIII. and of Francis I. In the first reformed Prayer Book of King Edward, prayers for the dead were commanded; and in the bishops' book of the last reign, disputes were forbidden about the pains suffered by those who died "under imperfect qualifications," though the name of purgatory is not once mentioned. Whether on these grounds or from want of confidence in the Protector, whose object was to enrich himself and to purchase partizans, or whether under the joint influence of doubt and distrust, Cranmer resolutely opposed the measure, when by the introduction into parliament of a bill for the dissolution of colleges and chantries Somerset sought to invest the council with the powers formerly conceded to Henry VIII. The preamble, intended by the Protector to win the support of the ultra-reformers who regarded him as their leader, went further than Cranmer was, on this head, prepared to go, in attributing "a great part of superstition

tered in their obitual or martyrology, and annually observed, in gratitude to their founders or benefactors. Guild signifies a fraternity or company, from the Saxon guildan, to pay, because everyone was to pay something towards the charge and support of the company."

and error in Christian religion" to the retention of masses for the dead; but it is certain that Cranmer saw through the unconscious hypocrisy of Somerset, who if he really felt, as he probably did, that the masses were superstitions which ought to be abolished, had no intention of applying the funds, when placed in his hands, to the objects specified in the bill. The Protector had to purchase the support or buy off the opposition of the ancient aristocracy, who viewed the advancement of the *novus homo* with no feelings of complacency; and he had to provide estates for those plebeians whom he designed to ennoble. His object was perceived in the House of Commons, and by the lower house the archbishop was supported. By the proposed act the clergy in the towns would have been impoverished, and the towns would therefore have had to support them; and though the bill proposed to meet this difficulty, it was felt that the difficulty would not be fairly met by the Protector. What Cranmer suggested was reasonable and politic. He would postpone the proposed measures until the king had come of age. Time would then be gained to discuss the doctrinal merits or demerits of the case, and the property, if confiscated, would be applied to the king's use. If power were given to the Protector and the Commissioners to sell or otherwise to alienate it, it would be sold to courtiers at a mere nominal charge, and it would afford a scramble, as was afterwards the case, to political reformers who, with the name of God on their lips, were possessed by the Demon of Avarice.*

The House of Lords was as quick-sighted to discern the purpose of the Protector as the House of Commons, but as the lords temporal were to divide the spoil, Somerset found no difficulty in carrying his measure.

* 1 Edw. vi. c. 14. Parl. Hist. iii. 223.

What Cranmer foresaw came to pass. The goods and lands were sold to the courtiers.*

Perhaps the funds thus passing into the hands of Somerset and his supporters averted a *direct* attack on the property of the Church as distinguished from that of the monasteries; although the Church was under Somerset's government plundered in various ways. The nomination to the higher preferments of the Church being in the hands of the Protector, he courted popularity by appointing reformers; but they were too frequently reformers who, like Somerset himself, made a gain of godliness. Men were nominated on the condition that as soon as they were in possession of the property they should either alienate the estates in favour of the nominees of the court, or let them on long leases, which amounted almost to a donation of the fee-simple. To such an extent was this dishonesty carried, that in Queen Elizabeth's reign leases for more than twenty-one years were made illegal.

The Protector did not always consult the Primate in his appointments, and consequently he sometimes involved him in difficulties. Among others we may cite the case of Hooper. Hooper, an extreme Calvinistic reformer, was certainly a generous, and was always regarded as a pious man. His opinions concurred with those of Somerset, and his appointment to an episcopal see, effected with difficulty by Somerset when he had ceased to be the

* Who forgot to pay or paid next to nothing; but who, as Hayward hints, were now pledged to the Reformation. But this was not all. Goods, chattels, plate, ornaments, and other movables being common goods of such colleges, free chapels, chantries, and stipendiary priests, were conveyed to the king, and in the king's name a rush was made upon all the movable property by hundreds who never accounted for the same to the King or the Protector, who were loud in their denunciation of all that was held sacred, and who in the name of God blasphemed.

Protector, was hailed with enthusiasm by the party which regarded Somerset as a saint. It is hardly to be supposed that, at a period when the object was to promote peace and harmony among the reformers, Cranmer would himself have selected a man so pertinacious in his opinions as to create a controversy on a subject so trivial as that of the sacerdotal vestments. As we happen to know that at this period Cranmer's caution was represented by many as lukewarmness, we can easily imagine the extreme party urging the Protector to nominate to the Episcopate a man who was more decidedly Protestant in his views than Cranmer ever became.

I have been led to connect some events, which took place at a later period of the reign of Edward, with the occurrences which marked its commencement, because the reader will remember that I am not writing a history of the Reformation, but the life of Cranmer, and I wish to show that although Cranmer and Somerset acted together and accorded in a desire to reform the Church, they were not associated by any congeniality of temper or character, or, to a certain extent, we may say even of principle. Such being the case, no blame attaches to Cranmer for sending in his adhesion to an opposite party in the council, when insurrections at home and disasters abroad, financial derangement and forebodings of a national bankruptcy, proved Somerset's inadequacy to conduct the affairs of the country.*

---

* I have not occasion to enter into an examination of the proceedings against Somerset; but I may say, that after a patient examination of all the documents which have come to light, I am inclined to acquit him of everything but incompetency to discharge the high duties in which he had been involved by his ambition. His first disgrace was merely a change of ministry. He was certainly dealt with leniently according to the customs of the age, when death frequently followed the deposition of a minister. The opposition had not taken Cranmer into their

At the coronation of Edward VI. the archbishop officiated. From the Saxon times to the reign of our present beloved queen, the Church of England has used at the unction and coronation of our sovereigns an office substantially the same. The primate is at liberty to make such alterations in details as circumstances from time to time may require; and Cranmer, with his usual distrust in his own judgment, consulted the Privy Council as to the changes which the youth of the king, only nine years of age, might render expedient. The ceremonial—followed, as it always was till the reign of William IV. by a banquet—was fatiguing to those who were in the vigour of their strength; and the question was whether to such fatigue the young king should be subjected. There were the precedents of Henry III. and Henry VI., who were

councils, but as soon as their intentions were made known to him, he cooperated with them. A timid counsellor he always was, but there is no reason to suppose that he did not now act upon his convictions. Certainly, as far as I can ascertain, he was not bound to the ex-minister by any ties of friendship. A man who like Somerset could sign his brother's death-warrant rather than sacrifice his ambition, was not a man likely to be trusted by his associates. There seems to be little doubt that the admiral deserved his fate, for he was a bold, bad man; but when his brother was his executioner, we suspect that the brother's heart was as tough as that of Henry VIII. Somerset's own death was brought about through measures the most iniquitous; but there can be little doubt that Warwick found him intriguing to be restored to power. This minister had treated Somerset leniently; he had permitted him to resume his seat at the council board, and then found that Somerset was manœuvring to supplant him. He determined to destroy him, and he resorted to the most iniquitous arts to accomplish his object. Still Somerset had provoked his fate. I am not aware that in this matter Cranmer was in any way mixed up, and therefore I pass it by. Some writers dwell on Somerset's personal piety. That is, of course, a point on which we can know nothing for certain, and the safest course is to believe its reality, when there is a profession of its existence; but a man may be fervent in devotion who in action is guilty of much which is culpable.

younger than Edward, and that of Richard II., who was not much older. This, however, was a period of change, and further alterations were suggested in the service. But I suspect that, after the publication of the programme— which is given in his "Records" by Burnet *ex libro concilii*—the council determined to adhere more closely than was at first designed to the ancient order. Certainly it is not correct to state, as Burnet does, that a new form was ordered to be drawn, unless mere omissions made it such. The account of the coronation which is printed by Strype from a MS. in the C. C. C. C. Library breaks off abruptly; but it does not follow that any of the ceremonies deemed essential to the service were omitted. It is certain that the king was anointed on his breast, on the soles of his feet, on his elbows, on the wrists of his hands, and on the crown of his head. A rich pall of red tinsel gold being held over his head by some knights of the Garter, the king "grovelled," as it is said, before the archbishop, and lying prostrate, was anointed on his back. There can be no reason for doubting that the usual investitures, such as are to the present time observed, took place. Seated on the chair of Edward the Confessor, the young king was crowned with three crowns. When the anointed head of the sovereign was decorated by the crown of England, each peer placed on his own head his coronet or cap of state. But, while remarking that all essentials were observed, we cannot justify Cranmer, even if he acted under the advice of the Privy Council, for an unwarrantable change in the ceremonial, which had more of significance at that period than it would have now. It had been the invariable rule for the king to take an oath to preserve the liberties of the Church and realm, especially those of the time of Edward the Confessor, before the people were asked whether they would consent to have him for their king; but, on the present occasion, not only did the address to the people precede the oath of the king, but in that address they were reminded that he held his crown by descent, and that it was their duty to submit to his rule.* Up to this period, although the crown of England was held to be hereditary, the people retained the power to reject the immediate heir, though, when once he was anointed, obedience and loyalty to him became an act of duty in all his subjects. There was no pretender to the throne at this time to be feared; but the evident intention was to meet the objection, sometimes urged, that obedience was not due to a king who was a minor. This difficulty it was attempted to meet by asserting that the king claimed the crown by descent; and that by right of inheritance he was in possession of all the prerogatives which that descent implied; nothing being added to his rights by the mere ceremony of the coronation. It is said that instead of a sermon, the archbishop delivered an address to the young king on the duties of his office. This *concio ad unum* was in accordance with the feelings of the age and with the sentiments of Cranmer in particular; but I more than doubt whether the speech attributed to Cranmer on this occasion is genuine. It partakes too much of the character of a later generation, and was evidently invented to give something like a Protestant tone to proceedings which, as adhering strictly to Catholic precedent, were peculiarly offensive to the Puritan mind.†

The very feeling which induced Cranmer and the Privy Council to keep out of view the popular origin of sove-

---

* Fœdera, vii. 158. Burnet, ii. Append. 63.

† It was first published in "Foxes and Firebrands," by Robert Wace, who professes to have found it among Archbishop Usher's papers. The MS. is nowhere to be discovered.

reignty, and assume the divine right of kings to rest upon hereditary claims, prompted them also to attend to all the minutiæ of the ancient ceremonial when the young king publicly assumed his office. The procession from the Tower to the Palace of Westminster was of the most magnificent description. None of the vestments of the clergy were set aside. The suffragans of Canterbury, all mitred and in rich copes, walked two and two, attended by their apparitors and chaplains, preceding Archbishop Cranmer, who walked alone. Over his scarlet rochet Cranmer wore an embroidered cope, the train of which was borne by gentlemen of his household; the mitre upon his head was resplendent with jewels; before him was borne erect his crosier, the cross of Canterbury. At the abbey door they were met by the clergy of the abbey, with the members and children of their choir and those of the chapel royal, then as now arrayed in scarlet tunics beneath their surplices or albs. When the homage was done, Archbishop Cranmer himself sang the mass of the Holy Ghost, the choir accompanying him, and the "organs playing." At the elevation of the host, Archbishop Cranmer paused, and the Lord Chancellor read a general pardon granted by King Henry VIII. to all who had offended before the 28th of January.

After the king had received the Holy Sacrament he again "grovelled" before the archbishop, and Cranmer intoned the Veni Creator and signed the king with the sign of the cross.

I have mentioned these circumstances to impress it still further on the reader's mind that although at the accession of Edward VI. Cranmer was a reformer, yet he was not even yet a Protestant. Although he was now enquiring into, and although he did soon after renounce, the dogma of transubstantiation, he certainly held it at this period. No one has ever accused Cranmer of hypocrisy; he acted honestly on his convictions. If indeed he had held the opinions of the Sacramentarians, he would have been supported by the Protector, and it is not improbable that a majority of the council would have permitted the coronation to have proceeded with the omission of the mass.

The legislation of the Protector, at the commencement of his political career, was generous, liberal, and such as must commend itself to the sympathy of the nineteenth century. The repeal of the statute of the six articles was a matter of course. It had done its work, and the result was favourable to Protestantism. It had, in the hands of Henry, restrained those excesses on the part of Protestants which were exasperating the country against them; it had fired the indignation of the Protestants themselves, who complained, though in murmurs, of the hardships to which they were exposed; it excited the sympathy of many who, first influenced by sympathy, became afterwards partizans; and there was no one prepared to entrust to the Protector the powers it conferred. If, indeed, they had been conferred upon him, *he* would have been the first to repudiate them. The acts of Henry IV. and Henry V. against Lollards were repealed; although heresy, whatever it was, remained by the common law of the land an offence to be punished by burning. The authority of parliament was re-established by the repeal of certain tyrannical acts passed in the late and the penultimate reign. The severity of Henry's vagrancy law was mitigated. When we compare the legislation and the acts of the government in Edward's reign with those of Queen Mary, we cannot fail to admire the mildness and leniency, comparatively speaking, of both Somerset and Cranmer. The more credit is due to them because for their lenity they were despised by their enemies and censured by their friends. Calvin, in writing to the Protector, advises that not only those who adhere to "the superstition of the Antichrist of Rome," but those also who "under colour of the Gospel would set all in confusion," should be punished by the sword. In the attack made by Warwick and his party upon the Protector, the miserable condition of the country was attributed to the encouragement they received from the well-known sympathy of Somerset with the lower orders.

At the same time we must admit, that, although Cranmer and Somerset were both of them merciful in their administration, they were nevertheless sufficiently despotic. Although the statute of Henry VIII. which gave to royal proclamations the force of parliamentary enactments was repealed, it was not repealed until Cranmer obtained, through its instrumentality, a power over his suffragans and the Church in general, which was almost papal and would have been intolerable if it had continued.

The first thing that Cranmer did, was to take out a licence from the king for the discharge of his duties as metropolitan, and to require all his suffragans to do the same. He had taken out a licence under Henry VIII., and they who had succumbed, as Gardyner and Bonner had done, to the royal supremacy, could not consistently oppose the measure.* Cranmer's policy is obvious. Being at the head of the regency, and knowing that the Protector was prepared to go all lengths in the direction of the Reformation, the royal authority would be wielded by him. The king or his representative who gave the licence could withdraw it, and every bishop was thus

* Of this inconsistency Gardyner was guilty in a letter to Paget; but we must remember that it was a private letter, nullified soon after by the fact that Gardyner appealed from his metropolitan to the council.

virtually placed under Cranmer's control, as some of them were soon after made to feel.

It is absurd to suppose, that this application for a licence was a denial of the Apostolical succession. It was indeed about this very time that Cranmer became convinced, as we gather from his Catechism, that the Apostolical succession was necessary to constitute a minister or ambassador of the King of kings. The licence merely related to certain rights of jurisdiction. A lord chancellor, as we have before remarked, becomes a barrister by one process and an officer of the crown by another. When the sovereign consigns to him the custody of the great seal, this act does not constitute him a barrister; *that* he was before, and unless he had been a barrister previously, according to modern custom, the great seal could not be confided to his custody. Before a man can exercise his functions as a clergyman he must be ordained; before he can act as a bishop he must be consecrated: the ordained man receives his living from the layman to whom the advowson pertains; to the bishop a particular see is assigned through an election overruled by the crown, or, as in Cranmer's time, and as is still the case in the Church of Ireland, by the direct nomination of the sovereign. What Cranmer contended for was, that a bishop was removable by the crown, not from his episcopal order, but from his diocese; just as a judge was removable, until the reign of George III., not from the status of a barrister, but from the judicial bench. It is necessary to recur to these elementary observations, because the case is sometimes in ignorance or in malice misrepresented.*

---

* Even Burnet admits what has been stated above:—"By these letters patent it is clear that the episcopal function was acknowledged to be of divine appointment, and that the person was no other way named by the king than as lay patrons present to livings; only the

It was on the same principle, that Cranmer sought to abolish the election of bishops. The government being weak, he thought that the deans and chapters might, in some instances, brave the Præmunire, and refuse to elect the government nominee. He obtained, therefore, an act of parliament which placed the Church of England in the same position with respect to the appointment of bishops in which the Church of Ireland and the Colonial Church are placed at the present time. Instead of permitting the deans and chapters to go through the form of election, the appointment to a vacant see was to be made through letters patent, on the receipt of which the metropolitan was bound to consecrate. The permission to elect or the *congé d'élire*, has been subsequently restored to the Church of England, though it is at present exercised as a form and nothing more. It is wise, however, to cling to a form which may hereafter be inspired with life. The ceremonial opening of Convocation was, for many years, a mere form, but by attending to the form, the Convocation was prepared to act when that liberty of action, permitted to all other institutions, could no longer be held from the Church of England. The time may come—much to be deplored—when, in a revolutionary age, it may be the duty of the English Church, in a popular movement, to take a decided part against the crown, and nothing is to be despised which gives to any institution the power of free action.

The most decided measure taken by the government, on the advice of Cranmer, was the formation of a commission

bishop was legally authorised, in such a part of the king's dominions, to execute that function which was to be derived to him by imposition of hands. Therefore here was no pretence for denying that such persons were true bishops, and for saying, as some have done, that they were not from Christ, but from the king." Burnet, ii. 448.

with power to visit the entire Church of England, to report on the state of religion, and to carry into effect the enactments of Convocation and Parliament, together with those injunctions of the crown which, in right of his presumed headship, the king from time to time had issued. The kingdom was divided into six circuits. To each circuit certain commissioners were appointed, two gentlemen, a civilian, a divine, and a registrar; they were accompanied by learned and pious preachers. While the visitors investigated the state of each parish and diocese, the preachers were to instruct the people.*

The injunctions delivered by the commissioners in this royal visitation of the Church are a valuable record of the state of religion at this period, and they show how far the reformation of the Church had advanced. All deans, archdeacons, parsons, vicars, and other ecclesiastical persons were to cause to be kept and observed all and singular laws and statutes, made as well for the abolishing and extirpation of the Bishop of Rome, his pretended and usurped power and jurisdiction, as for the establishment in the " Church of England and Ireland " of the royal supremacy. On this subject they were to preach at least four times in

---

* The clergy and churchwardens of St. Martin's, in Ironmonger Lane, London, had in a tumultuous manner removed images and defaced the pictures in their church. The Bishop of London, Dr. Bonner, and the Lord Mayor complained of these proceedings of the council. Cranmer reminded the council that Henry VIII. had decided on the destruction of all images which had been superstitiously used, and as it was difficult to determine what images had been superstitiously, he advised that the worship of images should be abolished altogether. The judgment given was, that the parishioners should provide another crucifix in the place of that which had been destroyed; but though the crucifix was allowed, no order was given for the replacement of the other images. Burnet, iii. 16, 23; Strype, Memorials, ii. 502-596.

the year. They were forbidden to set forth or extol any images, relics, or miracles, for any superstition or lucre, or to encourage pilgrimages to the same, that God only might be glorified and none other. One sermon at least every quarter was enjoined; in this sermon men were to be exhorted to works of faith, mercy, and honesty, and to be warned against works devised by men's phantasies "beside scripture," such as wandering to pilgrimages, offering of money, candles, or tapers, or relics, or images, or kissing or licking of the same, praying upon beads and such like superstition. The clergy, and not private persons, were to take down and destroy images that had been censed unto, and they were not henceforth to suffer torches or candles, or tapers, or images of wax, " to be set afore any image or picture ; but only two lights upon the high altar before the Sacrament, which for the signification that Christ is the true light of the world, they might suffer to remain still." When no sermon was preached, the Pater Noster, the Credo, and the Commandments were to be repeated in English from the pulpit. Within three months one book of the whole Bible of the largest volume in English was to be provided in every church, and as a catholic exposition of the same, a copy of Erasmus's " Paraphrase of the Gospels." These the people were to be encouraged to read. Every person who came to confession in Lent was to be examined whether he could recite the Pater Noster, the Credo, and the Commandments in English. Registers for baptisms, marriages, and burials were to be duly kept, together with a poor box for the reception of alms. Nonresident clergymen were to devote a tenth of their income to the poor of the parish ; and whoever had an income of a hundred pounds a year was to maintain a poor scholar at Oxford or Cambridge. In the time of high mass he who said or sang the same, was to read or cause to be read the epistle and gospel of that mass in English, and not in Latin, in the pulpit or in some place convenient for hearing. Every Sunday and Holy day, the clergyman was to read or cause to be read one chapter of the New Testament at Matins in English, and, at Even-song after the Magnificat, one chapter of the Old Testament. To avoid all contention and strife, which was frequently occasioned by those who sought precedence in processions, and to enable people to hear distinctly what might be said to their edifying, they were not henceforth to use any procession about the church or churchyard or any other place; but immediately before high mass, the priests with other of the choir were to kneel in the midst of the church and sing or say plainly and distinctly the Litany as it was set forth in English. All shrines, covering of shrines, all tables, candlesticks, trindles or rolls of wax, pictures, paintings, and all other monuments of feigned miracles, privileges, idolatry, and superstition were to be taken away and destroyed. Because in some places, through lack of preachers, the people continued in ignorance and blindness, certain homilies were provided, one of which each non-preaching curate was to read every Sunday. It will be recollected that in the Convocation of 1542 order was taken that homilies, with this object in view, should be composed. It appears that under the direction of the primate twelve sermons were prepared, and were now published. These form the book called in the thirty-nine articles, "The former Book of Homilies." They were for the most part of a practical nature; but they had also, according to Dr. Corrie, a direct reference to the doctrinal errors and Antinomian practices of the various sects which passed under the name of Anabaptist.*

We hear so much in the history of this period of

* Wilkins, iv. ii. 1417. Records. Collier, ii. 59.

certain men engaged in the affairs of the world, and while upholding religious opinions not always animated by Christian principles or sentiment, that it is necessary to remind the reader occasionally that the great, either in virtue or in vice, form the exceptional few; and it is pleasant occasionally to catch the tone of feeling in humbler and in common life. We have it affirmed by an unexceptional witness that "the mass of the people were at this time tractable, obedient and quiet, and of such a nature that they may easily be brought to do anything that is for God's glory and the king's honour." *

For such a people these injunctions were well adapted, and everyone must be struck with the moderation and sound judgment by which they were dictated.

Although we are by no means prepared to say that if a reformation was to be effected, the measures to which attention has just been called were not necessary; and although we are perfectly ready to admit that at a revolutionary period, we must not reduce everything to the ordinary standard of right and wrong, such as is received in ordinary times, yet, on the other hand, we are not to censure those who, suffering under the oppression of men in power, denounce their measures as despotic, and feel justified in resisting what, upon received principles, can only admit of palliation by being regarded as exceptions to a general rule. The opposition to Somerset, and especially to Cranmer, was headed by the Bishop of Winchester, Dr. Gardyner; and it would have been more formidable than it was, if Gardyner, had possessed the peculiar talent which enables some men to form a party and to inspire it with confidence. Gardyner was not calculated to act as a leader. But anyone who reads

* John Hales to the Lord Protector. State Paper Office, July 24. 1548. Tytler, i. 113.

his history with candour will concur in the opinion that, his conduct throughout the reign of Edward VI. was on the whole dignified and praiseworthy. He assumed the position taken on one occasion by Cranmer himself: he contended that no alterations or innovations ought to be made in the Church or the services of the Church, so long as the king remained a minor. Having been brought before the council and questioned, he promised to offer no factious opposition to the commissioners when they visited the diocese of Winchester; but he found fault with the doctrine both of the Homilies and of the Paraphrase of Erasmus, and at the same time he declined to promise that he would carry out or enforce the injunctions. Private friends entreated him to concur in the proposed reformation of the Church; a bribe was offered to him of being admitted to a seat in the Privy Council; the archbishop discussed with him in private and corresponded with him; but Gardyner remained firm to his principle. He would maintain all things in Church and State as they had been left by his wise old master, until the king came of age to act for himself.

"I am by nature," he said, "already condemned to die, which sentence no man can pardon, nor assure me of delay in the execution of it; and to see that of necessity I shall leave my bishopric to the disposition of the crown, from whence I had it, my household also to break up, and my bringing up youth to cease, the remembrance whereof troubleth me nothing. I made in my house at London a pleasant study that delighted me much, and yet I was glad to come into the country and leave it; and as I have left the use of somewhat, so can I leave the use of all to obtain more quiet; it is not loss to change for the better."

Finding him, however, impracticable, the Council committed him, about three weeks before the visitation of his diocese, to the Fleet prison for contempt of court. The warden of the Fleet was his friend, and, although Gardyner complained and made the most of his hardships, the only real hardship to which he was subjected was that he was under surveillance. We find him dining with the Dean of St. Paul's, and there meeting the archbishop and other prelates, having been invited to discuss amicably the great doctrine of Justification by Faith only— the doctrine now asserted in the Homilies and to which he was vehemently opposed. After the visitation of his diocese, and when certain bills had passed through parliament, which it was presumed that he would have opposed, the Bishop of Winchester was permitted to return to his diocese. Here he conducted himself with great decorum: he was active in the discharge of his duties, munificent in his charities, and so cautious in his proceedings, that no one could accuse him with any show of justice of having offered a factious opposition to the government.*

Cranmer, however, became aware that the Reformation could not be carried on effectually, if a statesman so experienced and resolute as Gardyner remained at large. Recourse was therefore had to a measure which had been fatal to others. The Bishop of Winchester was required to preach before the king on St. Peter's Day. Secretary Cecil gave him his subject, warning him what he should say, and what he should not say, the object being to compel him to recognise the authority of the council. The sermon did not give satisfaction, and the bishop was committed to the Tower on the day following, and there he remained a state prisoner till the end of this reign.

* Strype, ii. 71.

Several attempts were made to bring him to terms; but at length the council having, in the exercise of the Royal prerogative, the authority of withdrawing the Episcopal licence, first sequestered his bishopric, and then declared it vacant. Let us hope, and we may believe, that with this act of gross injustice Cranmer was not concerned. He did not shrink from recourse to measures which would render Gardyner impotent to oppose the Reformation; but the object of the council in seizing his bishopric was to divide the spoils among themselves. They appointed Poynet to be the successor of Gardyner, and this was a transaction which brings disgrace upon the Reformation, not more for the deed itself, than for the manner in which the partizans of Protestantism have defended it. Poynet was a very learned man, an eloquent and powerful advocate of ultra-protestantism, though ready to yield when it was his interest to do so. At one time he must have been a consummate hypocrite, for we cannot otherwise account for his having been made chaplain to a man so good, earnest, and upright as Archbishop Cranmer. He was an immoral and low man, who was at last so lost to all sense of shame that he lived in open adultery with a butcher's wife; and was compelled legally to separate by the ecclesiastical courts and to pay an annuity to the woman's husband.* The extent of his profligacy was only

---

* "On the 27th of July, 1551, Poynet, the Bishop of Winchester, was divorced from his wife in Paul's, the which was a butcher's wife, of Nottingham, and gave her husband a certain sum of money a year during his life, as was judged by the law." *Grey Friars Chron.* 70. The same is repeated by Maclyn in his diary. Poynet was, with the exception of his chaplain, Bale, one of the most foul-mouthed of men. Strype, I am sorry to say, eulogizes him, and says that "he was one of the episcopal order in this reign that cordially favoured religion." *Memorials,* II. ii. 166. He elsewhere speaks in his praise. To uphold

known to an interested few, when he was appointed to the see of Winchester; until which time he had played the hypocrite's part. That he was, however, an unprincipled man the Council must have known, for he agreed to reserve two thousand marks for himself, and divided the rest of the temporalities among those greedy courtiers whose zeal for the Reformation was of the same character as his own. Such was the man appointed to succeed Gardyner, who, with all his faults—and they were many —was a stern man of strict morality, and a man of learning in the law though not in divinity, and a gentleman.

The Bishop of London, Dr. Bonner, was a man very different from Bishop Gardyner, and the government had the more difficulty in dealing with him, because he was one of those unprincipled men who find delight

> To palter with us in a double sense:
> To keep the word of promise to the ear,
> And break it to our hope.

That Cranmer expected to win Bonner to his side is to be inferred from the fact of his inserting in the book of Homilies still in use, a sermon from Bonner's own pen; and as no one had been more zealous than Bonner in the late reign in upholding the Royal supremacy and in opposing all Papal aggression, the expectation was by no means unreasonable. But Bonner took the position which had been assumed by Gardyner: namely, that until the king came of age, all things were to remain *in statu quo*—even as they had been left by Henry. In vain did Cranmer argue, even from facts known to both of these prelates,

such characters from party considerations is to prefer party feeling to the claims of morality.

that Henry had designed further reforms. They maintained that the supremacy was a branch of the prerogative inalienable from the person of the king. Edward in his minority, it was said, could not exercise it; neither could he delegate it to the council. They were not insane enough, as they are sometimes supposed to have been, to contend that all legislation must cease during the minority; but they simply asserted that in matters of religion the Regency had no power to act. There could be no hardship, they said, in letting things remain for a few years as they were left by their wise old master; and this concession they demanded. The council overruled their objections: they ruled that the Court they formed had jurisdiction in things spiritual. If the two prelates denied this they were to be committed to prison for contempt of court. Gardyner consistently maintained his position, and remained, as we should now say, within the rules of the Tower,—for his imprisonment amounted to little more than this. But Bonner, less honourable and straightforward, after he had been committed to the Fleet for contempt, recanted and was released. He was a man who delighted in the kind of cleverness which distinguishes a pettifogging attorney: he found pleasure in placing himself almost within the power of his enemies, and of then extricating himself by some dexterous evasion. He only offered to all the measures of his metropolitan and the Government a passive resistance. When the English service was ordered, he did not oppose its introduction into his diocese, although in English he would never himself officiate. He did not attack those who conformed, although he patronised nonconformists. He evaded every law in every possible way, and yet defied his enemies to prove that he had transgressed it. He was known to be the encourager of insurrectionary movements, and was in some way supposed to be implicated in the manœuvres of Lord Seymour, the admiral. A more annoying opponent it was not easy to find; and at length it was determined to remove him. This was done with that appearance of justice which so often disgraced the despotic acts of an age, when men found satisfaction, while violating the spirit, in observing the letter of the law. He was first confined as a prisoner in his own house, and he was required at the same time to perform all the functions of his office appointed by law. He was directed to preach a sermon at Paul's Cross; in this sermon he was to consign to damnation all persons rebelling against their Sovereign Lord, whatever their religious persuasion may have been. He was to declare that Divine worship consisted in prayer to God, and that all other forms and ceremonies might be abrogated or changed at the will of the magistrate; and that if any man used, therefore, the Latin service when the English was ordered, the merit of his action was cancelled by the sin of his disobedience. He was to dwell especially upon the king's authority in affairs of the Church, as well as of the State, during the minority. These were extreme opinions, and it was probably supposed, that the Bishop would at once have refused to occupy the pulpit. This was not Bonner's mode of acting. He undertook to preach. An immense congregation gathered round Paul's Cross. On all the topics he was said to have been unsatisfactory, and he entirely omitted the last head, having, he regretted to say, somehow or other, mislaid his notes. On these grounds he was denounced to the government by no less a person than John Hooper, a man as ready to be burnt as he was to burn. Of Hooper we have remarked before, that he was an obstinate and disputatious, though a munificent and pious man. He caused no little trouble to Cranmer, when, contrary to Cranmer's wishes, he was preferred to the see of Gloucester. He was doubtless employed as the spy or public prosecutor on this occasion; and on his report, a commission was issued to the Archbishop of Canterbury, to Bishop Ridley, and the two Secretaries of State to sit in trial upon Bonner. The result was, that the Bishop of London was committed to the Marshalsea for contempt of court. In October he was deprived of his bishopric; and to the see of London Cranmer's friend and adviser, Bishop Ridley, was translated.* Although the conduct of Cranmer, abstractedly considered, was in these instances unjust and despotic, yet when we bear in mind the cruelties of which Crumwell was guilty when enforcing the act of supremacy, and the still greater cruelties of Queen Mary's reign, we must admit that Cranmer did not, in the plenitude of his power, forfeit his character as a humane man; and we may claim this character for him the more powerfully, since his disinclination to persecute was attributed by the foreign reformers to lukewarmness, on his part, in the cause of the Reformation.

The excesses of the Reformers caused but little annoyance to such ministers as Somerset and Northumberland. They seemed to justify these statesmen in the adoption of measures which enabled them to pay their supporters and enrich themselves through the forfeiture of ecclesiastical property.

* There appears to have been some jobbing about the estates, but I think that the biographer and namesake of Ridley clearly proves that Ridley only exchanged some lands of the see of London for lands equivalent of the suppressed see of Westminster. The see of London was benefited by the exchange. Bishop Ridley was so decided in his condemnation of church jobbery, that it was not likely that he should be guilty of it himself.

Even the emotional religion of Somerset evaporated towards the close of his life, and he was accused of having relapsed into carelessness. When Northumberland was in the ascendant, and Somerset was not likely any longer to share in the spoils if the Church were ruined, the reforming zeal of Somerset appears to have cooled.

Northumberland, the cleverer man of the two, was also the more unscrupulous. He was evidently a man of no religious principle at that period of his life when religion, if a reality, is a principle rather than a sentiment. If we believe his own confession, he became an advocate of reformation from motives base and sordid; and—perhaps still dissembling in the hope of a possible pardon to the last—he died an avowed papist.

Edward VI. was a youth of precocious talents, whom Somerset and Northumberland, for their own purposes, surrounded with Puritans. Through their influence he was prepared to carry out the Puritan notions to their extreme point, the object of the two statesmen being to find some plausible excuse for seizing upon the spoils of the Church. The young king's mind was framed like that of his sister Mary. There can be, he would say, as she was accustomed to say, only a right and a wrong; let those who are right be encouraged, let those who are wrong be restrained, and if they propagate their errors, be burned.*

In what related to the actual reformation of the Church, Cranmer was left by the Gallios of the council to act upon his own judgment, and he consulted the convocation. Somerset and Northumberland found it to be their policy to side with the ultra-Protestants, and to

* It was thus he argued on the subject of image-worship.

allow them to believe that the temporal members of the council could go much farther, if impediments were not offered to their proceedings by Cranmer. The probability is that this was a mere pretext, and that they perceived that the work of reformation was going on fast enough, if the peace of the country was to be preserved. They were not persons who could have permitted themselves to be restrained by the archbishop if their interests lay in the opposite direction.

It is now necessary to return to our review of the various reformations which were at this time effected. Of Cranmer himself we must be permitted to say, that sufficient allowance is, in these days, hardly made for the difficulties of his position. Only coldly supported, indeed clandestinely opposed, by a government greedy to enrich its members through the spoliation of the Church; appealed to through all the influences to which a kind heart is open by men whom he wished to please, but with whose opinions he only partially sympathised; having no theological principle to guide him, though fully aware of the necessity of a reformation; with no compass to direct him how to steer the Church in the midst of the wild uproar of discordant sentiments, he was so situated that we ought to be sure of our own steadfastness of purpose before we are unduly severe in our judgment; and the severity of our judgment must, under any circumstances, be mitigated when we remember that Cranmer did not himself seek, but was forced by circumstances into, a position, in which it was difficult to decide how to advance, or whether to recede.

One thing, however, is certain, that before the accession of Edward VI., Cranmer had perceived that it was impossible to remain stationary. He steadily, though cautiously, persevered in carrying out the measures already devised but kept in abeyance in the late king's reign.

One measure, indeed, would probably have met with the disapproval of Henry; and that was a measure nearest to Cranmer's heart. He obtained from Convocation, though not without some opposition, a vote that all such canons, laws, statutes, decrees, usages, and customs heretofore had or used, which forbade the marriage of the clergy should be utterly void and of none effect. A majority of fifty-three voted in the affirmative, thirty-two against it. It was remarked that even of the minority many entered into the holy estate of matrimony, when the marriage of priests became legal. Their concubines probably insisted on marriage when marriage was allowable.*

There was greater difficulty in procuring the consent of the laity to the marriage of the clergy; and it is a remarkable fact that, for two generations at least, a strong prejudice continued to exist in favour of clerical celibacy. The vulgar insolence with which Queen Elizabeth treated the wife of Archbishop Parker is well known; and is such as no one would have ventured to perpetrate, except a crowned head.

Immediately after the vote of convocation in favour of the marriage of the clergy, a bill was introduced into parliament having for its object to declare the legality of such marriages. It was read, indeed, three times in the House of Commons, but the large minority who formed the opposition procured the prorogation of the House of Lords before the bill could pass into a law. The synodical decision not having obtained the force of statute law, the subject was again brought under the notice of Convocation in the year 1548, when "it was thoroughly

---

* Strype, 136. Wilkins, iv. 16. Collier, n. 226.

debated and thoroughly sifted." The majority in favour of the marriage of the clergy had, during the recess, advanced from fifty-three to seventy in the lower house. A majority was also obtained in the upper house of convocation. There was still a party in the House of Commons opposed to any concession to the clergy; but at last an act of parliament was obtained "to take away all positive laws made against the marriage of priests."

The archbishop now sent for his wife, and, in his happy reunion with his family, he exposed himself to the complaint that he had become indolent, and that he was not sufficiently attentive to public affairs. This charge was more easily made than proved. Cranmer's mind was employed on the great work to which his attention had been for some time directed. He had determined on that revision of the ancient devotional offices of the Church which commenced in the reign of Henry VIII. and resulted in converting the Use of Sarum—its missal and its breviary—into the Book of Common Prayer. The Prayer Books revised and arranged in the reign of Edward VI. are not identically the same as the Book of Common Prayer now in use, or the Revision of 1661. But to the liturgical reformers of the reign of Charles II. Cranmer and his associates were, what to Cranmer and the reformers of Edward VI.'s reign were Osmond, the great Bishop of Salisbury, and the compilers of the Use of Sarum.

Cranmer was beginning to see that all the controversies of the day hinged upon the doctrine of the Eucharist. The Romanising party in our Church desired to retain the mass, the reforming party to convert the mass into a communion. We have already stated to the reader the merits of the case; and as a first step to liturgical reform, or to a revision of the missal, so as to make it a communion office, certain queries on the subject of the Eucharist were addressed to a committee of the bishops and deans, preparatory to legislation on the subject.

The answer to the queries which are still extant show that both parties knew the purpose for which they were questioned, and made their answers to bear upon the main subject.*

The subject of the Eucharist was brought under discussion in the upper house, soon after the meeting of Convocation; and on the 20th of November 1547, it was submitted for discussion to the lower house. Everything had been previously arranged. If there were to be a communion whenever the Eucharist was celebrated; if portions of the service, as it had been already settled, were to be in English; if the people were to receive in both kinds; then some alteration in the missal would be absolutely necessary. On the very day, therefore, that the subject of the Eucharist was formally discussed in the lower house of convocation, it is recorded " that Mr. Prolocutor exhibited and caused to be read publicly, the form of a certain ordinance determined upon by the Most Reverend the Lord Archbishop of Canterbury for receiving the Body and Blood of our Lord, under both kinds, viz. bread and wine. This the Prolocutor Archdeacon Gwent himself subscribed with the other members of the house." †

The next session was on the 2nd of December, when a synodical decree on this important point was carried without a dissentient voice. The lower house, numbering

---

* The queries and the answers are to be found in the Stillingfleet MSS., Lambeth, 1108, fol. They are published in Cranmer's Remains, ii. 178-181. They are too long for transcription here, but they are worthy of perusal to those who are studying the doctrine of the Eucharist.

† Strype, 156.

sixty-four * members, " did approve the proposition made in the last session of taking the Lord's body in both kinds "*nullo reclamante.*" The archbishop, still true to his principle of opposing the Protestant as well the Popish extreme, had almost simultaneously introduced into the House of Lords a bill which denounced in the strongest terms, the irreverent and profane language applied out of doors to the Holy Sacrament, and inflicting penalties on the offenders. The administration of the Eucharist in both kinds was authorised. This bill was read a second time on the 3rd of December. On the 27th of December a proclamation was issued in the king's name forbidding all contentions on the subject "until such time as the king's Majesty, by the advice of his Highness' Council and the clergy of this realm, shall define, set forth, and declare an open doctrine thereof."

The decree of Convocation—ratified by parliament and the Crown—that the Sacrament should be received in both kinds by all communicants, had necessitated, as we have observed, an alteration in the missal; and to effect this object, a royal commission had been issued, consisting of the Committee of Convocation appointed in 1543 to revise the offices of the Church and some others.† The Commission met at Windsor Castle, and were empowered

---

* The number sixty-four being mentioned, we may perhaps infer that the members of the opposition stayed away. We cannot otherwise account for an unanimous decision on a subject upon which opinions must have been divided.

† In the Convocation of 1547, a requisition was sent from the lower house to the archbishop to the effect that the labours of the committee appointed in 1543 to revise the services of the Church might be laid before the synod. Wilkins, iv. 15. The subject of Prayer Book reform had been for some time before the public. There was a good understanding between the Church and the State through Cranmer's position at the head of the regency. Heylin, i. 118.

to "consult about a uniform order for administering the Holy Communion in the English tongue, under both kinds, of bread and wine."

The revision of our liturgical and other sacred books is a subject of such great importance that I shall enter rather fully upon the subject; and it becomes my duty to do so, because, without having the facts of the case before us, it is impossible to understand the conduct of Cranmer and his fellow-labourers; what they did, and what they forbore to attempt. The reader who would do justice to the historical facts to be brought under his notice must bear in mind that our Prayer Book dates not from the era of the Reformation but from the year 1085. The reformers of the sixteenth century already possessed a prayer book in the "Use of Sarum," and the commission already mentioned was not appointed to compose or to compile a new Prayer Book. It consisted of men too wise and too modest to make an attempt so absurd. Their business was simply to revise the Prayer Book then in use; to adapt it to the altered circumstances of the Church, to compare it with Scripture and with primitive practice, to abbreviate it, to re-arrange it, and to erase those superstitious additions to the original forms which could not fail to have crept in, when no Act of Uniformity existed, and when every bishop, almost every priest, even if substantially adopting the Use of Sarum, might, according to his caprice or his carelessness, make alterations in the formularies. That the reformers of the sixteenth century did their work well, the voice of three centuries has declared. Some persons may think they were too free in their erasures, others may complain of their additions from foreign sources. But when we find that their work was adopted with a few alterations by our reformers in the reign of Queen Elizabeth; and again by our reformers in the reign of Charles II., by whom was completed our present Book of Common Prayer, we shall be prepared to accord to them the praise which is justly their due. We shall give them credit for the exercise of a sound judgment, combined with a resolute determination to employ their common sense in the rejection of unscriptural error however long established, and in the restoration of primitive truth however long neglected. As they reformed without revolutionising the Church, so they revised the ancient Liturgy without substituting a composition of their own. Although the exercise of much practical wisdom was required in their revision of services to which the people were attached, the reformers of the sixteenth century in point of fact did little; and because they did not establish anything new, because they had no occasion to give minute directions, because they took it for granted that the people for whom they legislated would do as they always had done except when expressly forbidden to do so, because, especially in rubrical directions, they were not enjoining new proceedings but regulating old practices, we are, at the present time, involved in some difficulties. We are referred to what was the usual practice of their age, and of the ages which preceded them in the existing Church; but unfortunately our Church was proscribed and its ritual was suspended for nearly a generation at the time of the great rebellion. What, in the sixteenth century, had been traditional practices, which the reformers assumed would be continued, had in the interval ceased to be observed. The reformers in Charles II.'s time had to begin *de novo*, but were hardly aware of their position. The divines who at that time revised the Prayer Book were most of them elderly men who had been brought up under the old traditions; and they forgot, too often, that they were legislating for a generation not habituated to the ancient liturgy. To them the rubrics required explanation, and the explanations given were not always sufficiently explicit. If we place in the hands of a sporting man a breech-loader, some few explanations might be necessary to show him how it should be used, but the explanations would be few, and he would know at once how to handle his weapon; but if we place such a gun in the hands of one unaccustomed to the use of fire-arms, we should have to descend to minute particulars in the one instance, which would be ridiculous, because simply unnecessary, in the other.

The reader who has attended the author through the preceding volumes of this work, when the Church of England, into which all the other Churches in Britain gradually merged, was first established, will remember that our great founder Augustine found considerable difficulty in arranging the offices of his church. This was occasioned by a fact of which, when he started on his missionary labours, he was ignorant; namely, that although all liturgies bore a strong resemblance in all substantials one to another, yet the several liturgies, all of them differing more or less from the Roman, were adopted in different churches.

By writers who have devoted their time and attention to liturgical subjects, the ancient liturgies are arranged under four general heads or families, and to one of these primitive or apostolic forms, although different churches had their own peculiarities, the origin of their liturgical forms was to be traced. They are as follows :—The liturgy of St. James, or of Antioch, from which the Russian liturgy of the present time is derived; the liturgy of St. Mark, or Alexandria, which is the origin of the Egyptian liturgy;

the liturgy of St. Peter, the basis of the Roman rite; the liturgy of St. John, or of Ephesus, which, under certain modifications, before and since the Reformation, has been the foundation of the ordinance as administered in the Church of England, having come into England from France. This liturgy of St. John, used throughout the episcopate of Ephesus, where St. John took up his abode during the later years of his life, passed over into Spain and Gaul, and so to the far West, and is known as the Gallican liturgy. With this liturgy we were doubly connected, because it was not only the liturgy of the British Church antecedently to the coming of Augustine, but also of the Normans. Augustine found this liturgy used in the church of St. Martin's, Canterbury, where Bertha, the queen of Ethelbert, had been accustomed to worship; and the British Christians carried the rite with them into Wales. Augustine had met with the Gallican or Ephesian liturgy before he arrived in England, and being himself a simple-minded man, he was perplexed by its divergence from the Roman liturgy, with which only he had been acquainted. On consulting Gregory the Great, Augustine was advised to proceed upon that principle upon which all who have subsequently revised our liturgical offices have been accustomed to act. Although Augustine was at first acquainted only with the customs of the Roman Church, in which he had been educated, yet Gregory's advice to him was,

—" if you find anything in the Roman, in the Gallican, or in any other Church which may be acceptable to Almighty God, you should carefully make choice of the same, and sedulously teach the Church of the English, which is at present new in the faith, whatever you gather from the other Churches. For things are not to be loved for the sake of places; but places for the sake of good things. Select, therefore, from each Church those things which are pious, religious, and correct, and having, as it were, made them up into one body, instil this into the minds of the English for their use."*

These were the wise and catholic principles adopted by the founder of our Church; and when, in the process of time, before the printing-press existed, the old forms were corrupted, these were the wise and catholic principles upon which our reformers were careful to act. These principles found an advocate in Archbishop Theodore, to whom the early English Church looked as a second founder, and who was naturally inclined to Orientalism. The Roman rite was thus not exclusively adopted in the early English Church, much attached to it though the Italian missionaries naturally were. The tendency was to form an amalgamation of the Roman, the Gallican, and the Eastern elements, which, however, was not effected until the great liturgical reformation under Osmund, Bishop of Salisbury, was accomplished.

The orderly mind of Osmund, with whom the reader of these volumes is already familiar, was shocked at the prevalent want of uniformity in the services of the Church of England, and especially in the province of Canterbury. He attempted to consolidate and remodel the services for his own church at Salisbury, so as to render them the model according to which the services in other dioceses might be arranged.† His object was the same as that of the reformers of the sixteenth century, not to form a new

---

* Bede, i. 27. Gregor. ii. 1151. A remarkable proof of our early connexion with the Gallican Church is to be found in the number of French saints in our calendar. The reader who would pursue this subject further, is referred to Sir William Palmer's Orig. Liturgicæ, sect. 1, and to Neale and Forbes' Gallican Liturgies.

† On account of Osmund's liturgical fame, the Bishop of Salisbury received the office he still retains of Præcentor to the Province of Canterbury.

ritual but to revise the old. So successful were the labours of St. Osmund, that although his Use was not avowedly adopted in every other diocese, yet there was no diocese in which the influence of his example could not be traced. There were the Uses of Lincoln, Hereford, and Bangor. In St. Paul's Cathedral, and probably throughout the diocese of London, there was an independent Use till the fifteenth century; and in the province of York it was only in the diocese of Durham that the "Salisbury Use" was followed. Nevertheless this discrepancy was more in appearance than in reality. There were provincials unwilling to sacrifice local customs to which they had been habituated and attached; and others there were who felt a pride in asserting their independence; but the differences here related chiefly to unimportant matters of detail, while the general resemblance to the "Sarum Use" and the constant reference to it when doubts on any specified subjects were entertained, attested the influence which it soon obtained in this country, until, as we shall presently see, it became in point of fact, the Prayer Book of the English Church.*

There can be no doubt, however, that with the growth of superstitious thought, there were continual additions made to the Salisbury and the other Uses. It was the knowledge of this that created a demand for revision in the sixteenth century.

The labours of Osmund had extended beyond the liturgy, which, strictly speaking, refers only to the Communion office,† and had reference to all the offices of the

* The monasteries, which prided themselves on being exempt from diocesan regulations, adopted generally the Roman system.

† It is so common at the present time to understand by the Liturgy the entire Prayer Book, or at least that part of it which relates to public prayer, that I shall not strictly observe a distinction, to which, however, the reader's attention must be occasionally directed.

Church through which an amalgamation was effected of the various rites, British, Celtic, Saxon, Roman, Gallican, and of which in our first Book we have spoken at length. It will be for the convenience of the reader if I enumerate here the principal office-books of Sarum; for to them I shall have occasion, from time to time, incidentally to refer.

CHAP. III.

Thomas Cranmer. 1533-56.

I. There was the Missal, which contained the ordinary and canon of the Mass, together with the Introits, Collects, Epistles, Graduals, Alleluia, Tracts, Sequences, Gospels, Offertories, Communions, and Post-Communions throughout the year.

II. The Graduale, or Grayle, which contained the musical notation to the Introits and other portions of the service of which mention has just been made, together with the musical notation to the Nicene Creed, Gloria in Excelsis, and such other points of the ordinary and canon as were sung.

III. The Processionale, containing such parts of the service as were sung in processions.

IV. The Ordinale, or book of direction for the priests.

V. The Portiforium, or Breviary, containing the service for Matins, Lauds, Prime, Tierce, Sext, Nones, Vespers, Compline, throughout the year, together with the Litany and the Vigils for the dead. It was divided into two parts: Pars Hyemalis, the services from the first Sunday in Advent to the end of Whitsun Week; Pars Æstivalis, beginning with Trinity Sunday, and giving the services from thence to Advent from the Roman service. The Use of Sarum differed from the Roman Rite by adopting only this twofold division. The Roman Breviary is divided into four parts: Pars Vernalis, beginning with the first Sunday in Lent, and Pars Auctumnalis, beginning with the Sunday nearest the Calends of September.

VI. The Legenda, containing the lessons to be said at Matins.

VII. The Pica or Pie, a kind of directory as to the order in which the services are to be said.

VIII. The Tonale, vulgarly called the "Tunnal," containing the Gregorian tones for the Psalms, with directions.

IX. The Antiphonarium, or Antiphones, containing musical notations of the Antiphons.

X. The Manuale, containing the offices of Baptism, Matrimony, Visitation and Anointing of the Sick, Burial of the Dead, &c.

XI. The Pontificale, containing the offices peculiar to the Bishop; as Confirmation, Ordination, and Consecration.

We are not surprised that a demand should have arisen for a simplification of these volumes, some of them of considerable dimensions, and all of them requiring an amount of study which was irksome even to those who had been accustomed to the manipulation of them, in whole or in part, from early life.*

In what relates to mediæval religion in general, we may trace the failure which attended holy purposes and praiseworthy endeavours to the fact that an end too high, and therefore unattainable, was aimed at. Too much was attempted. As regarded the whole monastic system, what idea could be more sublime! How irresistible its fascination to the mind whose ambition did not terminate with this world, but which aspired to a seat nearest to the Saviour in the kingdom of glory! But it was a system adapted for angelic beings, not for men; for holy creatures who had not fallen, and not for man who in his holiest condition is only a sinner saved. Men in despair either

* Carter's Liturgy of the Church of Sarum, Pref. p. 5.

raved in madness, or relaxed into worse than carelessness, while legends became lying legends representing them as doing what the system required them to do; taking it for granted that what they ought to do, that they did, though in point of fact they did it not.

Of the Ritual services we may also remark, that the ideal was grand; it was a grand idea, which understood almost literally the injunction that men ought always to pray and not to faint. But what was attempted was found to be physically impossible. Instead of a chapter of the Bible, one verse was frequently read, and other alterations were effected, still leaving the services so long, and, except to the enthusiast, so wearisome, that the daily service was almost confined to the cathedrals and the monasteries. There was no Common Prayer in the churches; there were masses said,—sometimes irreverently shortened,—to meet the requirements of the sportsman, the warrior, or the statesman, who thought only of the *opus operatum*; but for common prayer, to which allusion has been made, the worshipper had to go to the cathedral, or if at a distance from the cathedral, to some near monastery.

Even here, however, where leisure was great, and the attendance at Divine worship was the primary if not the only duty, men found it necessary not unfrequently to evade the laws, even when to evade them improperly was far from their inclination. The hours of the day were thus arranged to meet the requirements of the Use of Sarum and the other Uses then in vogue; there was a service before daybreak called Nocturns, or Matins; at daybreak there was another service, called Lauds; at six o'clock, there was Prime; at nine o'clock, Tierce; at twelve, Sexts; at three o'clock in the afternoon, Nones; in the evening, Vespers; at bed-time, Compline. These services were, to avoid practical inconvenience, blended together so as to form one office, like our Common Prayer and Communion office. They, however, had so many points in common, that the accumulation of them led to frequent and vain repetitions. All these practical inconveniences combined, with the gradual detection of erroneous doctrine resulting in superstitious practices, to induce men to desire a reformation; and this became a necessity when the monasteries were dissolved. No longer could persons, desiring a daily attendance at the divine worship, repair to a monastery near at hand; and in most cases the cathedral was at a distance. They now required daily service at the parish churches, and a service adapted to the circumstances, no longer of monks, but of busy men of the world. Hence the Breviary of the Use of Sarum was altered to make it serve for the daily service of the parish churches. As in other cases, the grievance was felt before it was declared, and attempts at reform were made before the demand for reformation became a popular cry.

The notion that the divines, who were appointed under a royal commission, with the sanction of Convocation and of Parliament—the clergy and the laity of the land—to make a revision of the Use of Sarum, set to work immediately, and in a short space of time composed, or, as it is said, compiled our liturgy, meaning by that word the whole Prayer Book, is certainly not in accordance with historical facts. Men speak as if these respectable committee-men acted under an immediate and special inspiration, and in producing the Prayer Book as the result of their labours, wrought a miracle. Whereas in point of fact, the subject had been mooted for years, and had been subjected to long deliberation and examination, and was not a composition or compilation, but simply a revision.

At an early period in the episcopate of Archbishop Warham, the reform of "the Use of Sarum"—and our Prayer Book, let it be remembered, is no more than this—had commenced. In 1516, a new edition of the Salisbury Portiforium was printed, and so many were the alterations which were tacitly made in it, that the student who collates it with other copies of the "Use of Sarum," will see that it deserves the character which has been given to it of a "reformed breviary."

Of the Salisbury Portiforium, thus reformed, there was a reprint in 1531; and so popular was this proceeding that in 1533 the Missal appeared, reformed on the same principle. It is not intended to say that much was done or designed. The doctrine of the Church had not been impugned. But admission was already made, that the time had arrived when a new revision of the offices of the Church had become necessary. In both reforms the rubrics had been simplified; and in both, the great demand of the age for the reading of Scripture had been met. In the Portiforium it was directed, that instead of single verses, entire chapters of the Bible should be read;* and arrangements were made, in the publication of the Missal, to enable the laity to find the places in the Epistles and Gospels. In the Primers, translations were to be found of various portions of the service, including the Litany, portions of the Psalms, and the Epistles and Gospels. A demand for the whole service in the vernacular was now made, and on various grounds resisted by Cranmer. Although he yielded to the judgment of others, yet he

---

* The pious attempt originally made to induce a copious reading of Scripture, because too much was enjoined, at length terminated in the perusal of one verse. One sees at once that this was to the pious and to men of leisure a suggestion, and that they could read the rest of the chapter at home. But we also see how easily it became, to the generality of persons, a mere form.

was adverse to a translation of any part of the Missal. He was willing to concede to the wishes of the public in all that related to the Portiforium or Breviary, but his unwillingness for a long time to touch the Missal, shows his deep reverence for the Sacraments. This remark is made, because it is well to bear in mind that difficulties presented themselves to the reformers on both sides. There were pious men who assumed that the people could not understand the services unless they were translated; and others there were who, like Cranmer until further advised, feared lest there should be a decrease of reverence if the mysteries of the Church were presented to the people in the vulgar tongue.

A re-arrangement of the Psalter had taken place, and in 1534 and 1540 the Psalter had been printed in Latin and English.

At length, in 1541, Osmund triumphed. He had hoped to provide one great service-book, or rather, a series of offices, for the use of the whole Church of England. Although the Use of Sarum was the basis of all the other Uses, still a variety of offices existed until the year just mentioned. On the 3rd of March, 1541-2, the Use of Sarum, purged, it was said on the title-page, from many errors, was, by order of Convocation, adopted throughout the province of Canterbury. After the Te Deum and the Magnificat, an order was made in this edition that the lessons should be read in English. On this point there were no differences of opinion.

These measures were adopted partly to satisfy an increasing demand for a reform, not only of the clergy, but also of the Church; and partly as tentative to ascertain what would meet the wishes of the public. It was desirable to act with caution and to take time; and by temporary arrangements the public were to be satisfied until the authorities were in a condition to proceed. That they were earnest in their intentions was shown by the appointment, in 1542, of a committee of Convocation, consisting of a certain number of bishops, with six clergy of the lower house, to examine, correct, and reform all mass books, antiphones, and portuises.* This committee continued its sittings, and with additional members formed the committee of 1549, who produced the revised Missal, Breviary, and Manual, which together form our Book of Common Prayer.

The violence and excesses of the reforming party, encouraged in all their iniquities by Crumwell, had rendered necessary the passing of the statute of the six articles, one of the decided but statesmanlike measures of Henry VIII. The penalties threatened were severe in the extreme, but I have stated, what will probably be the conclusion of every reader examining the subject with impartiality, that the king only desired through this statute—hung *in terrorem* over the heads of the Reformers—to compel silence for a time, with a view to further reform in due season. The continuance of the committee for the revision of the service-books may be adduced as a proof of Henry's intention to carry on the Reformation, as Cranmer asserted. He intended to put down the party violence, and then to introduce gradually such forms as his clergy in convocation might recommend.

Although this committee did not issue a report in the reign of Henry VIII., yet it was not inactive. The practices of the Church were investigated; and in 1543 a canon was prepared, though not published, on the ceremonies of the Church of England, together with an explanation of the meaning and significancy of them. In 1544 the committee

* The Portiforia, or Breviaries, were so called by the common people.

set forth, with the sanction of the king, the Litany in English. The Litany had for many years been published in the vernacular language; but this Litany was not merely a reprint of the old ones—in it may be traced references to the Ritual of Cologne, published by the celebrated archbishop of that place, the Elector Hermann.

Archbishop Cranmer was not the only Primate and Metropolitan of the Western Church, who had resolved, not, like Calvin, to establish a new sect, but, like our own predecessors, to reform the Church. His Grace the Lord Archbishop of Canterbury was in correspondence with his Highness the Archbishop of Cologne, who was also an elector of the empire and a sovereign prince. Hermann was a man of energy and zeal, of learning and prudence, and he endeavoured to do in Germany what the Archbishop of Canterbury succeeded in doing in England. He desired to establish within his province and electorate a pure system of devotion and worship. Archbishop Hermann had, for this purpose, courted the assistance of Melancthon and Bucer. It was probably through the influence of the Elector, Archbishop of Cologne, that Archbishop Cranmer was induced to offer preferment in England to Melancthon and Bucer. He sought the advice of the former and secured the assistance of the latter.*

* The Latin title of Hermann's great work was "Simplex Indicium de Reformatione ecclesiarum electoratus Coloniensis." According to the statement of Melancthon, the Archbishop of Cologne, in reforming his breviary, took for his basis a formulary of devotion known as the Nuremburg Liturgy. (Epp. 546.) This was drawn up by Melancthon, and professed to be an abridgment of the services of the Catholic Church, with such alterations and amendments as were judged necessary to purge it from error and superstition. It was a reformed breviary, as a Rule of Devotion revised on the same principle as our Book of Common Prayer: and I will take this opportunity of stating

There was also another work of considerable importance to which the attention of the English Reformers was called, and which made a considerable impression upon their minds, the work of Cardinal Quignon; for we find in the Preface of the Prayer Book of 1549 direct references to the Preface of Quignon's breviary.

This breviary was first published under papal patronage in the year 1536, and was extensively used in various European churches, until 1568, when it was superseded

that I refer generally for the statements relating to the revision of the offices of the Church of England, and their assuming their present form, to this and to the following works:—The Notes of Bishop Andrewes; Ang. Cath. Lib.; Bulley's Variations of the Communion and Baptismal Offices; the various publications of Cardwell, an accurate though a prejudiced writer; Collier, Burnet, Bishop Cosin; Archdeacon Freeman's Principles of Divine Service, a work of deep philosophical thought and of historical accuracy; L'Estrange's Alliance of Divine Offices; Liturgies of Edward VI.; Parker Soc.; Maskell; Merbecke's Common Prayer Book, Noted, 1550; Neale's Various Works; Sir William Palmer's Origines Liturgicæ; Sparrow's Rationale; Stephens' Edition of the Prayer Book. With Comber and Wheatley most persons have been acquainted from their early years; and we feel grateful to works which set us a-thinking when no more recondite publications existed. But although Wheatley evidently was aware that the Book of Common Prayer was a revision, and not a compilation, he did not pursue or examine the subject—perhaps he dared not. To have represented us as indebted for our Prayer Book to Osmund, who himself only revised what had come down from primitive times, would have exposed him to a suspicion of popery, and have imperilled his life. He has been superseded by Mr. Procter, who has done his work thoroughly well; still it is only a compendium, and it is to be hoped that he will continue his labours on a more extended scale in the same honest Anglican spirit by which his present book is distinguished. It is to be hoped that the ground will not be occupied by half-learned men—the men who confound Post-reformation Romanism with Pre-reformation Catholicism. No one has a right to dogmatise upon the Ritual question who has not been able to consult Durandus; the Sacramentaries of Gelasius and Gregory the Great; Goar; Catalani, and Zaccaria.

by a bull of Pius, who established the present rule in churches of the Roman obedience.

Quignon's breviary made the formulary more conformable to its title, by omitting or abbreviating all the more recent innovations and superstitions, together with many of those versicles, little chapters, and responds which interrupt the reading of the lessons and irritate the minds of all except the learned few. The learned, when a custom is once established, discover a reason for it which perhaps never occurred to the minds of those to whom it is indebted for its introduction. Quignon also omitted the *officium parvum* of the holy Virgin, under the pretext that although the Church was bound to adore her, she would be better pleased with a system which, "by a more convenient and expeditious method allured the clergy to the Divine Word of her Son Jesus Christ."*

The committee of revision appointed in the reign of Henry VIII. was considerably enlarged in the following reign, and, as we have before remarked, acted now under a royal commission. Of the upper house there were the Archbishop of Canterbury, Dr. Cranmer; the Bishop of Ely, Dr. Goodrich, afterwards Lord Chancellor; the Bishop of Lincoln, Dr. Holbeach; the Bishop of Chichester, Dr. Day; the Bishop of Hereford, Dr. Skip; the Bishop of Westminster, Dr. Thirlby; the Bishop of Rochester, afterwards of London, Dr. Ridley. Of the lower house the members were the Dean of St. Paul's, Dr. May; the Dean of Christ Church, afterwards Bishop of

---

* This was probably one main reason why this Breviary was suppressed. The character of Romanism after the Council of Trent was materially changed from what it had been before. The reformers of England set the first example of a revision of the Breviary in 1510. Quignon pursued the subject with greater boldness. The work is so extremely rare, that it reaches almost a fabulous price in the book-market.

Ely, Dr. Cox; the Dean, afterwards Bishop, of Lincoln, Dr. Taylor; the Dean of Exeter, Dr. Haynes; Archdeacon Robinson, afterwards Dean of Durham, Mr. Robertson; and Dr. Redmayne, the master of Trinity College, Cambridge.

A more judicious selection of learned and moderate men representing all classes and all schools could not have been made.

The result of their deliberations was an immediate reform of the Missal; which emanated in a Communion office substantially the same as that which is now in use.*

Inadvertently, indeed, a further liberty was granted to the members of the Church of England. Auricular confession was declared to be no longer obligatory before the reception of the Holy Sacrament. The communicants had become so very few, that measures were taken to increase the number, and one of the impediments to frequent communion, or to communion at all, was found to consist in the supposed necessity of confessing. Confession to God, being necessary, a general confession and an absolution were afterwards prepared; but at the present time, with a liberality worthy of commendation, the subject of confession was left an open question. Persons who adhered to the old system of auricular confession were exhorted to abstain from censuring their brethren, by whom a general confession to Almighty God was considered to be a sufficient preparation for the Holy Sacrament; on the other hand, it was required of

---

* Our present office was adopted in the Convocation of 1662, in the reign of Charles II. It is to be observed that the present Mass Book was not used in England anterior to the Reformation, as modern sciolists take for granted. Although all liturgies, using the term in its strict sense, were similar, and the English Communion office is no exception, yet, until the Council of Trent, which imposed (with some trifling exceptions) the Roman office on churches of the Roman obedience, they differed considerably, as has been shown above, in detail.

others who were contented with a confession to God only without the intervention of a priest, not to vituperate their brethren who set a value on sacerdotal benediction.

It was ordered that the ancient office, to which the people were accustomed, should be used without alteration, in the Latin tongue, to the end of the canon, and up to that point where the celebrant was accustomed to receive the Communion himself. An exhortation, in effect the same as the second of those now in the Prayer Book, was after this addressed to the communicants. They were to be prepared for the high privilege to which they were admitted by a warning and an encouragement; by confessing their sins to God, and by a general absolution; the comfortable sentences followed, and the prayer of humble access. The communicants having received in both kinds, were dismissed with the benediction.*

The order for the Communion was published by proclamation on the 8th of March; and the proclamation was followed by a royal letter requiring the bishops to distribute it without loss of time in their respective dioceses, in order that it might be in the hands of the clergy before the ensuing Easter.

A reform of the Breviary was a natural consequence of the reform of the Missal: from the liturgy, properly so called, attention was directed to the entire ritual of the Church of England. The additions made to the Missal with the view of bringing prominently forward the sacramental as distinguished from the sacrificial portion of the ordinance, had caused much annoyance to many who trembled for the safety of the ark when a portion of it so sacred was touched.

With the Breviary it was otherwise. The Breviary,

---

* The office may be found in Wilkins, iv. 11; Sparrow's Collections; L'Estrange's Alliance; and Cardwell's Two Liturgies.

itself an arrangement of offices previously existing, had, at various periods, received additions and alterations. It required to be translated, rearranged, compressed, and rendered more convenient for common and parochial use. To bring the whole within the compass of one volume was a great and important undertaking, rendered possible through the instrumentality of the printing-press. Before the art of printing was discovered, or rather applied to the fabrication of books, every set of offices formed a separate volume. The trouble and expense of transcription was great, and as all parts of the ritual were not in demand in every place, it was not easy to procure them. The parish priest did not require the pontifical; and the processional, which was studied in the cathedral and the monastery, was, comparatively speaking, of little importance in the rural parish. There were the Psalter, the Bible, the Antiphonarium, the Hymnarium, the Passionarium, the Martyrologium, and similar books, of which the use, respectively, like those enumerated, was denoted by their titles, to discuss which would occupy us long.

For all this a remedy was demanded. It was also discovered that valuable as was the Portease, Portuis, Portuasse, Porthoos, or Porfory, or Portiforium—(by all which titles the Salisbury Breviary was denominated, being a collection of lessons, collects, hymns, thanksgivings, and forms of prayer which have solaced the souls of the faithful and brought them into communion with God, from the earliest times)—it was nevertheless tinged and tainted with certain superstitions and errors of doctrine, which required the erasing hand of the cautious reformer.

But as Cranmer and his coadjutors observed :—

" There was never anything by the wit of man so well devised, or so surely established, which (in continuance of time) hath

CHAP. III.

Thomas Cranmer 1533-56.

not been corrupted: as (among other things) it may plainly appear by the common prayers in the Church, commonly called divine service: the first original and ground whereof if a man would search out by the ancient fathers, he shall find that the same was not ordained, but of a good purpose, and for a great advancement of godliness; for they so ordered the matter, that all the whole Bible (or the greatest part thereof) should be read over once in the year, intending thereby that the clergy, as especially such as were ministers of the congregation, should (by often reading and meditation of God's Word) be stirred up to godliness themselves, and be more able to exhort other by wholesome doctrine, and to confute them that were adversaries to the truth. And further, that the people (by daily hearing of Holy Scripture read in the church) should continually profit more and more in the knowledge of God, and be the more inflamed with the love of His true religion. But these many years passed, this godly and decent order of the ancient fathers hath been so altered, broken, and neglected, by planting in uncertain stories, legends, responds, verses, vain repetitions, commemorations, and synodals, that commonly when any book of the Bible was begun, before three or four chapters were read out, all the rest were unread. And in this sort the book of Esaie was begun in Advent, and the book of Genesis in Septuagesima; but they were only begun, and never read through. After a like sort were other books of Holy Scripture used. And moreover, whereas St. Paul would have such language spoken to the people in the church, as they might understand and have profit by hearing the same: the service in this Church of England (these many years) hath been read in Latin to the people, which they understood not, so that they have heard with their ears only; and their hearts, spirit, and mind have not been edified thereby. And furthermore, notwithstanding that the ancient fathers have divided the Psalms into seven portions, whereof every one was called a nocturn; now of late time a few of them have been daily said (and oft repeated) and the rest utterly omitted. Moreover, the number and harshness of the rules called the Pie, and the manifold changings of the service, was the cause, that to turn the book only was so hard and intricate a matter, that many times there was more business to find out what should be read than to read it when it was found out."*

The commissioners over whom the Primate presided, assembled at Windsor on the 9th of May, 1548. They continued to sit during the summer months, and brought their labours to a termination in the month of November. They removed from the Breviary all that was anti-scriptural, and they adopted an order of service very similar to that with which we are ourselves familiar. At the same time they carried on still further their reform of the Missal. The whole office was now to be in English, and it was styled, "The Supper of the Lord and the Holy Communion, commonly called the Mass." This reformed Mass is very nearly identical with that office which is still used by the Church of England.

The Act of Uniformity, by which parliamentary authority was given to the work thus accomplished by the Church, is so important, as corroborating the facts now laid before the reader, that it will be interesting to peruse it as an historical document. It commences with saying:—

"Whereas of long time there hath been had in this realm of England and Wales divers forms of Common Prayer, commonly called the Service of the Church, that is to say, the Use of Sarum, of York, of Bangor, and of Lincoln; and besides the same now of late much more divers and sundry forms and fashions have been used in the cathedrals and parish churches of England and Wales, as well concerning the mattens, or morning prayer, and the even-song, as also concerning the Holy Communion, commonly called the Mass, with divers and sundry rites and ceremonies concerning the same, and in the administration of other sacraments of the Church; and albeit, the king, by the advice of his Council, hath hitherto divers

---

* Pref. to First Liturgy.

times assayed to stay innovations or new rites concerning the premisses, yet the same hath not had such good success as his Highness required in that behalf; whereupon his Highness being pleased to bear with the frailty and weakness of his subjects in that behalf, of his great clemency hath not only been content to abstain from punishment of those that have offended in that behalf, but also to the intent a uniform quiet and godly order should be had concerning the premisses, hath appointed the Archbishop of Canterbury, and certain other of the most learned and discrete bishops, and other learned men of this realm, having respect to the most sincere and pure Christian religion taught by the Scripture, as to the usages in the primitive Church, to draw and make one convenient and meet order, rite, and fashion, of common and open prayer and administration of the sacraments to be had and used in his Majesty's realm of England and in Wales, the which by the aid of the Holy Ghost, with one uniform agreement, is of them concluded, set forth, and delivered in a book. entitled 'The Book of Common Prayer and Administration of the Sacraments and other Rites and Ceremonies of the Church, after the use of the Church of England:' Wherefore the Lords spiritual and temporal, and the Commons, in this present parliament assembled, considering as well the most godly travel of the king's Highness herein, as the godly prayers, orders, rites, and ceremonies in the said book mentioned, and the considerations of altering those things which he altered, and retaining those things which be received in the said book, and also the honour of God, and great quietness which by the grace of God shall ensue upon the one and uniform rite and order, in such Common Prayer and rites and external ceremonies to be used throughout England and Wales, do give to his Highness most hearty and lowly thanks for the same, and humbly pray that it may be enacted by his Majesty, with the assent of the Lords and Commons in parliament assembled, that all and singular ministers in any cathedral or parish church, or other place within this realm, shall be bounden to say and use the mattens, even-song, celebration of the Lord's Supper, commonly called the Mass, and administration of each the sacraments, and all their common and open prayer, in such order and form as is mentioned in the same book, and none other, or otherwise." *

With the exception of a reference to one of the rubrics, we of the nineteenth century, as Mr. Gladstone observes, are not more concerned with this Prayer Book than we are with any of the Breviaries preceding it. It is the basis of the Prayer Book adopted by the Convocation of 1662, but so were the antecedent Breviaries the basis of Edward's first Book of Common Prayer.†

It may be doubted whether Cranmer, and those who were associated with him, could appreciate to its full extent the work as it came from their hands. Without depreciating their learning or their piety, we know that their minds had been directed to doctrinal studies rather than to devotional exercises; and we also know that to liturgical subjects the learned mind of Europe was not directed before the middle of the seventeenth century. For the blessing which we possess in our liturgy, using the term in its most extended sense, we are indebted to that intuitive wisdom of the English mind, which objects to changes for the mere sake of changing, and which, while sanctioning reform, abhors revolution. Our first reformers dared not do more than they did; our last reformers, those to whom we are especially indebted, and who, in 1662, gave us our present Prayer Book, appreciated the blessing to the full extent, of having a Church not made new but reformed. They, as we do, felt a pride in being able to say:—" The English Prayer Book was not composed in a few years, nor by a few men; it has descended to us with the improvements and the approbation of many centuries: and they who truly feel the calm and sublime elevation of

* Phillimore's Burns, iii. 409.
† See the Introductory Chapter to this book.

our hymns and prayers, participate in the spirit of primitive devotion. The great majority of our formularies are actually translated from Latin and Greek rituals which have been used for at least fourteen or fifteen hundred years in the Christian Church; and there is scarcely a portion of our Prayer Book which cannot in some way be traced to ancient offices."*

By the Calvinists, who were beginning to form a party in our country, and who desired to substitute their sect on the overthrow of the Church, complaint was made that the commissioners in supplying the Church, in the Book of Common Prayer, with a mere revision of the ancient formularies, had done next to nothing. The Book of Common Prayer, it was said, was only the Missal and the Breviary in the English language. That this was not, strictly speaking, true, it is unnecessary to affirm. The slightest examination of these works will show that the reformers strictly observed the principle which in the Breviary as it then existed—except under the forms published by Cardinal Quignon and Archbishop Hermann—had been violated though it had not been repudiated. Provision was made for the reading of the entire Scriptures, which, in the unrevised formulary, had been rendered impossible by the introduction of legends now discarded. The Psalter was to be read or sung, in the course of a month instead of a week. The seven services were united so as to produce, what had of late become the practice through their unauthorised junction, two forms, one for morning, the other for evening prayer. The Ave Maria and Invocation of Saints were abolished, together with many superstitious observances. In the abolition of what they regarded as superstitions, it may be doubted whether the reformers did not go too far. The various consecra-

---

* Sir William Palmer, Origines Liturgicæ, ii. Pref. ii.

tions and exorcisms of bread, cheese, candles, incense, palms, bells and images, were very properly abolished. But there were various other customs to which the people were attached and which attracted them to the Church; and whether a reservation of some observances which, though not necessary, were at least innocent, might not have been permitted, is a question which occurs to the mind of those who, after the lapse of ages, contemplate with gratitude the good work which was accomplished as admirable in principle, even if not perfect in detail. Among the English reformers there were no men of a vivid imagination, and there were some who were influenced by the sarcastic wit in which the more violent partisans of the reformation indulged. Their single object was the refutation of error, and they did not perceive that religion has to deal not only with the logical faculty in man, but also with his affections and imagination.

The Common Prayer Book being intended for the service of the priests and people, the ordinal at first formed no part of it. But the desire to be able to bind up all our offices in one volume was reasonable. A reformation of the ordinal was accordingly required; and the revision was conducted by the same commission by which the other ordinances of the Church had been reformed, with the exception of the Bishop of Chichester. From the renunciation of the patriarchal authority, formerly assumed by the Pope, certain alterations had become necessary, and these were carefully framed in conformity with the rules recapitulated in the Council of Carthage, held in the year 401. When change was not necessary, the service followed the ancient ritual.*

It is observed by a distinguished ritualist that this was

* Collier, v. 376; Strype's Memorials, ii. 186; Heylin, 82; Origines Liturgicæ, ii. 246.

an important step, by which the apostolical succession was preserved to the Church of England. "The clergy," he says, "are proved to be the successors of the apostles and the true ministers of God, by the succession of apostolical ordination; by prescriptive, rightful, and original possession; and by the succession of apostolical doctrine.

"*First.* The bishops who rule the churches of these realms were validly ordained by others, who by means of an unbroken spiritual descent of ordinations, derived their mission from the apostles and from our Lord. This continual descent is evident to any one who chooses to investigate it. Let him read the catalogues of our bishops, ascending up to the most remote period. Our ordinations descend in a direct unbroken line from Peter and Paul, the apostles of the circumcision and the Gentiles. These great apostles successively ordained Linus, Cletus, and Clement bishops of Rome; and the apostolical line of succession was regularly continued from them to Celestine, Gregory and Vitalianus, who ordained Patrick bishop for the Irish, and Augustine and Theodore for the English. And from those times an uninterrupted series of valid ordinations have carried down the apostolical succession in our churches even to the present day. There is not a bishop, priest, or deacon amongst us, who cannot, if he pleases, trace his own spiritual descent from St. Peter and St. Paul. *Secondly.* These bishops are the rightful successors of those who ruled the Church in the beginning. The pastors who originally preached the gospel and converted the inhabitants of these realms to Christianity were legitimately ordained, and therefore had divine mission for their work. The ancient British bishops, who sat in the councils of Arles and Nice in the fourth century, were followed by a long line of successors, who governed dioceses in Britain; so were those prelates from Ireland, who in the seventh century converted a great portion of the pagan invaders of Britain; and so also was Augustine, Archbishop of Canterbury, who was sent by Gregory of Rome about the same time, and who preached to another portion of the Anglo-Saxons. The churches, deriving their origin from these three sources, were governed by prelates, who all filled distinct dioceses; and those dioceses have been occupied by a regular series of bishops, canonically ordained, from the beginning down to the present day. We can therefore not only prove that we are descended by valid ordinations from the apostles Peter and Paul; but can point out the dioceses which our predecessors have rightly possessed even from the beginning. We stand on the ground of prescriptive and immemorial possession, not merely from the times of Patrick and Augustine; but from those more remote ages, when the bishops and priests that were our predecessors attended the Councils of Arles and of Nice, when Tertullian and Origen bore witness that the fame of our Christianity had extended to Africa and the East."*

The Ordination Service was at first used, as the office for the consecration of churches is at the present time, by the sole authority of the bishops. But as, in those days of bitter controversy, the validity of the office, as related to the secular rights of the clergy, might have been questioned, an act of parliament was obtained: and a most extraordinary act it was, constituting that to be law which did not at the time exist.†

"Such form," it was said, "and manner of making and consecrating of archbishops, bishops, priests, deacons, and other ministers of the Church, as by six prelates and six other men of this realm learned in God's law, by the king

---

* Sir William Palmer, Origines Liturgicæ, i. 250.
† Statutes at Large, ii. 435.

to be appointed and assigned, or by the most number of them, shall be devised for that purpose and set forth under the Great Seal before the first of April next coming, shall be lawfully exercised and used, and none other."*

In the year 1553, the ordinal was annexed to the Book of Common Prayer, and so it has continued to be. Certain alterations were then made; the omission, for example, of some requirements as to vestments, of introits, of all appeal to saints and evangelists, of the delivery of a chalice and bread at the ordination of a priest; and of the laying the Bible on the neck, and of the placing the pastoral staff in the hand at the consecration of a bishop.†

These were concessions made to the violent clamour raised against the Book of Common Prayer and against all the work of our reformers, by the Calvinistic or Ultra-Protestant party, now rising into importance. Of the violence of this party we shall have occasion to speak more particularly hereafter. We have only occasion here to renew our remark, that Archbishop Cranmer had no very fixed principles to guide him; and that, though he was a man of great ability, he had no genius to mark out a line of his own. By the clergy generally, the Book of Common Prayer had been favourably received. No greater proof of this can be produced than the fact, that

---

* The principal writers in defence of the validity of our ordinations are Mason, Bramhall, Burnet, and Elrington. Amongst the Romanists, Courayer, Canon Regular of Ste. Geneviève, distinguished himself by a "Defence of the Validity of the English Ordinations," and by a masterly "Supplement" to the same work, in which he overthrows triumphantly all the objections of Père le Quien, and other Romanists, to our ordinations.

† Bulley, Variations of Communion and Baptismal Offices in the Church of England.

before the Whitsunday on which it was commanded to be used, it had been introduced into many churches by the impatience both of the clergy and of the people. But it was violently assailed by the party of the old learning, and more violently still by the Calvinists. At this time, the Archbishop, in his weakness, held parley with the Ultra-Protestants. He dared not do as they wished in all respects, for he knew that although the country would tolerate the reform of the Church, an attempt to overthrow it would cause a rebellion.* But the Calvinists were supported by a government, the members of which were anxious to make their own fortunes through the overthrow of the Church; and thus supported they could obtain a hearing, and they made an impression even on the clergy, though not at present to any great extent.

In his letters to the Protector, to Bullinger, and to the Archbishop himself, Calvin fiercely attacked not only the Prayer Book, but the whole principle of the English Reformation. He projected for this country a submission to his own code, and for this purpose he employed agents in the court, among the clergy, and in the two Universities.† It is an extraordinary fact, that although Calvinism consigns whole masses of people to perdition, there is such a fascination about the system even to the present time, that the most illiterate and even immoral Calvinist can secure an overflowing congregation, where an orthodox preacher can scarcely obtain an audience. To this

* An eminent writer uttered the paradox, that in our revolutions the English thought much of liberty, and nothing of religion. This historical falsehood has been reiterated by many an ignoramus pretending to that superiority of intellect which infidelity assumes to itself; though the slightest glance at the history of England would convict them of uttering what is a palpable untruth.

† Heylin, 107.

class of reformers, the retention of the name of Mass, which was the title of our Communion office when first it was revised, gave great offence.* Our reformers retained it, probably, without having considered the subject. There it was. It was one of the ancient names of the office. They merely revised the office, and permitted the old title to remain in the English Liturgy.

Nothing could exceed the violence of the ultra-reformers and the insolence of foreigners in seeking to dictate to the people of England. To such an extent was this violence carried, that it was found necessary to bring the whole subject of a revision of our offices before the Convocation which met in the year 1550. Of the debates in this Convocation no record has been preserved; we only know, from a letter written by Peter Martyr, that he had been informed by the archbishop himself that he had summoned the Convocation "about the business of the revision, and had concluded many alterations." †

---

* The word Mass, as applied to the Divine Liturgy, is, according to Bingham, who gives the authority, derived from the words, "Ite missa est," addressed to the catechumens, "Go, ye are dismissed;" or, as in the Eastern Liturgies, "Let us depart hence in peace." I believe that there was no doubt about this origin of the term in the early writers. In the middle ages, as the doctrine became corrupt, some of the schoolmen derived the signification of the word from its being a sacrifice, sent up, "dismissed to God." It was this, probably, which made it offensive to some Protestant divines. Certain it is, that it was used, at length, to distinguish the Roman idea of a *propitiatory* from the primitive idea of the *spiritual* sacrifice. Our reformers, dwelling on the Sacrament, spoke of the Communion office; the Romanists, dwelling on a corporeal sacrifice, spoke of the Mass. It is a misfortune to have permitted the Romanists to maintain and appropriate the correct name; but it cannot now be helped. The reader may find it convenient to be reminded or informed that the "ordinary" of the Mass was such part of the service as preceded the canon, which did not vary with the different festivals. The "canon," or rule, was the part of the service containing the actual consecration.

† Collier, v. 434.

The original commissioners, it appears, with the archbishop at their head, renewed their labours in 1550; and, proceeding carefully in their work, they were able to submit it to the Convocation on the 14th of October, and again at the session of the 5th of November. The parliament met on the 23rd of January, 1552, and on the 6th of April another Act of Uniformity was passed. The offices, thus further altered, came into use on the Feast of All Saints, and are generally known as the Second Book of Edward VI. The Ultra-Protestants were almost as much dissatisfied with the second book as they had been with the first. The ultra-party had got the ear of the young king, whose precocious talents were accompanied by the self-sufficiency and obstinacy by which the Tudor race was, for good or for evil, distinguished. There was, at the same time, a large party who were unwilling that the first book should be changed at all. Sufficient liberties, they thought, had already been taken with the ancient offices. The two parties have continued in the Church to the present hour. We have still to lament the bitterness of the controversial spirit as exhibited by either extreme; and we still find the strength of the Church in that large but unobtrusive body of Christian men and Christian women who, treading in the via media, are inflexible in principle, while exempt alike from the weakness of superstition and the reveries of fanaticism; who, active without ostentation, bring religion to bear on the relations of life, while their patriotism and churchmanship are neither warped by ambition nor tainted by faction.

Whether the alterations introduced into the second Prayer Book were all of them improvements, is a subject upon which opinion is still divided; and, as we know not the precise line taken by Cranmer, it does not fall within my province to discuss it. It may be convenient, however, briefly to state what were the chief variations from the first book which appeared in the second.

The first reformed Prayer Book enjoined what the second did not in the following particulars among others: It had its introits or psalms prefixed to the collects for the day. A second Communion was appointed for Christmas and Easter, and a service for the Feast of St. Mary Magdalene. The use of the terms "mass" and "altar" was omitted, and the mixture of water with wine in the Eucharist. A rubric was added for setting the elements on the altar, and the ancient form in delivering them was retained, together with an invocation—a verbal oblation,—and signing of the cross in the consecration. Transpositions of the *Gloria in Excelsis*, and some other portions of the services were ordered. In the first book, moreover, there were prayers for the dead in the Communion and Burial Service. There was a rubric for receiving the bread in the mouth, another for reserving the Sacrament, and others supposing daily Communion. A Communion was provided at burials. Anointing in the Visitation and Communion of the Sick was retained, with a form of exorcism, trine immersion, unction, and the chrism in baptism. There was a separate service for the consecration of the water. Signing of the cross was a ceremony observed in matrimony. The rochet, albe, and vestment, or cope, were authorised. The Athanasian Creed was to be read only on the great festivals.

In the second edition of the revised Prayer Book, various changes were made. In the Communion Service several transpositions took place, and a modern form, since rejected, was substituted for the ancient delivery of the elements. Prayers for the dead were no longer introduced. The festival of St. Mary Magdalene was discontinued. A rubric was added at the end of the Preface, requiring all priests and deacons to say daily the morning and evening prayer, either privately or openly, unless they were let by some urgent cause. The Sentences, Exhortation, Confession and Absolution, and the *Jubilate Deo, Cantate Domino,* and *Deus misereatur,* were added in the morning and evening prayers, together with the Commandments, and a third exhortation in the Communion Service. It contained the declaration relative to kneeling at the Communion. The ordinal of 1549 was now added to the Prayer Book, with the slight variations mentioned above; and the Athanasian Creed was appointed for several saints' days, as well as for the great festivals.*

Archbishop Cranmer entered cordially into the scheme proposed by Melancthon for drawing up a confession of faith, to be adopted by all those communities of Christians in the Western Church by whom the supremacy of the Bishop of Rome was denied. Cranmer desired to see all these communities united under the King of England as their protector—a kind of lay pope to be opposed to the Pope of Rome. Calvin, who, if there were to be a Protestant pope, aspired to that office himself, perceived and declared, with his practical wisdom, that such an attempt would be futile.† Cranmer, however, determined that,

---

* Bulley's Variations in the Communion and Baptismal Offices. Pref. pp. vi. vii. x.; Cardwell's Two Liturgies, Coll. v. 435–7; Pickering's reprint of Prayer Book. London, 1844.

† Of this great and good man, to whom even those who stand opposed to the views regarded as distinctly and peculiarly his own, are nevertheless indebted for much of their theology, Archbishop Laurence truly says that 'systematizing was his darling propensity, and the ambition of being distinguished as a leader in reform his predominant passion; in the arrangements of the former he never felt a doubt, or found a difficulty; and in the pursuit of the latter he displayed an equal degree of perseverance and ardour. Thus, in the

if on a large scale he could not succeed, the attempt, nevertheless, to enforce an uniformity of teaching on all important points of divinity should be made in England.

It was the more needful that some authorised confession of faith should be published, as in some quarters, the reformers were accused of heresy, and this accusation the English reformers resisted.

Hence the forty-two articles, which were afterwards reduced to thirty-nine, were prepared under the direction of the archbishop, accepted by Convocation,* and enforced by the king in council, every clergyman being required to sign them. The two Protestant parties, the Lutherans and the Calvinists—though the Lutherans were in after times designated in England, under certain modifications of doctrine, Arminians—have made the articles thus first drawn up, under the auspices of Cranmer, their ground of battle. The Calvinists have striven to give to the articles drawn up by Lutherans an exclusively Calvinistic meaning; and they have been justified in the attempt, for though the articles were drawn up by Lutherans, yet the Lutherans penned them with the express purpose of making concessions, wherever it was possible, to the Calvinists.

doctrine of the Eucharist, it is well known that he laboured to acquire celebrity, and conciliate followers, by maintaining a kind of middle sacramental presence between the corporeal of the Lutherans and the mere spiritual of the Zuinglians, expressing himself in language which, partly derived from one and partly from the other, verged towards neither extreme, but which, by his singular talent at perspicuous combination, could be applied (and not without success) to his own particular purpose.

* How far the forty-two articles had the synodical sanction of the Church of England has been questioned. The subject is fairly discussed by Joyce, 483, and by Cardwell, in his Synodalia. Although we depend upon indirect testimony, the point seems to be established that they were submitted to Convocation.

The Archbishop of Canterbury was, I think, again indebted to the Archbishop of Cologne. In that prelate's valuable formulary may be seen the groundwork of the articles.*

CHAP. III.
Thomas Cranmer.
1533-56.

There was not much labour required on the part of the archbishop in the preparation of these articles, for he did not attempt to draw them up himself. He was doubtless aware, that he had not sufficient theological learning or firmness of character to do so. What was required, was that which Cranmer pre-eminently possessed, a sound judgment, and that power of revision which enabled him to mould what was intended for one set of circumstances into the shape which, under different circumstances, might make it still useful.

As the assessors of Archbishop Hermann were Melancthon and Bucer, we find what we should expect to find, a close resemblance between the forty-two articles and the Augsburg Confession. If we refer to Hermann's work, it is impossible to deny to Cranmer the credit due to him for the soundness of his judgment, and for the skill which could separate from a mass of important statements the salient and necessary portions. Cranmer had the faculty of expressing other men's thoughts more clearly than the

---

* In the Library of Chichester Cathedral we have the copy of Archbishop Hermann's work, which was in the possession of Archbishop Cranmer. On the title-page there is Cranmer's autograph. I give the full title and the colophon:—" Nostra Hermanni ex gratia Dei Archiepiscopi Coloniensis et Principis electoris, &c., simplex ac pia deliberatio, qua ratione Christiana et in verbo Dei fundata Reformatio Doctrinæ, administrationis divinorum Sacramentorum, Cæremoniarum, totiusque curæ Animarum et aliorum ministeriorum ecclesiasticorum, apud eos qui nostræ Pastorali curæ commendati sunt, tantisper instituenda sit, donec Dominus dederit constitui meliorem vel per liberam et Christianam Synodum, sive Generalem, sive Nationalem vel per ordines Imperii Nationis Germanicæ, in Spiritu Sancto congregatos. Bonnæ, ex officina Laurentii, Typographi, anno MDXXXV."

original thinker himself. Every document that passed through his hands came out improved.

The articles were first published by Grafton, the king's printer, in July 1553, with the following title: "Articles agreed upon by the Bishops and other learned Men of England in the Synod of 1552." In the same year was published a Catechism to which the articles appeared as an adjunct, and the whole together usually went by the name of The Catechism. It does not appear that in framing The Catechism Cranmer bore any part, though it was published by his authority.

The last important work in which Archbishop Cranmer was engaged was one peculiarly suited to his talents, and congenial to his legal mind. From the commencement of his career he had felt that, as by the repudiation of the papal supremacy many of our canons had become a dead letter, so a codification of the old canon law had become, though not necessary, yet highly important.

The idea of a reformation of the canons did not indeed originate with him, but to this important subject his spare moments had for many years been devoted. So early as the year 1532, before Cranmer had begun to take much interest in church affairs, the clergy, in their submission to the king, declared that " there were divers constitutions, ordinances, and canons prejudicial to the prerogative royal and onerous to the king's subjects; and that they were content to commit the revision of them to thirty-two persons, sixteen of the upper and nether house of the temporality, and the other sixteen of the clergy to be chosen and appointed by his most noble Grace." *

By an act of parliament, passed in 1534, the king was empowered to nominate commissioners, the act being

* Wilkins, iii. 755.

renewed in 1536 and 1544.* The work of the commissioners, among whom the primate was the most active, had been nearly brought to a completion when the king died. In 1549 an act was passed enabling King Edward VI. to issue a new commission to thirty-two persons, lay and clerical, for the compilation " of such ecclesiastical laws as should be thought by him, his counsel and them, convenient to be practised in all the spiritual courts of the realm." For some reason or other, the commissioners were never nominated, and the number required by the statute being deemed unnecessarily great, a royal commission was issued in November 1551, entrusting the prosecution of the work to eight persons, with the primate at their head; these eight persons being to be regarded as a sub-committee to a greater commission to be appointed afterwards. It was a singular arrangement, designed probably to save the trouble of a fresh application to parliament. The work had been so nearly completed in the late reign, that revision and correction were now all that was required. The work of revision devolved chiefly on Cranmer, who was assisted by Dr. Walter Haddon, king's professor of civil law at Cambridge. The work was composed, but not published, in English; a translation into Latin was made by Dr. Haddon, who is supposed to have consulted Sir John Cheke—the style was certainly much superior to the style in which such documents are generally drawn up.†

CHAP. III.

Thomas Cranmer. 1533–56.

* 25 Henry VIII. c. 19; 27 Henry VIII. c. 15; 35 Henry VIII. c. 16.

† " Atque hoc modo confectæ hæ quidem leges sunt, sive eas ecclesiasticas sive politicas appellare libeat. Quarum materia ab optimis undique legibus petita videtur, non solum ecclesiasticis, sed civilibus etiam, veterumque Romanorum precipua antiquitate. Summæ negotii præfuit Tho. Cranmerus, archiepis. Cant. Orationis lumen et splendorem addidit Gualterus Haddonus, vir disertus, et in hac ipsa juris

Commissioners were engaged in this work during the year 1552, and they were prepared to submit it to the next parliament and Convocation, when their labours were brought to a termination by the death of Edward VI.

The work was a failure. No one can read it without being impressed by a feeling of Cranmer's great ability—a fact the more worthy of note since his learning and talents were depreciated by his adversaries; but it was not what it was designed to be—a codification of the ancient canons of our Church. It was a system of sectarian law, rather than the adaptation of the laws of the Catholic to the exigencies of a national Church. It was not what King Henry contemplated—a reformation; it was a new system based on the expedient, rather than on the eternal principles of law and equity.

The "Reformatio Legum Ecclesiasticarum" was, nevertheless, a work of high pretensions; that, probably, on which Cranmer thought his fame would rest. It was distributed into fifty-one titles, in imitation of Justinian's celebrated digest of the Roman law; and in imitation of the addition to the printed copies of the "Pandects," an appendix, "De Regulis Juris," was supplied.

We are only concerned with the work so far as it throws light upon the character and opinions of Cranmer. Cranmer's extreme opinions with respect to the prerogatives of the Crown were unchanged. As the foundation of all ecclesiastical law, he introduces the king as commanding all his subjects, everywhere and under every denomination, to be Christians. By Christianity is meant the Catholic faith. By the Catholic faith is meant the acceptance of

---

facultate non imperitus. Quin nec satis scio an Joan. Checi viri singularis eidem negotio adjutrix adfuerit manus. Quo factum est, ut cultiori stylo concinnatæ sint istæ leges, quam pro communi ceterarum legum more." Præf. ed. 1571. Ref. Legum. Cardwell, xxvi.

the fact of the Holy Trinity, and of the doctrines bearing
upon that fact.* The penalty for denying that truth, and
for not worshipping the Trinity in Unity and the Unity in
Trinity, is death.

The next title defines, rather vaguely, the notion of
heresy, and distinguishes the heretic from the schismatic.
Notice is then taken of various heretical opinions prevalent at the time, and the law is laid down that any heretic
who, having been found guilty, will not renounce his
heretical opinions, shall be handed over to the civil
magistrate, to be punished—but not necessarily by death.
Death awaited those who denied "the fundamental doctrine of Christianity, the Catholic faith, the doctrine of
the ever blessed Trinity;" but that in other cases punishments milder than death were intended, is evident from
the fact that the outlawry of one convicted of heresy is provided: he is incapable of being a witness or of making a
will—provisions which would be absurd if, on conviction,
he were to be burned as a matter of course. The magistrate might condemn any heretic to the stake, but he was
at liberty also to commute the punishment for any act of

---

* Thus under this title is included an acceptance of the three creeds,
of the canonical Scriptures, to the exclusion of the Apocrypha and of
the first five councils; but, it is added, " quoniam perlongum esset, et
plane opus valde laboriosum, omnia nunc distincte scribere quæ catholica fide sunt credenda, sufficere judicamus quæ breviter de Summa
Trinitate, de Jesu Christo Domino nostro, et de salute per Eum humano
generi parta, diximus." (Ref. Leg. 7.) It will be remarked and remembered, that death for holding heretical opinions was as much a part of the
Protestant code as the Roman. With a view to peace, we must never
forget that neither party had a monopoly in the right of persecution. Nor
may we deny the fact that the spirit of persecution still exists, as may
be seen in the proceedings against such churches as St. George's in the
East, and in the speeches of certain lords and gentlemen in either
House of Parliament. Alas for human nature!

"Iliacos intra muros peccatur et extra."

heresy, except in cases where the fundamental fact of Christianity was denied.*

On doctrinal subjects it may be presumed that Cranmer's opinions were at this time very nearly, if not entirely, what, in accordance with the existing formularies of the Church of England, we should regard as orthodox. The statements are lucid and decided with respect to regeneration in baptism and with respect to the Lord's Supper, as also with reference to the consecration of bishops, and the ordination of priests and deacons. Idolatry, magic, witchcraft, consultation with conjurors, and divination by lots are all denounced. Stringent canons were introduced on the subject of marriage and divorce, and the duties devolving upon parish officers were laid down in some detail. Perhaps the most objectionable thing in this document, after the sanguinary penalties attached to misbelief, is the chapter relating to predestination. Predestination and election are treated of in the Lutheran, and not, as has been stated by those who have not examined the subject, in the Calvinistic sense; and the subject was introduced to guard against the introduction of ultra-protestant views: but if such

* Cranmer was not in advance of his age; he thought that a heretic was as much deserving of death as a felon. I have laboured throughout this work to deal justly in the award of praise and censure to both Protestants and Papists. But if, looking to our own house, we must not throw stones in what regards the subject of persecution, we may safely affirm that no such disregard for truth has been of late years displayed by Protestants as there has been by their opponents. The conduct of the French translator of "Ranke's History of the Popes" has been branded by the indignation of Macaulay and Milman. The latter observes that the most unscrupulous bigot will hardly attempt to justify the publishing, as the sentiments and opinions of an author, sentiments and opinions which he has not authorised and would utterly repudiate as directly opposite to his own. But even worse than this was the infamous proceeding of hiring Cobbett to employ his powerful

subjects were to be introduced not only into confessions of faith—and many think that they are out of place even there—but into codes of law, other similar subjects could not be excluded, and the fetters placed upon the mind would become unbearable.

From the adoption of this Cranmerian code the Church was, in providential mercy, saved; when it was nearly completed, by the death of Henry VIII.; and again when it was ready for a royal proclamation to establish it, by the timely death of Edward VI. The Puritans having given a Calvinistic turn to articles and canons—designed to conciliate them, without, however, endorsing their opinions—attempted to have the proposed code established by act of parliament in 1571; but the wisdom of Queen Elizabeth, who would not permit parliament to legislate for the Church independently of the Crown and of Convocation, frustrated the manœuvres of a minority in the house of commons, and maintained the Church in the enjoyment of its ancient liberties. On the subjects relating to the Quinquarticular controversy, and many others, upon which the Puritans would have bound us, men are free to think, to speak, and to write, subject only to the moral persecution which leaves all but the temper and feelings intact.

The Church remained, as it still remains, under those ancient canons enacted in a long succession of synods "from the days of Augustine to the present time, modified

---

pen to write a "History of the Reformation," in which every refuted fact is asserted as an indisputable historical statement. But even worse than this is the fact that this book of lies is still industriously circulated by leading men of the Romish persuasion. It is represented to foreigners as the only authentic history of the English Reformation. We fear not the result, for we know who is the father of lies. But such conduct on the part of those who profess and call themselves Christians, afflicts the heart of all who serve the God of truth.

in their application by acts of parliament, by royal injunctions, by the constitutions and canons and ecclesiastical statutes agreed upon in 1603," and by the judgments given in our ecclesiastical courts.

If over our ecclesiastical courts, with a few splendid exceptions, judges have presided who have been unequal to the high position to which they have been called, who have been unable to distinguish what is catholic from what is papal, and who have unjustly interpreted our Prayer Book—a reform of the Missal and the Breviary—not by reference to ancient customs and canons, but by their own private opinions, formed in some ultra-protestant school—if the highest court has expressed a judgment under the direction of men who have hated the Church, because their deeds are evil—we can only say that the Church has been unfortunate in her members, and we may be permitted to hope that, as in the courts of common law and equity, men have been chosen, except in the case of Lord High Chancellor, not from political but from professional excellence—so the day may come when over our spiritual courts judges may be appointed to preside who will understand that the duty of a judge is to abide by a law, however imperfect, and not regard in his decision the favour of the crowd, the plaudits of a religious mob, or the smiles of aristocratic intolerance.

Cranmer's labours in this, as in everything else, were brought to a termination by the death of Edward VI.

It is sometimes presumed that Cranmer's influence was great in the court of the young king; but for this, as for many other historical conjectures, when made by incompetent persons, we look in vain for proof. From the young king's diary, indeed, we should draw the opposite conclusion. With a fanatical and wrong-headed boy a man so courteous, calm, and prudent as Cranmer, was not likely to be a favourite ; and we have many instances of an impatience of contradiction displayed by Edward. His dislike of Somerset most probably arose from the fact that the Protector, in coercing the boy, acted more with the authority of the uncle than with the flattery of the courtier.

The archbishop himself declares that he was so much out of favour with Northumberland, that he sometimes thought his life in danger ; and he expressly asserts that to the duke's intrigues to divert the succession of the Crown he was an entire stranger, until he was sent for to the court to perform an official act by appending his name to a document which had been previously drawn up.*

When Northumberland had succeeded, by an appeal to the fanaticism of the king, in his conspiracy to divert the succession to the Crown in favour of his daughter-in-law, he was aware of the obstinacy of Edward's character, and he thought he might with safety summon the archbishop to court. Cranmer's signature to the instrument, sanctioning the proposed resolution, was almost a necessity, because, although, being without ambition as a statesman, he had ceded the post of honour to others, he had been placed by Henry's will at the head of the Regency. Cranmer felt his responsibility and opposed the proceeding. The fact of his acting eventually against the dictates of his conscience, renders his weakness on this occasion the more inexcusable. At the same time we must in fairness admit, that when he began to waver, strong

---

* The archbishop expressly says: "The duke never opened his mouth to me, (to) move me to any such matter. Nor his heart was not such towards me (seeking long time my destruction) that he would ever trust me in such a matter, or think that I would be persuaded by him." Remains, ii. 362.

arguments could be adduced to palliate, if not to justify, his conduct. To a man of Cranmer's character, the fact that all the council except one, including the secretary Cecil, had yielded to the persuasions of the king, who had made the subject personal to himself, would have very great weight. He could not read men's hearts. He could not know that such a man as Cecil was belying his convictions by the course he was taking; and who was he that he should stand alone in an affair in favour of which his predilections could not fail to be strong? for he could not expect any favour from the daughter of Katharine of Aragon. This line of argument would come to him with greater force when he was informed that the Chief Justice and the judges who had entertained the same opinion as himself, had at length receded from it. Then, again, by several enactments in the late reign, the principle seemed to have been conceded that the sovereign, with the consent of parliament, had power to divert the succession to the crown from the immediate claimant. Mary, and Elizabeth also, though they had been appointed to succeed in default of issue from the king's marriage with Queen Jane, and afterwards with Queen Catherine (Parr), had nevertheless been declared illegitimate; and, even as it was, if either princess had married without the consent of the Privy Council, by the enactment of the thirty-fifth of Henry VIII., she was to be passed over, as if she had died without lawful issue. In the exclusion of the Queen of Scots, Edward merely followed the provisions of his father's will.

It is fair to Cranmer to mention these perplexities, and to remind the reader that the law of succession generally was not at that time as clearly defined as it is now. One of the difficulties arose from the doubt whether a female could succeed to the throne. The king's "device," in the first instance, would have excluded Jane, in favour of her heirs male. But, after all, Cranmer was too clear-sighted not to detect the sophistry by which the " device " was supported, and, as was usual with him, he did not yield at last, until an appeal was made to his feelings.

He was summoned to the royal presence. The young king lay before him in the last stage of a pulmonary consumption. His eye was still bright, and he was as self-willed as ever. He had just before overruled the Chief Justice Montague and the judges. When they declined to reduce the king's " device " into legal form, without the sanction of parliament, the despotic boy angrily exclaimed, " No; I will have this thing done immediately, and it shall be ratified by parliament afterwards. I therefore command you to fulfil my orders without further delay." Thus spoke the son of Henry. With his father's friend the Primate of all England, with more than his father's tact, he pursued a different course. He listened to the archbishop with patience. But the Marquis of Northampton and Lord Darcy were present, and in those perilous times, any expressions that might have escaped the archbishop's lips, would have been afterwards produced and perverted to his injury. The intimidated Cranmer wished for freedom of speech, and asked for a private interview. He would, in ordinary times, have had a right as a peer and a privy councillor to claim it; but the privy council now acted together as the regency, and it was not therefore permitted that one member should approach the king to speak to him on a political subject without the presence of others to represent the remaining members of the body. Northumberland had used the word traitor to Sir Edward Montague, and this implied a possible prosecution, for the offence, with its terrible consequences to the criminal. He rebuked the primate, telling him at the

CHAP. III.
Thomas Cranmer.
1533–56.

council-table that in endeavouring to dissuade the king from his will, he had exceeded his powers. Cranmer still hesitated. The intimidated judges produced the "device" in the proper form to receive the signature of the council. Cranmer said, "I cannot set my hand to this instrument without committing perjury, for I have sworn to the succession of the Lady Mary, according to the late king's testament." The answer was that the other members of the council had subscribed, and that in doing so their consciences did not accuse them of having committed the sin of perjury. Cranmer answered, "I judge no man's conscience, but my own. I cannot, however, allow my conscience to be guided by other men's acts." He was reminded that the legal authorities had pronounced the king competent to dispose of his crown by will. This was, of course, intended to silence him; it was an appeal *ad verecundiam*; but Cranmer saw that it was no valid answer to his objection, and he remained unmoved and inflexible. He was summoned again into the royal presence, and attended by the members of the council, he waited upon the king. The dying boy, pale and cadaverous, lay before him—the royal boy, his godson, whom he had loved as his own child, the son of his benefactor and friend, whom he had crowned and faithfully served; there he lay on his death-bed, too ill to argue, but resolute, determined, regarding this his last act as an act of duty to his God, his country, and himself. In justice to Cranmer, let us call all this to mind. Cranmer stood at the side of the couch to receive the last request of one whom he revered as a dying saint. "I hope," said Edward, "I hope that you will not stand out, and not be more repugnant to my will than all the rest of the council. The judges have informed me that I may lawfully bequeath my crown to the Lady Jane, and that my subjects may lawfully receive her as queen, notwithstanding the oath which they took under my father's will." The king had learned his lesson well. Cranmer still hesitated. He quitted the royal presence. He consulted the judges, who were in attendance. He returned to the sick chamber; he took a last look at his godson, and he signed the fatal document. This, considering the light in which Cranmer had regarded the subject, was an awful fall. He fell; but it was not from fear of death—he fell because he would not hurt the feelings of the dying youth.

Twenty-three names were attached to a written promise, pledging the oaths and honours of the subscribers to maintain the order of succession as limited in King Edward's "device." The perjury committed by all, including Cecil, was such as to involve the parties concerned in eternal disgrace. They swore to Edward that they would observe his will, they swore allegiance to Jane, and in swearing allegiance afterwards to Mary, they swore that they had originally designed to perjure themselves—all but Cranmer. When Cranmer had committed himself, he remained faithful to "the meek usurper" to the last.* The judges told him that he was exonerated from the oath he had made to observe King Henry's will; he believed them not, yet he acted on their dictum; and the same kind heart which yielded to the petitions of the dying Edward, induced him to remain loyal to Jane, though she, when she knew all, was free to admit that the proceedings which made her, as the French ambassador said, "a twelfth-day queen," were utterly unjustifiable and nefarious.

Whether Cranmer officiated at the funeral of Edward VI. is very doubtful. The interment took place at West-

* This was one of the charges brought against him when he appeared in the Star Chamber on the 14th of September, 1553.

minster Abbey on the 9th of August, and Bishop Day, who was soon after restored to the see of Chichester, of which he had been deprived by Cranmer, preached the sermon. He made an excuse for the conduct of the late king, in sanctioning the alterations in Church and State, which took place during his reign. He reviled Edward's advisers. He eulogized Queen Mary. According to Godwin, Day celebrated as well as preached.* The service was the reformed service, and the Communion administered in connexion with the service was in English. It is very probable, that Day may have objected to use this service, the only service which it was lawful to use, and that Cranmer may have been appointed to officiate that he might hear himself reviled by Day, who had formerly been his friend; and who, up to a certain point, had co-operated with him in the work of reformation.

But if this were the case, Cranmer must have had a special licence to leave the precincts of Lambeth. For immediately after the queen's arrival in London, he was summoned to attend the council; and having been reprimanded for the part he had taken in the revolution attempted in favour of the Lady Jane, he was ordered to confine himself to his manor at Lambeth, and to hold himself in readiness for another summons.

He was subjected to no other hardship, and many there were who now resorted to him for comfort and consolation; and among these came Peter Martyr. This distinguished foreigner had been suspended from his pro-

* Godwin, 110. Burnet and Strype assert that Cranmer officiated. Heylin is silent upon the subject. It is said that the queen had a mass of requiem celebrated next day in the Tower for the benefit of Edward's soul. (Noailles, ii. 109; Heylin, i. 298.) Sanders, 248, makes the same assertion, but remarks that the queen afterwards, " melius postea instituta," would not permit prayers to be offered for the soul either of her father or of her brother.

fessorship at Oxford, and sought a refuge at Lambeth. The archbishop could not offer him protection, and advised him to return home to Florence. Cranmer's advice to his friends in general was to fly the country, and there seems to be little doubt that the queen's government, scarcely knowing how to deal with an archbishop under his circumstances, purposely afforded him opportunities to escape. When urged by some of his friends to act upon the advice he had given to others, and to withdraw clandestinely from the country, he saw clearly the distinction to be made between his case and theirs. He said, "Were I likely to be called in question for treason, robbery, or some other crime, I should be much more likely to abscond than I am at present. As it is, the post which I hold and the part I have taken require me to make a stand for the truths of holy Scripture. I shall therefore undergo with constancy the loss of life, rather than remove secretly from the realm."

It was nobly resolved. No man knows his own weakness till he is tried to the uttermost. He directed his attention to the adjustment of his affairs, and arranged all pecuniary matters. But what strikes us as extraordinary is that he did not seem to think that he would be accused of treason for the part he had taken in the attempted revolution in favour of Queen Jane; and throughout the remainder of his life he was resolute in denying that he was a traitor.

It was now that the leading reformers of the Church of England seem to have laid down the rule on which they were to act, if the past reformation in the Church's discipline and doctrine were reversed, and practices renewed against which the leading men in Church and State had protested.

I. Those who, like Cranmer and Ridley, had made

themselves responsible for the series of reformations introduced in the reigns of Henry and Edward, very properly determined that their duty it was to remain in the country, to testify that they considered the changes they had introduced to be of vital importance. They were to abide in their respective stations, to vindicate the past, and to persuade the government to persevere in the principles of reform. Calm, dignified, truly religious, were they in their bearing. They did not court persecution; they did not fear it. They would escape if they could; but not at the sacrifice of any of those principles they had laboured to establish. They did not seek to introduce Protestantism, considered as a system, which in truth it never became; but they had raised their protest, and would continue to raise it, against the pope, and against those doctrines which were regarded as distinguishing papal from catholic Christianity.

II. Others there were, such as Cecil destined to become the great Lord Burghley, Sir Thomas Smith, and others, who were unjustly judged and considered as cravens or traitors in modern times. We are obliged to reiterate our warning against the supposition, that all who were in the sixteenth century opposed to the pope and popery must have been Protestants on the Exeter Hall pattern, and that they ought to have been ready to die for Protestantism. The statesmen of Cecil's stamp were men who, although they desired to see the Church reformed, did not feel called upon to defend, at peril of life and limb, the alterations in discipline or in dogma, which had taken place in King Edward's reign. Without agreeing in an approbation of all that had been done in the two preceding reigns, they had conformed under the regulations of Henry VIII.; they had rendered obedience to Edward's act of uniformity; and without weighing nicely the difference between consubstantiation and transubstantiation, they yielded obedience also to the ecclesiastical laws enforced by the government of Mary. They preferred a royal to a papal supremacy; but if the queen and the country thought otherwise, it was their business as good subjects " to do as they were bid." This was not high ground to take; but it was ground perfectly intelligible to men like Cranmer, Ridley, and Latimer, although they felt that it did not become them to take it. It is important to keep these cases before us, to render Cranmer's subsequent conduct intelligible. Men of this stamp were not molested, they only remained without preferment. The government had its eye upon them; they were suspected and watched; it was known that they would gladly see a change in the policy of the country, and that they were discontented; but still if they remained quiet, there was no wish to shed their blood.

III. There were impassioned zealots, men to be honoured for their sincerity and virtue; but who certainly had, many of them, a zeal without knowledge. When they saw men martyred, they became furious in their indignation; not distinguishing between the officer and the man, they fiercely attacked the magistrate or the official when performing his duty, and brought disgrace upon the cause they advocated by a violence and ribaldry, which at the same time provoked their opponents to acts of violence and deeds of blood, and brought disgrace upon the provokers and the provoked, upon the Christian cause in general.

IV. There were cold, avaricious, ambitious statesmen who cared for none of the things of religion; who advocated the cause of reform under Henry and Edward in order that they might enrich themselves by the spoils of abbeys and shrines; who were bribed under Mary, by permission given them to retain their spoils, to apply, or rather to misapply their statesmanship—their unquestioned abilities—to uphold the cause of the pope, so long as it was the cause of the queen, just as they had formerly encouraged the extreme licentiousness of the ultra-Protestants, in order that they might exercise dominion over the fanatical mind of King Edward. When they thought that the accession of Jane would be acceptable to the people, they were prepared for a revolution; when she was proclaimed under an ominous silence, they made their peace with Mary; and, the sincerity of their loyalty being suspected, they were violent partizans of the queen's religion; and to these men—the Arundels, the Pembrokes, the Russells and the Pagets, as well as to the queen herself—are to be attributed the persecutions which have stamped the reign of Mary with an epithet, which no power of sophistry will ever efface.

The attempt is made to fasten the blame of the persecutions upon Gardyner and Bonner. When we examine the facts of history, instead of relying on the statements of partizans, we must come to the conclusion that this is incorrect with regard to Gardyner; and, coarse and unfeeling as Bonner was, even with respect to him, it is only partially true.

Gardyner had been an opponent of the papal supremacy in the reign of Henry VIII.; but in his prison, during the reign of Edward, he had come to the conclusion that the exercise of the royal supremacy might be rendered more intolerable and unjust than that which the Bishop of Rome had usurped. He was, therefore, prepared to change his principles in regard to the supremacy, although it was with reluctance that he yielded to the re-establishment of a despotism which Henry had destroyed.

That he felt no more compunction at burning a heretic

than Cranmer, or Bonner, or Calvin, is certain; but as a matter of fact, there was not one person burnt when he was at the zenith of his power in 1553–54; and in the last year of his life fewer were burnt than at any other period of Mary's reign. His bitterest enemy in the preceding reign had been the Duke of Northumberland; yet he not only visited the duke, when this great traitor was in the Tower, but he pleaded for his life, and if it had not been for the interference of Charles V., he would have succeeded.* No one had been a more stanch opponent of the Bishop of Winchester than Peter Martyr; but when it was debated in Council whether that reformer should be detained in England to answer for his conduct, as an English subject, Gardyner, being Lord Chancellor, not only exerted his interest in his favour, but supplied him liberally with all things necessary to expedite his departure.† When we consider the treatment which Gardyner himself had received, this conduct is the more praiseworthy. The wise and witty, though we fear not highly moral reformer, Roger Ascham, when writing to another reformer, John Sturmius, equally zealous with himself, uses these terms:—"Stephen, Bishop of Winchester, High Chancellor of England, treated me with the utmost humanity and favour, so that I cannot easily decide whether Paget was more ready to commend me, or Winchester to protect and benefit me; there were not wanting some who, on the ground of religion, attempted to stop the flow of his benevolence towards me, but to no purpose. I owe very much therefore to the humanity of Winchester, and not only I, but many others also, have experienced his kindness."‡

---

* Burnet, iii. 222. † Wood, Hist. Univ. Oxford, 275.
‡ Ep. p. 51, ed. Oxon. 1703.

Hadrian Junius, a physician to Edward VI., and a zealous Protestant, is equally warm in the praises of Gardyner.* We have the highest evidence possible, that of Simon Renard, in a confidential letter to the emperor, that instead of being the enemy of Queen Elizabeth, Gardyner prevented her destruction as urged upon Mary by the Spanish ambassador and by Charles.† Although in Cranmer's answer to Gardyner there occur some bitter expressions which show that there existed between them feelings of personal hostility, and although Cranmer had deprived Gardyner of his liberty in the reign of Edward VI., yet to Gardyner Cranmer was indebted for his liberty, when, upon an occasion to which we shall

---

* Ep. 12. Speed, the chronicler, 828, attributes the advice to put to death the Princess Elizabeth, with great probability, to Lord Paget. Although I am of course opposed to Gardyner's principles, and although I regard him as a worldly statesman rather than a divine, I must remember that I am writing history, and I hope that the spirit of persecution will not be displayed against me for stating facts as I find them, though partizans have thought fit to suppress or torture them. Although Gardyner was a Papist, I do not forget that he was a Christian. Foxe, speaking of the death of Gardyner, says: "His death happened so opportunely, that England hath a mighty cause to give thanks to the Lord . . . . especially for that *he had thought to have brought to pass in murdering the noble queen that now is.* For, whatsoever danger it was of death, that she was in, it did, *no doubt,* proceed from the bloody bishop, *who was the cause thereof.* And, *if it be certain,* which we have *heard,* that, her Highness being in the Tower, a writ came down from *certain of the council* for her execution, *it is out of controversy* that wily Winchester was the wily Dædalus and framer of that engine, who, *no doubt,* in that one day, had brought this whole realm into woful ruin, had not the Lord's most gracious counsel, through Mr. Bridges, then the lieutenant, coming in haste to the queen, certified her of the matter, and prevented Achitophel's bloody device." (iii. 450.) This is a fair specimen of Foxe's style of writing history.

† See a transcript of the original letter at Brussels, dated March 14, 1553-54, in Tytler, ii. 336.

have presently to refer, every one expected that the archbishop would be sent to the Tower. So far from desiring the archbishop's death, Gardyner proposed to remove him from his dignity, and to allow him a pension.* By one of the exiles who was most opposed to Gardyner, the latter is accused of having strained his authority as chancellor, and, without the consent of the queen or council, to have offered Latimer a pardon if he would recant; that he laboured to save men from death by trying to persuade them to forsake what he regarded as their errors, is admitted by all.

Dr. Bonner was a very different man from Dr. Gardyner. He was convivial, vulgar, coarse-minded, unfeeling, and insolent. There was in him more humour than wit, and he could not at times refrain from making heartless jokes though the questions before him related to life and death. We may apply to him a vulgar term, and we shall best describe him by calling him "a bully." But this is no reason why falsehood should be invented for the purpose of blackening a character in itself sufficiently revolting; the falsehoods being propagated by the Puritans, because he was a bishop. There is no reason why it should be recorded as a fact, poetically adorned, that when a martyr perished,

"Bonner, blithe as shepherd at a wake
Enjoyed the show and danced about the stake."

Or take another specimen:—

"This cannibal, in three years' space, three hundred martyrs slew.
These were his food; he loved so blood, he spared none he knew." †

---

* Biog. Brit. iii. 2119.

† Dr. Maitland agrees with Hume in stating the number of legal murders committed in Mary's reign to be 277. Of these, not one-half came under the cognizance of Bonner. I have quoted a Protestant,

Dr. Maitland, whose "conscience acquits him of all sympathy with any person of whatever party or name (Cranmer, Calvin, or Bonner), in so far as he thought of maintaining or enforcing Christianity by fire and faggot," states that it has been proved that Bonner, instead of seeking for cases of reputed heresy, confined himself to the administration of the law—a most unrighteous law—within his own diocese; and when the justices from other counties sent heretics to him, he sent them back and refused to have anything to do with them. By the same writer it is shown, that the admitted coarsenesses of Bonner have been much exaggerated, and what was often nothing more than a vulgar jest, has been represented as expressing a reality. One thing is certain, that instead of urging the government to the adoption of more stringent measures, Bonner was more than once rebuked, in common with the other bishops, by Queen Mary and her government for not carrying on the bloody work against the heretics with greater severity.* A royal

who writes in the spirit of a candid enquirer; let me add what is said by Mr. Tierney, a Roman Catholic priest of Sussex:—"As to the number and character of the sufferers, certain it is that no allowances can relieve the horror, no palliatives can remove the infamy, that must for ever attach to these proceedings. The amount of real victims is too great to be affected by any partial deductions. Were the catalogue limited to a few persons, we might pause to examine the merits of each individual case; but when, after the removal of every doubtful or objectionable name, a frightful list of not fewer than two hundred still remains, we can only turn with horror from the blood-stained page, and be thankful that such things have passed away." Tierney's Dodd, ii. 107, *note*.

* Puritan and infidel writers are accustomed to transfer the blame of the persecutions from Mary and the council to the bishops. Sir James Mackintosh more justly remarks, that, "in the fourteen dioceses then filled, the bishops used their influence as altogether to prevent bloodshed in nine, and to reduce it within limits in the remaining five." ii. 328.

circular was sent to him and to all the bishops, in May 1555, expressing surprise and regret that greater strictness had not been used to suppress the prevalent errors; and commanding that all persons charged with heresy should be made to abandon their opinions, or, if they should continue obstinate, to suffer according to the order of the laws.* It is not true that Bonner deliberately sought for victims; what made him odious was the vulgar, bullying personalities in which he indulged when the heretic, brought before him as a judge, provoked his angry passions. He was irascible; but bad as that was in a judge, he was not the person most to be blamed.

The queen's council was composed of men who, many of them, had changed their opinions according to their interests, and who regarded as perverse and obstinate all who refused to do the same. They were not anxious for persecution, and would have advised the opposite course as the better policy; but, to save their places, they would do as the queen willed. An attempt is made at the present time to detach from the name of Mary the epithet which will cling to it for ever. The question is not whether she was in some cases an amiable woman; but whether she was a persecutor. It is no answer to this accusation to prove that she could be kind to those who obeyed her orders, that she cherished her mother's memory, that she braved her father's and her brother's tyranny, that she was able to love even to distraction the wretched profligate to whom she had unwisely given her heart. That heart which could be soft as wax under one set of circumstances, could under another set of circumstances be cold and hard as ice. Her conduct to Elizabeth was as bad as it could be, and she never would

---

* Burnet, Collections, No. xx. v. 431.

forgive Cranmer the part he had taken in the case of her mother's divorce. As to persecution, the course she took was such as often marks a weak intellect in connexion with a determined will. There can be but a right and a wrong, and wrong must be punished. Protestants are in the wrong; let them repent or be punished. The law must be obeyed. The law says that the punishment for heresy is burning; let the heretic be burned. The Church says that heresy is a crime which brings, if tolerated, ruin on a country; let the country be saved from ruin by searching for heretics and by destroying them. This was her principle of action. Such a person felt no compunctious visitings of nature when ordering the law to take its course; rather she felt that she was showing a becoming firmness; and the persons mostly to be blamed were those, her counsellors—Gallios themselves—who ought to have been prepared to die rather than to encourage her in her wrong doing by their ready obedience. No one counselled her to mercy. Renard cared not for heretics; but the execution of political offenders was to the politician a work to which the queen should be urged. The Lady Jane and the Greys were to be sacrificed to her passion for Philip; and nothing but a fear of the vengeance which awaited her from the whole kingdom prevented her from destroying the Lady Elizabeth. On one occasion, when the council, alarmed at the sensation caused throughout the country by the executions, persuaded Mary to release certain of the prisoners, she afterwards lamented her weakness to Renard. "The queen," says Renard, writing to the emperor in February 1553-4, " has granted a general pardon to a multitude of people in Kent, after having caused about five score of the most guilty to be executed. Numerous are the petitions presented to her Majesty to have the pains of death exchanged for perpetual imprisonment, but to this she will not listen."*

The same confidential correspondent of the emperor, writing to him in April 1554, says of Throckmorton:—

"He was acquitted by the twelve jurymen who had been chosen and impanelled, and who were all heretics; there being no doubt that in spite of the verdict he deserved to be condemned. And when they carried him back to the Tower (after his acquittal), the people with great joy raised shouts, and threw their caps in the air; which has so displeased the queen, that she has been ill for three days, and has not yet got quite the better of it."†

Of the persecutions themselves I shall speak in the words of a Roman Catholic clergyman, who, we would fain hope, represents the opinions of his class:—"To detail the atrocities would be a revolting task: the mind would shudder, the heart sicken at the recital. Suffice it, therefore, to say, that the persecution continued to rage until the death of Mary. At times, indeed, a momentary suspension of cruelty seemed to indicate the presence of a milder spirit. But the illusion was quickly dissipated. New commissions were issued, new barbarities were enacted, and a monument of infamy was erected, which, even at the distance of three centuries, cannot be regarded without horror."‡

The truth is that the Reformation was seriously damaged by the gang of unprincipled robbers, including Somerset and Northumberland, who had formed the council of Edward VI. The counsellors of Mary, equally unprincipled, were willing to concede everything to the stern policy of Queen Mary so long as they were not

---

* Simon Renard to the Emperor, Feb. 22, 1553–4; Tytler, ii. 309.
† Tytler, ii. 374.
‡ Dodd, Ch. Hist. of England, ii. 103, *note*.

compelled to disgorge their prey. A new generation learned wisdom under Queen Elizabeth.* Terrible times were these.

To return to Cranmer. We left the archbishop a prisoner at large, or rather not under restraint, in his manor-house at Lambeth. His resolution was taken to die, if need should be, a martyr's death. He was preparing his mind for the coming events by his favourite study of Scripture and by prayer. His wife, his children, were far away. It would be offering to his enemies a subject for attack, if he had retained them with him, though for their society at this period of anxiety his whole soul yearned. The calmness of his mind was interrupted by one of those cruel reports which, originating in the father of lies, are in themselves a persecution. It was reported, that in order to gain favour with the new queen, he had offered to celebrate King Edward's obsequies, not as the law required, according to the order in the book of Common Prayer, but with the old Latin

---

* We are not to suppose that the stern character of Mary's policy was confined to the prosecution or persecution of heretics; it equally marked the prosecution or persecution of all offenders against the law, especially traitors. A contemporary says:—" This day was ther set upp at every gate of London a galouse, and at the brige-fote one, in Southwarke ij paire, at Leaden-hall one, ij in Chepeside, in Fleetestrete and about Charing crosse iij or foure paire, and in many other places about the city. In Kent also, and many places more, ther was raysed gallouses, a great sorte. That day and on Thursday there was condempnyd of the rebelles to the nombre of cccc or thereaboutes. All the prisons of London was so full that they were fayne to keep the poorest sort by iiij^{xx} on a hepp in churches. On Wednesday following was hanged in sondery places of the citey to the nombre of xxvj^{te} or more. On Thursday, in Southwarke, and other places of the subburbes, there was hanged a great numbre; this day being the xvth of February, ther was x prysoners out of the Tower arrayned and caste, whose names doe followe." Chron. of Queen Jane and Queen Mary, ed. Camd. Soc. p. 59.

mass of requiem. This report might be easily refuted; but the fact was stated also that in the metropolitan church of Canterbury the mass had been already restored. The restoration, contrary to law, of the proscribed service in the primate's own cathedral, was adduced as a clear proof of the time-serving disposition of the archbishop, and what was worse, it tended to dishearten those conscientious persons who were waiting in anxiety to know what course of conduct the new government was about to pursue. It was generally supposed that Mary would be contented to place the Church on the same footing on which it had been left by her father. Did the archbishop mean to sanction this mode of proceeding? Was all that had been done in Edward's reign to be nullified at once? We are to remember that there was a large class of persons in every parish who were willing to do whatever their superiors in Church and State should decree. Cranmer felt his responsibility. He enquired, and found that the mass *had* been restored at Canterbury. So far, then, the report was true; but it was restored by the Vice-Dean—the dignitary in residence—Dr. Thornden, without consultation with the archbishop.* The archbishop saw the difficulties of the case, and fully appreciated the evil consequences which would ensue, if the reports were not contradicted. He sat down immediately, and in the first burst of his indignation he gave expression to his feelings in a letter to a friend. The letter was written, but not sent; it lay, probably for revision, on his study table, when on the 5th of September he

---

* It is sometimes stated that Dr. Thornden was a personal friend of the archbishop. If this was the case, it must have added to Cranmer's difficulties. But the authorities which dwell on this point, in general, confound Thornden with his predecessor Tregworth, who was certainly a friend of Cranmer.

received a visit from Bishop Scory. The prelate read the letter, and approved of it so much that he begged for a copy. It is probable that Scory, knowing the vacillating and timid character of Cranmer, who, like other men in high places, was afraid of acting on the spur of the moment, determined to give it to the public as it came warm from the heart and brain of the worried and angry archbishop. Certain it is that the letter was soon in other hands, and being again transcribed, was publicly read at Cheapside. All London was astir to obtain a copy of the manuscript. The sensation was great. It was not printed, but every scrivener was writing out a copy of it.* It ran thus:—

"As the Devil, Christ's ancient adversary, is a liar and the father of lying, even so hath he stirred up his servants and members to persecute Christ and His true Word and religion with lying: which he ceaseth not to do most earnestly at this present time. For as a prince of most famous memory, King Henry VIII., seeing the great abuses of the Latin mass, reformed some things in his time; and after, our Sovereign Lord King Edward VI. took the same wholly away for the great and manifold errors and abuses of the same, and restored in the place thereof Christ's holy Supper according to Christ's own institution, and as the Apostles used the same in the primitive Church in the beginning: so the Devil goeth about now

---

* The declaration is transcribed from the MS. copy in the Library of Emmanuel College, Cambridge. At the close of the Latin version of the declaration, published 1554, it is said:—"Lecta publice in vico mercatorum ab amico qui clam autographum surripuerat, 5 Septemb. anno Dom. 1553." This undoubtedly shows that the document was not published with Cranmer's sanction. We have his own authority for stating that he intended to publish it, but he would probably have softened some expressions; not that Cranmer was averse from using strong language when the occasion required it, as may be seen from his controversy with Gardyner. His eulogists think it necessary to apologise for the manner in which he speaks of the vice-dean; but when a man feels deeply he speaks strongly, and ought to do so.

by lying to overthrow the Lord's Supper again, and to restore his late satisfactory masses, a thing of his own invention and device. And to bring the same more easily to pass, some have abused the name of me, Thomas Archbishop of Canterbury, bruiting abroad that I have set up the mass again at Canterbury, and that I offered to say mass at the burial of our late Sovereign Prince King Edward, and also that I offered to say mass before the queen's Highness, and at St. Paul's Church, and I wot not where. And although I have been well exercised these twenty years to suffer and bear evil reports and lies, and have not been much grieved thereat, but have borne all things quietly, yet untrue reports to the hinderance of God's truth are in no wise to be tolerated and suffered. Wherefore these be to signify to the world, that it was not I that did set up the mass at Canterbury, but it was a false, lying, and dissimuling monk, which caused mass to be set up there without mine advice or counsel. *Reddat illi Dominus in die illo.*

"And as for offering myself to say mass before the queen's Highness, or in any other place, I never did, as her Grace right well knoweth. Nor no man can say to the contrary, and speak truth, that there is anything in the Communion set out by the most godly and innocent Prince King Edward VI. in his high court of parliament; but that it is conformable to the order which our Saviour Christ did observe and command to be observed, and which His Apostles and the primitive Church used many years. Whereas the mass in many things not only hath no foundation of Christ's Apostles or the primitive Church, but is manifestly contrary to the same, and containeth many horrible abuses in it. And although many, unlearned or malicious, doth report that Mr. Peter Martyr is unlearned, yet if the queen's Highness will grant thereunto, I with the said Peter Martyr and other four or five which I shall choose, by God's grace will take upon us to defend, that not only the Common Prayers of the Church, the ministration of the Sacraments, and other rites and ceremonies, but also that all the doctrine and religion set out by our late Sovereign Lord King Edward VI., is more pure and according to God's Word than any other doctrine that hath been used in England these thousand years: so that God's Word may be the judge, and that the reasons and proofs on both parties may be set out in writing; to the intent, as well that all the world may examine and judge therein, as also that no man shall start back from his writings. And where they boast of the faith which hath been in the Church three thousand years, we will join with them in this point: for that doctrine and usage is to be followed, which was in the Church fifteen hundred years past. And we shall prove, that the order of the Church set out at this present in this realm by act of parliament is the same that was used in the Church fifteen hundred years past. And so shall they never be able to prove theirs." *

Cranmer had now thrown down the gauntlet, and the government was obliged to act. On the evening of the 7th of September, on which day the declaration was published, he received an order to attend the Star Chamber.† On his appearance he was treated with great consideration and kindness. On the following morning he was interrogated about the declaration, and to afford him an opportunity to escape, or to justify themselves in letting the matter drop, it was insinuated through Bishop Heath that the court would be satisfied, if the archbishop would express sorrow for the circulation of a document which, according to his own admission, had been promulgated without his sanction. Cranmer acted with great

---

* Remains, iv. 1.

† The following is the minute from the Council Book:—"On the 8th of September, 1553, Thomas, Archbishop of Canterbury, appeared before the lords, as he was the day before appointed. After long and serious debating of his offence by the whole board, it was thought convenient that, as well for the treason committed by him against the queen's Majesty as for the aggravating of the same his offence, by spreading about seditious bills moving tumult to the disquietness of the present state, he should be committed to the Tower, there to remain and be referred to justice, or further ordered as shall stand with the queen's pleasure."

dignity. He would not deny that he regretted the premature publication of the declaration before it had been subjected to his revision. For, he added, that his intention had been to have enlarged it, and then to have had it fixed, authenticated by his archiepiscopal seal, upon the door of the cathedral church of St. Paul, and on the doors of all the other London churches.*

The archbishop's manner was conciliatory though his conduct was uncompromising, and he was permitted to return to his manor-house at Lambeth. The council, indeed, was composed of men who were quite aware that Cranmer, if pressed, might make revelations which would inculpate others besides himself. They still wished that he would fly the country, and with a view to expedite this proceeding, Bishop Gardyner, now Lord Chancellor, suggested that, proceeding on Cranmer's own principles, his licence to act as archbishop should be withdrawn, and that he should receive a sufficient maintenance to enable him to live as a private gentleman. There was probably a time when Cranmer would have listened gladly to such a proposal, but to have consented to it now would have been a manifest dereliction of duty. Cranmer remained at Lambeth, determined on a passive resistance. But the queen, who entertained towards him a feeling of personal hostility, used her authority with the council to have him committed to the Tower. This was accordingly done on the 14th of September.

Cranmer, though a prisoner, was still treated with respect, and even civility. He was not strictly confined; but had the freedom of the Tower. By a letter addressed by the council to the Lieutenant, that officer was "to suffer the late Duke of Northumberland's children the liberty of walking within the garden of the Tower, and

* Heylin, ii. 101.

also to minister the like favour to the Lady Jane and Dr. Cranmer."

In the Tower the archbishop found his friends Ridley and Bradford; and five days after, in came a venerable octogenarian, as light-hearted, as hard-headed, and as strong-minded as ever, Bishop Latimer. With the Lady Jane they formed a little congregation, as happy as circumstances would permit. The prison in the Tower became, after a time, so crowded, that it was found impossible to give to each prisoner a separate apartment; but although Latimer complained that he and his three friends were thrust into one chamber, "as men not to be accounted of," yet still some consideration was shown them, for they were not separated. The friends availed themselves of the opportunity to read over the New Testament, "with great delectation and peaceful study," thus deriving immediate comfort to their own souls, by communion with God and one another, and preparing themselves for peace in death, or, if life were spared, for the further maintenance of God's truth.

Up to this time Cranmer entertained hopes of pardon. He knew not yet how bigoted Mary was in her attachment to "the old learning," neither did he know how deeply rankled in her mind his conduct with respect to her mother's divorce; he only knew that persons far more seriously implicated in Northumberland's conspiracy than he had been, were pardoned. The Bishop of Winchester, in making his peace with the queen on the subject of the divorce, would naturally throw the chief blame upon Cranmer. The distinction to be made is clear, though the advocates of Cranmer, in their hatred of Gardyner, accuse the latter of "shamelessness" in attacking Cranmer on the subject. Mary could pardon a minister of her father, who, though holding a brief against her mother, was nevertheless prepared to yield if the pope had refused to pronounce the marriage null; but she could never forgive the man who, in her view of the case, took the law into his own hands, and did illegally what the law, as she understood it, would not have sanctioned. Gardyner was not a high-minded or a generous man, but I do not think that we should judge him harshly for pointing out the difference between his case and that of Cranmer. At the same time, we may join in those censures which he has justly incurred, for purchasing his pardon by receding from the high ground he once had taken on the subject of the royal supremacy. On this point, Cranmer maintained his position; and until Mary's extreme papistical notions were made known, he expected that his zeal in this respect would secure for him the royal favour. It was *the* subject uppermost in her father's mind, and Mary at first appeared anxious to tread in her father's steps.

But these hopes and expectations, after the meeting of Parliament and Convocation, were soon to be dissipated. Parliament met on the 5th, and Convocation on the 6th of September, 1553. It was not difficult for the government to pack both the Parliament and the Convocation. The feeling in favour of the Reformation, though latent, was strong. But leader the Protestants had none. They had not the means of ascertaining their strength, and consequently, to all appearance the Protestant cause was weak. And who was to rally them? Northumberland's apostacy had astonished and astounded them. If so zealous an ultra-Protestant could proclaim that he had played the hypocrite for political and party purposes, who was to be trusted? Such statesmen as Cecil might have placed themselves in the foremost ranks, but they, though they maintained that the Church needed reform in doctrine and in discipline, did not think it a cause for which they were called upon to imperil their lives or even to sacrifice their interest at court. Even Pole was a reformer, and these men contended, that though they sought reform, they had never been Protestants. The enthusiasm which afterwards led men to court persecution, and to offer their bodies to be burned for the sake of God's truth, had not yet to any great extent been awakened. The large class of quiet sober-minded persons who had accepted the changes of the late reign with thankfulness, had been so thoroughly disgusted with the avarice, the hypocrisy, the inefficiency of such men as the Somersets, the Northumberlands, the Arundels, the Russells, and the Pagets, that they felt no inclination to fight their battles, even if any one were prepared to summon them to the contest. While the zeal of Mary's friends, supported by a reaction to a certain extent in public feeling, was unabated, they found scarcely any opponent; for most men, if they did not accord with them in their opinions, thought it best to bide their time—to wait and see what would take place. The counsellors of Mary might have been bad men; but worse men than Somerset and Northumberland they could scarcely have been, though Somerset has come down to us in the character of a saint.

In the Convocation there was only a minority of six to defend the reformation. These six were dignitaries of the Church, who had right *ex officio* to a seat in the Convocation, and who determined, at all risks, to defend the various reformations effected in the synods of the late reign.

The Bishop of London, Dr. Bonner, presided with the vulgarity and vigour which were his characteristics. He thought it witty to observe, "As for Mr. Canterbury, he must be placed where it is meet for him." These words betrayed a spirit of revenge as well as of malice. He exulted in the downfall of one who despised and had maltreated him.

The Convocation was informed that it was the pleasure of the queen, who was compared to "a heaven-sent dove," that debate should take place on certain controverted points, in order that canons might be framed for her Majesty's satisfaction. In spite of the strenuous exertions of the minority, the Book of Common Prayer, though despised by ultra-Protestants for being a mere revision and translation of the Missal and Breviary, was pronounced to be "very abominable," and the forty-two articles "pestiferous and full of heresies." The discussion on the dogma of transubstantiation was fixed for the 23rd of October. The minority requested the attendance and assistance of Bishop Ridley, and of certain other divines whose special attention had been directed to the investigation of this subject. This reasonable request was refused. But, under the leadership of Archdeacon Chency, the six gallant reformers argued the cause with great force of reason; they defied their opponents to produce any authority of Scripture for the dogma of transubstantiation, and they proved that it was contrary to the teaching of the Catholic Church in primitive times.*

Dr. Weston, the prolocutor, a coarse-minded man, like Bonner, and afterwards suspended for immorality, brought the discussion abruptly to a conclusion with the remark: "It is not the queen's pleasure that we should spend any longer time in these debates." Then, alluding to the zeal of the reformers for the circulation of the Scriptures, he added: "Ye are well enough already; *ye* have the word, and *we* the sword."

It does not say much for the prolocutor's discretion or

* The reader may see the whole discussion in Joyce, 501. I have only to refer to the subject on account of its relation to Cranmer.

logic in not perceiving that by what he intended for wit he stultified himself and his party.

It was soon perceived that the overbearing intolerance of the majority of the Convocation, the insolence with which they sought to silence their opponents, and the unfairness of excluding from the discussion the men who, on the side of the reformation, were best qualified to conduct it, made an unfavourable impression upon the public mind. There was a large number of people who, unbiassed by party feelings on either side, suspended their judgment; and before recourse was had to persecution an attempt was first made to win them. It was arranged, therefore, that Cranmer, Ridley, and Latimer should be permitted to argue their cause; but not in London, lest a demonstration should be made in their favour. It was determined to transport them to Oxford. A university, it was pretended, was the fittest place for a doctrinal discussion, and Cambridge was invited to send delegates, that the conclusion might be represented as the judgment of both the Universities.*

But much was to be done before this measure could be adopted. The proceedings of Convocation were to be ratified by Parliament; and in the House of Commons a strong opposition was raised, when it was proposed to supersede the Book of Common Prayer and to revert to the Use of Sarum. The debate lasted for ten days. At length the queen's party succeeded in obtaining a majority, and it was enacted that after the twentieth day of December, no other service should be allowed but that which was in use at King Henry's death.† By

---

* Burnet, ii. 399.

† Mary, in conversation with Commendone, who had been sent to England secretly by the pope to confer with the queen, admitted that the very name of Rome was mortally hated by her people, and that

another act all King Edward's laws relating to religion were repealed. The feeling against Cranmer was apparent in the bill introduced to declare the legitimacy of Queen Mary, the preamble of which runs thus:—

"That truth, how much soever obscured and borne down, will, in the end, break out; and that therefore, they declared that, King Henry the Eighth being lawfully married to Queen Katharine, by consent of both their parents, and the advice of the wisest men in the realm, and of the best and notablest men for learning in Christendom, did continue in that state twenty years, in which God blessed them with her Majesty and other issue, and a course of great happiness; but then a very few malicious persons did endeavour to break that happy agreement between them, and studied to possess the king with a scruple in his conscience about it; and to support that did get the seals of some universities against it, a few persons being corrupted with money for that end. They had also by sinistrous ways and secret threatenings procured the seals of the Universities of this kingdom, and finally, Thomas Cranmer did most ungodlily and against law judge the divorce, upon his own unadvised understanding of the Scriptures, upon the testimonies of the Universities, and some bare and most untrue conjectures; and that was afterwards confirmed by two acts of parliament, in which was contained the illegitimacy of her Majesty; but that marriage not being prohibited by the law of God, could not be so broken, since what God had joined together no man could put asunder. All which they considering, together with the many miseries that had fallen on the kingdom since that time, which they did esteem plagues sent from God for it; therefore they declare that sentence given by Cranmer to be

---

until their feelings were mollified towards the Apostolical See she did not venture to recall Cardinal Pole. (Pallavicino, ii. 32.) The court encouraged the use of the Roman Missal, but the reprints of the Sarum books, which went on all through Mary's reign, prove that the attempt to discard the old service-books of the Church of England met with a passive resistance from the great body of the clergy.

unlawful, and of no force from the beginning, and do also repeal the acts of parliament confirming it." *

The feeling out of doors now was so decidedly against the government, that the proceedings against Cranmer, consequent upon the votes of Parliament and Convocation, were hurried over; and we have no detailed account of what occurred upon his impeachment. We only know that on the 13th of November he was arraigned in Guildhall for levying war against the queen, and for conspiring to set up an usurper. The Lady Jane and her husband were arraigned at the same time. All pleaded guilty. Sentence of death was pronounced upon them all. Cranmer, however, urged in extenuation of his offence that, until the judges and law officers of the Crown had given their opinions, he had not consented to the exclusion of Queen Mary. His attainder followed as a matter of course. His life was now at the queen's mercy, and he immediately transmitted a letter to the queen, asking for an exercise of mercy towards him in an urgent but still a very dignified manner. His conduct as compared with that of Crumwell, or even with that of Wolsey, is worthy so far of all admiration. Let it not be forgotten that he bravely refused to fly when flight was possible; and that though life was dear to him, there was not in him that abject cowardice which we lament in a man so really great as Wolsey, or in one who had acted so important a part in public life as Crumwell. The letter contains a lucid and to all appearance a candid statement of the manner in which he was seduced into the commission of that offence for which he was condemned. Of the facts stated in this letter I have already made ample use, and we shall therefore call attention

* Parl. Hist. iii. 293.

only to the concluding paragraph, which is peculiarly important as throwing further light on Cranmer's principles and conduct. It would seem that he thought a compromise might still be effected He entertained the notion that although King Edward's reformation were rejected, the queen might be persuaded to adopt some measures to secure the independence of the Church of England—of which she still declared herself the supreme head—and to effect the alterations which the position of ecclesiastical affairs rendered a necessity.* It was not unreasonable that he should expect this; for the queen, in her speech to the Lord Mayor in the preceding August, had declared, that "she meaned graciously not to compel or strain other men's consciences, otherwise than God should, as she trusted, put in their hearts a persuasion of the truth, through the opening of His Word unto them; *until such time as further order, by common consent, may be taken therein.*" This throws light upon the following paragraph in Cranmer's letter:—

"As concerning the state of religion, as it is used in this realm of England, at this present, if it please your Highness to licence me, I would gladly write my mind unto your Majesty. I will never, God be willing, be author of sedition, to move subjects from the obedience of their heads and rulers; which is an offence most detestable. If I have uttered my mind to your Majesty, being a Christian queen and governor of this realm (of whom I am most assuredly persuaded, that your gracious intent is, above all other regards, to prefer God's true Word, His honour, and glory), if I have uttered, I say, my mind unto your Majesty, then I shall think myself discharged. *For it lies not in me, but in your Grace only, to see the reformation of things that be amiss.* To private subjects it appertaineth not to reform things, but quietly to suffer what they cannot amend; yet nevertheless,

---

* A scheme of reformation was actually drawn up by Pole, and will be found in the "Life" of that Primate of our Church.

to show your Majesty my mind in things appertaining unto God, methinks it my duty, knowing what I do, and considering the place which in time past I have occupied. Yet will I not presume without your Grace's pleasure first known, and your licence obtained; whereof, I most humbly prostrate to the ground, do beseech your Majesty, and I shall not cease daily to pray to Almighty God for the good preservation of your Majesty from all enemies, bodily and ghostly, and for the increase of all goodness, heavenly and earthly, during my life, as I do, and will do, whatsoever become of me." *

If Cranmer expected an answer he was disappointed. No notice whatever was taken of the letter; but he was made to feel that the hour of danger had arrived. The Lady Jane, beautiful, learned, pious, and innocent, had laid her head upon the block, in meek reliance on her Saviour's merits. The regulars among the clergy who had married were suspended, on the undeniable charge that they, in marrying, had violated the vows which, as monks, they had previously taken. The secular clergy who had not taken a vow of celibacy, were required to put away their wives in twelve months' time, and to undergo penance for having violated the law; they were then to be restored to their preferments. The unwise, unconstitutional, and unorthodox measure by which Cranmer had obtained the means of depriving Gardyner and Bonner of their bishoprics, now recoiled on the head of the archbishop himself. As no bishop could exercise his episcopal functions without a licence from the Crown, so by the withdrawal of that licence from all prelates who favoured the Reformation, the bench of bishops, seriously reduced in number, became powerless against the Crown, whose deference to the tiara might be inferred from the marriage which the queen had determined to contract with Philip of Spain.

* Strype, Mem. Cranm. Appendix, 919.

While these events were in progress, alarming and perplexing the minds of the three illustrious men who were still permitted to take sweet counsel together in a prison converted by them into the house of God, an order came on the 8th of March, 1554, to the Lieutenant of the Tower, requiring him to deliver up to Sir John Williams " the bodies of the late Archbishop of Canterbury,* of Dr. Ridley, and of Mr. Latimer, to be by him conveyed to Oxford."

In order to understand the conduct of Cranmer at this juncture, the reader must realise to his mind the position of affairs. Cranmer and his two friends were state prisoners. The state prisoners, under a strong guard, were removed to Oxford. Why? Not, let it be remembered, to be tried; but as learned doctors, among other learned men appointed by Convocation, to enter upon a theological discussion. Such discussions were customary, if not absolutely necessary, until by the press these *vivâ voce* discussions on abstruse subjects were rendered comparatively, if not entirely, useless.

To simplify matters, the whole subject had been reduced by the Convocation in London to three points. The committee of Convocation was to maintain, and the three bishops were to oppose, the following propositions :—

"I. In the Sacrament of the altar, by virtue of the divine word uttered by the priest, the natural body of Christ, conceived of the Virgin Mary, is really present under the species of bread and wine; and also His natural blood.

II. After consecration, the substance of bread and wine no

---

* His description, as " the late archbishop," confirms the opinion of some lawyers that by Cranmer's attainder the archbishopric became, *ipso facto*, vacant. The dean and chapter had in fact taken upon themselves the administration of the province, regarding Cranmer as dead in law.

longer remaineth; neither any other substance, save only the substance of Christ, God and Man.

III. In the mass there is a life-giving propitiatory sacrifice for the sins of as well the dead as the living." *

There was a great gathering. The committee of Convocation had already arrived in Oxford. Delegates from Cambridge were expected, and soon after made their appearance.† Certain doctors of Oxford represented that University. And now Sir John, afterwards Lord Williams, was leading the three bishops to Oxford, that in the debate they might bear their part. The State was to take care that the prisoners did not escape; but when the discussion should take place all were to be, or rather ought to have been, upon an equality.

The three bishops do not appear to have been made acquainted with the object of their journey to Oxford. They were required to start at a moment's notice, and to take no luggage with them—nothing but what they had on their backs. It was generally supposed that Cranmer, who had now been attainted, was going to execution.

As he passed through London, a multitude came forth to look at him. It was reported that he appeared resolute and cheerful. The sympathy beaming through many a countenance darkened by sorrow must have been consolatory to one of the kindest hearts in England. But not a word was said. After the late insurrection every one was careful to avoid the possibility of being accused as a fautor of rebellion; and Cranmer, knowing that a demonstration in his favour might have been fatal to others as

* " In missa est vivificum sacrificium pro peccatis tam vivorum quam mortuorum propitiabile." Wilkins, iv. 98; Harl. MS. 3642.

† The instruments appointing the delegates and accrediting them to Oxford may be found lxxvii. and lxviii. in Strype.

well as to himself, entreated his friends to guard against any tumult.*

Firm, cheerful, grateful to the masses who sympathised with him, Cranmer passed through London, with his two beloved companions and friends. He was consigned to the custody of Sir John Williams at Brentford. They stopped at Windsor on the 10th of April. On the following day the gates of Bocardo, the common prison at Oxford, closed upon the three greatest men within the precincts of the city, now crowded with visitors from all quarters. The prisoners were soon after separated. Ridley was consigned to the custody of Alderman Irish, and was exposed to the vulgar insults of his wife. Latimer was lodged elsewhere. The archbishop remained in Bocardo.

The treatment these illustrious men received at this time was disgraceful to all concerned. Of the indignities, the insults, the hardships to which they were unnecessarily exposed, mention is frequently made. There may have been some exaggeration here; but to summon these prelates to a discussion with picked men from the Convocation and from the two Universities, and to allow them only two days for preparation, was itself an act of injustice as well as of cruelty. It was a cause on which the life or death of many depended, but they were to defend their side offhand. While to the one party all the libraries in the University were open, and learned librarians were ready for consultation, the archbishop and his two episcopal friends were debarred the employment of pen, ink, and paper, and were positively refused the use of their own books—those marked and annotated volumes the very dust of which was dear to them, and

* This is gathered from a letter of *à Lasco*, Gardesii Miscell. ii. 695.

every mark in which suggested an idea. While the representatives of the Convocation had summoned to their aid all the learning of their party, the three bishops were kept apart, and no conference between them was permitted. Each was to answer for himself; and it was hoped that one would be sometimes found, without knowing it, to contradict the other. This attempt at mental excruciation and torture we call persecution; this summoning of the unarmed man to fight with the beasts of Ephesus. Surely these persecutions, this disarming of the bishops before their combat; this endeavour to depress their minds by denying to their bodies the support to which they had been accustomed; all this was a tacit acknowledgment of conscious weakness, an admission that the learning of the age, old as well as new, was with the reformers. It was a confession of intellectual inferiority, when they who held the sword felt it necessary to avail themselves of every advantage of which physical force gave them the command. It was the misfortune, not the fault, of the Convocation, that, for having a wife whom he loved, the primate should be censured by one who, like Weston, the prolocutor, was soon after suspended for adultery.*

On the afternoon of Saturday, the 14th of April, Archbishop Cranmer was informed that he was placed under the custody of the Mayor of Oxford, who was waiting to escort him to St. Mary's Church, where the discussion was to take place. Surrounded by "rusty billmen"—javelin-men, as we now call them—the venerable prelate proceeded to the church, confident in the justice

---

* The whole of the ensuing narrative is derived from the original documents. There has been some little difficulty in arranging the order of the events, and I have made allowance for the one-sidedness of the narrator. See Cranmer's Remains, vol. iv.

of his cause, though called upon, thus imprisoned, to defend it. When he arrived at St. Mary's, he found the prolocutor, Dr. Weston, who was also Rector of Lincoln College, sitting in state before the high altar. On either side, arrayed in their scarlet robes or full academical dress, were the thirty-three commissioners—representatives of the Convocation of Canterbury and of the two Universities. Behind, the pyx, ostentatiously displayed on the high altar, declared a foregone conclusion. The primate was taken by surprise. He unexpectedly found himself, not as an equal come to discuss, but more like a criminal summoned to receive sentence. With his accustomed urbanity, however, he made a low obeisance to the doctors seated before him. Leaning upon his walking-staff, he looked around him, expecting to see his fellow-prisoners. But he stood alone, amidst his opponents. He was offered a seat; but not in the midst of themselves, not among the doctors, who sat as if forming a court before which he was brought as a criminal to be questioned. He did not expect them, after his attainder, to receive him as their primate; but if there was to be a fair discussion, he ought, in that place of conference, to be received as a doctor and their equal. He refused, therefore, the proffered civility. Standing in front of the doctors, supported by his staff, the archbishop listened patiently while the prolocutor delivered a discourse he had prepared on the Unity of the Church. In the course of his address, Weston turned towards Cranmer, and accused him of having violated this unity by the introduction of erroneous doctrines, and by making, as it were, every year a new faith. He concluded by saying, that it had pleased the queen to commission the doctors there assembled to send for him, and on his repentance to restore him once more to the unity of the Church.

CHAP. III.

Thomas Cranmer. 1533–56.

This was placing the whole matter on a footing different from that which had been proposed. It was now shown that the Archbishop and his friends, instead of being disputants, were only to be respondents. Against this mode of proceeding, as unfair to the cause of truth, the primate, at a subsequent period, protested. In order that " these weighty matters should be more diligently scanned and examined," he required that he and his companions might be permitted to oppose as well as respond; that they might be allowed to bring forth their proofs, and to receive such answers as their opponents might be able to advance. But, at present, he contented himself with accepting the truisms propounded by Dr. Weston; and he thought fit to make some display of his learning by showing how unity was the conservative principle among heathens as well as among Christians. There was an implied sarcasm on the uselessness of introducing such a discourse; and, as for himself, he was all for unity, provided it was in Christ and agreeable to His Holy Word.

The three articles which were to form the basis, not of discussion, but, as it now appeared, of examination, were now read to the archbishop, and a copy of them placed in his hands. He perused them carefully. Then, repeating the first article, " In Sacramento altaris virtute verbi Domini a sacerdote prolati, præsens est realiter sub speciebus panis et vini naturale corpus Christi conceptum de Virgine Maria. Item naturalis ejusdem sanguis," he asked what was meant by the terms " verum et naturale"—true and natural? " Do you mean," he asked, " corpus organicum—a sensible body?" The question seems to have perplexed the doctors; some said one thing and some another; but they all at last concurred in the answer, "Idem quod natum est ex Virgine," that which was born of the Virgin. This the Archbishop of Canterbury at once denied; and passing on to the other two articles which have been given above, he said that they were false and contrary to God's Word, and he concluded by saying. "If by unity you mean that I should join in approving these articles, I must wholly decline to follow that advice."

The prolocutor directed that he should write his mind on these articles, and be prepared to maintain his opinion on the following Monday; "Meanwhile," he added, "you will be supplied with any books you may require."

It is evident that the persons in authority had become aware that the injustice of their conduct so far had excited a feeling in favour of the reformers. Great decorum had been observed throughout the proceedings, if we overlook the unfairness of placing the archbishop, not among the disputants, but as a criminal called upon to answer any questions, within the prescribed limits, which might be put to him.

The dignity, the meekness, the self-command displayed by the archbishop had attracted the notice and excited the kindly feelings of the multitude who had "thronged" to see him. For twenty years Thomas Cranmer had been the counsellor of kings, the first peer of the realm, the friend—the only real friend—of a monarch whose vices were forgotten, and to whom all parties looked back with admiration, as to a sovereign who only could control a society so disorganised as England had now become. Of the fallen archbishop, no unkind word or action, when he was in the plenitude of his power, could be mentioned. He now came forth from St. Mary's Church, unsupported, without a friend, the prisoner of the mayor, surrounded by "rusty billmen," a venerable old man. Many were moved to tears as they thought of

CHAP. III.
Thomas Cranmer.
1533-56.

the past; and, contemplating the resigned and even cheerful expression of his countenance, witnessed the self-possession he had displayed under circumstances peculiarly provocative of indignation and anger. More than this, an eye-witness bears testimony that tears were seen to roll down the cheeks of not a few, who to his opinions and principles were most opposed.

Cranmer having now the power of consulting books, laboured diligently during the Saturday night and the Sunday. The prolocutor received the written comment upon the articles, from the archbishop, on the Sunday evening, when he was proceeding to a grand entertainment given to the dignitaries of the University at Lincoln College.

It is written in terse and elegant Latin, and asserts concisely the real state of the case and of the argument.* The great work which he had done was to bring back the Eucharist from the mediæval notion of a mass to the primitive notion of the Communion; or as the usual mode of expressing it at that time was, the reformers had changed the mass into a Communion. This was the real point. If, as we have seen before, there was a propitiatory sacrifice in the Eucharist,—the fundamental idea of the mass—then the corporeal presence of the victim offered was necessary. Hence, to simplify the debate, the stress was laid upon the dogma of transubstantiation. If, as Cranmer says in this document, there was only a μνημόσυνον—a memorial of the propitiatory sacrifice once and once for all made upon the cross—then, although a

---

* It may be found among the Collection of Records printed by Collier, lxxi., from a MS. in his own possession, transcribed probably from the official report in the British Museum. There is an English translation by Grindal in Harl. MSS. 422, f. 44, which is printed in most of the popular histories.

real presence of our Lord to the communicant was necessary and asserted, yet transubstantiation was an unnecessary demand upon faith, and was to be rejected.

It is necessary to remember, that the real question was between the Mass and the Communion; so that the debate between the papists and the reformers was not, as is sometimes supposed, a mere piece of logomachy.* We do not find in Cranmer, so far as I can perceive, any approach to the rationalism to which puritanism has unintentionally given rise, when it rejects transubstantiation because of its apparent absurdity. The great question with our reformers was whether the sacrifice of the Cross was all sufficient, and not to be repeated; and their appeal was not to the opinion of men, whether it were reasonable or not, but to the Bible, interpreted by primitive practice.

At eight o'clock, on Monday the 16th of April, the mayor and his javelin-men appeared again at Bocardo, and the most reverend prisoner was marched to the Divinity School. Here he found the prolocutor and the other commissioners apparelled in their scarlet gowns, having come in procession, with the usual formalities, from Exeter College, where they had met the Vice-Chancellor of Oxford. The prolocutor was seated on the chair of the Professor of Divinity, a kind of pulpit,† between two other pulpits, one of which was, in the University exercises for the Doctor's degree, occupied by the respondent, and was now assigned to Cranmer, the mayor and aldermen of the city keeping guard. Dr.

---

* The whole subject is concisely, and with a thorough acquaintance with the whole subject, stated in "The Eucharistic Doctrine of the Holy Scripture and the Primitive Liturgies," by the Rev. William Milton, Curate of Newbury, formerly Curate of Leeds.

† Wood calls it "that lofty professor's chair, not long since demolished."

Weston opened the proceedings in his usual blundering manner. "Brethren," he said, in Latin, "we are assembled here to confound the detestable heresy of Christ's body in the Sacrament." An exordium so ludicrously equivocal was received with an unusual burst of laughter. When the prolocutor proceeded in his address, he still went on unconsciously blundering; for the drift of his argument was to show that it was not lawful, by God's Word, to controvert any of the three articles: such persons doubted the words of Christ, and might well be thought to doubt both the truth and power of God.

It is evident that the thought in Weston's mind was, that he was to give sentence against Cranmer; he forgot that the form of proceeding adopted was not that of a trial but of a discussion. Cranmer perceived and availed himself of the prolocutor's mistake. Having requested permission to make a few observations on the opening address, he said: "We are assembled here for the purpose of discussing these doubtful controversies, and to lay them open before the world, being subjects on which we think it lawful to dispute." He then went on to remark that if the end were to be taken for granted, or if there were a foregone conclusion, there could be no ground for dispute. "If," he concluded, "the questions be not called into controversy, surely my answer is then looked for in vain."

Did Cranmer expect to convince the gainsayers? or did he say this sarcastically? He determined, at all events, to go on with the discussion, for the sake of those who were outside.

When the reader remembers that Cranmer was standing alone, confronted to the *élite* of the men of the old learning from both of the Universities, he must marvel at the great ability displayed on this occasion by Cranmer, and the extreme readiness of reply which shows that the learning displayed in his written works was not "got up" for the occasion. When I mention that the report of this discussion, called, from the name of the chief of the disputants opposed to Cranmer, "The Disputation with Chidsey," occupies more than sixty pages, I shall be excused from transcribing what will interest no modern readers except those who really wish to convince themselves of the learning and ability of the celebrated archbishop, who was never so great as when he was thus baited by many assailants. A proof of the impression made upon the auditors by the calmness and superior arguments of the archbishop may be found in the irritation which he caused in the ranks of his opponents. Weston was wholly unable, even if he desired, to preserve order. He permitted Cranmer to be subjected to continual and rude interruptions; he did not repress the hissings, and hootings, and peals of laughter, and clapping of hands, to which the packed assembly resorted in the hope of silencing or of intimidating the undaunted, unabashed defender of the Reformation; and he so far forgot himself as on one occasion to call the archbishop an unlearned, unskilful, and ignorant man. Amidst the wrangling and the clamour, Cranmer stood facing the storm, calm, collected, unmoved. He asked for more time to consider the questions at issue, and to prepare himself for meeting his adversaries by a reference to the various works of which mention had been made in the course of the discussion. He pointed out the unfairness of requiring of him and his friends that they should act only as respondents; and he desired permission to press upon his adversaries those arguments which he defied them to answer, while he affirmed that he could produce citations from the fathers which they would be unable to explain away.

At two o'clock the storm was at its height; and the meeting was dispersed by the prolocutor, shouting "Vicit veritas!" The voices of the party really defeated re-echoed the shout through the streets of Oxford. The solitary victor returned to his prison.*

A temporary reaction took place, and the abettors of Weston were ashamed of their conduct. John Harpsfield, the newly appointed Archdeacon of London, was to perform his exercises for his Doctor's degree on the 19th of April; and, as the custom then was, the exercises consisted of a disputation. Cranmer having complained of the unfairness of those proceedings which made him and his friends, in every case, the defendants, was now offered the opportunity of appearing as the opposing party. There were several reasons for adopting this course. The disputation was not considered a real one; the object was to bring out the ability of the person attacked, the assailant producing arguments against him, without pledging himself to hold them in reality. The moderator might close the discussion whenever he thought fit, and was expected, whether right or wrong, to give judgment in favour of the disputant who professed to maintain the cause of orthodoxy. We cannot but suspect also, that a feeling existed in the mind of Weston and the other commissioners that there was truth in the report industriously circulated, that Cranmer was not a man of learning; and that, consequently, when opposed to a man of such unquestionable erudition as Harpsfield, he would be disgraced in the eyes of all scholastic pedants.

To follow the disputants through their logical subtleties would be to the reader neither amusing nor instructive,

---

* Of the shameful manner in which the discussion was conducted we have an account under the hand of Cranmer himself, in a letter which will be given to the reader.

but the student in mental archæology will peruse the discussion with interest. A report of it is preserved in the "Remains" of Cranmer,* and whoever consults it will be persuaded that Cranmer's ability was equal to his learning, and that both were considerable. When he concluded, the moderator addressed him, saying, "Your wonderful gentle behaviour and modesty, good Dr. Cranmer, is worthy much commendation; and that I may not deprive you of your right and just deserving, I give you most hearty thanks in mine own name, and in the name of all my brethren."†

Upon this, all the doctors present "quietly took off their caps." These were the last worldly honours paid to Thomas Cranmer. There is something gratifying in the tribute of respect thus forced from his adversaries by one, whose many faults have been freely admitted, but of whom it may be said that he fully sustained the character of a gentleman, and thus contrasted favourably with his opponents.

From his prison the archbishop was soon after summoned again. On the very next day he had to appear before the commissioners at St. Mary's Church. There he had the happiness of seeing, though only in public, and without any opportunity of conference, his two friends Bishop Ridley and Bishop Latimer. The conduct of Weston the prolocutor was still urbane. He was to pronounce the three bishops guilty of heresy, if they would not subscribe to three articles which the Convocation had appointed as the test of their orthodoxy. But he was anxious to save them from the penalty of the law by persuading them to yield. Not being an earnest man himself, he could not understand earnestness in others. They were not now to discuss; the time for discussion had passed; the three bishops had simply to say

* Remains, iv. 67.   † Ibid. iv. 76.

yes or no. Weston had them one by one called before him, and he entreated them, even as Cranmer had entreated Fryth and Lambert, to yield to the decision of Convocation. They one and all refused to subscribe the articles which had just been adopted by the committee of Convocation, and the prolocutor had only therefore to resume his seat and let matters take their course. The doctors, in full array, sat in a semicircle on either side of the chair occupied by Dr. Weston, whose seat was on the step in front of the altar. The prisoners were placed before them. It was a novel sight, never seen before or after in the Church of England, or in any branch of the Catholic Church: three bishops were standing to hear sentence pronounced upon them by a commission consisting exclusively of presbyters.

There stood the octogenarian Latimer, bending beneath the weight of years and infirmities, and leaning heavily upon his staff, with two or three caps and a handkerchief on his head; his spectacles, without a case, hanging by a string on his breast. There stood Ridley, the clear-headed, resolute, but pious polemic; knowing that there was no one there present who, with weapons not carnal, could venture to enter into the lists with him without suffering a defeat. There too stood Cranmer, the scholar, the lawyer, the statesman, the accomplished gentleman, the courtier, the affectionate husband and father. Always blundering, Dr. Weston, in addressing them, had ventured to say that the prisoners had been defeated in fair and open disputation. This roused the archbishop, and, referring to what had occurred on the Monday, he replied, "Whereas Doctor Weston said, he, Cranmer, hath answered and opposed, and could neither maintain his own errors, nor impugn the verity; all that he said was false: for he was not suffered to oppose as he would, nor could answer as he was required, unless he would have brawled with them, so thick their reasons came one after another: ever four or five did interrupt him, that he could not speak."*

The officer of the court prepared to read the sentence, but he had scarcely commenced, when the prolocutor compassionately stopped him. Now, for the last time, he would put to the prisoners collectively the question he had urged upon them in private, whether they would turn or no. "Read on," they said, one and all; "in the name of God, read on." We seem to hear the voice of Ridley uttering the words which the other two made their own by repeating them. When the officer of court ceased, there was a brief pause. The three prelates said deliberately, "We are not minded to turn." Their doom was pronounced.

There was another solemn pause; the silence was broken by the archbishop: "From this your judgment I appeal to the judgment of God Almighty, trusting to be present in heaven with Him, for whose presence in the altar I am condemned."

Bishop Ridley said: "Although I be not of *your* company, yet doubt I not but my name is written in another place, whither this sentence will send us sooner than we should by the course of nature have come."

"I thank God most heartily," exclaimed Bishop Latimer, "that He hath prolonged my life to this end, that I may in this case glorify God by that kind of death."

Dr. Weston was heard to mutter, "If you go to heaven in this faith, then will I never come thither, as I am thus persuaded."

Let us hope that he was misunderstood or misrepresented; for considering the character of the man, the sentiment he uttered is as sad as it was uncharitable.

The court broke up. Bishop Ridley was taken to the house of Alderman Irish, Bishop Latimer to the bailiff's house, and Archbishop Cranmer to Bocardo. From the

* Remains, iv. 77.

windows of his prison he witnessed the solemn procession which was made to celebrate the act which had doomed him and his two friends to the stake. The sacrament was carried by Dr. Weston, four doctors of divinity holding the canopy over it.

Cranmer immediately wrote the following letter to the council, which may be regarded as winding up this scene of the tragedy, not yet to be brought to its final conclusion.

"In most humble wise sueth unto your Right Honourable Lordships Thomas Cranmer, late Archbishop of Canterbury; beseeching the same to be a means for me unto the queen's Highness for her mercy and pardon. Some of you know by what means I was brought and trained unto the will of our late Sovereign Lord King Edward VI., and what I spake against the same; wherein I refer me to the reports of your honours.

"Furthermore, this is to signify unto your Lordships, that upon Monday, Tuesday, and Wednesday last past, were open disputations here in Oxford against me, Master Ridley, and Master Latimer, in three matters concerning the Sacrament. First, of the real presence. Secondly, of transubstantiation. And thirdly, of the sacrifice of the mass. How the other two were used I cannot tell: for we were separated, so that none of us knew what the other said, nor how they were ordered. But as concerning myself, I can report that I never knew nor heard of a more confused disputation in all my life. For albeit there was one appointed to dispute against me, yet every man spake his mind, and brought forth what him liked without order. And such haste was made, that no answer could be suffered to be given fully to any argument before another brought a new argument. And in such weighty and large matters there was no remedy, but the disputations must needs be ended in one day, which can scantly well be ended in three months. And when we had answered them, then they would not appoint us one day to bring forth our proofs, that they might answer us again, being required of me thereunto: whereas I myself have more to say than can be well discussed in twenty days. The means to resolve the truth had been, to have suffered us to answer fully to all that they could say, and then they again to answer to all that we could say. But why they would not answer us, what other cause can there be but that either they feared the matter, that they were not able to answer us; or else (as by their haste might well appear) they came, not to speak the truth, but to condemn us in post haste, before the truth might be thoroughly tried and heard? for in all haste we were all three condemned of heresy upon Friday. Thus much I thought good to signify unto your Lordships, that you may know the indifferent handling of matters, leaving the judgment thereof unto your wisdoms. And I beseech your Lordships to remember me, a poor prisoner, unto the queen's Majesty: and I shall pray, as I do daily, unto God for the long preservation of your good Lordships in all godliness and felicity.—April 23, 1554."*

The friendliness shown by Weston, notwithstanding occasional outbursts of insolent passion, induced Cranmer to entrust the letter to him to be delivered to the council. Weston took the liberty of opening the letter, when on his journey, and finding not the compliments which he expected to be paid to himself, but a statement of the case which exposed his incapacity, indecision, and want of temper, he returned it to Cranmer, who found other means of transmitting it.†

To this letter no answer was returned. The queen and council had acted precipitately, and were now in a difficulty. During the whole of the Tudor period nothing surprises us more, than the daring violation of the spirit of the law, united with a scrupulous, even a pedantic observance of its letter. A reverence for law is indeed a characteristic of our race. What was to be done under

* Remains, i. 365.
† We may infer from this that Weston, whose insolence was remarkable at the commencement of the proceedings, had received a hint from head-quarters to adopt a more conciliatory tone. Hence the change which certainly took place in his conduct.

existing circumstances? This was the question which the council could not answer, and the judges, when consulted, found it difficult to decide.* The papal authority, and with it the canon law, had been rejected in England. Queen Mary, being accounted supreme head of the Church of England, could have lawfully ordered the execution of the prisoners. But to exercise her powers as supreme head was against her religious principles; although, in opposition to those principles, she had, with an inconsistency not unusual, to secure some immediate and important end, not unfrequently acted. She would not, however, go so far as to order the execution of three prelates of her Church; and how far a sentence pronounced by priests upon their bishops could be, even in an extreme case, defensible, was a question which could not fail to occur to a conscience hardened on the one side, but scrupulously sensitive on the other. By the common law, it is true, a heretic might be executed; but the common law could not act until the accused had been convicted in the ecclesiastical court. Cranmer's life, as that of one who had been attainted of treason, was indeed made forfeit to the law; but if, on that ground, he were to be sent to the block, who in the council would be safe?

Thus all things were working in the course which the queen desired. The affairs of the country, she and her immediate friends remarked, could not be properly conducted until the authority of the pope was restored, and the canon law established.

It was finally determined to treat the proceedings at Oxford as a nullity. Eighteen months were therefore to elapse before Bishop Ridley and Bishop Latimer were consigned to the flames. There was an interval of five months between their execution and that of Archbishop Cranmer.

* Council Book. Archæol. xviii.

That prisoners should be subjected to hardships was a thing, in those days, only to be expected; and that the three venerable prelates were subjected occasionally to insults from the low and vulgar-minded, is what, from our own experience of the excesses to which religious partisanship will hurry even good men, we should greatly fear. But from Bishop Ridley's complaint that the "manner of their treatment did change as sour ale doth in summer," I should infer that they were not systematically ill-treated. Occasionally a fanatic was in office, or a report came that they were planning their escape, and they were subjected for a season to annoyance and restraint; but the government had certainly given orders to the Mayor of Oxford to provide them with food and raiment. They were not, at all times, prohibited from visiting each other; they were, in fact, associated. We happen to have their bill of fare for the 1st of October, 1554:—

Bread and ale	ij*d.*	Item, ling		viij*d.*
Item, oysters	i*d.*	Fresh salmon		x*d.*
Item, bread	i*d.*	Wine		iij*d.*
Item, eggs	ij*d.*	Cheese and pears		ij*d.*

It is added that they constantly ate suppers as well as dinners, that their meals usually amounted to three or four shillings, never exceeding four; that, at both meals, cheese and pears were the last dish; and that they had wine, of which the price was always threepence, and no more.*

They were permitted to receive and send letters, and therefore when it is said that they were prohibited the use of pen, ink, and paper, the reference must be to some order given on a special occasion; and not to any

---

* Todd, ii. 405.

general regulation extending over the whole time of their confinement. They also received pecuniary assistance from their friends. By the letters they received, expressive of the most touching piety and sympathy from fellow-sufferers or from men expecting to suffer, they must have been comforted and supported. The great support and consolation to their souls, however, came from above, for, of their deep and sincere piety no man has dared to doubt. I mention the whole state of the case, because, where there is so much cause for pity, and even indignation, there is no object that I can perceive in trying to make things appear worse than they were: bad enough in due time they became.

The burning had not actually commenced in 1554; but in all parts of the country men were imprisoned—holy, pious, learned men, prepared to endure hardship and to suffer death itself in their Great Master's cause. They had means of communication; and describing themselves as prisoners of the Gospel, they drew up an address to the queen and king,* and to the high court of parliament, in which they eloquently avow their principles in language which attests their orthodoxy as well as their courage. They conclude with saying :—

"This, therefore, our humble suit is now to your honourable estates, to desire the same, for all the mercies' sake of our dear and only Savior, Jesus Christ, and for the duty you owe to your native country, and to your own souls, earnestly to

---

* The reader will remember that Mary was married to Philip on the 25th of July, 1554. The act of parliament, 1 Mar. Stat. 2, c. ii., Fœdera, vol. xv. p. 394, provided that on the celebration of their nuptials, Philip should, during their marriage, "have and enjoy, jointly together with the queen his wife, the style, honour, and kingly name of the realm and dominions unto the said queen appertaining, and shall aid her Highness, being his wife, in the happy administration of her realms and dominions."

consider from what light to what darknes this realm is now brought, and that in the weightiest, chief and principal matter of salvation of al our souls and bodies everlasting, and for ever more. And even so we desire you at this your assembly, to seek some effectual reformation for the afore written most horrible deformation in this Church of England. And touching yourselves we desire you in like manner, that we may be called before your Honors; and if we be not able both to prove and approve by the Catholic and Canonical rules of Christ's true religion, the Church Homilies and Service set forth in the most innocent K. Edward's days; and also to disallow and reprove by the same authorities, the Service now set forth, since his departing; then we offer our bodies, either to be immediately burned, or else to suffer whatsoever other painful and shameful death that it shall please the King and Queen's Majesties to appoint. And we think this trial and probation may be now best, either in the plain English tongue by writing, or otherwise by disputation in the same tongue. Our Lord for His great mercy sake, grant unto you all the continual assistance of His good and Holy Spirit. Amen."*

In drawing up this address, the " prisoners " at Oxford must have concurred ; whether they assisted in drawing it up, or who were the authors, is not known.

All petitions and remonstrances, however, were in vain. The reforming party was still without a leader ; and to that circumstance we may attribute, to a certain extent, the number of martyrdoms. If the reforming party could have been rallied, the government, alarmed at its strength, would have adopted milder measures. But now they thought that they were only a few fanatics here and there, by making an example of whom, the many who knew not how to decide—the quiet, humble, pious, uncontroversial Christians who always form the bulk and the strength of the Church—would have submitted to

* Strype, Appendix, lxxxiv.

any regulations made by the government, whether they entirely approved of them or not.

In the existing condition of the country, it was easy, as we have before remarked, to pack both the parliament and the Convocation. In former reigns we have seen that parliament was only strong when the executive was weak. A strong government appointed the returning officers, and these officials, supported by the government, intimidated opposition candidates, and sometimes falsified the returns. We are not, therefore, surprised to hear that the Convocation petitioned the queen and king, that Cranmer's treatise on the Sacrament, the late service-books, and other books, pronounced by them to be heretical, might be burnt; or that in parliament there was only an opposition of one in the House of Commons, to the vote by which the papal authority was re-established in the Church and realm of England. The lords and others of her Majesty's privy council—many of them great reformers in the last reign, some of them the ready instruments of Mary in the work of persecution—were reconciled to the abolition of the royal supremacy, when a pledge was given that the papal supremacy should not be exercised to rob them of the abbey-lands of which they had robbed the monks.

It was at the close of 1554 that Cardinal Pole arrived in England, a legate, at that time, à latere; and on the 23rd of November he took possession of the archbishop's residence at Lambeth—a sufficient indication that it was never more to be occupied by Cranmer.

The imprisoned prelates at Oxford were aware that things were now coming to a crisis, so far as they themselves were concerned. They were not mistaken; for a commission was soon issued by the legate to examine, with a view of absolving or degrading, and after degradation, if degradation were decided upon, of delivering over to the secular arm, Bishop Ridley and Bishop Latimer. With respect to Thomas Cranmer, an archbishop, the commission issued from the pope himself.

No cheering prospect was before the prisoners. In the year 1555, the persecutions commenced in earnest. Their hearts, though saddened, must have been strengthened and refreshed when they heard of the power of endurance exhibited by many who had been with them the standard-bearers of the Reformation.

For maintaining the doctrine of a Communion instead of the mass, and in fact for the Prayer Book, the protomartyr Rogers, a prebendary of St. Paul's, and one of the most eloquent preachers of the day, was consigned to the flames on the 4th of February, 1555. All differences between the pious, though fanatical, Bishop Hooper and Archbishop Cranmer were forgotten when, for having a wife and for upholding the Communion against the mass, by denying the dogma of the corporeal presence, Hooper suffered on the 9th of the said month. Rowland Taylor, Rector of Hadley, and Ferrar, Bishop of St. David's, were friends whom Cranmer, Ridley, and Latimer loved, lamented, and admired. No wild fanatics were these. Men were afterwards maddened by fanaticism, and rushed upon death with a madness of which we have seen instances in less worthy causes; but these were men who felt that to belie their convictions would be to sin against their own souls, and that to God and His truth they owed a debt. Ridley and Latimer experienced something of the enthusiasm which induces a noble nature to share in the sufferings, as well as to sympathise in the sorrows, of those we love. If there were one among the prisoners at Oxford who felt that life, even at three score years and five, was dear to him, let us remember that Cranmer, knowing how severe the trial was to which the martyrs would be exposed, had all along advised his friends to fly, unless, from the prominent part they had taken in the Reformation, their flight might appear as a denying of their Lord. Nobly did Cranmer, feeling thus, determine, when the power of flight was allowed him, to stand at his post and to dare the worst. If he miscalculated his strength and courage, let him not be severely censured by those who are untempted and untried.

Although Cranmer conducted himself bravely at his trial, yet the reader who will attend to the details will be inclined to think that his opponents surmised his weakness before it was known even to himself, and that they hoped that one who had so frequently changed his opinions was still open to conviction.

The papal authority having been restored in England, immediate measures were adopted to secure his condemnation in proper form. On Saturday, the 7th of September, 1555,* he received a citation to appear at Rome before the expiration of eighty days, to make answer to such matters as should be objected to him by the king and queen. He was informed that at the suit of the king and queen, the pope had issued a commission to Cardinal de Puteo. He was aware that all this was matter of form, and that his real judge would be the prelate whom the cardinal appointed as his subdelegate, and who as such was commissioned by the pope — the Bishop of Gloucester, Dr. Brookes.

In the commission from the pope it was ordered that the archbishop should have charity and justice shown to him, and that the laws should be interpreted, in the most

---

* There has been some misunderstanding as to the date of citation, but Cranmer himself states that he received it on the 7th of September. See his letter to the queen, Remains, i. 369.

ample manner, in his favour.* It was decreed that the archbishop should appear before the Bishop of Gloucester, as subdelegate of Cardinal de Puteo or high commissioner of the pope, and that Dr. Martin and Dr. Story should, in the name of the king and queen, demand his examination.†

On the 12th of September, 1555, the archbishop was again led as a prisoner, in custody of the city guard, to St. Mary's church. There, at the east end, he saw the altar decorated and the Sacrament exposed. Beneath and in front of it, on a throne raised ten feet from the ground, sat, *in pontificalibus*, the Lord Bishop of Gloucester, the commissioner—all indicating a foregone conclusion. On seats, lower than the throne of the papal commissioner, sat the proctors of the King and Queen of England. On his right sat Dr. Martin, a man of the world, keen, as a lawyer, to win the cause for which he had been retained and to secure the conviction of the prisoner. He was, so far as the religious question was concerned, a perfect

---

* Strype, i. 533.

† Of this examination we have three contemporary accounts. There is the official report sent by the Bishop of Gloucester to the Cardinal de Puteo, which is called the "Processus contra Cranmerum," and may be seen in MS. in the Lambeth Library, No. 1136. It has been printed in the Addenda to the Oxford edition of Strype. There are two reports preserved by Foxe. The longest of these, written by an opponent of the archbishop, is, though the longest, the least to be depended upon, as some of the statements are inconsistent with historical facts. It is written, however, in a fair and kind spirit. I have minutely examined them all, and compared them with the archbishop's letter to the queen (letter ccxix. in the "Remains"), which Dr. Jenkyns remarks may be considered in the light of a corrected report of his speech. I have presented the reader with a harmony of the reports, and though there may be room for some discussion on the exact sequence of some of the events, I think that I state to the reader a report quite as accurate as that which is given us of the proceedings in a court of justice in the present day.

Gallio; but that did not prevent him, unprincipled as he was, from uttering the most sarcastic remarks, and putting the questions which he thought to be the most annoying to the accused. Dr. Martin was, at this time, retained to argue in favour of the papal, as opposed to the royal, supremacy. We are justified in speaking of him as a Gallio; for when it was his interest, in Queen Elizabeth's reign, to uphold the royal, in opposition to the papal, supremacy, Dr. Martin did not hesitate to take that oath, for taking which he would now consign Cranmer to the stake.

On the left of the subdelegate sat Dr. Story, the friend of Bonner. He was a man whose piety had degenerated into fanaticism. He regarded as an enemy to God everyone whose theological opinions differed from his own, and he thought he was doing God service when he caused an enemy of God to die the death of a heretic. Stern as his features were, they showed that he was a man who rejoiced in the work which it was his duty as a lawyer to perform.

Below these, three officers of state, the authorities of the University, and the other distinguished personages, including the pope's collector, were arranged in a semi-circle, all arrayed in their scarlet gowns or robes of office. Beneath them, on the floor, crowded the graduates of the university and persons of low degree described as the " rabblement."

In contrast to all this splendour stood the dark figure of the Archbishop of Canterbury, for so was Cranmer still regarded.* He stood at the entrance of the choir, in

---

* When the archbishop was attainted, he could no longer exercise authority in England, and the Dean and Chapter of Canterbury assumed the administration of the province as if he were defunct. But in the eye of the Church he did not cease to be Archbishop of Canterbury until he was formally degraded.

his gown and cassock, with his doctor's hood on his shoulders, and his square cap on his head. The solemn silence was broken by the voice of the apparitor: "Thomas, Archbishop of Canterbury, appear here and make answer to that which shall be laid to thy charge; that is to say, for blasphemy, incontinency, and heresy, and make answer to the Bishop of Gloucester, representing the pope's person."

The archbishop, attended by the officers of the court, was paraded up the choir until, standing before the throne, he confronted the Bishop of Gloucester. As he drew near, he doffed his cap and made a genuflexion first to Dr. Martin and then to Dr. Story. Then raising himself, with his usual dignity, and looking motionless at the representative of the pope, he deliberately and in a marked manner replaced his cap upon his head.

The action was so marked, that the Bishop of Gloucester observed, that considering the authority he represented, it might beseem the archbishop right well to make his duty to him. But the cap remained on the archbishop's head, his knee was unbent: not in discourtesy to Dr. Brookes, but because the Bishop of Gloucester represented on this occasion an authority which the archbishop refused to recognise. He observed that "he had once taken a solemn oath never to consent to the admitting of the Bishop of Rome's authority into this realm of England again; and that he had done it advisedly, and meant by God's grace to keep it; and therefore would commit nothing, either by sign or token, which might argue his consent to the receiving of the same; and so he desired the said bishop to judge of him, and that he did it not for any contempt to his person, which he could have been content to have honoured as well as any of the other, if his commission had come from as good an authority as theirs." *

The dignified reluctance to give offence, combined with a modest determination to do his duty and maintain his principles, which he thus evinced, the gentlemanlike deportment—we can use no more fitting term—which marked the speech and conduct of the archbishop, created, as an eye-witness informs us, a strong sensation in the assembly, though doubtless in the minds of others besides Dr. Story angry and vindictive feelings may have been excited. At the same time, let justice be done to the Bishop of Gloucester; he did not resent what some would have regarded as a personal insult. After waiting to see whether the archbishop could be persuaded to show the customary respect to the court, he proceeded to deliver an address, which, too long for transcription, I have read attentively; and I must pronounce it to be a kind, a charitable, a considerate, and a learned discourse. He, of course, assumed that he was right, and that Cranmer was wrong; he was obliged to condemn, *ex cathedra*, as the pope's representative, what he regarded as the archbishop's wrong doings; and, at the same time, in the pope's name, and therefore in the language of a superior, he admonished one whom the University had already condemned as a heretic. If he had not done this, he must have remained silent; but it is no mean praise to say, that he laboured to discharge an unpleasant office without giving more offence than was absolutely necessary. He certainly displayed no attempt to wound the feelings of his opponent or to irritate him to make some angry retort in doing which such men as Bonner took delight. Addressing the archbishop, he said:

"My Lord, at this present we are come to you as com-

* State Trials, i. 773.

missioners, and for you, not intruding ourselves by our own authority; but sent by commission, partly from the pope's Holiness, partly from the king and queen's most excellent Majesties, not to your utter discomfort, but to your comfort, if you will yourself. We come not to judge you, but to put you in remembrance of that you have been *and shall be.** Neither come we to dispute with you, but to examine you in certain matters; which being done, to make relation thereof to him that hath power to judge you. The first being well taken, shall make the second to be well taken. For if you of your part be moved to come to a conformity, then shall not only we of our side take joy of our examination; but also they that have sent us. I would think good somewhat to exhort you, and that by the second chapter of Saint John in the Apocalypse: ' *Memor este unde excideris, et age pœnitentiam, et prima opera fac. Sin minus,*' &c.. Remember from whence thou art fallen, and do the first works, or if not, and so as ye know what followeth."†

He then adverted to many of those actions in Cranmer's history which we regard as reflecting an honour on his memory, but which were disgraceful in the eyes of the pope's representative. All the common-places on his own side of the question are reproduced by Brookes, and all the hackneyed quotations from the fathers which had been from time to time refuted or explained; the argument, nevertheless, throughout is that of a man who, if not deeply read, was well up in the controversies of the day.

The following passage is one of those to which allusion has been made before as exciting a suspicion, that from conversation with Cranmer, the agents of the government

---

* Throughout the proceedings insinuations were thrown out that if Cranmer recanted, he would be restored to power.

† State Trials, i. 773.

had already concluded that a recantation on his part was not a thing impossible.

"What should stay you, tell me, from this godly return? Fear, that ye have gone so far, ye may not return? Nay, then I may say as David said, '*Illic trepidaverunt ubi non erat timor.*' Ye fear where ye have no cause to fear. For if ye repent and be heartily sorry for your former heresy and apostacy, ye need not to fear. For as God of His part is merciful and gracious to the repentant sinner, so is the king, so is the queen merciful, which ye may well perceive by your own case, since ye might have suffered a great whiles ago for treason committed against her Highness, but that ye have been spared and reserved upon hope of amendment, which she conceived very good of you; but now (as it seemeth) is but a very desperate hope. And what do you thereby? '*Secundum duritiem cordis thesaurizas tibi iram in die iræ.*' According to the hardness of your heart, ye treasure up to yourself anger in the day of wrath. Well what is it then, if fear do not hinder you? shame, to unsay that you have said? Nay, it is no shame, unless ye think it shame to agree with the true and the Catholic Church of Christ. And if that be shame, then blame St. Paul, who persecuted the disciples of Christ with the sword; then blame St. Peter, who denied his Master Christ with an oath that he never knew Him. St. Cyprian, before his return, being a witch, St. Austin being nine years out of the Church. They thought it no shame after their return of that they had returned. Shall it then be shame for you to convert and consent with the Church of Christ? No, no. What is it then that doth let you? glory of the world? Nay, as for the vanity of the world, I for my part judge not in you, being a man of learning, and knowing your estate. And as for the loss of your estimation, it is ten to one that where you were Archbishop of Canterbury and Metropolitan of England, it is ten to one, I say, that ye shall be as well still, yea, and rather better."*

The Bishop concluded thus:—

"And thus much have I said of charity. If this poor simple exhortation of mine may sink unto your heart and take effect with you, then have I said as I would have said, otherwise not as I would, but as I could for this present."†

The subdelegate was followed by Dr. Martin. In a succinct speech, he stated, that the process against the archbishop had been ordered by the pope, on a petition from the king and queen, which empowered his colleague Dr. Story and himself to act as proctors for their Majesties on the occasion. He concluded by exhibiting articles of accusation against the archbishop. Cranmer was accused of adultery and perjury; and certain books of heresy were laid upon the table, "made partly by him, and partly set forth by his authority," and here "I produce him as the party principal to answer to your good lordship."

Without moving his cap from his head, the archbishop rose. He enquired whether he was expected at the present time to make his answer. Dr. Martin, the accuser, replied, "As you think good; no man shall hinder you."

When the archbishop raised his eyes, he beheld, peering above the subdelegate's throne, the pyx, and he knew that if he knelt down, facing the consecrated wafer he should be afterwards accused of worshipping it. He turned therefore to the west. There was a breathless silence throughout the court. The archbishop knelt, and said in

* State Trials, i. 773. † State Trials, i. 777.

English the Lord's Prayer. Rising from his knees he distinctly and slowly repeated the Creed. At the conclusion he said, solemnly: "This I do profess as touching my faith, and make my protestation, which I desire you to note. I will never consent that the Bishop of Rome shall have any jurisdiction within this realm." Dr. Story said, "Take a note thereof," and Dr. Martin, losing all patience, exclaimed: "Mark, Master Cranmer, how you answer for yourself. You refuse and deny him by whose laws ye yet do remain in life, being otherwise attainted of high treason, and but a dead man by the laws of this realm." The archbishop replied, "I protest before God I was no traitor; but indeed I confessed more at my arraignment than was true." "That is not," replied Martin, "to be reasoned at this present. Ye know ye were condemned for a traitor, and *res judicata pro veritate accipitur*. But proceed to your matter."* The archbishop proceeded by first of all denying the authority of the court.

"My Lord," he said, "I do not acknowledge this session of yours, nor yet you as my lawful judge; neither would I have appeared here this day before you, but that I was brought hither as a prisoner. And therefore I openly here renounce you for my judge, protesting that my meaning is not to make any answers as in a lawful judgment, (for then would I be silent), but only for that I am bound in conscience to answer every man of that hope which I have in Jesus Christ, by the counsel of St. Peter, and lest by my silence many of those which are weak here present might be offended. And so I desire that my answers may be accepted as *extrajudicialia*." †

The speech of the archbishop and the forbearance of the Bishop of Gloucester stirred up the proud spirit of

---

* Remains, iv. 83. † Ibid. iv. 110.

Dr. Story. In an angry speech, he vindicated the authority of the court, and, almost in terms of rebuke, certainly in an unbecoming spirit of dictation, he addressed the Bishop of Gloucester:

"Wherefore, my good Lord, all that this Thomas Cranmer (I cannot otherwise term him, considering his disobedience) hath brought for his defence shall nothing prevail with you, nor take any effect. Require him, therefore, to answer directly to your good lordship; command him to set aside his trifles, and to be obedient to the laws and ordinances of this realm. Take witness here of his stubborn contempt against the king and queen's Majesties, and compel him to answer directly to such articles as we shall here lay against him, and in refusal, your good lordship is to excommunicate him."*

The Bishop of Gloucester, whose conduct throughout the trial was impartial, and, so far as circumstances permitted, considerate, only signified "gently," it is said, that the archbishop might proceed. His Grace thus resumed:—

"My Lord, you have very learnedly and eloquently in your oration put me in remembrance of many things touching myself, wherein I do not mean to spend the time in answering of them. I acknowledge God's goodness to me in all his gifts, and thank him as heartily for this state wherein I find myself now, as ever I did for the time of my prosperity; and it is not the loss of my promotions that grieveth me. The greatest grief I have at this time is, and one of the greatest that ever I had in all my life, to see the king and queen's Majesties, by their proctors, here to become my accusers, and that in their own realm and country, *before a foreign power*. If I have transgressed the laws of the land, their Majesties

* State Trials, i. 785.

have sufficient authority and power, both from God and by the ordinance of this realm, to punish me; whereunto I both have, and at all times shall be content to submit myself." *

He proceeded to show, that between the papal laws and the laws of the realm there is such a repugnancy, that no man can be loyal to both pope and king. He argued this point very ably and at some length; he showed that if to deny the pope's authority and the religion which the Church of Rome had published to the world in these later years were heresy, then "all the ancient fathers of the primitive Church, the apostles, and our Lord Himself had been teachers of heresy;" then coming to his own doctrine, he said:—

"As concerning the Sacrament, I have taught no false doctrine *of the Sacrament of the altar;* for if it can be proved by any doctor above a thousand years after Christ, that Christ's body is there really—*i.e.* corporeally—I will give over. My book was made seven years ago, and no man hath brought any authors against it. I believe, that whoso eateth and drinketh that Sacrament, Christ is within them, whole Christ, His nativity, passion, resurrection, and ascension; but not that corporeally, that sitteth in heaven." †

He distinguished between the *real* and *corporeal* presence. When the rays of the sun are illuminating, quickening, warming some creature upon earth, we say that "here the sun is *really* present," though still the sun is *locally* in the firmament. So, although the Lord Jesus Christ is locally in heaven, yet, by the rays of His grace, He is really and truly, verily and indeed, present to the believer's soul. Looking at the Eucharist in the sacramental point of view, there is a presence—a presence in

* Remains, iv. 110. † Remains, iv. 85.

the believer, which is sufficient for sacramental purposes. The elements are consecrated; they are prepared to become the body and blood of Christ; and such, when endorsed by the believer's faith, they become in the believer. According to Cranmer's doctrine, the real presence of our Lord is effected by consecration *and* worthy reception; and the sanctified believers offer themselves, with the whole Church, a living sacrifice to God. The opponents of Cranmer, looking at the Eucharist as an ordinance in which Christ is sacrificed, were not content with this real presence: they required a corporeal presence, that Christ should be on the altar, in order that He, by the celebrant, might be offered a sacrifice for the quick and the dead. Christ's presence, in their view, is effected, not by consecration *and* worthy reception, but by consecration alone. Hence they worship Christ in the elements. The subject is so important that no apology is necessary for repeating it.

The archbishop's speech was an unprepared reply to the well-considered and carefully elaborated address of the Bishop of Gloucester, and we must again be impressed with a sense of the ability and ready learning of Cranmer. He spoke as if he had been irritated by the patronising tone, which was the really offensive part of the subdelegate's address. Cranmer undoubtedly used no "mincing phrases" when he described the pope as Antichrist, and he concluded thus:—

"This enemy of God and of our redemption is so evidently pointed out in the Scriptures, by such manifest signs and tokens, which all so clearly appear in him, that, except a man will shut up his eyes and heart against the light, he cannot but know him; and therefore, for my part, I will never give my consent to the receiving of him into this Church of England. And you, my Lord, and the rest that sit here in commission, consider well and examine into your own consciences; you have sworn against him; you are learned, and can judge of the truth. I pray God you be not wilfully blind. As for me, I have herein discharged mine own conscience towards the world, and I will write also my mind to her Grace touching this matter." *

The Bishop of Gloucester good-naturedly remarked, "We come to examine you, and you, methinks, examine us." The archbishop's powerful address had been very provoking, and he gave proof that now, as on other occasions, he could make use of very strong language when he chose. During his speech, the two proctors would have interrupted him several times; and on one occasion, Story, regarding what he heard as blasphemy, called upon the commissioner to silence the archbishop; but the Bishop of Gloucester kept his temper, and "suffered Cranmer to end his tale at full."

And now, as was customary at that time in courts of justice, a desultory conversation was permitted to take place between the law officers of the crown and the accused. Of what occurred we have only a partial account; but some things were said which throw light upon the character and conduct of Cranmer.

Before answering any questions, the archbishop declared that every question was answered under a protest that he denied the legality of the court held in the pope's name. Dr. Martin then led him on to a discussion on the nature of an oath, with the view of convicting him of perjury under the circumstances under which Cranmer accepted the archbishopric. As we have already availed ourselves of all the information to be derived from the

* Remains, iv. 114.

assertions and admissions of the archbishop on that point, it will be unnecessary to report the colloquy between his Grace and the learned proctor. The archbishop repeated what he had frequently declared, that the archbishopric was not sought by him, but that it was forced upon him by the king.

Martin accused him of having held three doctrines with respect to the Eucharist, which the archbishop denied. Martin persevered.

"What doctrine was taught by you when you condemned Lambert, the Sacramentary, in the king's presence at Whitehall?"

The archbishop answered: "I maintained then the Papist's doctrine."

Mart. "That is to say the Catholic and universal doctrine of Christ's Church. And how when King Henry died? Did you not translate Justus Jonas's book?"

Cran. "I did so."

Mart. "Then there you defended another doctrine touching the Sacrament, by the same token that you sent to Lynne, your printer, that whereas in the first print there was an affirmative, that is to say, Christ's body really in the Sacrament, you sent then to your printer to put in a 'not,' whereby it came miraculously to pass, that Christ's body was clean conveyed out of the Sacrament?"

Cran. "I remember there were two printers of my said book, but where the same 'not' was put in I cannot tell."

Mart. "Then from a Lutheran ye became a Zwinglian, which is the vilest heresy of all in the high mystery of the Sacrament; and for the same heresy you did help to burn Lambert, the Sacramentary, *which you now call the Catholic faith*, and God's word."

Cran. "I grant that then I believed otherwise than I do now; and so I did, until my Lord of London, Doctor Ridley, did confer with me, and by sundry persuasions and authorities of doctors drew me quite from my opinion."

Mart. "Now, sir, as touching the last part of your oration, you denied that the pope's Holiness was supreme head of the Church of Christ?"

Cran. "I did so."

Mart. "Who say you then is supreme head?"

Cran. "Christ."

Mart. "But whom hath Christ left here in earth His vicar and head of His Church?"

Cran. "Nobody."

Mart. "Ah! why told you not King Henry this, when you made him supreme head? And now nobody is. This is treason against his own person, as you then made him."

Cran. "I meant not but every king in his own realm and dominion is supreme head, and so was he supreme head of the Church of Christ in England."

Mart. "Is this always true? and was it ever so in Christ's Church?"

Cran. "It was so."

Mart. "Then what say you by Nero? He was the mightiest prince of the earth, after Christ was ascended. Was he head of Christ's Church?"

Cran. "Nero was Peter's head."

Mart. "I ask, whether Nero was head of the Church or no? If he were not, it is false that you said before, that all princes be, and ever were, heads of the Church within their realms."

Cran. "Nay, it is true, for Nero was head of the Church, that is in worldly respects of the temporal bodies of men, of whom the Church consisteth; for so he beheaded Peter and the Apostles. And the Turk, too, is head of the Church in Turkey."

Mart. "Then he that beheaded the heads of the Church, and crucified the Apostles, was head of Christ's Church; and he that was never member of the Church, is head of the Church by your new-found understanding of God's Word."*

It is easy to understand what Cranmer meant; but if the report of the proceedings be correct, it is equally clear that Martin conducted his argument with the greater skill.

The court being called to order, Dr. Martin, as proctor for the king and queen, proceeded to exhibit certain articles of accusation against the Lord Thomas Cranmer, Archbishop and Metropolitan of Canterbury, all of which, if required, he was prepared to prove.† On account of its verbiage, the document is of considerable length, but its statements may be briefly given. Having affirmed the undeniable fact that Cranmer had succeeded Warham as Archbishop of Canterbury, the proctor, *ad invidiam*, adverted to Cranmer's life, not only before his consecration but before his ordination, when " he married a certain woman called Joan, alias *Black Johanne of the Dolphin* at Cambridge." Cranmer, as a layman, had a right to marry; and to make this marriage an article of accusation against him was a mere act of malice—worthy to be noted as showing the animus of Martin. The proctor proceeds to notice the archbishop's second marriage, in a most offensive and unjustifiable manner. "After the decease of his first wife,

---

* Remains, iv. 96.

† The interrogations and the answers are usually taken from Foxe. On comparing them with the "Processus contra Cranmerum," in the Lambeth Library, I find that they are not accurately given by Foxe, but we have in the document only the substance of Cranmer's answer.

the said Thomas Cranmer, having been made a priest and placed in the sacred apostolical order, took to wife another woman, *named Anne, or perchance otherwise called, de facto*, when *de jure* he ought not to have done so." The proctor affirms his readiness to prove " that he secretly retained, paid, and kept the woman aforesaid, taken by him as his second wife, until the death of Henry VIII., as covertly as possible." The proctor would prove that in the reign of Edward VI. the archbishop avowed his marriage, and without shame or reserve treated her as a wife " as well *in mensa* as elsewhere."

A list of Cranmer's works was put in, from which the proctor was prepared to prove him to be a heretic, especially in what related to the Sacrament of the altar. The proctor was also enabled to prove that, by the authority of the most serene Lady Queen Mary, the archbishop had been committed to the Tower for his enormous and nefarious wickednesses, offences, and crimes; that he was condemned as a heretic by the University of Oxford; and that he continued to re-assert and defend his heretical tenets. The archbishop was accused of having instigated " Henry VIII. and many bishops, prelates, nobles, magnates, and persons of either sex to recede from and renounce the authority of the pope," although, the proctor alleged, he had at his consecration professed fidelity and obedience to the Apostolic See. The archbishop was accused of usurping and arrogating to himself the authority of the supreme Pontiff, among other things by consecrating as bishops persons whose election had not been confirmed at Rome. All these things were laid to the charge of the archbishop, and he had shown no signs of repentance or change of mind. The articles were publicly read in English and in Latin.

The archbishop rose and signified his readiness, under

protest, to put in his answer at once. The facts he generally admitted to have occurred as was stated; he had only to offer certain explanations.* He did not deny his marriages, or that he concealed his second marriage, until, by the laws of the realm, he could place his wife at the head of his establishment. He asserted that he received his archbishopric, not, as had been said, by favour of the pope, but through the favour of King Henry VIII. He explained that, as regarded some of the books on the list, he published them, but was not in every case the author; nevertheless he maintained that the doctrine they propounded was catholic and true. He admitted that he had "receded from the authority of the Roman pontiff," and had persuaded others to do the same, on account of the enormities committed in the papacy; but he denied that by so doing he was a schismatic, or that by receding from the pope he had receded from the Catholic Church. He offered the explanation of the circumstances under which he accepted the archbishopric, of which we have availed ourselves when speaking of his consecration. As archbishop he had for all that he did the authority of Convocation and of Parliament, of Church and State.

Although the words of Cranmer were taken down by a notary, and a promise was made to the archbishop that he should be permitted to correct the report, the promise was not kept, and we have only a garbled statement of what he really said. That he spoke boldly and bravely, without shrinking from the assertion of any truth he had already advanced, that he manfully defended his conduct, we may infer from the behaviour of the high commissioner. It appears to me quite clear, that the Bishop of Gloucester hoped and expected that the archbishop would make

* Strype, Memorials, ii. 1077.

some concession, and enable him to interfere in his favour. Brookes was chagrined at the bold and courageous manner in which Cranmer defended himself and his cause. This is apparent in the bishop's manner. Hitherto he had addressed Cranmer as "my Lord"; he now said:*—

"Master Cranmer—I cannot otherwise term you, considering your obstinacy—I am right sorry, I am right heartily sorry, to hear such words escape your mouth so unadvisedly. I had conceived a right good hope of your amendment. I supposed that this obstinacy of yours came not of a vain glory, but rather of a corrupt conscience, which was the occasion that I hoped so well of your return. But now I perceive by your foolish babble, that it is far otherwise. Ye are so puffed up with vain glory, there is such a *cauteria* of heresy crept into your conscience, that I am clean void of hope, and my hope is turned into perdition. Who can save that will be lost? God would have you to be saved, and you refuse it. '*Perditio tua super te, Israel; tantummodo in Me salvatio tua, ait Dominus per Prophetam.*' 'Thy perdition is only upon thyself, O Israel; only in Me is thy salvation, saith the Lord by his prophet.' You have uttered so erroneous talk, with such open malice against the pope's Holiness, with such open lying against the Church of Rome, with such open blasphemy against the Sacrament of the altar, that no mouth could have expressed more maliciously, more lyingly, more blasphemously. To reason with you, although I would of myself, to satisfy this audience, yet may I not by our commission neither can I find how I may do it with the Scriptures. For the Apostle

---

* It is to be surmised that the officials received instructions from head-quarters to obtain a recantation from Cranmer if possible; and they were unduly irritated whenever Cranmer gave indications of his firmness.

doth command that such a one should not only not be talked withal, but also shunned and avoided, saying : ' *Hæreticum hominem post unum aut alterum conventum devita, sciens quod hujusmodi perversus est et delinquit, quum sit proprio judicio condemnatus.*' ' An heretical person, after once or twice conferring, shun, knowing that he is perverse and sinneth, being of his own judgment condemned.' Ye have been conferred withal not once or twice, but oftentimes, ye have oft been lovingly admonished, ye have been oft secretly disputed with. And the last year in the open school, in open disputations, ye have been openly convict, ye have been openly driven out of the school with hisses : your book which ye brag you made seven years ago, and no man answered it, Marcus Antonius hath sufficiently detected and confuted, and yet ye persist still in your wonted heresy." *

" Athough," he said, " I do not intend to reason with you, but to give you up as an outcast from God's favour, yet because ye have uttered to the annoying of the people such pestilent heresies as may do harm among some rude and unlearned, I think it meet and not *abs re*, somewhat to say therein."

He then with considerable ability repeated, *ex cathedra*, the oft-repeated fallacies by which his party supported their opinions, and concluded in these words :—" Thus much have I said, not for *you*, Master Cranmer, for any hope that I conceived of you is now gone and past, but in somewhat to satisfy the rude and unlearned people, that they perceiving your arrogant lying and lying arrogancy, may better eschew your detestable and abominable scheme."

Dr. Story called certain witnesses to give evidence to the truth of the articles exhibited; the Dean of Christ

* State Trials, i. 792.

Church, Dr. Smith; a Canon of Christ Church Dr. Tresham, Dr. Crooke, Mr. London, Mr. Curtop, Mr. Warde, and Mr. Serles.

It was notified to the Lord Thomas—as he was again called by the public officer, who read the names—that he might take exception to any of the witnesses so named. He declared that he excepted to them all, as all were perjured, and, as he expressed himself, "not in Christian religion." "If in times past to swear, as they had done, against the prince were unlawful, they should rather have given their lives than their oath. But if it were lawful, then are they perjured, to defend him whom they forsware before."

This was more than the fiery temper of Dr. Story could stand. He burst out :—

"Master Cranmer, you have made a goodly process concerning your heretical oath made to the king, but you forget your oath made to the See Apostolic. As concerning your oath made to the king, if you made it to him only, it took an end by his death, and so it is released; if you made it to his successors, well, sir, the true successors have the empire, and they will you to dissolve the same, and become a member of Christ's Church again, and it standeth well with charity."

To this the archbishop, says the reporter, answered again; but the answer is not given: it was indeed only commenced, for Dr. Story insolently interrupted him, exclaiming :—" Hold your peace, sir, and so shall it right well become you, considering that I gave you licence before to say your fancy. Your oath was no oath; for it lacked the three points of an oath, that is to say, *judicium, justitiam, et veritatem.*"*

* State Trials, i. 797.

The prisoner was ordered to be removed.

The archbishop again made a genuflexion, and removed his cap to each of the proctors for the crown. Dr. Story, with an angry frown, pointed to the Bishop of Gloucester as the person to whom the compliment was due; but the archbishop immediately replaced his cap, and as he passed the commissioner of the pope, no genuflexion was made.

The court met the next day in New College. It is not necessary to go through the evidence given by the witnesses there summoned. The facts were not denied, though the inferences from them were controverted.

Dr. Martin, with a soft and silky mode of speaking, delighted to give as much annoyance and pain to an opponent as he possibly could. Knowing what would amuse the vulgar, he inquired of the archbishop, sarcastically, whether his children were bondmen to the see of Canterbury. The archbishop asked, whether, if a priest at his benefice kept a concubine and had illegitimate children, those children were bondmen to the benefice or not; then, smiling, he said, "I trust you will make my children's cause no worse."

Not abashed, Dr. Martin next, reverting to their former dispute, asked him again, who was the supreme head of the Church of England. The archbishop was glad to have an opportunity of explaining his former rather strong assertions on this point:—

"Marry," he said, " Christ is head of this member, as He is of the whole of the body—of the universal Church." " Why," quoth Doctor Martin, " you made King Henry the Eighth supreme head of the Church." " Yea," said the archbishop, " of all the *people* of England, as well ecclesiastical as temporal." " And not of the Church?" asked Martin. " No," said Cranmer, "*for Christ is only head of His Church, and of the faith and religion of the*

CHAP. III.

Thomas Cranmer.

1533–56.

same. The king is head and governor of his people, which are the visible Church." "What!" quoth Martin, "You never durst to tell the king so." "Yes, that I durst," quoth he, "and did, in the publication of his style; *wherein he was named supreme head of the Church there was never other thing meant.*" *

The proceedings against the archbishop were now suspended, until the report of what had taken place had been sent to Rome. Cranmer was remitted to prison, there to await the final judgment of the pope. He was not, however, without hope, that if that decision were against him, the country, so long opposed to papal interference, would not permit a papal sentence against an Archbishop of Canterbury to be carried into execution.

Cranmer appears to have been infatuated by the notion, that on account of the good offices he had, when in power, rendered to the queen as the Lady Mary, he should, in his time of need, receive mercy and consideration from her Majesty. This may have been one of the reasons why he so particularly resented the charge of treason, whenever it was brought against him. According to modern notions, nothing can be more clear than his treason, when he joined in the proclamation of the Lady Jane. But according to the ancient feudal notions, which still lingered in the public mind, a man was not guilty of treason to the sovereign unless he had sworn allegiance to him, or until the sovereign had been anointed by the Church. Cranmer had been among the first to advance what afterwards became the Jacobite principle, that by right of primogeniture and by that right only and without limitation, the crown descended from sire to son. Under the old feudal idea the counsellors of Mary pleaded their cause and were pardoned; but it is difficult to understand how Cran-

* Remains, iv. 117.

mer could have urged this plea in his own favour, after the speech he made, if indeed he made it, at the coronation of Edward VI. It also appears strange, that he should be so little acquainted with Mary's character as to suppose that, if his conduct with respect to the Lady Jane were overlooked, she would pardon him for the part he had taken in the great divorce case and in the religious reformations in the late king's reign. He evidently thought that the Reformation was still an open question, and that after a free discussion both parties might make concessions. Though he might be deposed, still he thought his life would be spared. Reginald Pole, as we shall see in his "Life," was a reformer. Although Pole was opposed to the reformation conducted by Cranmer, it still appeared to be on the cards that the two prelates might come to an agreement.

The archbishop, immediately after the trial, wrote the following letter to the queen's proctors:*—

"I have me commended unto you; and, as I promised, I have sent my letters unto the queen's Majesty unsigned, praying you to sign them, and deliver them with all speed. I might have sent them by the carrier sooner, but not surer; but hearing Master Bailiff say, that he would go to the court on Friday, I thought him a meeter messenger to send my letters by; for better is later and surer, than sooner and never to be delivered. Yet one thing I have written to the queen's Majesty enclosed and sealed, which I require you may be so delivered without delay, and not be opened until it be delivered unto her Grace's own hands. I have written all that I remember I said, except that which I spake against the Bishop of Gloucester's own person, which I thought not meet to write. And in some

* Although it is not without difficulties, there is, as Dr. Jenkyns observes, a strong presumption that two letters to the queen, which have been preserved, and are numbered ccxcix. and ccc. in the "Remains" are the letters referred to in the letter to the proctor.

places I have written more than I said, which I would have answered to the Bishop, if you would have suffered me.

"You promised I should see mine answers to the sixteen articles, that I might correct, amend, and change them, where I thought good; which your promise you kept not. And mine answer was not made upon my oath, nor repeated; nor made *in judicio*, but *extra judicium*, as I protested; nor to the Bishop of Gloucester as judge, but to you, the king's and queen's proctors. I trust you will deal sincerely with me, without fraud or craft, and use me as you would wish to be used in like case yourselves. Remember that '*Qua mensura mensi fueritis eadem remetieter vobis*,' i.e. *What measure you mete, the same shall be measured to you again.* Thus fare you well, and God send you His Spirit to induce you into all truth.—(September, 1555.)"

In the letters to the queen there is no want of boldness nor the slightest indication of a wavering mind on the part of the archbishop. We should describe the allusion to the fact of the king's being a foreigner, as peculiarly bold, for it was a fact which had strongly excited the jealousy and fears of the English people. He thus describes the proceedings at Oxford:—

"So it is, that upon Saturday, being the seventh day of this month, I was cited to appear at Rome the eightieth day after, there to make answer to such matters as should be objected against me on the behalf of the king and your most excellent Majesty: which matters the Thursday following were objected against me by Dr. Martin and Dr. Storie, your Majesty's proctors, before the Bishop of Gloucester, sitting in judgment by commission from Rome. But, alas! it cannot but grieve the heart of any natural subject, to be accused of the king and queen of his own realm, and specially before an outward judge, or by authority coming from any person out of this realm, where the king and queen, as if they were subjects within their own realm, shall complain, and require justice at a stranger's hands against their own subject, being already condemned to death by their own laws. As though the king and queen could not do or have justice within their own realms against their own subjects, but they must seek it at a stranger's hands, in a strange land; the like whereof, I think, was never seen. I would have wished to have had some meaner adversaries; and I think that death shall not grieve me much more, than to have my most dread and most gracious sovereign Lord and Lady, (to whom under God I do owe all obedience,) to be mine accusers in judgment within their own realm, before any stranger and outward power. But forasmuch as in the time of the prince of most famous memory, King Henry the Eighth, your Grace's father, I was sworn never to consent that the Bishop of Rome should have or exercise any authority or jurisdiction in this realm of England, therefore, lest I should allow his authority contrary to mine oath, I refused to make answer to the Bishop of Gloucester, sitting here in judgment by the pope's authority, lest I should run into perjury." *

He then proceeds to show, at considerable length, that the papal laws are opposed to the laws as well as to the authority of the crown imperial of this realm. He shows that the laws of the pope are transgressed in England, always have been and always must be, if the laws of the realm are to be enforced; and he points out, therefore, that since the pope anathematises all who disobey his laws, the whole realm, including the king and queen, are under the papal curse. He sums up this part of his subject thus:—

"And if I should agree to allow such authority within this realm, whereby I must needs confess that your most gracious Highness, and also your realm, should ever continue accursed, until you shall cease from the execution of your own laws and customs of your realm; I could not think myself true either to your Highness, or to this my natural country, knowing that I do know. Ignorance, I know, may excuse other men, but he that knoweth how prejudicial and injurious the power and authority,

* Remains, i. 367.

which he challengeth everywhere, is to the crown, laws, and customs of this realm, and yet will allow the same, I cannot see in any wise how he can keep his due allegiance, fidelity, and truth to the crown and state of this realm." *

After this he censures the ritualistic and doctrinal errors of the papacy. He attacks first, the Latin service; asserts it to be contrary to Scripture; and in proof that it was opposed to the practice of the primitive Church, he makes a long and apposite quotation from Justinian:—

"Therefore," he says, "when a good number of the best learned men reputed within this realm, some favouring the old, some the new learning, as they term it (*where indeed that which they call the old is the new, and that which they call the new is indeed the old*); but when a great number of such learned men of both sorts were gathered together at Windsor, for the reformation of the service of the Church, it was agreed by both, without controversy (not one saying contrary), that the service of the Church ought to be in the mother tongue, and that Saint Paul, in the fourteenth chapter to the Corinthians, was so to be understanden." †

He refers with equal learning to the sin of the papacy in withholding the cup from the laity in the Sacrament of the Holy Communion:—

"Christ," he says, "ordained the Sacrament in two kinds, the one separated from the other, to be a representation of His death, where His blood was separated from His flesh, which is not represented in one kind alone; so that the lay people receive not the whole Sacrament whereby Christ's death is represented, as He commanded." ‡

Reverting to the assumption by which the pope represents himself as the universal bishop, Cranmer points

* Remains, i. 373.   † Ibid. i. 375, letter ccxcix.   ‡ Ibid. i. 377.

out how any such assumption had been denounced by Gregory the Great. The archbishop dwells upon the inordinate pride by which the papacy was disgraced, and hesitates not to describe the pope as Antichrist. With respect to his own doctrine relating to the Holy Sacrament, he repeats what he had often said before:—

"Herein, I said I would be judged by the old Church, and which doctrine could be proved the elder, that I would stand unto. And forasmuch as I have alleged in my book many old authors, both Greeks and Latins, which above a thousand years after Christ continually taught as I do; if they could bring forth but one old author, that saith in these two points as they say, I offered six or seven years ago, and do offer yet still, that I will give place unto them." *

After complaining of the manner in which the statements of the fathers had been falsified by the Papists, he continues:—

"In the beginning, the Church of Rome taught a pure and a sound doctrine of the Sacrament. But after that the Church of Rome fell into a new doctrine of transubstantiation; with the doctrine they changed the use of the Sacrament, contrary to that Christ commanded, and the old Church of Rome used above a thousand years. And yet, to deface the old, they say that the new is the old; wherein for my part I am content to stand to the trial. But their doctrine is so fond and uncomfortable, that I marvel that any man would allow it, if he knew what it is. But howsoever they bear the people in hand, that which they write in their books hath neither truth nor comfort." †

A portion of another letter, addressed to the queen, is still bolder, for he points out in strong language the opposition between the oath which she had taken to observe the laws and statutes of the realm, and the oath she had

* Remains, i. 380. † Ibid. i. 381.

taken to the pope, and entreats her to weigh the two oaths together—

"and to see how they do agree: and then to do as your Grace's conscience shall give you; for I am surely persuaded that willingly your Majesty will not offend, nor do against your conscience for so doing. But I fear me that there be contradictions in your oaths, and that those which should have informed your Grace thoroughly, did not their duties therein. And if your Majesty ponder the two oaths diligently, I think you shall perceive you were deceived; and then your Highness may use the matter as God shall put in your heart."*

In this letter he complains that he was kept from the company of learned men and books, from counsel, from pen and ink, "saving at this time to write to your Majesty, which all were necessary for a man being in my case." He also says that for his appearance at Rome, "if your Majesty will give me leave, I will appear there."

It was beneath the dignity of Cranmer's character to make a point, as he did, of the impossibility of obeying the citation. He knew, as well as anyone, that the citation was a mere form—one of those legal fictions, such as he himself was guilty of, when, in pronouncing sentence on a heretic, he handed him over to the civil power, knowing very well what such handing-over meant.

His complaint as to want of companions was soon remedied; he had ere long a greater number than he desired, though not exactly the persons he wished to see. Pen and ink he had, for he employed his active mind, when in prison, by preparing a vindication of his book upon the Sacrament, in the shape of an answer to Bishop Gardyner, by whom, under the pseudonym of Marcus Antonius, it had been attacked. Of this he finished three parts in prison: two of these parts were lost at Oxford; one part

---

* Remains, i. 383.

fell into the hands of John Foxe the martyrologist; but though a copy was sought for, with his usual diligence, by Strype, it has never been discovered.

Cranmer's powerful letter to Mary, written under these difficult circumstances, and his readiness, away from his own books, to undertake to answer an elaborate treatise, are a further confirmation of the vigour of Cranmer's mind and of the soundness of his learning. His intellect was solid rather than brilliant, but he never decided upon a subject till he had investigated it fully; his memory was retentive and what he had once mastered was always ready for use.

There is one passage in the archbishop's letter to the queen, which, as contrasted with what afterwards occurred, is remarkable.

After describing the pope as Antichrist, he says:—

"This that I have spoken against the power and authority of the pope, I have not spoken (I take God to record and judge) for any malice I owe to the pope's person, whom I know not; but I shall pray to God to give him grace that he may seek above all things to promote God's honour and glory, and not to follow the trade of his predecessors in these latter days.*

"Nor I have not spoken it for fear of punishment, and to avoid the same, thinking it rather an occasion to aggravate than to diminish my trouble; but I have spoken it for my most bounden duty to the crown, liberties, laws, and customs of this realm of England, but most specially to discharge my conscience in uttering the truth to God's glory, casting away all fear by the comfort which I have in Christ, who saith, 'Fear not them that kill the body, and cannot kill the soul, but fear him that can cast both body and soul into hell fire.' He that for fear to lose this life will forsake the truth, shall lose the everlasting life: and he that for the truth's sake will spend his life, shall find everlasting life. And Christ promiseth to stand fast with them

* Remains, i. 379.

before His Father, which will stand fast with Him here. Which comfort is so great, that whosoever hath his eyes fixed upon Christ, cannot greatly pass on this life, knowing that he may be sure to have Christ stand by him in the presence of His Father in heaven." *

The office of preparing an answer to this letter the queen assigned to Cardinal Pole. To Pole's character, I have sought to do justice in his "Life." But although he took his time for his reply, which did not appear till the 6th of November, the document he produced is so immeasurably beneath the standard of his ability, that we must conclude that he composed it under constraint, and that probably what he wrote was elaborated by other hands before it reached those of Cranmer.† The letter closes with the usual reproach of perjury against Cranmer, and it attributes all his sins and calamities to the Divine vengeance for the violation of the pledges he had made to the pope, antagonistic as those pledges were to the oath of allegiance which he made to the king.

A tone of bitterness and severity pervades the letter. As a matter of course, a hope is expressed that his arguments will convince the archbishop of his iniquities; but the letter was evidently written for the public rather than for the person to whom it was addressed. The commonplaces of his party, in vindication of his tenets, are adduced and heartily supported by Pole. There are no traces in the composition of the Ciceronian latinity which the cardinal affected, not very successfully, in his other writings. For a controversy with Cranmer, he was certainly not the man.

If Pole had given up the hope of converting Cranmer, his despondency on the subject was not shared by those who were with the archbishop at Oxford.

* Remains, i. 380.
† The letter may be found in the Appendix to Strype, ii. 972.

Cranmer always desired discussion, not for the sake of victory, but in order that he might form an impartial judgment of doctrines and of persons. On the morning of the 16th October he was engaged in earnest conversation with a friar. Their conference was suddenly interrupted. It was abruptly announced to the archbishop that Bishop Ridley and Bishop Latimer were passing the prison on their way to execution. Cranmer rushed to the window. It was too late. He was told that, when they were passing a few minutes before, Ridley, his dear, his best beloved friend and chaplain, had looked up to the window of the archbishop's room to exchange a last but not a long farewell, with the honoured friend who had been to him as a father. The agony of Cranmer's mind can be imagined, not described. Up to the roof of the prison he hurried to catch if possible a sight of his friend. He saw much, but nothing in detail. The chief magistrates of the city were assembled at Canditch, over against Balliol College, surrounded by a military force. He could just see the two illustrious martyrs conferring together, and taking their last embrace. A pause ensued, during which Dr. Smith, formerly one of Cranmer's friends, was preaching, but not as Cranmer would have wished. A long pause it seemed, though the service only occupied a quarter of an hour. He saw the authorities trying to persuade his two illustrious friends—saints, martyrs—to recant; he saw Bishop Ridley distributing little keepsakes to those who were weeping around him; he saw men scrambling for relics of the martyr; he saw him who had come neatly dressed in the garments he was wont to wear as Bishop of London, stripping himself to his shirt; he saw him standing upon a stone at the stake and lifting up his hands in the attitude of prayer; he saw the brave old octogenarian Latimer, throwing off his old frieze coat, "standing bolt upright" in his shroud; he saw the iron chains brought out, and Ridley was seen to be *rattling* his chain, ere it was fastened round his middle. He saw a faggot kindled and laid at Bishop Ridley's feet. Cranmer closed his eyes. He could look no longer. He was on his knees in prayer. What Cranmer's prayer at that dread hour was we may leave it to the reader's heart to suggest.

The next two months were months of deep anxiety to Cranmer. The news arrived at Oxford in December, or the beginning of January, that the administration of the see of Canterbury had been conferred upon Reginald Pole. The fact was, that when the eighty days appointed for the appearance of Cranmer at Rome had elapsed, Cranmer's case was heard in the consistory. Counsel *pro forma* had been assigned to him; Cardinal de Puteo (du Puy) prosecuted the archbishop in the name of the King and Queen of England. The excommunication of the Archbishop of Canterbury was pronounced on the 4th of December. By a bull, dated the 11th December, 1555, the pope collated or *provided* Pole to the archbishopric of Canterbury.* Thus was defied the English nation. Thus was set at nought not only later statutes but the statutes especially of Provisors and Præmunire. Pole was only a deacon; he could therefore be only administrator of the see until he was ordained and consecrated.† Directions were, at the same time, given for Cranmer's degradation. The Bishop of London, Dr. Bonner, and the Bishop of Ely, Dr. Thirlby, were appointed papal delegates to carry into effect the mandate for his degradation. Thirlby was selected, as exhibiting in his own person the honours to which, by recantation, any one who would conform to the new regulations of our Church might expect to be advanced. Thirlby would have shrunk from this

* Parker, 511.
† Pole was not consecrated till the 26th of March, 1556.

painful office which, as a penance, he was required to discharge. Among the many censurable actions of the government, Thirlby's appointment to this office may be regarded as one of the most cruel. Cranmer, in the days of his prosperity, had been more than the patron, he had been the affectionate friend of Thirlby. He had treated him with the confidence of a brother, he had been to him a generous benefactor; it was a saying in the archiepiscopal household, that " Thirlby's commendation of any valuable article in the possession of the primate was a plain way of winning it." * During the whole process, Thirlby was dissolved in tears. He had done what Cranmer was about to do, he had recanted. He retained his bishopric; but he had a severe penalty to pay. It rather shocks one's sense of justice, when we find those very persons who seek for excuses for the recantation of Cranmer, utterly unable to pity Bishop Thirlby. The weakness was venial or criminal in both or in neither.

With respect to Bonner, we observe that the worst features of his harsh character displayed themselves on this occasion. He delighted in triumphing over a man who was a rival cordially hated.

On the 14th of February, 1556, the archbishop was brought under a guard to Christ Church. Here the Bishop of London, the Bishop of Ely, and other persons in the commission had already taken their places on an elevated platform before the high altar, in the choir, in full pontificals. The commission was read. In the body of the document it was stated, that in the consistory at Rome, the case had been fully and impartially examined, both the articles laid to the charge of the archbishop, and his replies; and it was added that counsel had been heard

* Morice.

both on the part of the king and queen, and also in behalf of the party accused, that nothing had been omitted which pertained to his defence. The archbishop could not restrain himself; under considerable excitement, he exclaimed:*—

"O Lord, what lies be these that I being continually in prison, and never could be suffered to have counsel or advocate at home, should produce witness and appoint my counsel at Rome! God must needs punish this open and shameless lying."

The officer of the court continued to read the commission, which was to be considered as supplying all defects in law or process, and which invested the commissioners with full authority to deprive, to degrade, and to excommunicate Thomas, Archbishop of Canterbury; and on his degradation to deliver him up to the secular power, *omni appellatione remota*.

With solemn step and slow the procession moved out of the church to a portion of the adjoining yard. Here stood a credence table in the shape of an altar. The candlesticks were upon it, but the candles were not lighted. It was covered with the habiliments of the clergy, and the various utensils made use of in their ministrations. On either side were sedilia for the two bishops and other persons included in the commission; for the officer appointed by the government,—when to the tender mercies of the State the criminal should be committed,—and for a notary public. There was a faldstool placed, at which the archbishop knelt, while the Bishop of London, in the name of the blessed Trinity and by the authority of the Church, declared him deposed, degraded, and cut off from all the privileges attached to his clerical order. This was not enough, however, for Bonner. With unfeeling inso-

* State Trials, i 803.

lence he turned to the assembled multitude, and exclaimed in triumph :—

"This is the man that ever despised the pope's Holiness, and now is to be judged by him. This is the man who hath pulled down so many churches, and now is come to be judged in a church. This is the man that condemned the blessed Sacrament of the altar, and now is come to be condemned before that blessed Sacrament hanging over the altar. This is the man that, like Lucifer, sat in the place of Christ upon an altar, to judge other, and now is come before an altar to be judged himself."*

Throughout the proceedings against him, Cranmer was sometimes unfortunately provoked to an altercation with his accusers or his judge; and this somewhat detracts from the dignity of his position. He was naturally disgusted and justly provoked by Bonner's vulgar air of triumph; but it would have been more dignified to have remembered the example of his Master, and when he was reviled not to have reviled again.

Instead of this, he told the Bishop of London "that he belied him; as in other things, so in this. For that which was now laid to his charge was no fault of his; but if fault there were, it was to be laid to Bonner's own account; 'for the thing you mean, was in Paul's Church,' said he, 'where I came to sit in commission; and there was a scaffold prepared for me and others by you and your officers; and whether there were any altar under it or not, I could not perceive it, nor once suspected it, wherefore you do wittingly evil to charge me with it.'"

But Bonner's proud wrath was not to be silenced; he went on railing against the archbishop, commencing each sentence with "This is the man." Bishop Thirlby was

* State Trials, i. 804.

seen pulling him by the sleeve, to make him sit down; and we are informed that he upbraided Bonner, when they afterwards met at dinner, for a breach of promise in reviling the prisoner. The Bishop of Ely had entreated him to treat the archbishop with respect. Bonner, however, did not restrain himself, until the scarcely suppressed murmurs of the indignant bystanders signified their disgust at conduct unmannerly as it was cruel, vindictive, and heartless.

Nearly three and twenty years had elapsed since Cranmer had been oppressed for the first time by the gorgeous apparel pertaining to his office, arrayed in which he had frequently, at subsequent periods, appeared before the public. All the vestments which he as an archbishop was privileged to wear lay outstretched on the credence table, though made of canvas and other coarse stuff:— the purple cassock, the amice, the rochet, the alb, the stole, the tunicle, the dalmatic. the maniple, the chasuble, the mitre, the gloves, the episcopal ring, the sandals, the buskins, the gremial, the pastoral staff. the crosier, and the pallium. Two or more mocking priests proceeded to vest him. There stood the venerable man, the mitre on his head, in his left hand the pastoral staff. The grace of his manly face, the dignity of his figure, prevented men from noting the materials of which the vestments had been made. From the top step which led to the credence table, standing in imitation of an altar, the Primate of all England and Metropolitan looked down upon his suffragans, who, contrary to all law, were sitting in judgment upon him. The archbishop proudly demanded who among them all had himself a pall, to justify him in removing the pall from the neck of the metropolitan to whom they had all sworn allegiance.

For the moment Bonner himself was awed. The

answer at length came in a low voice, probably from Bishop Thirlby. They acknowledged themselves to be his inferiors, in that they were bishops; but as the pope's delegates they had power to degrade the metropolitan by taking away his pall.

The archbishop did not prolong the discussion. He could not resist the temptation to show how his judges were, on their own principles, self-rebuked; but he had determined what to do. He directed the persons appointed to vest and to divest him to proceed in their work, he would give them no trouble, for with this gear, he said, he long since had done. One by one all the ornaments and distinctions of office were taken off. All was done in solemn silence, except when the crosier was taken from his hand; then the voice of the archbishop was once more heard. Drawing from his sleeve a document hitherto concealed, "I appeal," he said, "to the next general council; in this paper I have comprehended my cause and the form of it. I desire the appeal to be admitted." He handed the document to the Bishop of Ely, and called upon the bystanders to be witnesses of what he had done. The Bishop of Ely had received instructions how to act if, as was possible, such a proceeding should take place as had just occurred. He replied, "My Lord, our commission is to proceed against you *omni appellatione remota*, and therefore we cannot admit it." "Why then," was the archbishop's reply, "you do me the more wrong, for my case is not the case of a private person; the matter is immediate between me and the pope, and none other. I hold that no man should be judge in his own cause." Thirlby had hitherto kept his feelings under control. He now fairly broke down. Bursting into tears, he determined to dare the worst of his employers, and he exclaimed: "Well! if it may be admitted, it shall." He received the appeal contrary to his instructions, and having once given way he could command himself no more, but, weeping still, he entreated and implored the archbishop to consider his case, while it was yet in his power to do him good. If Cranmer would recant, Thirlby promised to be a suitor to the king and queen in his behalf. As he adverted to the love and friendship which had been between them, his tears impeded his utterance. He solemnly assured the archbishop that nothing but the express command of the king and queen would have induced him to undertake his present office. He could not disobey; but in obeying he had become the most unhappy of men. Cranmer's heart was moved, but he was master of himself. Confronting his judge, he stood nobly firm in his integrity. The condemned man was heard exhorting his judge to suppress his grief. Of the two which was the really degraded man?*

The act was drawing to a close. In the lowest depth a lower deep was found. A barber clipped the hair round the archbishop's head; and Cranmer was made to kneel before Bonner. Bonner scraped the tips of the Archbishop's fingers to desecrate the hand which, itself anointed, had administered the unction to others. The threadbare gown of a yeoman bedel was thrown over his shoulders, and a townsman's greasy cap was forced upon his head. The Archbishop of Canterbury, or, as he was now called, Thomas Cranmer, was handed over to the secular power. In the lowest and most offensive manner the innate vulgarity of Bonner's mind displayed itself. Turning to Cranmer, he exclaimed, "Now you are no longer my lord;" and he thought it witty ever afterwards to speak of him as "this gentleman here."

* The original authority for the whole transaction is to be found in Wilkins.

Cranmer's appeal commences thus :—

"In the name of the Father, and of the Son, and of the Holy Ghost. First, my plain protestation made, that I intend to speak nothing against one Holy, Catholic, and Apostolical Church, or the authority thereof (the which authority I have in great reverence, and to whom my mind is in all things to obey); and if anything, peradventure, either by slipperiness of tongue, or by indignation of abuses, or else by the provocation of mine adversaries, be spoken or done otherwise than well, or not with such reverence as becometh me, I am most ready to amend it." *

He assigns for his appeal six reasons :—

"1. Being cited to Rome, he says, he was kept in most strict confinement, so that he could in no wise be suffered to go thither, nor to come out of prison; that, in so important causes concerning estate and life, no man is bound to send a proctor; that though he would never so fain have sent his proctor, yet by reason of his poverty he was not able (for all that ever he had, with which he might bear a proctor's costs, was taken from him); and that whether he appeared or not, the Cardinal de Puteo had declared the intention to proceed in judgment against him. 2. That being cited to appear at Rome before the cardinal's delegate, Bishop Brookes, he had been denied what was necessary for his defence, the aid of counsel. 3. That he had not received from the royal proctors, as it was promised that he should, copies of his answers for amendment, if requisite, to the charges produced against him. 4. That he disowned the papal authority, as well in consequence of his oath against it, as of its discordance with the English constitution. 5. That the usurped authority of the pontiff had consumed the riches and substance of the realm. 6. That it had not only caused the national laws and customs to be trodden underfoot, but also to the decrees of councils and to the precepts of the Gospel was repugnant." †

He concludes with the following important sentence; which may be regarded as the final enunciation on the

---

* Remains, iv. 121.   † Todd, ii. 465.

part of Cranmer of the principles on which he acted or wished to act:—

"Touching my doctrine of the Sacrament, and other my doctrine, of what kind so ever it be, I protest that it was never my mind to write, speak, or understand anything contrary to the most holy Word of God, or else, against the Holy Catholic Church of Christ; but purely and simply to imitate and teach those things only which I had learned of the sacred Scripture, and of the Holy Catholic Church of Christ from the beginning, and also according to the exposition of the most holy and learned fathers and martyrs of the Church.

"And if anything hath peradventure chanced otherwise than I thought, I may err, but heretic I cannot be, for as much as I am ready in all things to follow the judgment of the most sacred Word of God, and of the Holy Catholic Church, desiring none other thing than meekly and gently to be taught, if anywhere (which God forbid) I have swerved from the truth.*

"And I protest and openly confess, that in all my doctrine and preaching, both of the Sacrament and of other my doctrine, whatsoever it be, not only I mean and judge those things as the Catholic Church and the most holy fathers of old, with one accord, have meant and judged, but also I would gladly use the same words that they used, and not use any other words, but to set my hand to all and singular their speeches, phrases, ways, and forms of speech, which they do use in their treatises upon the Sacrament, and to keep still their interpretation. But in this thing I only am accused for an heretic, because I allow not the doctrine lately brought in of the Sacrament, and because I consent not to words not accustomed in Scripture, and unknown to the ancient fathers, but newly invented and brought in by men, and belonging to the destruction of souls, and overthrowing of the pure and old religion." †

When Cranmer, arrayed, by Bonner's order, like a poor layman, was led from the court, a stranger, a Gloucester-

---

* The sentiment is that of St. Augustine.
† Remains, iv. 126.

shire gentleman, brought him his clerical gown, and said it had been sent to him by order of the Bishop of Ely! Cranmer replied that he might have done a great deal more for him, and never have been worse thought of; for, he said, "I have well deserved it." Of Thirlby's friendship the stranger assured Cranmer he might feel secure; and then he asked the archbishop whether he stood in need of any assistance or refreshment. "I would willingly eat something," was the reply; "for having been troubled with this day's business, I had little inclination to eat till all was over; and now that all *is* over my heart is quieted." The stranger's purse was opened to Cranmer, for in Cranmer's purse not a penny remained. Having left a sum of money for the maintenance of the archbishop, the mysterious stranger vanished.*

There can be little doubt that Thirlby found other means of communicating with Cranmer. Permission was granted to the archbishop to receive visits from his friends and acquaintance in the University in the prison to which he had been consigned. Cranmer, always moved by manifestations of kindness and sympathy, was consoled by the commiseration his visitors, men of all parties, expressed; while, with his usual readiness, he entered into a discussion on the theological controversies by which the Church was divided.

There had been no time to communicate with the government; but Thirlby, we know, was anxious to intercede in behalf of his friend, if Cranmer could be by any means persuaded to make a submission to the government. Cranmer was willing to save his life if he could, and the

---

* Foxe says that the stranger left Oxford for fear of being put into prison by Bonner and Thirlby. The more probable conjecture is that he was a secret agent employed by Thirlby, who disappeared as soon as he had executed his mission.

only question was as to the terms of submission with which the government would be satisfied. There must have been many discussions on this subject. To Cranmer's Erastian or High Tory principles an appeal was made. The sovereign was, according to Cranmer's view, the supreme head of the Church in England. He had himself subjected Bonner and others to punishment for refusing to yield obedience to the laws enacted by the authority of the supreme head. The king and queen, as supreme head, had, through parliament, obtained the repeal of certain laws which former parliaments had passed for the abolition of all papal power in the Church of England, and the two sovereigns had subordinated their own authority to that of the Pope of Rome. Cranmer, as a loyal subject, ought therefore to yield obedience to what had been ordered by the sovereign, by parliament, and by Convocation. To the force of these arguments Cranmer so far yielded as to sign what is called his first submission.

"Forasmuch as the king and queen's Majesties, by consent of their parliament, have received the pope's authority within this realm, I am content to submit myself to their laws herein, and to take the pope to be the chief head of this Church of England, so far as God's laws, and the laws and customs of this realm will permit.*

THOMAS CRANMER."

On consideration, it was found that this was not sufficiently definite. Perhaps within a few hours, certainly on the same day, the submission was signed in the following form:—

"I, Thomas Cranmer, doctor in divinity, do submit myself to the Catholic Church of Christ, and to the pope, supreme head of the same Church, and unto the king and queen's Majesties, and unto all their laws and ordinances.†

THOMAS CRANMER."

* Todd, ii. 572.   † Ibid. ii. 473.

When this point was gained, it is probable that Thirlby found means of softening Bonner, who—coarse, violent, and vulgar as he was—nevertheless preferred the recantation of a heretic to his execution.

Bonner determined to call on the ex-primate himself, and he did so, probably, on the evening of the 15th.* It did not escape him that Cranmer had said nothing on the subject of the Holy Sacrament. This was the point to be discussed, and on this point it was less easy for Cranmer to yield. His Erastianism might enable him to submit to the authority of the pope, when to that authority the crown had succumbed; but he had been, even in prison, writing an orthodox defence of the doctrine of the Eucharist, thereby, as the Papists would assert, persevering in his heresy. It was at last, however, agreed that the submission should take the following form:—

"I am content to submit myself to the king and queen's Majesties, and to all their laws and ordinances, as well concerning the pope's supremacy as others. And I shall from time to time move and stir all other to do the like, to the uttermost of my power; and to live in quietness and obedience unto their Majesties, most humbly, without murmur or grudging against any of their godly proceedings. And for my book which I have written, I am contented to submit me to the judgment of the Catholic Church, and of the next general council.

THOMAS CRANMER."

We may presume that among those who were anxious to save Cranmer's life the terms of this document were thoroughly canvassed, and the question asked whether the queen would be content with this. At last a fourth form of submission was suggested to Cranmer. It was, in all pro-

---

* The third submission is not dated. I think it more probable that it was signed on the 15th, and that the fourth submission was signed on the 16th, than that both were signed on the same day.

bability, the suggestion of Bishop Thirlby, who was well acquainted with the subtlety of Cranmer's mind. It is so evidently equivocal, that it strikes one as more offensive than any of the recantations that preceded it. Cranmer had maintained that he adhered to the primitive catholic doctrine of the Church, that he would at once accept what was admitted to be catholic, what would abide the test of the *quod semper, quod ubique, quod ab omnibus*. The object of his writings had been to show that his view of the Eucharist, that of a communion instead of a mass, was the catholic view; that the papal view was mediæval and comparatively modern. Such being the case, surely, it was said, you cannot object to sign the fourth demand, which will probably satisfy the queen. At all events, in point of fact, the following was signed:—

"Be it known by these presents, that I, Thomas Cranmer, doctor in divinity, and late Archbishop of Canterbury, do firmly, steadfastly, and assuredly believe in all articles and points of the Christian religion and Catholic faith, as the Catholic Church doth believe, and hath ever believed from the beginning. Moreover, as concerning the Sacraments of the Church, I believe unfeignedly in all points as the said Catholic Church doth and hath believed from the beginning of the Christian religion. In witness whereof I have humbly subscribed my hand unto these presents, the 16th day of February, 1555-6.

THOMAS CRANMER."

This was a dishonest document. It is quite true, as we believe, that what Cranmer contended for was catholic truth, as opposed to popish error; but we can hardly doubt that the intention in this document was to convey a very different meaning to the royal mind. In the queen's mind the catholic truth implied the supremacy of the pope, though, by the major part of Christendom, comprehending in that title the Greek Churches, that supremacy was rejected and denied. The authorities at Oxford, however, were satisfied, and they felt themselves justified in removing Cranmer from Bocardo to the deanery of Christ Church. Here he was kindly received and hospitably entertained. His University friends rallied round him, and every one had a right to expect that the pardon conceded to other reputed heretics would be extended to him, especially as he was not in the position of a relapsed heretic. He was visited also by the Spanish foreigners, who had replaced at the University, through the influence of the Crown, the German foreigners appointed by Cranmer. Among these the most distinguished were Petrus a Sotho, of the order of St. Dominic, an eminent theologian, and Johannes de Villa Garcia, or Garcina, commonly called in England Johannes Fraterculus, who was regius professor of divinity.* These were unflinching supporters of the papacy. To one who had, like Cranmer, always found recreation in the sports of the field, and had been accustomed to much horse exercise, his long imprisonment must have been extremely irksome. Though under surveillance, he now thoroughly enjoyed his liberty; and we find him eager in the game of bowls—that game which, until of late years superseded, continued long a fashionable game among the clergy. By Cranmer's degradation, the archbishopric was open to his rival Reginald Pole, and, as it was not the interest of any one to make him suffer further, he felt secure of his pardon. Having conceded much, he evidently became reckless. He had lost character, and having no character to sustain, he was ready to do anything that might be suggested.

It is my business to state historical facts, and not to impute motives. The honesty of a man's own heart may be

---

* Wood, Annals, ii. 27.

doubted, when he is continually suspecting corrupt motives in others. I can find no facts to show that there was any insidious attempt to entrap Cranmer into a recantation, and then to betray him. Taking the facts as they come before us, all seems to have occurred through a natural sequence of cause and effect. Thirlby and Cranmer's other friends had been full of hope that they could secure the pardon of Cranmer, if he could be persuaded to follow Thirlby's example and to recant. They all rejoiced together now when the act of submission was signed. At the same time, there is not a particle of evidence to show that they acted on the queen's authority. They assumed that her sentiments were in accordance with their own. The queen's stern determination had not as yet been displayed; and Cranmer and his friends, all along, believed that her clemency was greater than it really was. They also expected that a petition presented in his favour by foreign exiles would tell in his behalf. They made a further very common miscalculation; Cranmer, had on more than one occasion, befriended the queen when she needed a friend, and he had interposed between her and her offended father. The merit of the good offices thus rendered to the Lady Mary was overrated on the one side; and by the queen, who resented wrongs longer than she remembered benefits, it was felt that Cranmer would not have hazarded the king's favour by pleading on her behalf, if he had not found, that by doing so he would not give offence. It is quite clear, that Mary never afforded any ground whatever for the hope that she would pardon Cranmer, and she never intended to do so. She never gave authority to those who effected his recantations to hold out to him hopes of pardon. Mary, who was always opposed to the reformations effected in her brother's reign, had become fanatical on the subject. Of those proceedings she regarded Cranmer as the chief author, and, since the death of Somerset and Northumberland, he was the only person surviving who was to be held responsible. He was led to the course of conduct which had brought the country to the verge of a revolution, by holding doctrines which were now denounced by the Church of England as heretical. He was doomed, as a heretic, to the death which he himself admitted to be, of heresy the proper punishment. She would be glad, as a religious person, to hear of his recantation. If he died a heretic she thought that his soul would go straight to hell: if he were reconciled to the Church, it might only go to purgatory. She would cheerfully, therefore, grant time for him to be persuaded of his errors. But this was perfectly consistent with a secret determination, that, as a warning to others, whether he recanted or not, he should die.

However much we may condemn Mary's principles and conduct, there is not the slightest proof of her having held out false hopes, or of her having sought to entrap the unfortunate Cranmer. She was determined; and, in her determination to sacrifice Cranmer she was, doubtless, encouraged by those of her privy council who, having been reformers in the late reign, had now conformed, and were eager to represent their former aberrations as the result of Cranmer's artifices.

In regard to those who had taken such interest in his perversion, if we except Bonner and the foreigners, they seem to have acted in sincerity and with good faith; their fault being that they were too sanguine as to the mercy of the queen.

Rumours soon reached Oxford that the submissions had not been such as to satisfy the royal mind; and Cranmer had now fallen into other hands. The foreign professors were supposed to have greater influence at the court than any other persons; but they had no affection for Cranmer; so far as they were concerned, their object was, through him, to bring discredit upon the cause of the Reformation. They also, like the English divines, overrated their influence; they talked to Cranmer not only of the preservation of his life, but also of a restoration to his lost dignity. His former friends had not succeeded; they, the foreigners, would now act on his behalf; but they would not undertake to plead his cause, unless, besides accepting the pope and the dogma of transubstantiation, he would denounce Protestantism, and assert more fully his acquiescence in all those mediæval fallacies which in the late reign he rejected. Meanwhile Cranmer, having lost his self-respect, had, as we have just remarked, become reckless. The descent was easy; to return was difficult. Intimations must have reached him of the indignation with which his recantations had been received by those who were preparing to die for the opinions which they derived from his authority and teaching. He, in his heart, despised Thirlby and others who had done what they were exhorting him to do. The good opinion of those holy men, the great and glorious army of martyrs who were waiting to glorify God in the "burning fiery furnace," which the queen was heating with sevenfold fury, Cranmer, at one time their leader and their chief, had lost. In the loss of honour among those for whose good opinion he only cared, Cranmer had lost all in this world. The lost man had nothing to care for; if his life was spared, he could hereafter make his peace with a God more merciful than man. It requires very little acquaintance with human nature to enable us to understand the misery of Cranmer under these circumstances, without a friend to encourage or to warn him,—goaded almost to madness.

When his new friends approached him with a fuller

submission, he must have sickened as he saw the smile of scarcely suppressed contempt upon their lips. "You have only," they said, "to put a few words"—that is, to sign his name—"on this little leaf of paper, and life and wealth are yours." And Cranmer took the pen and wrote the words, without perhaps even reading the document, which ran thus :—

"I, Thomas Cranmer, late Archbishop of Canterbury, do renounce, abhor, and detest all manner of heresies and errors of Luther and Zuinglius, and all other teachings which are contrary to sound and true doctrines. And I believe most constantly in my heart, and with my mouth I confess, one Holy and Catholic Church visible, without the which there is no salvation, and thereof I acknowledge the Bishop of Rome to be supreme head in earth, whom I acknowledge to be the highest bishop and pope, and Christ's vicar, unto whom all Christian people ought to be subject. And as concerning the Sacraments, I believe and worship in the Sacrament of the altar the very body and blood of Christ, being contained most truly under the forms of bread and wine; the bread, through the mighty power of God, being turned into the body of our Saviour Jesus Christ, and the wine into His blood. And in the other six Sacraments also, like as in this, I believe and hold as the Universal Church holdeth, and the Church of Rome judgeth and determineth. Furthermore, I believe that there is a place of purgatory, where souls departed are punished for a time, for whom the Church doth godlily and wholesomely pray, like as it doth honour saints and maketh prayers to them. Finally, in all things I profess that I do not otherwise believe than the Catholic Church, and the Church of Rome, holdeth and teacheth. I am sorry that I ever held or thought otherwise. And I beseech Almighty God, that of His mercy He will vouchsafe to forgive me whatsoever I have offended against God or His Church; and also I desire and beseech all Christian people to pray for me. And all such as have been deceived, either by my example or doctrine, I require them, by the blood of Jesus Christ, that they will, return to the unity of the Church, that we may be all of one mind, without schism or division. And to conclude, as I submit myself to the Catholic Church of Christ, and to the supreme head thereof, so I submit myself unto the most excellent Majesties of Philip and Mary, King and Queen of this realm of England, &c., and to all their laws and ordinances, being ready always as a faithful subject ever to obey them. And God is my witness that I have not done this for favour or fear of any person, but willingly, and of my own mind, as well to the discharge of my own conscience as to the instruction of others. Per me,

"THOMAM CRANMER.

"Witnesses to this subscription:
"FRATER JOHANNES DE VILLA GARCINA.
"HENRICUS SIDALLUS." *

So Cranmer fell. A degradation more pitiable it is impossible to imagine. The triumph over him was complete. The zeal of Villa Garcia and Sidallus or Sydall was greater than their discretion. Eager to proclaim their victory, they caused the recantation to be printed in London. This was done without the permission and to the great displeasure of the privy council. By the council the printers were required to deliver up every copy of the recantation, in order that they might all be burned. The queen had determined on Cranmer's death as a heretic. But if he recanted the whole nation might rise to demand his pardon; pardon was seldom refused on recantation, unless the person accused was a relapsed heretic. This serves to exonerate Mary's government from the charge of duplicity, though the cruelty of not extending pardon to Cranmer, under the circumstances, was as marked as was the impolicy.

So far had Cranmer degraded himself, that when it was

---

* Todd, ii. 477. The fifth recantation in Bonner's account appears in Latin, bearing, however, an English title.

notified to him that, notwithstanding his recantations, he had only received a respite, he actually forwarded the document he had just signed to Cardinal Pole, begging the respite of a few days, that he might give the world a more convincing proof of his repentance; in other words, he was prepared to make, if possible, a more complete recantation, in the hope that, when this was done, the respite might be converted into a pardon.

The queen, acting on the principle just stated, is said to have granted what was asked for—a respite of a few days. But she neither promised nor intended, on Cranmer's fuller recantation, to remit the sentence of death. The following, called the sixth recantation, was now laid before Cranmer:—

"I, Thomas Cranmer, late Archbishop of Canterbury, confess, and heartily lament, that I have most grievously sinned against heaven and the English realm, yea, against the Universal Church of Christ, which I have more cruelly persecuted than Paul did of old, I who have been a blasphemer, a persecutor, and contumelious; and oh! that I, who have exceeded Saul in malice and wickedness, might with Paul make amends for the honour which I have detracted from Christ, and the benefit of which I have deprived the Church. But yet that thief in the Gospel comforts my mind. For then at last he repented from his heart, then it irked him of his theft, when he might steal no more; and I, who, abusing my office and authority, robbed Christ of His honour, and this realm of its faith and religion, now, by the great mercy of God, having returned to myself, acknowledge myself to be the greatest of all sinners; and to the utmost of my ability, to God first, then to the Church and its supreme head, and to the king and queen, and lastly, to the realm of England, to render worthy satisfaction. But as that happy thief, when he was not able to pay the money and wealth which he had taken away, when neither his feet nor his hands, fastened to the cross, could do their office; by heart only and tongue, which were not bound, testified what the rest of his members would do, if they enjoyed the same liberty that his tongue did, by that he confessed Christ to be innocent; by that reproved the shamelessness of his fellow; by that detested his former life, and obtained the pardon of his sins, and as it were by a kind of key opened the gates of Paradise; by the example of this man, I do conceive no small hope of Christ's mercy, and that He will pardon my sins. I want hands and feet, by which I might build up again that which I have destroyed, for the lips of my mouth are only left me. But He who is merciful beyond all belief, will receive the calves of our lips. Animated by this hope first of all, therefore, I choose to offer this calf, to sacrifice this very small part of my body and life.

"I confess my unthankfulness against the great God. I acknowledge myself unworthy of all favour and pity; but not only of human and temporal, but divine and eternal punishment most worthy; for that I exceedingly offended against King Henry VIII., and especially against Queen Katharine his wife, when I became the cause and author of the divorce; which offence of a truth was the source of all the evils and calamities of this realm. Hence so many slaughters of good men; hence the schism of the whole kingdom, hence heresies, hence the destruction of so many souls and bodies which it bewilders my mind to think of. But after this commencement of mischief I confess that I opened a great inlet to all heresies, of which myself acted as the chief doctor and leader. First of all, indeed, it most vehemently torments my soul, that I did dishonour to the holy Sacrament of the Eucharist with so many blasphemies and reproaches, denying Christ's body and blood to be truly and really contained under the species of bread and wine. By certain publications also I did impugn the truth with all my might. In this respect indeed not only was I worse than Saul and the thief; but the most wicked man ever born.

"Lord, I have sinned against heaven and before Thee; against heaven, as I am the cause of its having been deprived of so many saints, in that I have denied most shamefully that heavenly benefit exhibited to us; I have sinned against the earth, which hath so long miserably been deprived this Sacrament; against men, whom I have called from this super-substantial food; the slayer of so many men as have perished for want of nutriment. I have defrauded the souls of the dead of this daily and most solemn sacrifice.

"It is manifest, moreover, how greatly I have been injurious, next after Christ, to His vicar, whose authority I have damaged by my publications. Wherefore I do most earnestly and urgently beseech the pope, that he, for the mercy of Christ, forgive me the things that I have committed against him and the Apostolical See. And I humbly beseech the most serene sovereigns of England, Spain, &c., Philip and Mary, that by their royal mercy they will pardon me. I ask and beseech the whole realm, yea, the Universal Church, that they take pity of this wretched being, to whom, besides a tongue, nothing is left whereby to make amends for the injuries and damages I have introduced. But especially because against Thee only I have sinned, I beseech Thee, most Merciful Father, who desirest and commandest all to come unto Thee however wicked, that Thou even vouchsafe nearly and closely to regard me, as thou didst look upon Magdalen and Peter: or certainly as Thou, looking upon the thief on the cross, didst vouchsafe by the promise of Thy grace and glory to comfort a fearful and trembling soul so; by Thy wonted and innate pity, turn the eyes of Thy mercy towards me, and deign me worthy to have that Word of Thine spoken to me, *I am thy salvation;* and in the day of death, *To-day shalt thou be with me in Paradise.* Per me,

"THOMAM CRANMER.

"Written this year of our Lord, 1555, the 18th day of March."*

This was transcribed and signed by Cranmer. The whole transaction is disgraceful to all parties concerned. We pity the unfortunate Cranmer; but still we regard him as entirely disgraced. Yet more disgraceful still was the conduct of those foreign papists who had led him to

---

* For the Latin see Cranmer's Remains. The translation is corrected from Strype.

expect that by thus far disgracing himself he would save his life, for they must have known that at this very time, the warrant for his execution was already signed! We can conceive nothing more base than conduct such as this.*

Cranmer was anxiously waiting the result of his last submission and expecting his pardon, when, on the evening of the 20th of March, he received a visit from the Provost of Eton, Dr. Cole. The provost had come to Oxford, appointed by the crown to preach at the execution of Cranmer, which was fixed for the following day. This intention of the government had been kept a profound secret. All that Cole desired was to ascertain, that Cranmer remained firm in his determination to abide by his recantations. The result of his visit was satisfactory to Dr. Cole. Alluding to some former discussions, of which no record has been preserved, he asked the prisoner, "Have you continued in the Catholic faith, *wherein I left you?*" Cranmer solemnly answered, "By God's grace I shall be daily more confirmed in the Catholic faith." The provost took his leave, perfectly satisfied.

The next day, Saturday, the 21st of March, was a rainy day, but multitudes might be seen from the prison window, flocking into the town; while the sound of the trumpet announced from time to time the arrival of troops. This must have awakened the suspicions of Cranmer, although he seems almost to the last to have entertained hopes of pardon. The cause of the disturbance was, however,

* Some modern writers, from internal evidence added to their desire to injure the character of Pole, represent him as the author of " the sixth submission." In the absence of other proof, I cannot state as a fact what is simply the conjecture of party writers. But this cannot exonerate him from his share in the iniquity of the proceeding. He must have seen the document, and he must have known that Cranmer was to die; what was done must have been done by his connivance, if not under his direction.

soon explained by Dr. Cole, who again paid Cranmer a visit. Finding him without money, he gave him fifteen crowns, and informed him that he would have to submit to further degradation, orders having come that the ex-primate should read his recantations to the public. It was so usual to require this of pardoned heretics, that Cranmer expressed no surprise at the course pursued, though probably it excited a recoil of his feelings, and the idea suggested itself of seizing this opportunity to recant his recantations.

We may presume this from what occurred, when, soon after, Villa Garcia arrived at the prison, to submit to him what is sometimes called his seventh recantation; but which was in fact the form, according to which what he had already subscribed in private was to be publicly read. He was to request the people to pray for him; to use a prescribed prayer for himself; to exhort the bystanders to lead a virtuous life; to declare the queen's right to the crown; to make a confession of faith, and to retract the doctrine in his book on the Eucharist. Cranmer transcribed the paper, giving one copy to Villa Garcia and keeping the other himself; but he resolutely refused to sign them.

It is an act of justice to Cranmer, to state that up to nine o'clock of the 21st of March he had no suspicion that he was to be executed. He still expected a pardon; yet as soon as Villa Garcia had left him, he changed the entire character of the document, substituting in lieu of the confession of faith dictated by the Spaniard, a disavowal of the six retractations already made. He probably expected to have to carry his faggot, and having done that, to receive his pardon at the stake. It is believed that he determined to avail himself of this opportunity for making a public profession of his sin in recanting, for recalling his recantations, and for refusing the pardon which, in the hour of weakness, he had made such sacrifices to obtain. I think that we are justified by the facts of the case, when considered as a whole, in arriving at this conclusion. It is certainly the only ground on which the honours of martyrdom, in any sense of the word, can be claimed for Thomas Cranmer. But even then one is shocked by his want of truthfulness.

The clock had struck nine. At the gate of Bocardo appeared Lord Williams with Sir Thomas Bridges, Sir John Browne, and a large array of noblemen and magistrates attended by their retainers, all armed. The intentions of the government with respect to Cranmer had become known. It was feared that between the two religious factions which divided the country, there might be a collision. Against this, the government had directed that precautions should be taken. There was a great concourse of spectators, supplied by the University and from the country round, and by not a few from a distance.

A deep silence expressed the sympathy, the awe of the multitude, as, pausing for a moment in the portal, the venerable prisoner, his long white beard flowing majestically over his black and ragged gown, moved his old square cap in courtesy to Lord Williams, and exposed his bald head to "the pelting of the pitiless storm." * The rain was descending in torrents. A multitudinous sob was almost audible. Whether there was a feeling of triumph in those who were papistically inclined, or of deep humiliation on the part of others who felt themselves forsaken by their leader, or of breathless hope entertained by not a few, who still expected him to declare that his recanta-

---

* "*Thomas Cranmer, aspectu venerabilis,*" says Campion the Jesuit, though he adds, "*cætera lævissimus et corruptissimus regiæ libidinis et voluntatis assecla.*"

tions had been wrung from him, and that they did not express his real sentiments, none could repress the kindlier feelings of our nature which many encouraged. They could not but regard with commiseration one who had walked humbly when on the dizzy height of prosperity, and whose firm step still showed that if he had stumbled he was not yet prostrated on the slippery descent of adversity.

It had been originally intended, that from Bocardo the prisoner should be taken immediately to the place of execution; a pyre having been prepared on the spot already consecrated by the blood of Ridley and Latimer. But owing to the state of the weather it was felt that if to this plan they adhered full effect would not be given to the provost's sermon, or to that seventh recantation which Cranmer had already transcribed and was expected to read. Fresh arrangements were consequently made at St. Mary's Church, where the first, and in truth the most painful, part of the ceremonial was to take place. The troops lined the streets. The mayor and the aldermen headed the procession as it moved from the prison. The prisoner walked immediately behind them, with a Dominican on either side. Certain psalms were chanted antiphonally, the two monks taking the lead on either side. At the porch of the church they paused. The choir from without was silenced. The choir from within the church took up the note.

As he crossed the threshold the whole choir, in a jubilant triumphant strain commenced the *Nunc Dimittis*, and Cranmer no longer doubted what the end would be. The jubilant chant was designed to tell forth the faith— the inward joy as it was supposed—of their victim. He admitted that his sin had been great; his prosecutors assumed that it had been so great that his pardon in this world was impossible. But he was invited to join with them in the happy thought that he might now be pardoned in the other world. Having recanted, and having received absolution, he would go not to hell but to purgatory. This was a ground for rejoicing. Death, it was said, was disarmed of half its terrors. When they reached the platform, which, facing the pulpit, had been prepared for the prisoner, the Dominicans, with their respective choirs, branched off on either side. The prisoner ascended the steps alone. All eyes were upon him. He was seen to lean against a pillar, where, like another Jacob, he was evidently wrestling with God in prayer.

The preacher, perhaps purposely, kept him waiting, the gazingstock of many eyes. When the sermon commenced the archbishop composed himself and listened attentively. He sat, "the very image and shape of perfect sorrow." Once or twice he raised his eyes towards heaven or cast a sad look downwards, but his whole deportment was quiet, grave, dignified, though the tears, "like the tears of any child," dropped down abundantly from his "fatherly face." *

In the course of the sermon, the preacher remarked:— "That although pardon and reconciliation were due to the prisoner, according to the canons of the Church, seeing that he had repented him of his errors, yet there were causes why the queen and council at this time judged him to death. He was a traitor, having when metropolitan dissolved the lawful marriage of Henry VIII. with the queen's mother. He was an heresiarch, to whom all the late troubles in the Church were attributable, and further," he added, "It seems meet, according to the law of equality, that as the death of the Duke of Northumberland of late made even with Thomas More,

---

* I have quoted the expressions of an eye-witness.

Chancellor, that died for the Church, so there should be one that should make even with Fisher, of Rochester; and because that Ridley, Hooper, Ferrar, were not able to make even with that man, it seemed that Cranmer should be joined to them, to fill up their part of equality."

"Besides these, there were other just and weighty causes, which seemed to the queen and council, which was not meet at that time to be opened to the common people." *

He then exhorted the bystanders to profit by the melancholy example before them. Seeing the queen's Majesty will not pardon so notable a man as this, much less, he continued " in like cause she would spare other men; that no man should think to make thereby any defence of his error, either in riches or any kind of authority, they had now an example to teach them all; by whose calamity every man might consider his own fortune: who from the top of dignity, none being more honourable than he in the whole realm and next the king, was fallen into so great misery, as they might now see, being a man of so high degree, sometime one of the chiefest prelates in the Church, and an archbishop, the chief of the council, the second person in the realm of long time; a man thought in greatest assurance, having a king on his side, notwithstanding all his authority and defence, to be debased from high estate to a low degree, of a counsellor to become a caitiff, and to be set in so wretched a state, that the poorest wretch would not change condition with him; briefly, so heaped with misery on all sides, that neither was left him any hope of better fortune, nor place for worse."†

Cole then addressed his discourse to Cranmer himself.

---

* Remains, iv. 133.   † Remains, iv. 133.

Reminding the prisoner of the mercy of God, who " will not suffer us to be tempted beyond what we are able to bear," he expressed a good hope that he would, like the penitent thief, be that day with Christ in Paradise; encouraged him to meditate on the deliverance of the three children, to whom God made the flame seem like a pleasant dew; on the rejoicing of St. Andrew in his cross, and the patience of St. Lawrence on the fire. He assured him, that if, in his extremity he should call on God, and on such as have died in the faith, God would either abate the fury of the flame, or else would give the sufferer strength to endure it. He was glorified in the final conversion of Cranmer to the truth, which could only be regarded as the work of God; and concluded with many expressions of commendation, and with a promise that masses should be sung for his soul at every church in Oxford." *

The congregation was about to disperse, when Dr. Cole addressed them again :—

" ' Brethren,' he said, ' lest any man should doubt of this man's earnest conversion and repentance, you shall hear him speak before you; and, therefore, I pray you, Master Cranmer, that you will now perform that you promised not long ago; namely, that you would openly express the true and undoubted profession of your faith, that you may take away all suspicion from men, and that all men may understand that you are a Catholic indeed.' " †

The archbishop no longer looked the picture of despair. He assumed a determined and resolute attitude, and replied : " I will do it, and that with a good will." He took off his cap, he turned towards the people, and he said :—

* Le Bas, ii. 212. † Remains, iv. 135.

"Good Christian people, my well beloved brethren and sisters in Christ, I beseech you most heartily to pray for me to Almighty God that He will forgive me all my sins and offences, which be many without number, and great above measure; but yet one thing grieveth my conscience above all the rest, whereof, God willing, I intend to speak more fully hereafter. But how great, and how many soever my sins may be, I beseech you to pray God of His mercy to pardon and forgive them all."

He knelt down and prayed. There was silence—a space, for prayer. The silence was broken by the deep voice of the archbishop:—

"O Father of heaven, O Son of God, Redeemer of the world; O Holy Ghost, proceeding from Them both; three Persons and one God; have mercy upon me, most wretched caitiff and miserable sinner. I have offended both heaven and earth, more grievously than any tongue can express. Whither then may I go, or whither should I flee for succour? To heaven I may be ashamed to lift up mine eyes, and in earth I find no refuge or succour. What shall I then do? Shall I despair? God forbid. O good God, Thou art merciful, and refusest none that cometh unto Thee for succour. To Thee, therefore, do I run; to Thee do I humble myself; saying, O Lord God, my sins be great; but yet have mercy upon me for thy great mercy! O God the Son, this great mystery was not wrought (that God became man) for few or small offences; nor Thou didst not give Thy Son unto death, O God the Father, for our little and small sins only, but for all the greatest sins of the world, so that the sinner return unto Thee with a penitent heart, as I do here at this present. Wherefore have mercy upon me, O Lord, whose property is always to have mercy; for although my sins be great, yet Thy mercy is greater. And I crave nothing,

CHAP. III.
Thomas Cranmer.
1533–56.

O Lord, for mine own merits, but for Thy name's sake, that it may be glorified thereby, and for Thy dear Son Jesus Christ's sake. And now, therefore, Our Father which art in Heaven," &c.*

Rising from his knees he resumed: he exhorted the people to eschew worldliness; to obey the king and queen; to live together in brotherly love, and if rich, to abound in alms deeds. He proceeded to declare his faith, at a time when, whatever he may have said or written in times past, dissimulation would be worse than folly. He repeated the Creed, and added, "I believe every article of the Catholic Church and every word and sentence taught by our Lord and Saviour Jesus Christ, His apostles, and prophets in the New and Old Testaments."

He paused; there was a breathless expectation of what was coming. With peculiar solemnity he proceeded:—

"And now I come to the great thing that so much troubleth my conscience, more than any thing that ever I did or said in my whole life; and that is, the setting abroad of writings contrary to the truth, which now here I renounce and refuse, as things written with my hand, contrary to the truth which I thought in my heart, and written for fear of death, and to save my life, if it might be; and that is, all such bills and papers which I have written or signed with my hand since my degradation; wherein I have written many things untrue. And forasmuch as my hand offended, writing contrary to my heart, my hand shall first be punished therefore; for may I come to the fire, it shall be first burned." †

The whole assembly was electrified. A moment of astonished silence was succeeded by a babel of confused voices. Dr. Cole, and all who had taken part in the proceedings against Cranmer, expecting their final triumph

* Remains, iv. 136.   † Remains, iv. 139.

over their prostrate victim, were livid with rage. Protestants were seen silently weeping for joy; they were saying to themselves, that they had been almost sure that so it would be; at all events, their prayers had been heard.

Language the most violent now reached the archbishop's ears—"traitor, dissembler, liar."

Lord Williams remonstrated with him, and reminded him of his having recanted what he had said of the Sacrament. "Alas, my Lord," said Cranmer, "I have been a man that all my life loved plainness, and against the truth I never did dissemble until now. For this my fault I am most sorry, but now is the time to strip off all disguise. I say, therefore, that I believe concerning the Sacrament as I taught in my book against the late Bishop of Winchester." On this the clamour increased, and some, as a contemporary remarked, began "to cry out, yelp and bawl." Lord Williams, raising his voice, called upon him to remember himself and to play the Christian man. "I do so," was the reply, "for now I speak the truth." The exasperation increased, and amidst the infuriated University mob, the loud voice of Dr. Cole was heard, "Stop that heretic's mouth and take him away."

There was a rush to the scaffold; Cranmer was pulled down. But Lord Williams assumed the command and protected the prisoner from violence, and the procession outside the church was formed again.

Cranmer was once more himself. He had done what he had determined to do, and he had done it well. He came forth from the church with a happy smiling countenance. His gait was manly. His eye was bright. It was no longer fixed upon the earth, it was peering through the crowd, where he saw many an approving smile on many a tearful face. He felt the grasp of many a moistened hand. Two Spanish friars walked by his side, and tried to inveigle him into controversy; but he heeded them not, he was busy with the people who around attended him as it were to the field of battle, to witness the last struggle, and who were secretly praying that he who had at last confessed his Saviour, would not be by that Saviour denied.

They stood at the place where a few months before his dear friends Ridley and Latimer had glorified God by their deaths. He knelt and prayed. When he arose the friars were preparing to renew their argument; but Lord Williams in his impatience, or in his pity to Cranmer, commanded the proceedings to be cut short. Cranmer obeyed with alacrity; he threw off the ragged vestments by which they had sought to insult him, and stood in a long shirt, reaching to his heels. His bald head, his white shirt, his long and yet whiter beard flowing over his breast, betokened a victim whose sins had been pardoned. An iron band or chain was attached to his body, and he was bound to the stake. There was an eagerness shown to press his hand for the last time by those who gazed on the dying man. Among the multitude Cranmer saw one Ely; let his name be mentioned, for there are some who desire, and many more who deserve to be cursed to fame. He had cringed before the primate in his day of power. He had lately reviled him for disavowing his recantations. Cranmer put forth his hand to Ely, not wishing to be "at un-peace" with anyone. Ely refused to touch the hand of a heretic. What Ely rejected, the penitent Cranmer devoted to God. The pile was ignited, though the flame had not yet reached its victim. Over the flame Cranmer stretched forth his right hand, with a loud voice saying, "This hand hath offended." The other parts of his body were for a while uninjured; but steadily over the flame the offending right hand was held. As the devouring flame approached him, once or twice, in forgetfulness, when the perspiration was on his brow, the burning hand was withdrawn to wipe the face, which it only served to scorch. The left hand was pointed upwards, and with upturned eye the poor penitent exclaimed: "Lord Jesus, receive my spirit." But still the right hand was burning; still, amidst his agonies, was heard the cry, "Oh! this unworthy hand!" The body was motionless; not once did it swerve from its position; it seemed to be as insensible of pain as the stake to which he was bound. The flames rushed on him in charitable fury. His sufferings were short. His spirit was set free.

He died a martyr's death; but to die bravely when death is inevitable is not sufficient to constitute a martyr. The noble army of martyrs consists of those who, rather than deny the truth, have offered themselves *voluntarily* to torture or to death. By calling our attention from his offending soul to his unoffending right hand, Cranmer has excited our feelings of commiseration; but charity itself will sometimes doubt whether the right hand would have suffered, if the enemies of Cranmer had not proved themselves to be among the basest of mankind. We are disgusted by the falsehoods to which they had recourse, in order that they might rob their victim of his honour before they took his life; but of persecution the friends of Cranmer have no right to complain, for he had acted, and was still prepared to act, on the principle that the magistrate, justified in condemning to the gallows the wretch who deprived a fellow creature of life or property, was equally bound, for the good of society, to consign to the stake the unhappy person who, himself mistaken, had laboured, through the propagation of heresy, for the destruction of an immortal soul.

Of the merits and demerits of Archbishop Cranmer

CHAP. III.
Thomas Cranmer.
1553-56.

the reader has had in these pages an impartial description. Before he can be spoken of as a hero or a saint, the reader's estimate of the heroic and the saintly character must be ascertained. That he was time-serving as a politician, his warmest admirers must admit; in his worst actions, Henry VIII. found an instrument in Cranmer, whose remonstrances, if they evince the kindness of his heart, at the same time display a culpable weakness both of character and of principle. As the primate of an ancient church, while he laboured to remove the abuses by which, in the lapse of ages, it had been encrusted, he was careful to preserve its continuity, and he resisted successfully the attempts incessantly made to supplant, by the introduction of a modern sect, the church of Augustine; nevertheless, it cannot be denied that by the precedent set through his timid concessions to the civil power, Cranmer bequeathed to us an ecclesiastical atmosphere so charged with Erastianism, as to render it difficult, at certain times, to extricate the religious from the political element. In doctrine, Cranmer drifted from Erasmus towards Luther, but a Lutheran he never became; he is described in a Lutheran publication of the present day, as "having lacked the central living principle of justification by faith only, and a clear perception of other Gospel truths."* Of his morality in a profligate court we must ever speak with respect; if he was not always faithful in rebuking vice, he encouraged and rewarded the virtuous; if he was timid in the defence of his friends, his placability and gentleness towards his opponents became proverbial; if his imbecility and indecision prevented him from rallying around him many partisans, yet, charmed by the gentleness of his temper and the suavity of his manners, his friends were numerous. In literature, he had no originality; he would

* Bomberger's Protestant Encyclopædia.

never have been impelled to authorship by the mere irritation of genius. But if his writings indicate no independence of research and are never quoted as an authority by the modern divine, his professional reading was extensive, and he exhibited much readiness and skill in the use of his materials. The flames which consumed his body have cast a false glitter upon his character; but this is no fault of his. Cranmer, in the last act of his life, with his burning right hand, appealed to the Church, not for honour, but for pardon—'as a beacon upon the top of a mountain, and as an ensign on a hill.'

END OF THE SEVENTH VOLUME.

LONDON
PRINTED BY SPOTTISWOODE AND CO.
NEW-STREET SQUARE

www.ingramcontent.com/pod-product-compliance
Lightning Source LLC
Chambersburg PA
CBHW020546300426
44111CB00008B/813